Wanderjahr:

an odyssey of sorts

Richard Bevis

Memorials and Reconstructions III

Illustrator: Vivian L. Bevis
First Edition – February 2013

ISBN
978-1-4602-0563-1(Paperback)
978-1-4602-0564-8 (eBook)

Produced by:

FriesenPress
Suite 300 – 852 Fort Street
Victoria, BC, Canada V8W 1H8

www.friesenpress.com

Distributed to the trade by The Ingram Book Company

Memorials and Reconstructions

> Great is the power of memory, a fearful thing ...a deep and boundless manifoldness; and this thing is the mind, and this am I myself.
>
> St. Augustine, *Confessions*

It goes without saying that I was not always conscious, didn't always write - but I was not fully conscious until I began to write my story. Of those first seventeen years, what remains? Unreliable memories, traces in the neurons, snapshots and flickering home movies, stories and papers I wrote because someone told me to, a few letters: just glimpses, cameos, giving no sense of a life in time, a continuous, subsistent self. If I sought materials for an autobiography, I would not be much better off for those years than a scholar of the pre-papyrus Old Kingdom, gathering a shred here, a shard there. Of course I had reflections and feelings - was introspective to a fault, my father said - but it did not occur to me to *record* them until I was almost eighteen. *Great Expectations* begins with Pip receiving his first "impression of the identity of things" in a cold, windy cemetery. Mine came when my parents took me straight from prep-school graduation to Europe. Without knowing why, I realized then that there were thoughts I needed to articulate and preserve, so I bought a journal in which to set down *my* impression of the identity of things. This turned out to be a trait of character.

For some reason, though, travel was the one activity that could be depended upon to make me write; when I tried to keep a journal at home, it soon shallowed out and dried up. As a boy I did some small-bore travel - family car trips north, south, west

- of which my parents would say, "Travel is broadening." Yet that was not what caught my attention. It seemed to have something to do with relative motion: the still self at the center of the world-carousel spinning past. Both were interesting, the self known more clearly *per se* amid the flux, the world sensed in all its whirling variety. That is certainly self-centered, and perhaps sounds callous. I mean, the world known by its motion and difference from the turning axle. It also had to do with stress. Anyone who has traveled hard knows about that. Travel used to be, can still be, *travayle*, travail; it tries and tests, and in that testing you learn more about yourself and your companions than in a month of Sundays at home.

What I did not realize until later was that as memories of travel - like all memories - faded, my journal-records of them (along with pictures, books and maps) could become the means of restoring to life and consciousness what had otherwise all but perished. They were the memorials from which I might reconstruct vanished days and places, time machines in which to visit the past. If I am not mistaken, that is one of the basic functions of literature.

Contents

List of Illustrations

For Hector,
for our Benefactors,
and to all those who were so
incautious as to ask, when I
returned, "How was your trip?"

...perception is not whimsical, but fatal.

- Ralph Waldo Emerson

If I now feel that I have come to a turning point in my life, this is not because of what I have won but because of what I have lost.

- Albert Camus

I am a part of all that I have met.

- Ulysses, in Tennyson's "Ulysses"

I. First, Principles

> I should not talk so much about myself if there were anybody else whom I knew as well.
>
> - Henry David Thoreau

Why *do* young people turn their backs on love and money to go a-roving? What treasure do they bring back? Such an inquiry must begin where all ladders start: down in the foul rag-and-bone shop of the heart. When I graduated from college, with no clear idea of what to do next, I had already made two mistakes *vis à vis* the part of the world that holds the purse strings. ("It's the old men what got the money / And the young ones that need it so," as the song went.) I had failed to Interview for a Job, not knowing of one I wanted, nor believing that the process would move me toward the Good as I then understood it. Worse, perhaps, I had taken a backward step from gainful employment by acknowledging a desire to travel abroad in a manner not easily distinguished from vagabondage. At that time I wanted to go to East Africa: a bold though vague plan that lived long enough to alarm The Establishment.

The idea was hardly original, yet the reverberations up and down the eastern seaboard after I disclosed my intentions made it seem radical. In the pine woods of North Carolina and the suburbs of New York there were mutterings of dismay and disapproval. "What, travel in Africa on your own? Go *bumming* after graduation? What about a job? Who'll know you when you come back? Those college references won't last forever, you know. You can't just throw away years as if they didn't matter," and so on. This was in 1959; you would have thought that no young American had ever gone abroad except on a tour with parents or chaperones during school holidays. One friend shared my inclinations, however, so Hector and I decided to travel together. This was a great help and comfort: one man might be crazy; two could start a movement. By March of our senior year, we were discussing an African journey lasting six to twelve months. The college newspaper even did a story on us ("Bold Journey"), but the older generations were not impressed - in fact were further alarmed - by romantic phrases. "Bold, indeed," said my father darkly.

Those whose formative years had been conditioned by the economics and psychology of the Great Depression, or whose interest in other lands was perfunctory, could not be expected to endorse the idea that a young man completing his education, with the whole world before him but no specific plan for igniting it, would embark on a costly and time-consuming foreign adventure unlikely to yield tangible rewards; nor to have much patience with his own soul-searching on the issue. Whatever their personal sympathy with me, relatives and friends had serious misgivings about our plan that I could not alleviate. Either you feel the attraction we felt or you do not; dropping out for a year is either worth the sacrifices to you or it is not. I must have seemed a far-out eccentric, yet would have been glad to "keep in my place" if I had had one.

Whether congenital itchy feet prevented me from choosing a way more traveled by at 21, or wanderlust rushed into a vacuum of uncertainty, is hard to say. The two seemed to co-germinate like twins, each implying or necessitating the other. Or was the right metaphor tension and release? I don't know. But when my father, deeply concerned, said, "Do your work and wait until you're older; I travel a good deal on business now," I discovered within myself a fully-formed mystique of travel (as distinguished from transportation) that I tried unsuccessfully to explain to him. Four years earlier my parents had shown me some interesting places in Europe, but not a mode of travel that I could afford, enjoy, or endorse. A summer working in Yellowstone, however, had given me some idea of how a young man *might* visit other places. Gradually I formed a desire to marry the kind of travel I had practiced in the west with an old-world itinerary.

Sometime during that preparatory spring or summer, our cards being on the table, I came across an "Aha!" passage in Hendrik van Loon's *The Arts* (recommended by an esteemed music professor at Debrew). It introduced me to the mediaeval-Renaissance institution of *Wanderjahre* or "years of traveling, that took the young student to many different parts of Europe." Along the way, aspiring craftsmen or artists like Albrecht Dürer sought out the best that had been built or painted, and the best teachers, in order to learn the various skills of the field.

As a rule, such a wandering scholar was as poor as a church mouse, but that was the least of his worries. His worldly belongings he carried in a little bundle on his back, together with his sketchbooks and notebooks. He slept wherever he happened to be, in a haystack or in the attic of some charitable citizen who remembered his own Wanderjahre…in every town there were a number of houses where such a hungry youngster could count on a handout and occasionally on a small gift of money…. Meanwhile he would use his eyes and ears and everything he saw or heard went down in his notebooks.

That was the concept I had needed when faltering through an improvised distinction between *travel* and *transportation* for my father the previous fall - though if he had retorted, "What's your craft?" I could not have answered. Here again, my central problem was that I did not yet know what I wanted to study or achieve; I lacked direction, had no goal. That, I admit, gave my *Wanderjahr* a floundering appearance at times. Inverting the tradition, I would have to find a vocation in the course of my travels, and study its mysteries after my return.

Nevertheless, here was an old and honorable idea that seemed worth dusting off for modern use, one with which I felt a degree of kinship. I too would be a poor wayfaring student with a knapsack and notebooks, though I hoped to ride my own vehicle, not walk, would not expect handouts or free lodging along the way, and – American draft boards being what they then were - could manage at most only a *Wanderjahr*, singular.

That the notion of a 'wander-year' is *European* explains both the uncomprehending resistance we met before setting out, and why such a trip seemed natural and even obvious once begun. For it was not a dead idea; you just had to take the leap to land among hundreds of kindred souls, happily wandering. (There were also a few young Americans who, having chosen a career and demonstrated some talent for it, were making underwritten academic forays to Europe. I am glad that mine was a personal rather than an institutional venture, without interviews or formal obligations, less distant from the spirit of the original than those of the *fellows* and *grantees*.) At any rate, the *Wanderjahr* was an influential concept and precedent for me, however inapplicable it might seem to others.

Not only encouragement but useful information was difficult to obtain. AAA - the ranking travel agency in Broadleaf, NC, and the US - told us that passable roads would be hard to find in East Africa, and pointed to large blank spaces on the map between Cairo and Nairobi. Negley Farson's book about his recent travels through those spaces seemed to offer some hope, but my father declared him an unreliable source, *a novelist*, and his scepticism was widely shared. It was difficult to answer others' questions about why we were willing to spend all our savings on this project, when we were having loud internal dialogues on the same issue. The more we were challenged, the more confident we tried to sound, though between ourselves we discussed whether it might be better to volunteer for the service, discharge our military obligation and maybe see a bit of the world that way. Dad, however, advised against that as a waste of time. Well, I didn't want to waste time!

Our intentions being, then, in the open and unhindered - though not unquestioned - by authority figures, we decided to use the summer after graduation to earn what money we could before embarking. Hector found a job in the south, near home, while I pondered the invitation of a friend to work at his father's canoeing camp in Minnesota, using the time to prepare mentally and physically. I decided to accept, not only for the (modest) remuneration, but to learn some "outdoor skills" that might be helpful. Possibly I would also come to understand more about what I was doing, other than indulging a notion that there should be more to life than employment. Our commencement speaker, Ralph McGill, editor of the *Atlanta Constitution*, reminded us that a "commencement" is a beginning. A beginning of what? Of education in other forms, he said. I clung to that. Hector and I kept hearing that we were being "escapist" and "unrealistic," but the Pyramids and Kilimanjaro seemed more real to me than graduate school or a job. Blame Richard Halliburton and Ernest Hemingway.

Further revelations did not come easily. It may have been that they were blocked: much else - having to do with vocation, love, nature, and myself - was fermenting inside me. And as my search was almost random, so was my reading. Four books went into my Minnesota duffel: *The Arts*, which had already helped, *The Oxford Book of English Verse, Walden,* and Philip Wylie's *The Innocent Ambassadors*. The poets were occasionally stimulating but more often seemed irrelevant; I was surfeited with older English texts. *Walden* spoke nearer to the point, and frequently pleased me: "The sun is but a morning star" and all that. But Thoreau was so sure, so settled - and he advised against travel! We argued frequently. Wylie, though, whom a solicitous friend had urged me to read, helped clarify and articulate several of my "principles" of travel - if so high-sounding a term can be applied to the esoteric and intellectually sparse notions with which I set out.

Wylie's biting treatise lectured Americans on proper conduct abroad. He preached a kind of secular missionary ethic (don't be vulgar, ignorant, or insular; be well-informed and open-minded), attacked itinerant bigots with more money than taste, and demanded in their stead a generation of young travelers who would create a new image of America abroad. Yes, I thought, *that* was how one should travel: no first-class hotels, no American bars, organized tours or fixed itineraries. Mix with the people, try to speak to them in their own language, avoid all forms of "tourism," get out from behind the observation window and open yourself to the world. I swallowed a lot of what Wylie served up, much of it confirming what I had already felt or sensed, and came to think that, with all due modesty, the time asked travelers like…*us*. Somewhere between the bumbling tourist and the touring bum I hoped to find a middle ground, the domain of Wylie's enlightened ambassadors, as well as of van Loon's wandering students.

I saw no reason why foreign travel should not still produce new syntheses within, bringing about self-(re)creation, as it once had. At the very least it might be a post-graduate course from which one could derive more than complacent anecdotes and pictures. My ideal was the "scholar-gypsy," but in deference to the attainable I would settle for the itinerant student. Some of this I wrote to Hector after we parted for the summer. From the caution and reserve with which he replied, warning that we mustn't set our sights too high and try to know *everything*, I realized that I had spoken too ringingly. He seemed embarrassed or worried by my ideals, and lost no time in reasserting *his* idea of our trip. The label "tourist" held no horrors for him, though he would doubtless elevate that category before he finished. Hector, I realized, was less given to flights of imagination, and a good deal more practical, than I. A strong person, he had the advantage of me in experience of travel. Upon his stubborn will and stout heart I would have to depend heavily in our first cold plunge.

In this book I quote many passages from my original journals, holding the eclectic's belief that material from multiple sources will produce a more rounded view of a subject than the monolithic "historical past" can do. My own observations of fifty years ago constitute a second source, quite distinct from what I think and feel now. Generally, what was said of the past *in* the past may be as valid and useful as what we can say now with the aid of "perspective." Distance in time or space *does* lend a kind of perspective, yet also inevitably distorts what the observer wants to remember or perceive. When we try to magnify an object or reconstruct the past in order to examine it more fully, we also magnify the distortion. In optics, the distorting medium is the atmosphere; in history, it is emotion, change, partial oblivion and theoretical preconceptions that form a "distance haze" between us and the past.

A related problem is that some writers deny there can be an "objective truth" about the past, arguing that there is only the multiplicity of views about it, none of which may be "privileged" over another. In a way this carries eclecticism to its logical (or illogical) conclusion. If I protest that the truth about the past is "what really happened then," they ask not only "How do you know?" but "What 'really happened' *for whom*? And why canonize *then*? An event's 'truth' is the totality of what is made of it, then and later." Though I insist that our tires actually ("as acts") met roads in Europe, Asia and Africa - "Something happened" - it is true that Hector and I, and the people we met, may remember events differently, and certainly had different feelings about them, then and now. But that is part of my story; a pluralistic view of history is not at odds with what I have done in using my journals as one basis of this reconstruction of events that occurred in 1959-60. If there are thirteen ways of looking at a blackbird, there ought to be more than one way of understanding a *Wanderjahr*.

That summer of 1959, for instance, much of which I spent paddling the lakes and camping in the forests of Minnesota and Ontario, I now remember as the time of my (re)discovery of nature, of the earth, after years of trivial pursuits: a reorientation of my very self. It shames me to recall how foolish and misled I had been, and how long it took me to learn what the more whole of my contemporaries had known all along. That is, I think of Windhome (the canoe camp) as an adventure in its own right, not as part of the longer expedition that followed. But that is not how I felt nor what I thought I was doing just before my departure for the midwest. I know this because that was when I began to keep a journal, which often surprises me.

> Nothing reveals more with respect to ourselves, than when we again see before us that which has proceeded from us years before, so that we can now consider ourselves as an object of contemplation.
>
> \- Johann Wolfgang von Goethe

II. Garden Lake

Travel can be one of the most rewarding forms of introspection.

Lawrence Durrell

The night before leaving for Windhome I said *au revoir* to Penny for the summer, then drove home and sat down to inaugurate my journal into the orgy of self-examination.

June 14, 1959, Suburb, Conn. - Before I get caught up in the Minnesota trip, I want to set down some reasons for spending the summer in this way.

I can't discuss Minnesota without bringing in my proposed trip to Africa. The former is a stepping-stone to the latter. Why am I doing either, rather than settling into a career or the service? I don't know what I want to do in the long run, so why not do what appeals to me at the moment? I'm a searching, restless person. Or, more honestly, not having found anything yet, I'm not searching as hard as I should. The African venture, besides its basis in love of travel, was born of [a] need to stimulate myself into a war on complacency, conformity, [and] shallowness. I want to be deeper.

There are other reasons. Africa is a tremendously exciting place now, beautiful & fermenting...an experience I'll never forget. Hector, my traveling companion, is a longtime Africaphile, & his motives for going are more objective than mine.

Why Camp Windhome? It offers a "gateway to the silent places" & a chance to know myself better. It's $300 for two months: not too bad for a recession summer. I'll need the camping experience, the woodscraft, & the physical toughening to stay alive & well in Africa.

My defense of including such material notwithstanding, it is difficult not to be embarrassed by its naivety and facile rationalizations. Can anyone who cares about writing look at any piece of old work - even a journal - and not wish to improve it? But, in principle at least, I reject embarrassment and revision. These are my raw materials, my scriptures; they were *there*, like the aging veterans who march in parades on memorial days, clumsy but authentic. If there is anything more awkward than youthful attempts to write coherence into one's life, it is trying to disown them later. My editing shall be minimal, my commentary temperate.

My wanderings began within a week of graduation. Penny, along with Hector's girlfriend Andrea, went off to work in Germany. Mom and Dad gave me $50 so that I could fly, which allowed two more days at home, during which I bought a summerweight Dacron sleeping bag (well, Africa was hot, wasn't it?) and a long, heavy air mattress with the world's slowest valve. On June 15th I flew west. Even under a quilt of brown factory smoke, Detroit looked neat from the air, amidst green, fertile farmland. During our stop there I procured a forward-facing window seat: now "*the visual world could expand outward on my retina*" (my last psych course had been in brain physiology). I enjoyed the scenery and good weather on the next leg of the flight, to Minneapolis via Milwaukee, over extensive dairy farms. A friendly stewardess ("*with whom I had an informative talk about her job*") gave me a copy of the *Official Airlines Guide*, which had useful-looking travel information.

A "*typically alert traveling salesman*" – had I met any others? - gave me a lift from the airport to the bus terminal, where I boarded the first departure for Duluth. As late as 10:30 PM I could see lush, heavily treed farms and pastures, turkey pens, and countless acres of onions, tomatoes and cabbage, but it was dark before we reached Duluth. Barry – my friend, the camp director's son - was waiting. We spent the night 20 miles away at Camp Baganemon, of which Windhome was the outpost. In the morning I could see that Baganemon had a goodly spread in the woods by a lake: it looked like all the other camps of which I had seen pictures (I'd never been to one). We met its head man, Nathan, who was polite to us but snapped at his hirelings. Barry and I spent the morning loading assorted gear into the car and trailer, and half the afternoon running errands in Duluth and Superior, before starting the two-hour drive to Ely.

We headed north alongside the vastness of Lake Superior, varied in color and mood, having glimpses of the great docks and iron ore carriers at Duluth. Pastures and farms gave way to forest, resting on a backbone of rock and interspersed with lakes. A glance at the map tells the tale: nothing but a moving ice sheet could have gouged all those small basins, many of them oriented NW-SE. Camp Windhome proved to be a scratch in the woods near Ely, a hundred miles from Duluth. It clung to the shore of Garden Lake, spilling out onto a small island tucked into a cove and connected by a plank footbridge to the mainland. There were four wooden buildings, a trailer, two outhouses, a large tent-frame platform, and ample space to pitch tents.

June 17, Windhome - We came to Windhome about 6. Mr. & Mrs. Biel (David & Jennifer), handyman Rex Carpenter & wife Elaine, Barney & Jean Delacroix, & Barry's brother & sister are natural, wholesome, intelligent people. I think I'll profit by knowing them.

After portaging goods to the island, beating mattresses, assembling beds & de-bugging, Barry & I moved into the "resident campers' cabin." Though tiny, it will be comfortable enough. He & I took a canoe paddle at dusk (9:30). The environs are beautiful, green & peaceful. I want to get to work & toughen up.

Indeed. Once the Biels saw me around camp, they must have worried. My physical condition had deteriorated in the two years since compulsory P.E. ended at Debrew, and I possessed no relevant skills (they had to show me how to paddle a canoe). The Biels were all well-built athletic types who kept active year-round and had "always" camped. Rex was a woodsman, and Elaine, who did most of the cooking, had been around places like this most of her life. Only Barney and Jean, academics who taught French at Antioch, where David taught P.E., were "like me." The thought of all I needed to learn, and doubts that I could do it quickly enough, gnawed at me.

June 18 - A cloudy day: the air cool & brooding, the [lake] metallic & rippled. We worked on the campers' lean-to, nailing the table-top & benches onto uprights, stretching the tarp over the roof frame & pitching the rusty old stove into the lake. Afterwards, Barry & I paddled the nine canoes around the point to the campers' landing. I learned the rudiments of picking up, launching & paddling a canoe single-handed. Tonight, dinner with the Delacroix in French.

The Delacroix were friendly, and invaluable to me: an island of art and culture in this formidable sea of nature, and a bridge to the realms where I was heading. It was no small advantage to be able to speak a useful foreign language - and to be challenged in it - anytime that summer.

When camp had been prepared for the boys - garbage and outhouse pits dug, a soccer field laid out, the mess hall ready for action, etc. - we set off to prepare ourselves.

June 20, island in Basswood Lake on the U.S.-Canada boundary - A big day. The canoeing staff took off at 10 this morning on a shakedown cruise. I've been in a canoe with Barney & David all day; Barry & Hal are in the other.

Windhome lay that close to Canada and real wilderness: less than a day's paddle. Hal was a young counselor who arrived the day after I did, completing our staff.

The first hour my shoulder got sore (paddling from the middle you have to reach out farther), & on the first portage I fell carrying two packs (hard to see over the chest pack) & cut my knee on a stone. But in Fall Lake & on the next portage I got my second wind; by the third - Pipestone Falls - I was carrying a canoe. Skinny-dipped & ate lunch on an island in Pigeon Bay. After a siesta we pushed off again. This time I took the stern & navigated all the way to here.

We have camped on a small island in mammoth Basswood Lake. The rocks, lichen, trees, animal life are fascinating. The fishermen are having some luck, & we have seen beaver & deer. The tents are up; the woodsmoke from our dinner fire smells good. As I'm not cooking tonight, I have leisure to enjoy sun, water, nature, & thoughts.

Someone took a black-and-white picture of me that evening: alone, barefoot, unshaven, leaning against a rock as tall as myself, gesturing and talking to the air. Composing a journal entry? Pondering a career? Or (as someone scrawled on the back) "ESP'ing to Penny." The interiority, the obliviousness, is frightening. Perhaps I was trying to learn the part they had unaccountably given me. David must have realized that I was overmatched and was bringing me along carefully. At each stage something new was introduced - a canoe to carry, stern-paddling to master with its sweeps and J-strokes, a map to navigate by - and gradually my confidence increased, even that first day.

June 21, Basswood River - A bend in the torrent, a canyon of foam:/ For one brilliant evening, a paradise home.

I wish Penny were here to share this. To lie in the warm sun, to lean against the wind, deafened by the roar of the stream, to live off the forest & feel the tingle of cold water on glowing skin! What an idyll this country is! I feel myself growing hard enough again to be capable of sensuality.

Clearly this is not rational. "Live off the forest"? Our packs held at least 50 pounds of food, cookware, cans of hash, staples, powdered milk, soup mix, etc. We did catch fish, drink lake and river water, cook over wood fires and gather blueberries (Quetico-Superior Wilderness Area rules forbade more aggressive use of the flora and fauna). The country seemed less idyllic that night as the cold crept into my thin bag; I stayed awake shivering for an hour or two, hoping Africa really *was* hot. As for the remark about "hard enough to be sensual," I probably meant that I was feeling healthier than I had in a long time. What truth the entry has is that of feeling: how caught up I was in that moment and place.

We left at a gentlemanly 10:45, arrived here 2 hours & 2 portages later, pitched camp upstream of the end of the second portage & skinny-dipped in the river. After a large, grossly satisfying lunch, we dispersed to various esoteric tasks: fishing, sleeping, reading. My state of mind is more than ever focused on the moment.

This last remark was very nearly true. Most of my past life appeared to have little bearing on this existence, and my future was dark and uncertain: a cipher. The present *did* seem to deserve attention, and as an inability to enjoy the moment had been identified by friends as one of my problems, I was happy to indulge the inclination.

June 22, Lower Basswood Falls - Purple dusk of White Water Day. A hollow of green sheltered behind bluff rock, acrid smoke twisting over dark tents, a campsite drowning in the thunder of the falls. A day I'll remember for the thrill of my first ride through white water.

I cut my teeth on rapids today. The first was just below last night's campsite. I paddled bow for Barry, then took it alone. Easy, really. Kneel in the center, coast slowly (paddling steadily for control) into the vortex of the dark, smooth "V" (feeling its power and seeing, peripherally, the shore rush by), then glide straight into wild, foaming haystacks, take a little spray, cut right & you're out, milling in the eddy, looking back at white water.

The next rapids we ran without baggage. I paddled bow for Barry, then we portaged back, loaded the packs & ran it again. This time I rode bow for Mr. Biel. I paddled bow for him in the next & most exciting rapids, too: a canyon, channeling its current with a roar from dark V to white haystack. We made two or three sharp turns during the half-minute run. A real thrill.

If I went back to what has become the Boundary Waters Wilderness Area now and saw these chutes and riffles that so impressed me then, I would laugh at all the fuss - which seems to me an excellent reason for not going back.

Found a small lake today. It is on the map, unnamed. I came on it after a hike over a hill through Green Mansiony forest. Don't know why I kept walking: I was looking for a stream & had given up on that. But I kept exploring the moss-grown forest (there were piles of stones to mark an old trail) until I saw Penny's Pond.

When I told David about the place, he talked of adopting it as a wildlife study area and possible shortcut for Windhome. At once I realized that I liked it the way it was: unknown and deserted. Did I see the selfishness of that? Probably not. At any rate, I promised myself that I'd return.

After this initial high of wilderness canoeing with peers and elders, I - we - had to come down to reality: this was a camp, and a camp has campers. Each week a bus arrived from Camp Baganemon and deposited thirty loud teen-age boys. After a night of camping on the island, they left the next morning for a five-day canoe trip, returning in time to sleep another night at Windhome and catch the bus bringing up next week's quota. The first busload also brought three resident campers: 16-year-old returnees who would spend the whole summer at Windhome. Barry moved out of our cabin to bunk with Hal in the stores house, and the residents moved in. It was a poor exchange: while not wholly uninteresting, they were no more thoughtful than most high-school boys, and I was never off duty unless asleep. Still, it gave me a chance to see the camp - and to some extent, life - through their eyes. One thing I learned from them was that "pretty well everybody" at the camp was Jewish, which made me feel like more of an outsider.

With my cabin no longer a place of refuge, I went looking for privacy. At the southwest end of the island a high granite bluff faced the length of Garden Lake, where on sunny afternoons the west wind scuffed the face of the lake into bright wavelets and swept away chaff of all kinds. It could have been the place that inspired the camp's name. Here, dazzled by the sun, braced against the wind, I read and wrote in my spare time - and considered my future, whose only apparent certainty soon dissolved.

June 26 - The last two days I have alternated between depression & hope. The main factor is the uncertain fate of the Africa trip. Two letters from Hector, & a phone call yesterday, have confirmed my fear: he is not willing to make the necessary sacrifices. It's a matter of judging values, of course, & I respect his. But this project is so tied up with my hopes & plans now as to be inextricable.

A trip to New York & a AAA "road book" have convinced him that the money we have ($1500 apiece) won't take us where we want to go. He may be right. I say go anyway: perhaps our sources are at fault. Hector says he may want to use the money elsewhere: grad school, a photo shop. So I hang in the balance, not to know the fate of our plans for a few days more.

Fate! It seemed that I wanted our safari worse than Hector did. Hey, my life savings were going into the project, too! The real difference between us was that this was the best use *I* could think of for them. Hector had promised to consider my arguments, but the axe fell a few days later.

June 29 - Today is, from a short-range point of view, le jour catastrophe. Hector writes that he is bowing out. I have little hope that my proposals for a change of plans will be effective. I have written suggesting that we use orthodox transportation between key points in Africa, or confine ourselves to the Mediterranean. If he does not rise to either of these lures, it means a solo trip or the Marines for me.

The Marines?! Yes: in 1959 a healthy 22-year-old American male who was neither a father nor a student was liable to be classified

1-A and drafted into the Army. Both Hector and I had to face this obligation. His draft board was, he said, not hungry, but mine was ravenous; any 1-A's number would come up in a few months, they said, so to take a long trip I needed a student deferment. I applied for graduate work in English at Debrew, where my references would assist admission, in the *second* semester. But if there was not to be a trip - and the prospect of a solo effort was daunting - I would have to "serve my country," and the most attractive version of that was the Marines, who would teach me to fly.

Another front of concern opened that day:

The other blow is a letter from Penny...they found no jobs waiting in Germany, as [had been] promised. She makes light of it - they're off on a vagabond tour - but with no income & little money of their own, I don't know how they're to live. I hope she gets the $20 I sent.

Although I took any opportunity to evade them, the campers had the effect of drawing me out of such problems into my duties. The north woods helped too, in a different way, and now the two had to be combined. To me they seemed oil and water. My first trip, with David and a group of 14-year-olds, went to the big lakes northeast of Ely. The boys' unreflecting coarseness and indifference to nature annoyed me, yet there were also moments of beauty that dissolved my cares in a welcome fashion.

July 1, 11 p.m., North Bay, Canada - Titans rode the sky tonight: great dark cloud shapes, driven by devils of wind & rain. The sky was a multicolored battleground as the forces of good & evil [met]. It was like the war of the worlds. After the storm, fantastic rose-orange glowed in the sky, & the evening star appeared.

July 2, Shade Lake, Canada - The pies are cooking! The sun, still 20 degrees above the horizon at 6:30, is cutting a brilliant path across this lake. Our campsite's center is a rock point, with tents pitched under nearby trees. The lake was a welcome sight after the sluggish waters we traveled this morning. An hour-long swim this afternoon washed away the sludge & replaced it with a warm glow. We toppled a canoe, paddled on air mattresses....

This was David's way of rewarding fairly good behavior and making sure the boys enjoyed themselves. It is good to be reminded that I did sometimes have fun with the campers, and that, while I regarded this as the *domestic* part of my travels, most of the canoeing took place in Canada.

The next day I lost my pen and could not find another (David brought neither book, journal nor pen on trips: they were distractions from nature), so I did not write about a deserted stretch of the Quetico. For two days after portaging into Canada we saw no one at all. Private seaplanes were not allowed to land, so anyone there had come as we had: paddling and portaging. Every portage stopped another *outboard-fisherman*, another *gentleman camper* with his Colman stove and portable radio. David didn't have to say what was wrong with these styles: his tone of voice did that, and our mode of travel demonstrated the alternative.

On this trip I learned to appreciate David as a mentor. The boys, who seldom had a good word for anything, rarely had a bad one for him. He was a Thoreauvian athlete, a Paul Bunyan with sensibilities, an intermediary between the wilderness and the campers, who seldom failed to profit from their exposure to both. His ideal was to move through the land respectfully, a *tabula rasa*, without announcing his arrival, creating a stir, or leaving a trace. We were fortunate interlopers, to be neither seen nor heard (I did not realize then how much of this he had imbibed from writers such as Aldo Leopold and Sigurd Olson). A certain amount of animal spirits - such as joyful swims in isolated lakes - he permitted, but these indulgences were balanced by an hour at a time of paddling and portaging in silence. Even at Windhome, David believed that clean lakewater, firewood, and gas lanterns made electric lights and running water unnecessary as well as inappropriate, so we had none.

The last day of the trip was formidable: 25 miles into headwinds and through squalls on big lakes separated by long portages. At lunch we could still see the beach where we had camped the previous night. There we remained, windbound, for hours. Later came tailwinds, and I learned to dislike following seas that slopped water into the canoes and pushed them off course even more than headwinds. We reached Windhome dinnerless at 11 PM, but in style. There was just enough light to see by as our once-noisy horde ghosted in silently around the back of the island at David's behest. We came within ten yards of Jennifer, who was washing her hands on the float by the footbridge, before David softly called her name. Too calm a person to be much startled, she flashed her dazzling smile and invited us to a late supper of soup and spaghetti. To me she said quietly, "You have a couple of letters."

They were as good as the last pair had been grim. One was from Penny, reporting that she and Andrea had procured jobs in Konstanz, Germany, after all, so that crisis was averted. The other was from Hector, who wrote, "*I like your 'plan B': the Mediterranean & North Africa, for as long as we find it rewarding, independently on two cycles. We each go where we like when we like, & if one of us feels he's not getting his money's worth, he's free to leave. On these conditions (if I don't change my mind again!), count me in.*"

So our trip was on again, but for how long? Hector's letter, as careful as a lawyer's, stressed *independence*. Not sure how far to trust his change of mind, I nevertheless replied warmly and resumed my reading on Africa. Though I now concentrated on *North* Africa, especially Egypt, I continued to raid the Ely Library – whenever we were in town - for books about the continent in general, hoping that some door might open once we were abroad.

July 9, a campsite in Fraser Lake - If I owned an island, I'd do what someone did with this one before the wilderness area: a cabin, an outhouse, a stone fireplace, some tent sites. It's as good as the place on Knife Lake last night. Must mark these on a map to come back to. I'm on a seven-day trip with Barry & the resident campers.

At this point I began to combine journal-keeping with letters to Penny, and found the extra dimension that gave interesting. To her I wrote:

I envy you & everyone who has had the experience of camping all their lives. I am tempted to hold against my parents the omission from my education of harmony with the wild. I shouldn't have to be learning at 22 how to cook, pitch a tent, portage, etc.

This new audience, and events on the trip, made me even more introspective, more susceptible to self-doubt. At Adams Lake I felt "very down on myself, for I seem to be a farce." It took me a while to locate the source of these feelings; at first it was just existential flailing.

It is as if the world continued to turn & I rode along outside, beating my wings. I need a great task to which I can give all my energies, & stop having to make excuses to the world. Specifically, I am doing a bad job of counseling my three charges. I have never done any counseling before, & [am] learning my way around the wilderness.

Again, and more strongly, I felt that my expensive education had no use, no relevance, in the north woods. This was a steep learning curve! But recognizing a specific problem did not dull the pain - just allowed deeper analysis.

July 11, Adams Lake - I'm disenchanted with myself. I have been overrated. I am failing in my work here, after a propitious beginning. I have been a miserable influence on the boys, as Barry pointed out yesterday. The lessons I am learning here are hard ones, & they hurt.

A college girlfriend showed me a comic strip that her father had sent. A shopkeeper hands a broom to a young man, telling him to sweep the floor. "But I'm a college graduate!" Shopkeeper: "OK, I'll show you how." I felt like the guy being taught to sweep. Only later did it occur to me that these feelings did not occur on the first two trips with David, but only on the third, with Barry. David's style was to build confidence; he had had to show me many things, of course, but never implied that I should have known them. His only comments on my work had been positive. Barry, on the other hand, was a critic, and I was on his turf. That he was three years younger, and knew more about this work than I, made his criticism more painful.

My relationship with the resident campers was part of the problem: I didn't know how to behave towards them. Since we shared a cabin, I had been treating them more or less as roommates, as younger equals; now it seemed that I was to establish some distance and be exemplary to them. I thought that that point might have been made when Barry moved out and they moved in. Maintaining the right balance between authority and amity under those conditions would have challenged an experienced and gifted counselor, let alone an insecure neophyte.

I did manage to step outside my own problems long enough to contemplate my environs at Adams Lake:

One "great truth" emerges from this summer: Life Abounds. The glacier-pocked, granite-hard face of Minnesota & Ontario is alive with every species I've ever known, & more. There are fish, beaver, deer, bear, moose, ducks, loons, herons, eagles & snakes, not to mention leeches. The insect population seems infinite. If I wake up with a crawling sensation, it's because spiders & ants are exploring me. The wilderness teems with life, & thereby sets us an example.

This glance outward was fleeting. Penny had suggested that I make time to be alone, and to reflect. The opposite of my father's view, it coincided with my impulse, especially amidst campers. In another culture I would have gone on a spirit quest or retreat. I did retreat whenever possible, and as a result, "certain vague mental images" came to seem "startlingly clear facts." Mainly this meant trying to assess who I was and where I was going.

I have emerged most of the way from adolescence, & need convictions. Perhaps I have now had enough time to think things over. Perhaps this is the time when I answer Peer Gynt's question: who am I? Perhaps I can no longer postpone the pressure to decide my beliefs about religion, politics, morality, a vocation. Adolescence is a torrent of undirected emotions, impressions & influences: a period of change, of development, a debut in the world of nuance. It was not for me a happy time. Perhaps it ends when one gets insight into its dilemmas. Perhaps it ends only when one can say, "I'm happy." If I have emerged from that cocoon, then the relief from pain brings with it an obligation to assume responsibility. I have not yet done this.

What strikes me now is how often "perhaps" occurs in this entry, and how optimistic I was about post-adolescent existence. Aristotle wrote that character is formed by the age of six or seven, and many modern educators agree. I was already very nearly the person I was going to be, though I might evolve in some ways.

July 13, Kawishiwi R. Forks - About the time I finished my entry on the 11th, the fishermen returned & we started dinner. After that it was clean-up, then ghost stories around the campfire until bedtime. The next morning we got up at 6 & covered 20 miles, including 5 portages, several rapids to wade & 2 to shoot. Camped last night within the limits of "civilized" influence: the Great American Public was much in evidence. Today we covered 12 miles & pitched camp on this pleasant island in a little-traveled section of the Kawishiwi.

[Philip] Wylie, who attacks organized religion generally, says that man's immortality is his children. He is more secular than I, but he gives child-raising the importance it deserves.

9 PM - I cooked again tonight. My efforts, bumbling at first, have met with some success. A macaroni & cheese dinner 3 nights ago, spaghetti tonight, & an apple pie have all been applauded.

Why hadn't I tried cooking before? It was satisfying and even fun to produce a meal, especially when the diners liked it. I *enjoyed* rolling pie crust on the bottom of an overturned canoe (using a tin can of apple filling, and brushing off any leeches first), then baking it in the folding reflector oven.

The sun is going down & the bugs are out. This is the last day of our trip: we should get back to Windhome tomorrow. It has been a trip that has taught me much & straightened me out somewhat.

It is startling to see that this week-long outing with the resident campers and Barry, during which I had a miserable crisis of confidence, ended on a mellow note.

In high-summer mode now, we spent less than 48 hours at Windhome between trips. We would try to arrive early in the afternoon, clean up and check for mail: in my case, the latest report from Penny or Hector. On the morrow we packed for the next trip, saw off our veteran campers and received the tyros in their stead. There was usually time for volleyball, and David had the staff and resident campers road-running. The next morning we were off again.

July 16, S. Kawishiwi R. - This is the time of day I love: evening, with tents pitched, garbage & toilet pits dug, firewood gathered & cookfire smoke trailing pungently through the firs & spruces. I've had my swim & feel clean. It's a healthy existence.

This trip is with younger boys (12 & 13), with whom I have not tripped before. Although their lack of strength & size means extra work for [us], they are an amiable bunch. They look up to counselors, seem interested in us, & are not the thorns in the side that some of their older confederates are. In general, I prefer being with them.

Teachers and coaches are permitted to smile. I had discovered for myself that the pleasures of hero-worship are more likely to be found in pre-teens than in older boys.

July 18, Clear Lake - There was much for a counselor to do yesterday. Barry & I took our 8 charges to a nearby rapids, which we ran & swam in. After I cooked dinner we moved camp to this lovely island.

Today Barry & I stayed on the island; the junior counselor [is] taking the little monsters for the day (we took them yesterday). We have been swimming, talking, reading & writing. He told me about David's plans to make Windhome autonomous. He wants to have 75-100 campers living in cabins on the island [which] will be a base directing trips to Mexico, British Columbia & ocean sails. There will be instruction in literature, languages, the arts, & an artist in residence.

I knew David was no ignorant woodsman: Barry says he was first a physics, then a divinity, then a phys ed student at Wisconsin. He nearly made Phi Bete while working to support his mother & sister. He is an outstanding family man, which he gives top priority. David has been asked to head 5 or 6 camps, & [ran] the last National Phys Ed Conference. I hope he thought carefully before mentioning to me the possibility of my working here again.

Barry was my only source for most of this, but David did run an Outward Bound school some years later, and became a respected figure in his field. It is good to see that Barry and I were still having friendly exchanges - when the campers were not an issue. I had time to write more that afternoon.

Another Truth of the wilderness: Variation is Infinite. I look down a stream at myriad trees & bushes & see dozens of different species, a hundred shades of green & brown, thousands of plants, millions of leaves. Everywhere is lush profusion, an endless array of life, proof that we don't <u>need</u> anything "new under the sun." A rapids pours a torrent of green-brown water against a rock, forming first a hollow like a lock of dark hair, then a glimpse of speckled granite as through a plastic case, then a bright explosion of froth. Always the same, yet never for an instant the same pattern of light & shade on the droplets. Ten million molecules an instant, changing from hollow to billow, the infinite river made of infinitesimal droplets. Man, passing through, can only wonder at the land & its Creator, feel vague stirrings of kinship & yearn for the wisdom to see relationships.

Although there is much in this passage that I would revise today, I still find the attempt (by a novice woodsman who had not read Heraclitus) to express the paradox of flux within stasis interesting.

Perhaps influenced by a senior-year zoology course, I was trying to dig in and understand my environment. The introduction of "the Creator" shows that despite everything - Nails Bradley's course in Non-Christian Religions, Philip Wylie, my own lapsed church-going - I was still a theist, not yet prepared to drop a capitalized Creator in favor of the creative forces of nature.

The season was short enough. I made only six trips: one with the staff, three with visiting campers, the week with the three residents, and a glorious return to the Basswood region with more staff than campers, which made me feel more competent and relaxed. We had to make this excursion in order to relieve a two-man trip (Barry and one of the residents) who had totaled their canoe in a rapid, but had managed to send word of their loss to Windhome. The canoe could not be salvaged or even reached, and was still hung up on a rock in the main channel at summer's end. Of this outing I have just one memorial:

July 27, Basswood River - Have you ever risen from bed in the early morning light & eased naked into cold, running black water? Whatever you're doing now, do you? I did this morning, & the glow of sensual health is pure delight. Civilization & business should not take these pleasures from man.

The challenge was directed at my later self, but s/he may accept it who will. Obviously not everyone will be able to *afford* the situation in which to achieve such "delight."

On this trip I returned to Penny's Pond, abandoning camp on a sleepy afternoon and paddling to a portage into the opposite end of the lake from the one I had seen before. Stowing the paddle, I shouldered the canoe and crossed a low rise on the moldering remains of a corduroy road (David knew of no logging around there since the 1920s). The road ended at a cove. I waded into grey mud, placed the canoe in black water in which fallen trees were rotting, and paddled out past stumps and water plants. In a minute the canoe was rocking slightly in the blue, wind-rippled center of the pond, and I stopped paddling to look about.

Water had collected in a shallow basin among low hills that rose gently in every direction except north, where I later found the outlet. Wild undergrowth and dense conifers crowded to the very edge of the water and discouraged any exploration of the shore. Yet as I watched, a yearling deer materialized from the green wall to drink in a weedy shallows, raising his head in alarm after the first sip when the sun glinted on the canoe. I remained motionless, and we regarded one another. A strange conviction came over me that I was the first human to see, or be seen by, him. What did he think of that alien, flesh-and-aluminum creation in his water supply? Not much: I had the satisfaction of seeing him drink his fill and step away in his own sweet time before I moved. Being a deer, he probably did not trouble himself with half the reflections I devoted to him.

For an hour I paddled around, nosing into various coves and shallows, searching for other life. What intrigued me about the place was its pregnant hush, as if unseen thousands were watching my intrusion. Eventually I beached the canoe in another cove, hoisted it and marched away on a faint trail over the hill. I paused once in a rocky clearing, leaned the canoe against a branch, stepped clear and told the forest how glad I was to have found it and why I had come. Then, having repaid as much as I could of what the wilderness had offered, I took the canoe on my shoulders again and continued along an ill-defined, venerable aisle in the scented green cathedral. A bit late to dinner, I told only a vague tale about the dark lake I had found.

Soon after, my own "tripping" was over for the summer. I spent the final three weeks in camp as the person responsible for the three resident campers. The Big Trip, a two-week gala for all-stars chosen from those who had come on earlier trips, was out most of this time, leaving only a few of us at Windhome. My charges were free to go on this expedition if they desired, but they couldn't be bothered, choosing to stay behind – despite my pleadings – to "get in shape" for fall sports, play cards, and occasionally go into town. I had to stay with them, reading more but communing with nature less than I would have on the "trail." This turn of events finally soured me on the boys, a process that had been simmering for most of the summer.

All high-school athletes of some sort, they came from well-off, upper-middle-class families, like most of our campers. They therefore represented, in theory, the upper crust of young American manhood (I hear Barney and Jean speaking through me here). If so, the nation was in trouble. Each boy's family had paid $600 for the summer, in return for which they took two trips and did some conditioning (calisthenics and running twice a day, plus touch football or volleyball) that they could have done at home. When they read, it was letters from home or from a girl, comic books, pulp fiction, occasionally a best seller. Card games and bull sessions - endless exchanges of gossip and opinion - were their preferred means of killing time. *As if,* writes Thoreau, *you could kill time without injuring eternity.* They were, Barney said, "about as intellectual as cabbages."

Perhaps this is harsh. Barney, an academic, naturally assigned a high value to intellect, of which these privileged young men might have no great need. I don't ask brain power of everyone; they may have some other saving grace - and I'm open to suggestions. But in these three I found neither sensitivity, spirit, geniality, nor any intimations of a higher nature. Trying to discuss with them how they were spending their summer, I encountered first incomprehension, then resentment. With time on our hands and little to do, we got on each other's nerves (incredibly, I almost came to blows with one of them, which would certainly have ended my hopes of future employment with the Biels). Was this how our power-brokers-to-be prepared themselves? It occurred to me that, by definition, only the idle would spend the summer at camp, i.e. that my charges were a self-selected mediocrity, but that was no consolation.

August 5, Windhome - The Big Trip left today, as well as a regular one. I'll be here with the residents the rest of the season. Good conditioning, reading & writing, but I'd like to trip once more.

Now that I have been in the wilderness awhile, nothing that I can write about it seems important. What is meaningful is the stream of thoughts & reflections it provokes, & these have an outlet: letters to Penny. There seems little sense in duplicating these here.

What *did* go into my journal in August were "Questions and Sore Points" about Africa gleaned from my reading. "Do Africans feel that the USA is living up to the Atlantic Charter, the UN Charter, and the responsibilities created by its wealth?" Had Egypt achieved a balance of cotton vs. food production? Was Kenya still a "White Man's Land"? Where did the Mau-Mau fit in? Was South African apartheid worse than American Jim Crow? What about taxes on natives? Land expropriation? Pass systems? And so on, country by country, page after earnest page: agricultural staples, exports, political and social problems, possible dangers for us ("Tanganyika: tsetse flies; Germans"). If I was going to be an ambassador, I didn't want to be an ignorant one. On the outside, I went about doing my chores and interacting with the few people around, but I lived in books about the exotic places I still hoped to visit.

Aug. 15, Windhome - I feel the urge to halt for a moment this fast-closing summer. Times of peace & gear-shifting like this may someday be rare. The Big Trip has been out for ten days; the last small trip has returned & gone home. Barney & Jean left this morning: memories of stimulating talk, singing, & European nostalgia.

I've spent the time well, I think. The conditioning is taking effect. I've continued to read, keep up my correspondence, meditate. The older folks here are good to me: Rex & Elaine are fine people, & Jennifer talks as if she wants me back. I could stand that!

Underneath the peace, however, is Africa, with its growing psychological importance. I still search for the deepest rationale for going. Perhaps I wish to give back all that has been given, start with nothing & see what happens. It's akin to the motive for mountain-climbing I read somewhere. My reading on Africa has re-engendered a desire to get to the heart of the challenge. The knowledge of how I'll change during the trip forbids me to make lasting decisions now about marriage, the service, a job.

Letters from Penny yesterday & Dr. Pelham today. Hers was wonderfully loving: I read it on the point this morning & was in its spell. The doctor's contained welcome tidings: our report has been attached to his Committee's report to the University. He had high praise for the "style" & "intellectual analysis."

Harleigh Pelham, a respected professor in Debrew's History Department, chaired part of the university's Long-Range Planning Committee. A senior men's group that I belonged to had submitted a report on undergraduate housing that criticized living conditions on the men's campus as inimical to learning and civilization. And he endorsed it!

I did make a final, unplanned excursion into the north woods. Barney's last trip returned with a bag of human bones that some campers had taken from an old Indian burial ground. When Rex found out about this he was very upset, and told Jennifer (David being out) that they must be returned to the grave site: if the local Indians learned of this desecration they would be angry. If we buried them near camp or tried to sink them in the lake, they might come to light sometime, and then the police would be asking questions. They must go back immediately.

Fortunately the grave was not too distant, about 10 miles away; we could get there and back in a day. Jennifer, Hal and I undertook the mission. With three strong paddlers and a light load we made fast work of it: by midday we had reached the deserted site, where we replaced the bones amid others under some weathered boards - forming a sort of low roof - on a mound. After lunch we paddled home, moving easily but quickly. Despite the ghoulish nature of our task, it was a welcome break from camp routine and a joyous return to the wilderness, in which I now felt very comfortable. But it was only for one day.

A week later my sojourn at the "gateway to the silent places" ended and I carried my duffel across the wooden foot-bridge to the mainland for the last time. Although I was finally going where I had long desired to go, a bittersweet nostalgia flattened any tendency to jubilation. Plants of a rare kind had grown from dormant seeds at Garden Lake, and I had reaped much more than I had sown. I felt that my life had been changed, that I would never be quite the same after those months in the north woods. If so, my *Wanderjahr* was not about to commence, but had already begun. Also I was taking leave of some people I really cared about, and might not see again.

Nature was charitable at parting and did not flaunt her beauty. No sun, no ripples, no wind sweeping the birches. There was a hint of fall in the dull sky and leaden lakewaters. I said my brief goodbyes, got into a friend's car and shut the door on Windhome.

Aug. 23, Breezeway, PA, 11 PM - Hitchhiking home from camp. Got a ride to Detroit with Artie, spent night at his home & hit the road at 9 AM. First 3 rides (Detroit - Ohio Pike) in Ford wagons. One to Cleveland exit, a sizzling 2-hour wait, a lift to Akron exit, an hour wait, a ride to Warren, where I took time for a meal, & then a skyrocket here in 3 hours. Rain. During the last stretch, kicking myself into meeting the challenge of Africa.

Artie, a counselor at the main camp who had come on a Windhome trip as an assistant, gave me a fine start. I had decided to save money by hitchhiking home, which might also show me a different America. Most of the people I met were ordinary middle-class midwesterners, though, and the waits were boring. Three drivers in a row picked me up because they saw my guitar, and I played for my ride. In the middle of the night, on the Pennsylvania Turnpike, an Army vet who was searching for America - and himself - in a strap undershirt spent an hour begging me to "convert to Christ." He had found Jesus and was anxious to share the Good News; I tried to interest him in Buddhism. His proselytizing was benevolent, however, and my expressions of scepticism were gentle. The ride moved me well eastward and the debate kept us awake through the wee small hours, so I considered it a positive encounter. He sent me *Christ*mas cards for several years.

My last ride left me in the heart of Brooklyn. Weary from a sleepless night, I covered the last 30 miles to Suburb by train - probably. The hitchhike took 24 hours and cost me $7. At *that* time I would have recommended the experience to any male without dependents, stipulating that he not carry much money. Today, of course, is another matter.

At home I read, exercised, scanned the shipping notices and looked at outdoor equipment while waiting for Hector: planning to camp when possible, we needed a tent, backpacks and cookware. I obtained Able-Bodied Seaman's papers in case a marine opening occurred; we still hoped for a free passage. The doctor who examined me for the New York Maritime Board asked kindly, "And why are you going to sea, son?" I was Saul Bellow's "dangling man," suspended between the end of school days and the next step. By preference, that would be our trip, though we had made no irrevocable plans yet. On paper, I would start graduate work at Debrew in February, but the US Army draft would be watching from the wings.

After two weeks, Hector came north and our ladies returned from Europe. There were still major decisions to be made about equipment, modes of travel, a destination! The time of operating on my own was over. Our big adventure was about to start. It was September: harvest time.

It has come to this,--that the lover of art is one, and the lover of nature another, though true art is but the expression of our love of nature. It is monstrous when one cares but little about trees and much about Corinthian columns....

- Thoreau

III. Count Whitehand Goes to Napoli

"What does Africa, - what does the West stand for? Is not our own interior white on the chart?

- Thoreau

Dear Henry,

I agree: spirit-travels are most important, and unexplored territory can symbolize the unmapped regions within - but then we diverge. If Africa "stands for...our own interior white on the chart," you say, why bother to go? Yet it isn't *only* a symbol, is it, and where better to conduct the personal exploration? How likely am I to do any serious adventuring along my inner byways amid the dull round of daily cares? *You* always strove for a correspondence between soul and environment. Where was my Walden to be found? At school? You know better. At work? Not yet! You saw that your bean-field labor was just material for parables, yet you did it, because you liked sowing seeds. If Africa is a parable of inner questings, why should I not search there for my mirror? You know there are other bean-fields than yours. If we must live on two levels, make them harmonize, let them mesh, not grind in peace-destroying friction! It is always the inner world that loses.

No, whatever you meant by that remark, let me act out my allegory as you did yours. It matters little that we finally did only a bit of Africa or that the continent has now been explored; the curious man makes his own maps. I was a student of civilization, not geography. What you in your 30s found among ponds, books and friends in Massachusetts, I in my 20s sought among the peoples of the middle of the world, the *Medi-terranean*. After all, I think, you would not have been so displeased with that as to withhold your blessing - but I would not go without making my peace.

Great bursts of spray fly up perpetually from the western cliffs of the Azores. Nine mountains whose tops pierce the sea, green and arable only in scattered places, the islands present the rolling sweep of the Atlantic with its first obstacle in 2000 miles. Night and day through the centuries these headlands have endured the blue-green ocean's onslaught in a cannonade of white explosions: the charge and repulse of ranks of two-ton warriors, caught in mid-step and smashed to froth. Nothing in nature had stirred me like that meeting of wave and cliff. On passing ships the report is audible as a delayed crack and a sigh; even miles at sea the air is filled with a fine spray, so ethereal that it cleanses ship and passengers, as if that epic clash had the power to purge: a kind of natural catharsis. If ever irresistible force met immovable object, it is on those sheer windy bluffs, yet I wondered whether the islands were actually withstanding the charge, as it appeared, or if they were imperceptibly retreating toward their colonizers' homeland, and might someday find themselves cornered and *driven into the land.* Seeing them was already worth the passage-money. I would have tried to write heroic sea-poetry there, had I known Anglo-Saxon or Old Norse.

The month between the windswept cliff on Garden Lake and those in the Azores was hectic and disorderly. Once Hector, Penny and Andrea arrived, the pace quickened to a blur of many gestures. He and I spent three days haunting New York maritime offices and Hudson River piers in search of a job in the merchant marine, but the recession was at its height; even experienced seamen were on the beach. I grew uneasy at the idea that I might actually find a job, becoming a cheap replacement for a career sailor with a family. Our hunt acquired faint but unpleasant overtones of class struggle for me. Hector too became discouraged.

Every contact proved useless, every lead a dead end. The editor of the *Suburb Times* didn't think he needed to have his own man in Africa, or to read my collegiate essays. We spent an afternoon with well-dressed, idealistic people from Moral Re-Armament at an estate in North Suburb, hoping that *they* might send us abroad, as someone had suggested. They asked if we believed in world peace through shared moral revival. From what I had read, heard in my courses, and seen in Europe, we did not share a morality with Russia, China, or Germany, and after Suez, could we even say that we understood Britain, France and Israel? The thought of posing as some kind of moral re-armorer horrified me. Their faces fell; obviously I had botched that question. We said polite good-byes and departed in frustration. It seemed that we were going to be on our own.

It was a confusing period of uncertain, sidelong movements: plans, arguments, decisions and revisions, side trips, spending time with our lady loves, trying to select gear with our destination still unknown, simultaneously doubting our chances of reaching Africa and sending to Kenya for gun permits. Penny and I went off for a weekend in Boston, and another in the Adirondacks with Hector and Andrea. Hector made a brief trip home to say goodbye to his family and look into a scholarship to graduate school.

One by one we made the choices that reflected our ideal trip and shaped the real one: a butterscotch two-man tent with floor and screening ($26) on Long Island, an Army surplus cook kit ($2.98) on 42nd street. Our olive-drab backpacks ("assbreakers") were also Army issue. Then, accepting the final defeat of the free-passage idea - our only hope of reaching East Africa on the money we had - we cast our lots with Plan B: circle the Mediterranean. Our "Bold Journey" was now less so – but might be possible. Much then fell into place. We could choose clothes for a specific climate, and had some idea of the roads we would have to negotiate (though we knew less of both than we imagined). Motor *scooters,* cheaper than 'cycles, should suffice to circumnavigate Our Sea. Italy, scooter capital of the world, became a logical goal, though in theory any city around the Med *might* do (we nearly took a prison boat to Morocco). When we found an Italian Line ship, the *Conte Biancamano*, that would take us to Naples for $185 (4th class), sailing September 25th, it looked like destiny.

Logistics became the science of the moment; everything had to be crammed into our backpacks, to be lashed onto scooters somehow. On the night of the 23rd we made our final choices, paying close attention to the volume and weight of each item: clothes, camping gear, cameras, books, etc. It seemed miraculous that they all fit - but in fact we took only what did. On the morning of the 24th we went to a travel agency on Suburb Avenue to book our passage. The man at the counter was astonished: "You want to leave *tomorrow*?!" At that moment, however, we knew more about ships in New York than he did, knew that this was the best deal in town and that there was space. A wave of exultation washed over me. We were doing the right thing! Then I went off to spend the rest of the day with Penny.

Auspicious omens and generous gestures of support graced our last days. Uncle Gene gave me his old Exa, which Peerless Camera finished repairing on the 24th, and my parents donated film: more items to stow! Mom also gave me $200 (forgoing piano lessons that fall to do so), which I appreciated as both moral and financial support. Letters and calls bidding us *bon voyage* kept arriving from friends and relatives. On the morning of the 25th, after a few hours' sleep, I was awakened by the news that Phillip and Melissa, my Boston friends, had had a daughter. Dad took a rare morning off work so that he and Mom could drive us to the Hudson River pier - close to where we had been job-hunting a week earlier - for our noon departure.

Hector and I looked odd enough on the pier and on deck, dressed in wash-and-wear suits (our only good clothes), carrying the bulging packs. No matter! We might be walking contradictions, but we were on our way, *our* way. Hector remarked that Lindbergh's plane looked ungainly as *it* took off. We were outfitted for scooter travel, not fashionable embarcations. Dad went below to inspect our dormitory quarters and came back shaking his head. "Well, you'll be roughing it, all right," he said. Not until I saw his expression at that moment did it hit me how hard this must be for him. To have raised himself from the small-time South of 1930 to the pinnacle of his profession in New York, and now to have his elder son sail off to see the world at the end of his expensive education instead of getting a job…for the first time I viewed it all through his Depression-colored spectacles, and felt contrite, and sorry for him. But he left with a good word. As did Mom, of course - mothers always do - and the word was, "Write!"

Anchors Aweigh: the *Conte Biancamano*

> You are the great Western Barbarian, stepping forth in his innocence and might, gazing a while at this poor effete Old World, and then swooping down on it.
>
> - Henry James, *The American*

Our sailing was almost totally eclipsed by that of the S.S. *United States*: the huge, elegant speedster on which my family had returned from Europe in 1955. This had to be classified as a symbolic concurrence, since *our* mode of travel was meant to be less extravagant, lower-class, but more vital and demanding than that of the standard tourist. As we passed Battery Park - rolling in the wake of the *United States* - my Italian Tourist Class-mates were making musical whoopee on the afterdeck. The afternoon was mostly fair but cool; upstate there would be some fall color in the trees by now. I changed into less formal clothes and brought out my new snap-ring journal.

Sept. 25, 1959, Conte Biancamano, Lower N.Y. Bay - Thirty-three days after my return from Windhome, we are off to Napoli. Events have moved too fast to be recorded here. The Windhome journal will have to stand as preface to this trip.

This voyage, which has started with Italians playing accordions, singing & dancing on deck, promises plenty of interest. After calling at Boston, we stop in the Azores, Lisbon, Casablanca, Gibraltar, Barcelona, the Maiori Islands [sic], Cannes, Genoa [and] Naples.

The "Maiori Islands"? The ship's itinerary I unaccountably preserved does not mention them. Was I trying to remember an earlier version in which we were scheduled to call at Palma de Mallorca (which can also be spelled Majorca or Maiorca)? And confusing Maiorca with Maori? There was much to learn. Both sides of the itinerary are overwritten with Italian paradigms and vocabulary, grouped by parts of speech. There are adverbs from *quando* (when) to *ieri* (yesterday); conjunctions from *che* (that) to *perche* (why); idioms from *cader del sonno*, be very sleepy, to *stringere la mano*, shake hands; and verb conjugations: *bere*, to drink, *dire*, to say, *piacere*, to please, *fare* (do, make), *potere* (can, be able to), etc. The languages I had studied were Latin, French, and a year of Spanish; the languages we now seemed likely to need were Italian, Greek, Turkish, and Arabic. Evidently Ralph McGill had been right: "commencement" meant the beginning of education.

At lunch that first day, hungrily munching Italian rolls as the Lower Bay fell behind, I met *Signore* and *Signora* Russo, recently retired and returning to the Old Country to live on their savings. He had been a barber in Akron and Youngstown for thirty years. His hobby was the *mandolino*, on which he twanged classical melodies and Italian songs. Over pasta he announced, "I have forgot more than I'll ever know." I imagined gigantic mental transactions, casual gains and losses of Dow Jones magnitude. Small, neat and white-haired, he contrasted strikingly with his hefty wife, a mighty trencherwoman. They resembled stereotypes of Italian-Americans so closely that at first I was suspicious, yet they remained true to the end. I borrowed a guitar later and accompanied *Signore* Russo on some of his melodic flights. Improvising an accompaniment to Schubert's *Serenade* was beyond my reach, but our soulful version of *Torna a Sorrento* seemed to move the assembled listeners deeply.

Music, in fact, flourished in 3rd and 4th class, which dined together. Any number of uneducated, ill-mannered and frequently drunken slobs turned out to have glorious tenor or baritone voices; at dinner we were frequently regaled with winey duets by a tall-thin and short-fat pair a few tables away. The only bass I met, a ne'er-do-well who was often seasick, hearing me praise *Don Giovanni*, treated me to an impromptu performance of *Non voglio piu servir* on deck as we coasted the dark capes of Spain one grey, gusty afternoon. But that is getting far ahead.

Sept. 27, Conte Biancamano, at sea - Yesterday we docked in Boston as fireboats sprayed & tugs tooted [the ship's first visit there]. Hector & I paid a visit to a surprised Phillip. H. & I walked around Beacon Hill, the Esplanade & Commonwealth Ave. After dinner, we all went to Boston Lying-In Hospital & saw Melissa, who looks fine & happy, & Susan, who is incredibly small & very rambunctious. Then Phillip walked us to the ship, which sailed at 11. This morning is perfect: cool, clear weather, calm sea, a good pace, & a string of trawlers on the southern horizon.

For the first few days east of Boston we would see long lines of fishing boats in the distance. Later there were steel-blue flying fish, 6 to 8 inches long, gliding through the wave-troughs on triangular fins. As the vast ocean and blue sky grew familiar, I turned to reading, language study, and new acquaintances. Occasionally I held puzzling conversations with a young Mexican priest whose English was, if anything, worse than my Spanish. Each of us spoke in our weaker language, resorting to French at semantic crises. Mutual good will saw us through, along with the good offices of a husky young Spanish cleric who also spoke French, English, and German, and was learning Portuguese. He was returning to a monastery in Asturia after some years of Jesuit training in the U.S. Everyone was impressed by his quiet strength and pleasant humor. I found him admirable, and wished him well when we parted at Barcelona.

Sept. 29, 7 PM, C.B., 620 miles from Boston - Life at sea is proceeding as per intent: reading, language study & exercise. I study Italian & Spanish 2 hours apiece per day, & read another hour or two. 100 push-ups, 30 chin-ups & other calisthenics. Do laundry every day in the shower. Have finally encountered the semblance of a sea, to which the C.B. responds with an energetic rock & roll.

My Berlitz Italian phrasebook was useful (though I disliked its icon of the bald, bespectacled American tourist in his frock coat), and I evidently had something with verb paradigms. I. A. Richards's *Spanish Through Pictures* was interesting, if by then a bit elementary. We had brought an assortment of books to be read, traded, or given away. I was reading Aaron Copland's *Music and Imagination*, while Hector, a history student, was engrossed in Will Durant. As for conditioning, Hector's influence replaced the Biels's; without him I might have lapsed.

A week's sailing brought us to the thousand-mile sprawl of the Azores, breaking the pleasant monotony of our shipboard regime. We were to call only at San Miguel, but a day earlier we passed Flores, over a hundred miles west of the next island.

(1 Oct.) It was very rugged & precipitous, & revealed four small white villages & high green fields through the bluish haze. The air

smells fresh here, the sun is warm, & it looked very inviting. This is a milestone: we have now passed our first European possessions.

Here I first saw the great wave-lashed cliffs that impressed me so much. As in the Quetico, it seemed an unequal exchange to receive such bounty and be able to give back only words. An American prophet, though, had tried:

We can never have enough of nature.
We must be refreshed by the sight of inexhaustible vigor,
vast and titanic features,
the sea-coast with its wrecks, the wilderness with its living and decaying trees, the thunder-cloud....
We need to witness our own limits transgressed.

This is Thoreau, not Walt Whitman, and here it does not sound as if Concord and Walden by themselves will quite do the job for him. I do not wish to belabor this point, but it seems unlikely that one place can give everything we need. That at least was my fervent belief at the time.

Oct. 2, 3 PM, aboard C.B., east of Azores - On deck at 5:15, but no light for another half hour. Dawn revealed San Miguel as rugged & mountainous, with a scattering of white dwellings & straight, dark stone walls cutting across green fields & plowed earth. An island of shades of green, & many levels.

Punto Delgado crowded around a harbor, its houses & stores mostly white clay or brick, with some yellow & rose thrown in. Hector & I walked through the town & in the fields for 2½ hours, hounded by (usually friendly) kids begging. My Spanish was not understood. They speak a dialect of Portuguese.

High chimneys & storage vats by the harbor indicate some manufacturing, but the island as a whole is agricultural. S. Miguel produces corn, pineapple, & sugar beets; the other Azores wine, grain, & vegetables. The people are poor, though not desperately so. There is enough food, but little money. Oxen, cows, horses, etc., do much hauling in the city streets.

I don't trust this far too innocent ambassador: naïve, presumptuous, and shallow. Such facile readiness to generalize about economic conditions on San Miguel and palliate the locals' poverty after a three-hour visit! It takes time to learn how deceiving appearances can be, how little a visitor can trust such first impressions. I should have stuck to poetic descriptions of how the sun created the island from nothing as we ghosted in toward its dark mass before dawn. The entry goes on:

Our high point was an athletic scurry to the top of a hill, about 500 feet high, behind the city. There were no roads, so we crossed fields. Some Portuguese soldiers manning a gun battery gave us a Cook's tour of the fortifications.

These affable, bored young men hailed us as we descended, insisting that we come over. They managed to make us understand, despite the language barrier (we had only a few Spanish words in common, and friendly enthusiasm), that the battery was built for the island's defence ca. 1940. This scramble was the "high point" of our visit, and probably of their day. The top of the hill - a verdant forest of mostly unfamiliar trees and shrubs - gave a vista of the town below and our ship riding at anchor on the blinding ocean beyond (the shallowness of the port forced it to anchor offshore). An autumnal tang made the air exciting.

We caught the last launch back (round trip $1). Fruit vendors in brightly-painted rowboats were rocking in the clear blue water alongside; a basket on a rope, operated by someone on deck, raised fruit and lowered money. I bought a delicious pineapple for 25 cents: my only contribution to the local economy, other than postage. The island could dispatch airmail from its wartime fields, so I was able to report to family and friends.

We could see the island for two hours more. I spent the afternoon watching its sheer grey-brown cliffs, like ramparts of a bastion, act as breakwater-general to the Atlantic, throwing up diaphanous veils of spray.

Lisbon

Two days later we made our first port on the European mainland: Lisbon. The long slow approach up the Tagus River provided attractive and varied views of the city and its environs. A huge statue of Christ, spread-armed on a slitted trapezoidal base, seemed to welcome us to Europe from atop the bluffs on the south shore opposite the city. More or less across from it on the low north shore is the intensely white Tower of Belem, a picturesque old fortress-castle of which we knew little. Baedeker gives its date (1520), describes its architecture ("six tasteful turrets") and function (defence of the Tagus and political prison), but I enjoyed its mystery. To me it was a semantic as well as a geographical foil to the Good Shepherd across the water.

Oct. 4, 10 PM, C.B., off the Spanish coast - We have reached Europe, & spent the day in Lisbon. It was all new to me: I have never been to Spain or Portugal or seen Moorish influence. We left at 6, & are heading south for Casablanca in somewhat rough seas.

Lisbon is a beautiful city: I've read that, those who took the bus excursion said so, & I did see some evidence thereof. But that is not the whole story! Hector & I left the ship about 10:30 & returned about 4. We tramped 8 or 10 miles, mostly down narrow cobblestone streets, sometimes on broad boulevards, & saw, I think, the gamut: edifices, monuments, semi-slum areas on the hills east of the city, one expensive residential area, & a large slice of the business district.

I was preoccupied throughout by my inability to generalize about Lisbon. It seemed a jumble of architectures & districts, an unzoned pot pourri. There seems no plan, although the city falls into definite zones: commerce & industry near the docks, the wealthy on the gentle slopes, & the rest on the hills.

The place swarms with grey-uniformed police. The children beg universally & persistently. Meticulous workmanship has been used in building sidewalks, curbs & gutters, which are almost rough mosaic. Was struck by the similarities between this city & others. The human element must be everywhere much the same: suspicious & outwardly hostile to aliens, yet eager for close contact; playing & working much the same in all surroundings; showing its face most clearly in its children. The Human Element, in Lisbon as in Paris or Omaha, striving, deceiving itself, rising & falling, suffering & reproducing, chattering over the wash, hurrying to work in a suit, sleeping on a park bench - destined to die, but living today. Do I imagine all this?

I imagined a great deal in Lisbon, starting with the illusions that a new arrival *should* be able to generalize about a large city, and that it really ought to exhibit a "plan" or "zones." As for the "human element," over time I found the notion of the universality of humanity less and less helpful (as C. S. Lewis said of the "Unchanging Human Heart"). The beginning or superficial tourist sees similarities first, and rejoices in the secure feeling that everyone is much like himself after all. Veteran travelers treat the interesting (if sometimes disturbing) *differences* between themselves and other people as the real reasons for moving about the world. Months passed before I stopped trying to find mirrors, and learned to prize the Other as what I had come for.

In Lisbon some of the drawbacks of our mode of travel became apparent, when its merits had not yet been demonstrated. We were keenly aware that our shipmates who paid a couple of dollars for a bus tour of the city saw more of it than we had, and could have answered many of our questions. I felt that I could point to nothing specific on our walk that offset those advantages. We were still neophytes, without the finesse to discover memorable places or the *savoir faire* to achieve the breadth of commercial tours on our own. Yet our disgruntlement may have been excessive. The tourists got exactly what they paid for: being taken to the places that someone thought they should see and told what someone thought they should know. I did not hear that they saw slums, encountered poor children, or had dockworkers shout pro-Communist, anti-American slogans at them. One thing that your tourist dollar buys is insulation. We were feeling our lack thereof, but the advantage of "breadth" was with us.

At about this time came news of the deaths of Mario Lanza and Bernard Berenson. A student from Michigan lamented that he had been going to Italy chiefly on the hope of meeting Berenson, "but here, the women cry over Lanza, and the men ask, 'Who is Berenson?'" Another admirer of Berenson's aesthetics - Skip, an aspiring young writer just out of the US Army - was more philosophical; he claimed that we were fortunate to have retained the best part of the man: his writings ("So long as men can breathe or eyes can see, / So long lives this, and this gives life to thee"). He met with silent reproach from those who were grieving. Skip was en route to Rome with his wife, two children, and $2000 of Army savings to have a one-year fling at writing. I wished him success and *buon corragio* - but have never heard of him again. Perhaps he took a pen name.

At mid-morning the day after our call at Lisbon, the first unofficial lookout discerned a thin white line of sand across light blue water: the coast of Africa, by God! A faint haze materialized above that, suggesting the Moroccan highlands. A curious tremor of excitement passed through the ship. Long before it could possibly have been surf, I thought I heard drums. Morocco might be more Mediterranean than African, but to me the part bespoke the whole: to touch Africa anywhere was to feel some of the vast bulk and power of the entire continent. I was Michaelangelo's languid Adam, reaching for the galvanizing touch.

At this charged moment, we received an unkind cut from a sister ship of the Italian Line, the *Julio Cesare*. Newer, sleeker, and whiter, she was coasting Morocco on a run from South America to Genoa. "*Attenzione, attenzione, signori i passagieri*," blared the loudspeakers, and the captain announced this meeting in proud tones. We then gave three ear-splitting blasts of our *basso* whistle - perhaps a trifle too soon. The *Julio Cesare* was still a mile away, and though it could certainly hear us, did not respond. We were the overeager, over-the-hill uncle, jumping from his chair to welcome the handsome and successful nephew. A decent interval passed and gradually became indecent. Passengers began to squirm and titter. The gap diminished, but still silence as she slid by to port, a half-mile off, and began falling astern. The tension was terrible: this was the Lie Direct. That the *C.B.* was a tub whose command was tantamount to exile, while the master of the *J.C.* would be a Bright Young Star, made it worse.

At last our captain gave his opposite number the benefit of the doubt – or cracked under the strain - and began a new salute, as if to suggest that his previous hail *might* not have been heard. But the first had hardly sounded when the *Julio Cesare* at last began to reply – as if *it* had only been awaiting our pneumatic concession in order to create one of those awkward moments when two slight acquaintances blurt out simultaneous banalities. We watched in wounded silence as the white stern diminished northwards. *Et tu, Julio*?

Casablanca

Oct. 5, 10 PM, C.B., off Casablanca - an apt name for a city whose characteristic structures are white clay Arab dwellings & tall white

European office buildings & apartment houses. We were in port from 1:30-8 PM. Hector & I covered a great deal in that time.

Started out with Hubert, Norbert [German students] & Madelaine [French student] in a cab. Driver charged $3 for an ostensible 7 kms. to the city center, which was more like a mile. Tourist rot! We gave him his money, & insults, & left. We'll be glad to get our scooters.

After changing some money into Moroccan francs, the five of us walked through the Medina, or native market. It is really the Casbah, we later learned: an indescribable place, about as much above the surface as an iceberg. The narrow streets - not winding, but cutting at angles - enclose a mass of market stalls, produce, merchandise & life. The place sometimes brings to mind a stockyard, sometimes a sardine net hauled to the surface, spilling its burden. You cannot go through the medina and see its faces without reflecting: Are we the same species? Can their goals & my goals belong to the same animal? Or you wonder, "Why me?" There are no answers.

It had not taken my outlook long to swing from universalism to radical separatism. "Why me?" probably meant "Why was I born well-off in America, instead of poor in a squalid Arab ghetto?" - which would have been a radically different "I," of course. Not that I needed to go abroad for such a question to be raised. The geographical description here is somewhat misleading. The *medina* (market) adjoined - and often melted insensibly into - the *kasbah*, the residential quarter of the Faithful, which (unlike the market) was off limits to infidels. Once, Hector and I blundered into it down a narrow, stone-paved street, and were politely but quickly ushered out. If they thought we were lost they were right.

Hector & I took off on our own & walked about 2 miles to the Nouvelle Medina. We were the only white people in the area. The dwellings are more in evidence than in the old Medina: one unlighted room for 5, 6, or more. It's incredible. We found Casablanca immensely interesting, & beautiful. The general impression was of a thriving Arab community overlaid with a veneer of French civilization. French was usable almost everywhere. There were virtually no beggars. The first contact with Africa was titillating -

"White" here meant "non-Arab"; few foreigners came to the *Nouvelle Medina* (located in a lower-middle-class district of mixed population and peeling yellow paint), less exotic than the old, so we were stared at and followed everywhere. The glimpses we had into dark earthen rooms shocked me deeply. Often a woman would be cooking over a wood or coal fire on the floor in the corner, filling the room with smoke and flickering shadows. It was like a glance into Dante's Inferno, at once unreal and vivid. I had never had such a powerful sense of the Other. Of course *I* was the Other: a ragged, squatting Arab woman started fearfully to see me pass. Yet downtown, only minutes' walk away, high-heeled working girls chatted in French as they walked, looking as chic and attractive as their counterparts in Paris.

If Lisbon showed some of the disadvantages of our independent approach to travel, Casablanca revealed some of its strengths. As soon as we broke out of the standard tourist orbit and committed ourselves to the unknown, we began to find interesting places, to observe and feel freely, to enjoy ourselves. The keys, it seemed, were initiative, a willingness to take risks, and a wise use of our liberty. It helped, of course, that we could operate in French, a language we had studied, instead of in Portuguese.

I stayed on deck to observe how they extricated the ship from the harbor: the basic facts and how-to's of seamanship had begun to intrigue me. Each port, each ship, each pilot meant a different approach to particular problems. I was becoming an *aficionado* of nautical virtuosity! After we cleared Casablanca I watched the moon gleam on the sandy coast for awhile before descending to the stuffy dormitory and dropping into my bunk. We went down there only to sleep, or to sort gear one more time.

As we steamed north toward Spain I recalled the prediction of Antonio, a trilingual Neapolitan at our table, that I would "speak perfect Spanish in ten days." This would coincide with our arrival in Barcelona, and time was fast running out. Antonio tried to assist with lessons, but perfection still lay at some distance. (He made no better progress with the French I tried to teach him.)

In truth, though, I was studying less and girl-watching more. While a reserved American beauty with a negligent husband attracted some attention, European and Mediterranean women were more interesting. I could resist Madelaine, who had an admirable figure and was friendly – we sat on her bed while she sewed a button on my shirt – because she was rather plain and I was not ready for the unshaven look. But at Casablanca a raven-haired Cleopatra came aboard into whom all the beauty of the Mediterranean peoples seemed to have been poured, and I began to feel like Antony: smitten and torn. I had never been close to anything this glamorous, unless on a movie screen. She was a chemistry student in Naples, and since she spoke all the Romance languages I could pass her off (to myself, anyway) as a language teacher.

Gibraltar would have been more impressive if my expectations had not been so high. The Strait is quite wide, offering none of the narrow, towering, Scylla-and-Charybdis effect I had imagined. Morever, the Rock faces to the *inside*, toward the east, so that we saw it only after we had gone by. Worst of all, the face is half covered with great slabs of concrete to counteract its tendency to crumble and slide. So much for "As solid as the Rock of Gibraltar" and its use as an icon of stability by the insurance industry! We anchored in the harbor, besieged and entertained by multilingual hawkers in colorful skiffs.

Beyond Gibraltar we were finally in the Mediterranean, Homer's "wine-dark sea." If our wanderings had a hero, this was it. About its salutary waters we would now begin to wheel, reveling in its climate, the agriculture it fostered and the landscapes it touched, wondering at the civilizations it had nursed, sometimes straying from its side but always returning to it with relief. *Medi-terraneum*, 'the middle of the lands,' as the Romans called it (or "*mare nostrum*," 'our sea'), had (in those days) a multitude of lovely vistas, seascapes, cove-palettes, peaceful beaches and unspoilt islands. For having so much loveliness it has since paid. The *N.Y. Times* discovered Greek islands in 1960, and within a decade the crowding, development and pollution had reached problematical levels. Over the centuries, cold outlanders *have* pushed toward its warmth; perhaps only ignorance of its blessings or inability to travel there have kept even more of the world's population from its shores. Most of this I felt only later. At the first moment of entry I just knew that the Sea was of a fine blue, and that its breezes told tantalizing tales of discoveries to come.

Barcelona

Oct. 8, aboard <u>C.B.</u> in the Med. - A fabulous half-day & night in Barcelona produced impressions I treasure for their evanescence. The *approach to this city, which lies on & around a large hill behind the harbor, is beautiful. Most of the dwellings are light-colored; the tallest edifice we saw was a statue of Columbus in a square near the port.*

We left the ship at 4 with Madelaine, Cleo, Hubert, Norbert & Bruno, but split up while walking along the broad central sidewalk, the Ramblas. Bruno, Hector & I went shopping for knives & guitars. What a selection the city has! One guitar shop had a couple of dozen Spanish classical guitars, the most expensive of which cost $24. The quality was high, & I vowed to return. While knife-shopping for Bruno, we saw magnificent leather & metal goods. Barcelona's womanhood was also much approved, although it does not measure up to Casablanca's, with its French influence.

After dinner aboard ship, our group went music-hunting. We stopped in two places, & were well soaked for the privilege of hearing good flamenco. Also took a bus to the Plaza de España, which is really impressive. All in all, a cool night in a great city.

Barcelona evoked many feelings I could not articulate. It was the most exciting city I had ever seen, a high from beginning to end. I left the ship conversing in French with Madelaine and Cleo (trotting out a few subjunctives) and never came down. The Ramblas hummed with vitality at dusk, the glow of its lights vibrating like a Van Gogh. "Everything about it was appealing": couples strolling under the plane trees, shops selling excellent workmanship for low prices, eateries with *caracoles* (snails) and other treats, bistros with cheap cognac and flamenco, cozy *pensiones* in narrow cobbled lanes. The only sour note was the venality of the gypsy flamenco artists, who begged smokes and drinks between numbers. Bruno, Cleo's worldly brother, who spoke fluent Catalan, was an excellent guide to shops, bars, and trams, which we rode to the *Plaza de España* and the towering old *Palacio Royal*; he shielded us from feeling the inadequacies of my Spanish. The lure of the city was palpable that evening, but… not yet!

After that I wrote little until Naples, so preoccupied was I with being one of Cleopatra's courtiers. There is only one brief, hedonistic entry from our next stop:

Oct. 8, Cannes - A fine evening of drink, talk, etc., in the bistros. La ville est assez jolie. I'm with Hector, Hubert, Norbert, Bruno, Cleo

& Raymond in a little café enjoying after-dinner snifters. Tonight, la condition humaine seems pretty good. There is much to do (not see) in Cannes, & the French women are Nice (that's nearby). I'm a bit high, & the world looks good. That's shallow, but for now all the depth I need.

At least I had some insight into how I was living. Well, this *was* the Riviera! During the day and on excursions I had to share Cleo with others or admire her from a distance (though she looked so good in her *pull-ouvert* and sheath skirt that even distant admiration was rewarding), but at other times, mainly in the evenings, I had her to myself. In Cannes we held hands, and later conversed on the highest deck during the midnight sailing, alone between the stars and the scintillating water. I talked some existential drivel to her about the beauty of an *acte gratuit*, such as jumping over the stern at sea: an idea she was pleased to pronounce *trés profonde* - a pun, perhaps. And what, other than Camus (or Hart Crane, or Jimmy Dean) and cognac, suggested that idea? Probably the realization that this was a shipboard fling, transient by nature and doomed to end in a few days - unless I could see her in Naples. Yet how were we to become better acquainted if I couldn't *tutoyer* her? I had never learned the familiar verb forms. *Diable*!

We stopped in Genoa the next day long enough to walk its hilly streets, look into some statuary gardens and visit the museum. I made a date with Cleo for after dinner, but stayed long at my place, drawing out the meal. At length she finished and came over from her table to confirm arrangements. We spent a bittersweet final evening together, full of ambiguous looks, doubtful words and long silences - usually because I lacked the French to express myself. Finally I escorted her to her cabin and kissed her hand. "Why do you kiss my hand?" she asked. "That is for old women." While I looked at her, trying to gauge her meaning and formulate a reply, she smiled demurely and went into her cabin. It was a defining moment. If I had instead kissed her on the lips with all the fervor I was feeling and whispered *Je t'aime*, would my life have been different?

Probably not, nor would that "I" have been I. It would only have been to err on the other side - she probably expected to be kissed on both cheeks, European style - and *aimer* would have been the wrong verb. Besides, this Italian-Moroccan Catholic, who spoke virtually no English, already had commitments, it turned out, and I doubt we would have passed each other's meet-the-family test, had it gone that far. But I'll never *know*: what might have been is the Road Not Taken, of which life is full. She is one of my untaken roads, as I am one of hers. A kiss is but a kiss!

The next morning the hills and Bay of Naples materialized from a light haze, whose emotional equivalent hung over my feelings. The *Count Whitehand* eased to her berth all too soon for me. The time of farewells had come: to friends, to the ship and the sea, to a pleasure cruise disguised as an Atlantic crossing. Seldom has $185 (about 3 weeks of manual labor in 1959) bought more. And these few recollections are all I have left of this voyage, other than an itinerary and the "Daily Ship's Activities" for 7 *Ottobre*, both overwritten with Italian vocabulary and verb forms. Now it was over. Time for Hector and me, dressed more roughly now, to shoulder our packs and hit the streets of Naples. There was again much to be done.

Naples

> Newman caught the eye of the marquis looking at him heavily; and thereupon, for a single instant, he checked himself. "Am I behaving like a d__d fool?" he asked himself. "Am I stepping about like a terrier on his hind legs?"
>
> Henry James, *The American*

Oct. 10, Albergo Astoria, NAPLES - We have reached the end of the first leg of the trip. Disembarked at 9 & were ensconced here by noon after lugging our packs a mile or so. American Express provided city maps & mail. The Albergo, I think, is a house of ill fame.

Spent day doing errands & wishing for scooters. Changed money, went to the P.O., ate lunch, ogled the scooters through the window *[during siesta], & slept out the PM. At 4:45 met Giancarlo, who was very helpful at the Lambretta place. We can get 150s with everything we want for $298.*

G. took us around in his Fiat for awhile. We met Bruno, Cleo, & friend Pietro at 6 at the university. Drove around at a maniac pace, were told that camping around Naples was foolish & shown another pensione. But since it was far away & not much cheaper, we decided to remain here until scooter time - probably Tuesday. They dropped us at the funicular; we descended to Via Roma, ate dinner & came back here. Since then we have made two decisions: not to go to East Africa, and to sail from Italy to Greece.

If we thought there was still enough life in the East Africa idea at this date to require a formal rejection, it was *merely* formal: a kind of wake. We had known for weeks that the plan was dead unless we found cheap used motorbikes (the faint hope that succeeded "free passage"), and we did not see or hear of any in town. The big decision made that day was to buy 150cc Lambrettas, the middle size (125s would be underpowered, and 175s too costly). Vespa scooters were more common, but they looked funny as they leaned to balance the off-centre engine, while Lambretta had just come out with a sleek new design. No other rivals were visible, at least in Naples. So we would buy Lambrettas, cross to Brindisi and sail to Piraeus, thus avoiding the reportedly awful roads of the long land route via Yugoslavia. It seemed that things were starting to fall into place.

Giancarlo was a shipboard acquaintance: an apparently well-heeled young Neapolitan returning from two years in the U.S. He volunteered to help us at the Lambretta store, where no English was spoken, and we gratefully accepted. There was so much we did not know during those first days in Naples, beginning with our choice of a hotel whose rooms were rented by the hour. I often felt like one of Henry James's American innocents, painfully learning the ways of the Old World. Giancarlo himself was an education: a blend of charm, generosity, and gutter morals. His idea of recreation was driving around our neighborhood (the red-light district) at night, shouting obscenities - which he considerately translated for us - at the voluptuous streetwalkers. He claimed to have seduced two-thirds of the Copacabana chorus line ("They have no class. They do it like dogs") and one-third of the singing McGuire sisters while in New York. My eyes must have been as wide as Hector's. I did not doubt that Giancarlo at least tried. Yet he gave freely of his time during our stay.

Our first night in Naples was one of painful deprivation for me: my little shipboard romance was over, and I could no longer keep my feelings bottled up inside.

I believe I am being tested. I am strongly attracted to a beautiful Moroccan. She speaks Arabic, Spanish, French, Italian. We communicate chiefly in French, but disturbingly well. I like her a lot. I had no intention of being attracted to anyone else. I was content to love Penny. I still do, but this is disturbing. I have promised not to look back, to accept what came. But is this going too far? Am I being unfaithful in actively chasing this girl? Yes. But I am responding to what I feel: something I've wished to do. What gives the affair its near-crisis aspect is that she likes me, too. She apparently considers me something of an artist, because of the guitar & our talks.

Agonizing self-flagellation darkened my stay in Naples, with guilt, honesty, and love taking turns as torturer-in-chief. As we parted, Penny had, with great tact, returned the only piece of jewelry I had given her so that I would not feel *bound* to her on my travels. She had, then, foreseen that something like Cleo might happen. I did not imagine this to mean that she would take it calmly, or that it would not hurt her, but she seemed very distant and our love an abstraction compared to my present feelings.

Strangely, I did not see the true nature of the threat, was unable to place it in context. This temptress - who *said* she had embarked at Casablanca - appeared to me just as we entered the Mediterranean, home to some of the great *femmes fatales* of western culture: Circe, the Sirens (note the sibilant serpentine hisses), Calypso, Cleopatra. Seducing men away from solemn prior commitments was their forte. My blindness in that regard was a part of the powerful charm, or charms, they possessed. I even found myself wondering if my *felt* bonds to Penny were the real problem.

So I wrestled with my dilemma as we waited, becalmed, for the Lambretta winds to blow. Fortunately we found a few distractions. On a gray and gusty Sunday morning we took the *motoscafe* out to Capri. A storm was passing, roiling the Bay of Naples – famed for its beauty since classical times - and not only the waves but the clouds and Capri itself had a leaden, metallic tint. The cliffs of Amalfi, darker than sea or sky, loomed to the east, threatening, it seemed, to block our way to Brindisi. Yet would the scenery have impressed me as much on a fine day? It would have been less dramatic, and less congruent with my inner state.

Oct. 11, the wharf, Capri - They say that Capri during the summer is mobbed. The mob can be excused, for the island is a beautiful combination of blue-green water, stark cliffs, narrow streets & pastel houses. Yet now it is much more pleasant for the relative lack of people. The streets, dwellings, vineyards, cloisters & gardens all suggest simplicity & solitude, yet with the tangled skein of human relationships also possible. Capri is, as we saw it this morning, a subtle & rare suggestion. I could write & play guitar here.

Mediterranean islands - Capri, Ischia (also off Naples), and Ibiza in the Balearics – had begun to loom large in our thoughts as alternatives to a long hard journey, places where our money might buy a lot of time if scooter travel did not work out. It did occur to me to wonder if I really could "write and play guitar" here better than elsewhere, say at home. *Would* it be different here? Why? I had no answer. It was not a thought but a feeling.

The excursion was also notable for our meeting with Jeff Garibaldi, a likable and sophisticated Neapolitan bachelor working for Pan American. We fell to talking on the boat, and he walked around the island with us, teaching us bits of Italian and tricks of survival. To hawkers he would say, "*Dopo, forse*": 'Later, perhaps.' Subsequently he watched over us in Naples. As upright as Giancarlo was sleazy, Jeff forestalled any facile generalizations about "Italians."

So it was a good day on the whole, but that night, back in our room – quiet except for occasional, ambiguous, muffled noises from the hourly users behind the thin walls - I again gave way to what was churning around inside:

Oct. 11, Albergo Astoria - God help me, I am ready to make a fool of myself by falling in love with a girl I just met. She likes me - I don't know to what extent - & my way of life. I'm in need of guidance & I can't find it. I've never felt this lightheaded before, I see her face everywhere & hear her voice. It's a damn shame but you can only tell your heart no for so long...what will happen I don't know but why does it hit me like this? If she shows she doesn't care for me I'll just go off on the trip & lick my wounds, but if she gives me any sign the feeling is mutual I don't think I can control myself.

This raw, self-indulgent entry shows how disturbed I was, how incapable of clear thought, how isolated (it wouldn't do to open up to Hector: Penny and Andrea were good friends in close touch). At my wits' end, I saw a means of dealing with the pain that was, in some ways, inexcusable, but seemed the only way. My question should have been "Am I giving pain?", not "Am I being truthful?" I had yet to learn the limitations of "pure truth" in relationships.

Oct. 12, Albergo Astoria - I've just done a thing I didn't think possible - wrote Penny confessing about Cleo - & I feel much better for it. Giancarlo said today that she likes me a lot but has a boyfriend, who must be Pietro. Okay, I know my competition, & don't think much of him. The air is clearer. I will escape relatively unscathed, I think, if I have a chance to see her & tell her how I feel.

Today we shopped; bought a haze filter. Scooters tomorrow -

The letter might have been written - and torn up, leaving Penny in blissful ignorance while the thing ran its course, but I wanted a partner in pain. Hearing this egoist slide so quickly from hurting Penny to cutting Pietro to shopping is like seeing an unflattering old photograph. Giancarlo struck me as another possible rival, so I asked him about Cleo. He said that he did not care for her "body type." This stunned me. What did he want, Gina Lollabrigida? More height, perhaps: another dancing girl. It may have been just a lie, though he would have known what I did not: that Mediterranean women tend to bloom early, be goddesses from 13 to 30, and then decline into fleshy shapelessness.

The shipment of Lambretti did *not* arrive the next day, however, nor the next. We stewed in the Albergo or paced the streets, angry, frustrated, powerless. We had meant to stay here no longer than it took to buy scooters (which we assumed would not be long); still dreaming of Greece and Africa, we thought Naples banal. Friends helped fill our evenings - Giancarlo came by to take us out to pizza, and again to meet his friend Enrico and play his guitar - but we were soon and easily convinced that we had seen everything of interest in the city that could be reached on foot, and retired to read and chafe. What we did not care to visit was dismissed as not worth visiting. The streetwalkers were amazing - and we had the right accommodation - but we rejected that pastime. It was an unsatisfactory interval, during which my thoughts *would* turn to friends who were by now a month into graduate school, or married and starting a job and perhaps a family. What *was* I doing?

Yet we did not entirely waste the time, studying Italian, reading European and ancient history, taking long walks. Twice we tramped up the hill to *Castel Sant'Elmo* (then a military installation) for its panorama of the city. I came to enjoy the shady *tipos* who would accost us on the seaside promenade, opening their coats to show stolen watches and trinkets. One day, hearing footsteps behind me, I removed my wristwatch and wrapped it in a handkerchief. When Carlo hove alongside, I opened the hanky and proffered the watch. He was startled, but only for a second - you don't get far in his line of work by being caught off guard. "*Quanto*?" he asked, ready to deal. We tried to stretch our *lire* by paring down our meals. Like many before us, we discovered that pasta was filling and *gelato* (Italian ice cream) delicious. I always looked forward to a small cone (8 or 16 cents) with some exotic treat on top. Cinema billboards were delightful and instructive; I learned how to say "Some Like It Hot": *A Qualche Piace Calda*. It might come in handy.

One night we went to a concert at the old *Teatro San Carlo*, Naples' premier symphonic venue. A modest charge gained us a precarious perch up "in the gods": the 7th tier (no elevator). It was flaky in both senses. Sound lagged about half a second behind sight, making entrances and cut-offs appear ragged. I set down some impressions:

"Il Viaggio a Reims": typical Rossini, bright, clear, precise, distinct notes, effective use of orchestral counterpoint (clarinet vs. violins)... Dvorak's Cello Concerto in C: best in orchestral sections, lost interest in many solo passages...tutti sound rich and deep, polished mahogany ...some group entrances weak, and soloist (Kurtz) flat on some ascending scale passages...Beethoven's 7th Symphony: 2nd rate Beethoven, to my mind - only 2nd & 3rd movements really good.

If nothing else worked out, perhaps I could write music reviews? At any rate, we agreed that the concert was "worth much more than 50 cents," which was what 300 *lire* cost us at the current exchange rate. Naples was cheap – except that we had no income, only outgo.

About dusk on the 15th our lives changed. Walking in a glitzy district at some distance from the Astoria, we passed a Lambretta dealership, its lights glowing warmly in the soft twilight. Workmen were wheeling shiny new scooters into the showroom. Were doing *what*?! After a moment we realized what this meant and rushed to *our* dealer, where a similar scene was unfolding. The factory had come through! In our primed condition, a brief look and a test ride behind a mechanic were sufficient: we purchased on the spot.

Oct. 16, Albergo Astoria, noon - Scooter Day is bright, warm, & cloudless, as befits an auspicious occasion. The truck from Milan arrived yesterday afternoon, bringing many 150s to Naples & joy to our hearts. We got our temporary documents at the Auto Club of Naples & paid $285 each last night. We are scheduled to pick up the <u>*maquinas*</u> *at 3:30. Tomorrow we will take them to Ischia, returning Sunday for the Stravinsky concert, then make other excursions until we can get our EE (export) papers Tues. or Wed.*

I had not yet learned the Mediterranean wisdom of avoiding predictive statements, or prefacing them with a genuflection to fate. That would be the work of the Arab countries.

Yesterday I spoke with Cleo on the phone. It was good to talk to her again, & made me want to see her. Maybe what my fickle psyche really craves is an emotional experience, & she is the first to undulate along. She put me off till Sat. on my invitation to the concert, but agreed to a 4-person 1-day tour of the environs. If I can see her alone & set things straight, I think I'll be OK.

"Fickle psyche" indeed! Was I actually beginning to recover, or did I just finally have other things to do? But I was in no mood or condition to analyze my problems.

Late that afternoon we took possession of our sleek, blue-grey and cream Lambrettas, which started easily with the kick-pedal. Shrugging off the proffered assistance of grinning mechanics, I steered shakily out into the chaos of *Corso Victor Emmanuele.* My qualifications for driving a motorscooter consisted of having ridden around on the back seat of cousin Tommy's on dirt roads in Tennessee one afternoon, and years of bicycle riding. It was like sending a child out into rush-hour traffic to play. On my second low-gear circuit of the roundabout the motor died. Traffic shrieked to an irate halt (barely) as I wheeled the heavy machine to the curb. Hector was doing better and yelled encouragement as he whirled past in the stream. Tasting adrenaline, I restarted and puttered away. By the fifth circuit I had achieved third gear and decided to call it a day. I jerked to a stop before the *albergo*, more scared than pleased. How would it feel in the mountains, with a heavy pack tied on back? What if I couldn't learn to handle the damn thing, shift gears, keep it running? Well, I had to.

That night Giancarlo, "very worried" about us, came over to see our new toys. He drove and I rode postilion as we roared off into the evening crush of central Naples. With awesome bravura and enough gall to divide into three parts Giancarlo slipped through fleets of grey Fiats, trucks, taxis and gesticulating pedestrians, shouting back superlatives about the scooter, meeting every crisis with the horn and a burst of gas. Halfway up the hill to Sant'Elmo I asked his opinion of the brakes. "Don't know yet," he yelled. "Coming back, perhaps." *Dopo, forse.* I kept my eyes closed much of the time, and we survived. Giancarlo pronounced the test a solid success, said that he felt much better about Lambretta and us, and approved our plan to go test our equipment on Ischia and learn to handle the scooters while awaiting our travel documents.

Oct. 18, Albergo Astoria, 4 PM - After a day & a night of camping on spectacular Ischia, we are back here for a final night before moving to a campground outside of town.

We got the scoots at 5 p.m. Friday & spent the next few hours learning to drive them. They're sharp-looking, run well, shift stickily, & are much fun.

Coordinating that "sticky" shifting was my first big problem. The clutch lever and gear selector were on the left handlebar and the throttle was on the right; there were no pedals involved, so automobile skills did not transfer. To shift, you closed the throttle with your right hand, squeezed the clutch lever and rotated the handgrip to the new gear setting with your left, then released the clutch (not too fast!) while re-opening the throttle. Seeing Giancarlo and thousands of other Italians perform this with such *brio* proved that it could be learned, but the tightness of the gearshift and the novelty of the operation puzzled me initially.

With G. that night, we went up to Bruno & Cleo's. In a quiet moment aside, I found out from Cleo why she put me off about the concert: she must ask Pietro, to whom she's engaged! Incredible!! He must have a side I haven't seen. I'm shocked. I would have liked to take her out, but as a long-term aimant, I'm inexplicably well again.

The Jamesian education of a naïve young American moved onto a new level that night: I had been courting an engaged woman! But why hadn't she told me before? Perhaps that would have been to presume too much about my feelings, or maybe it had just happened. But engaged to Pietro! He looked like a hood, a surly one at that (though he probably saw my clumsy rivalry as justifying surliness to me), and treated Cleo negligently, I thought. Well, life was full of surprises and sharp lessons. My swift recovery must be taken *cum grano salis*; it was partly rationalization.

The next morning we packed up, tied on, and went to Ischia, an excursion marred by mistakes and misadventures. The freight rates and handling charges for the Lambrettas seemed exorbitant, but when we demurred and tried to unload them ourselves at the Ischia wharf, we almost dropped one off the narrow gangplank. Humiliated, we then had to ask - and pay for - help. As poor as we thought ourselves, just scrimping along, we were apparently expected to dispense largesse everywhere. A crowd of wise-cracking spectators gathered. Then my scooter wouldn't start, kick as I might. A bystander offered to assist, and started it on the first try. He may have meant well, but at that moment I hated him, the scooter - everything Italian. People stared, laughed, snarled, begged; I felt like both a cash cow and an ass. The world was definitely too much with us. Of course we were "dudes" writ large, from our red crash helmets, fancy windshields, and bulging packs slipping off baggage racks to our awkwardness with the scooters.

Yet once off the pier we had good moments on Ischia, which was as lovely as Capri, but more rugged and less frequented. I learned the rudiments of driving the Lambretta on its two-lane loop road, which undulated from sea to mountaintop and back down. Having luggage on the rack made little difference to the handling (until it began to slip), and mountain roads were preferable to city traffic. We ate lunch on the terrace of a nearly deserted restaurant on top, looking through a lattice of grape vines to pellucid green coves a thousand feet downslope. The island's only campground had closed for the winter, so we pitched our yellow tent for the first time on a beach in one such cove, which we shared with a pleasant middle-aged German couple on a camping holiday. A swim before dinner in the milky sapphire sea beyond a few breaking waves compensated for many of the day's problems.

Here, though – and without any help from Italians - we made or discovered a series of blunders, which I anatomized the next afternoon in Naples:

Our first camping experience was bad. To find decent camping places - away from people, with good water - is going to be difficult. Last night we made many mistakes. 1) Camped too late (need 2 hours of daylight). 2) Didn't have fresh water (can't count on finding it). 3) Camped on a sandy beach (messy). 4) We need box matches, salt & pepper, spoons, a grill & a cooking utensil. 5) Didn't have enough toilet paper. There will be other learning experiences. These were pretty bitter, but I may look back and laugh.

And that, of course, is why we have shakedowns! But how could I be such a bad camper after camping all summer? Well, I had not been in *logistics*; someone else had thought that through, and given me food and equipment to carry. Still, by the time we returned to Naples on Sunday, I thought we had probably identified, if not solved, our main logistical problems. We also located a campground outside of Naples to which we could now move.

On the social front, I heard from Bruno that Cleo had a physics exam the next day and would not be going to the Stravinsky concert, nor on our projected excursion to Sorrento. Pietro must have vetoed these plans; I certainly would have in his place. It was over, then, not with a bang or a whimper, but only the creak of a closing door. Part of what I felt was relief, along with a chilly realization that it had *always* been impossible, out of the question. It helped not to be seeing her every day.

Hector and I also took time that day to discuss our feelings about the current state of our joint undertaking:

The trip is not going well. I must admit this: we are not happy with what we are doing. We keep saying, "It'll be better when..." But it stays the same, so far. We get stared at, begged from, cheated. We spend money. We are not excited, enchanted or carried away. We don't like Italy. Hector & I agreed that it would be time to reassess our goals & attitudes after Greece & perhaps Constantinople. We might, for individual reasons, write finis to travel & go somewhere, perhaps Spain, to live & think. The feeling is stronger now that we want the most for our money.

This was obviously a premature and myopic assessment, reflecting post-Ischia depression and general disillusion, not a balanced analysis. We were feeling what it meant to do without insulation, to be travelers rather than tourists. True, it was more serious than earlier complaints, because now we had our scooters - yet the trip we had been planning had not even begun. At least we were still committed to Greece: maybe it would hook us.

Despite our grousing about Naples, we returned to the *Teatro San Carlo* that night and, for 65 cents each, saw Igor Stravinsky conduct. He had been the star of a modern music course that was a highlight of my senior year, and this turned out to be the only time I ever saw him. Ironically, I was disappointed in the part of the program he conducted, the *Apollon* and *Pulcinella* suites; late Stravinsky (*Apollon*) left me cold. I preferred the first half, in which his *protégé* Robert Craft conducted Haydn and Berg. Still, just to see the Great Man from our perch up in the gods was a thrill.

The next morning we moved to a campground out in *Pozzuoli*. It was pleasant to lie on the grass in the shade of fruit trees and daydream about possible futures. The place was almost empty, except for a passionate Scandinavian couple (as demoralizing as the streetwalkers) who seldom left their tent, and a friendly USAF lieutenant from North Carolina, based in Germany, who was vacationing with his family. Pleased by our plans and footloose style, he gave us much loot - an electric stove, a gas stove, cord, a converter socket - that he insisted he didn't need, thus becoming the first of our benefactors. That evening we scootered into Naples for dinner with our Capri friend Jeff Garibaldi - another benefactor - who took us to a restaurant by the bay for delicious clams. On our way back, about midnight, the scooter's weak headlight and confusing reflections in my windshield led me into the pebbly roadbed between the streetcar tracks. I was lucky to escape unhurt, and resolved to avoid night driving if possible.

On our last day we drove out to Pompeii on the far side of the Bay of Naples. Pompeii would be almost on our way southeast, but we thought we could see it better on a day trip, without packs, while awaiting our "papers." The scooters ran and shifted better - either parts were breaking in or I was learning to drive - so I enjoyed the ride. Pompeii was virtually deserted. Its "air of death & stilled activity" reminded me of Ostia, port of Rome, the only comparable ruin I had seen, but its setting "under the volcano" was much more spectacular. (Oddly, it did not occur to us to *climb* Vesuvius; a few years later that would have been my top priority.) We wandered the ancient streets by ourselves, taking pictures, absorbing the mood. Grass grew up between the old paving stones, polished to a dull sheen before the volcano, and by generations of walkers since Pompeii was uncovered in the eighteenth century.

We returned to Naples in time to pick up our vital "EE" export papers: now we could leave Italy. I also got a haircut and reclaimed my sunglasses, which had been repaired after breaking – after I broke them - on Ischia. That evening we said goodbyes to friends all over Naples, nodding humbly to their dire admonitions, and in the morning collected the last official documents and bounced over the cobblestones of south Naples onto the *autostrada. Andiamo!*

> The counsellors of Uruk...answered him, "Gilgamesh, you are young, your courage carries you too far, you cannot know what this enterprise means which you plan."
>
> *The Epic of Gilgamesh*

1. First base camp: Naples, Italy

2. Pompeii and Mt. Vesuvius

3. First day on the road: the Amalfi Drive

4. First camp on the road: near Bari

5. The Parthenon, Athens, Greece

6. The theatre and Oracle of Apollo, Delphi

7.The author and Mt. Parnassos (Winter Wright)

8. Mykonos countryside at dawn

9. Mykonos camp at dusk

10. The horse in the ruins, Delos

11. Sunset from the green house, Mykonos

12. Arcadia in the central Peloponnesus

13. The ruins of Knossos near Heraclion, Crete

14. A pause on the road north (Winter Wright)

15. Mts. Olympus and Pelion, northern Greece

IV. Odyssey on a Scooter

> What gives value to travel is fear. ...when we are so far from our own country...we are seized by a vague fear...we are feverish but also porous, so that the slightest touch makes us quiver to the depths of our being. ...I look upon it as an occasion for spiritual testing. ... Travel...brings us back to ourselves.
>
> Albert Camus, *Carnets*, 1935-1942

The commencement - there had been several, but this seemed the *real* one - remains extraordinarily vivid in memory. The day was fine, with a few white clouds, but a gusty wind almost blew me over several times as we rounded the bay. Even fully dressed and sitting behind the windshield on a mild day, I was cold at 35 mph. How would November feel in the Greek mountains? And where would December find us? Clearly I needed to redefine "fully dressed." No wonder we were not seeing other travelers like ourselves: the sensible ones had gone home or south. On the luggage carrier my pack caught the gusts and shifted with every bump. When large cars or trucks whooshed by, the 240-pound Lambretta tried to skip sideways. The mountainous Amalfi coast looked menacing ahead. A small voice in my head kept up a running commentary: "Idiot! What have you gotten yourself into now? Watch it!" Up ahead, stalwart Hector, also bouncing and swaying, pressed on regardless.

Oct. 21, Avellino, Italy, Albergo Patria, 6:30 PM - The trip is now under way & consequently going better! Already so much has happened that I know I won't be able to keep up with the writing. Yet the urge to set it down, to solidify the evanescent, is strong.

This morning we broke camp, bought gas coupons & set out about 11. Today's drive was one of the most spectacular I've ever seen. Sorrento - Amalfi Coast – Amalfi...green hills reaching bony fingers down to the surf - the road winding around green-brown cuts, through terraced vineyards: grapes, olives, limes. Startling vistas of sheer cliffs & surf 300 feet below. Then Salerno - big, dirty, poor, but beautiful parks (all the little towns have parks). Hills shone in the sun farther south. We roared higher into the mountains, through fields & tiny villages, as dusk fell. We are comfortable here in the Albergo, warmer than in hours, & the minestrone is boiling

- on our benefactor's electric stove, which we should not have been using in our room. The *Signora* came to our door: did we smell something burning? Hector said no; I thought it might be coming from the house next door.

As soon as we hit the road my journal could not keep up; each day beggared description, and our Neapolitan depression began to thaw. The Amalfi coast is a well-known beauty spot, of course, featured on many a postcard and poster. My favorite picture shows our scooters posed like prize greyhounds at a scenic pullout on the winding cliffside road that day. We ate lunch in Amalfi's empty plaza, quiet at that season; then went on through Salerno, which I knew from war stories and films had been a battleground only fifteen years earlier. Up in Avellino Hector sent me in to bargain for the room, but thought I could have done better than 80 cents apiece. I did some laundry in our washbasin to get my money's worth.

One advantage of a motorscooter over a car immediately became apparent: the sensory input is enormous. Besides the panoramic vision, you are open to all the smells of the countryside. They would prove one of the great delights of the trip, and scent - located in our ancient brainstem - seems to be the longest remembered and most evocative of the senses. The acrid odor of leaf-smoke and the sting of chilly air as we climbed in the late afternoon dominated that day, but every stage was different.

Oct. 22, campground near San Giorgio - A few hours drive today sufficed to carry us through topography that would have spanned the U.S. Leaving Avellino in full regalia at 7:45, we drove through beautiful mountains; large looming peaks formed a backdrop for smaller, inhabited hills close by. Gradually the country opened & lowered into something reminiscent of E. Colorado, then flattened into crop-rich Ohio. The final 2 hours were spent rolling down the shore of the aquamarine Adriatic, with a seacoast all its own.

It was the heart, soul and backbone of Italy that we passed today: peasant, agricultural, "Bread, Love & Dreams" Italy, growing grapes, olives & grain, staring from the roadside, going back to work.

I was still trying to understand what I saw in terms of what I already knew, i.e. looking for similarities. More time would have to pass before I learned to prize differences.

On our first full day of driving (about 100 miles) I learned more about the little machine that was carrying me. Driving it in the mountains was glorious sport - a carnival of the senses - but also cold and often humbling work. The limitations of a 6½ hp engine quickly became clear; I was often reduced to first gear during the morning's climb. Expectations of performance based on years of automobile driving had to be lowered. We stopped in a hill-town, Ariano, for our 500-km. service, during which shiny metallic shavings were noted in my oil bath. Apparently I was whittling my transmission down to size, but whether this was bad or normal, my fault or the scooter's, the mechanic would not say. After lunch we dropped down the eastern slopes of the Apennines, passing road-repair crews (a uniformed foreman and two workers), and went through Cerignola on the coastal plain to the Adriatic.

After a brief glance at Bari (using Hector's Michelin *Guide Verte*), we hummed down the flat coast road between vineyards and the sea to a large, attractive, nearly deserted campground at San Giorgio, which charged us 15 cents apiece. Here the intimations of autumn around Naples were more explicit; the solitude and quiet, the colors of leaves, sea, and sky all connoted the waning of the year, the departure of seasonal travelers, the return of the countryside to natural pursuits. It felt odd to be commencing a long trip in such an atmosphere. I tied a cord between the scooters and hung out the still-damp Avellino wash. The setting sun streamed golden through my underwear: a ludicrous offering to Apollo. After we pitched the tent, Hector left to buy victuals in a nearby hamlet while I took the laundry in out of the dew and made a wood fire on the beach. Overcoming some difficulties running the gas stove, we prepared soup and omelets, then sat quietly in the sand, watching coastal steamers leave horizontal trails of smoke in the calm air and trawlers gather their nets, and ate dinner.

As night fell we maintained the fire and had another serious talk. As conscientious a man as lives, Hector was now questioning the morality of his travels. He thought often of what he *should* be doing, of how he had been to Europe before while his mother never had and would love to go, and wondered if he was doing right. News had come recently of the death of a close friend in an airplane crash, and somehow this too brought his present course into question. He sounded shaky again, and I wondered if I was about to lose a good travel companion.

So I began to talk - hesitantly at first, for he was suspicious of abstractions, then more confidently as he let me run on - about my view of travel as existential knowledge; about our responsibility, once embarked, to make the most of what we were doing, to report faithfully to those left behind, to try to enrich them, and with luck improve ourselves, through our experiences. I suggested the eventual value to him as a person of seeing places long considered extraordinary, of meeting more foreigners, of making one's way by ingenuity and small means through a not-so-grand tour. I felt inarticulate and beset, nor did Hector respond then, but some days later he told me that my views had carried weight, and that for the present he was reconciled to the worth of travel.

The next morning we had to wait until 10 for the dew to dry off the cotton tent (realizing that this could prove inconvenient at times) before packing it and puttering off south along the smooth highway past yellowing vineyards.

Oct. 23, Brindisi - Our first cross-country jaunt (493 km.) is finished. We spend the night in this Adriatic port before embarking tomorrow night for Athens. With student discount that trip will cost $25 each, deck passage, for 1½ days.

Passing through beautiful agricultural S. Italy made me wish I knew some botany. The farmers utilize virtually every square inch of land, to live on or to raise crops. I saw good brown earth, plenty of grape arbors, olive trees, fields of hay & grain, carrots & radishes.

The scooters are doing fine & making 85+ mpg. I have spent $705 to date, including the boat passage & $25 in Greek money.

I think of traveling east as symbolizing mysticism. In my present mood this appeals to me, & I hope I have the guts to go on east & to Africa after H. drops out. I believe in the intrinsic value of travel, but I can see the other point of view. Time is money, & the value you receive depends on the value you place.

At this point it appeared unlikely that Hector would continue the trip for much longer, and the possibility of his defection permeated my thinking and planning.

Baedeker assures us that Brindisi "was a very famous place in ancient history," but I saw only an excellent harbor and a rather poor, crowded neighborhood adjacent to it where we found a *pension* for the night. Like most towns, it was less enjoyable than open countryside where we could roll freely and enjoy the space. In Brindisi we were already turning away from Italy - of which we had had more than enough - and looking east across the Adriatic.

Brindisi to Piraeus: the *Miaoulis*

Oct. 25, S.S. Miaoulis near Corfu, 7:45 AM - The isles & mainland of Greece had much the aspect of San Miguel [Azores] in the first light, but in full sun they appear much older: the mainland mts. are worn smooth, their slopes & the islands' cliffs are eroded & gnarled. The colors are light brown near the tops, darker brown & faint green-brown lower down. Death Valley.

Within a few hours I corrected my latest error: it was not Greek but Albanian mountains I had described at sunrise. By midday, however, we were passing Greek ranges, and they had the same appearance. Death Valley was, of course, my standard and shorthand for gnarled, barren mountains.

We slept adequately in deck passage last night, & met three interesting Americans headed for Greece: Jim, a free-lance photographer, Jerry, an artist, & Charley, a self-styled "shithead."

The key to surviving an overnight deck passage was to command a flat place where you could stretch out. A bench was great, if you could find one; a hatch cover or a patch of floor was more likely. But how to *hold* six feet without lying on it the whole time?

Depositing your pack and sitting beside it restricted your mobility, leaving the pack was risky, and folks were apt to encroach on any vacant space. If the interloper spoke English you could negotiate, but most deck passengers were poor Greeks and Italians, some with domestic fowl. Sixty or seventy "deckies" occupied the available space in the forward hold, one level below main deck, when the *Miaoulis* weighed anchor at midnight (Jim said five might be a record number of Yanks for deck passage). Hector and I found room for our sleeping bags on the big cargo hatch, where we catnapped amid lights, noise, and the curiosity of our shipmates, which we tried to bear with equanimity. At dawn, most of us moved up to the main deck (despite music blaring from the ship's speakers) to enjoy the sun and mild breezes.

1:45 PM, off the Greek coast - We docked at Korfu for an hour & a half this morning: a tiny port set amid pastoral scenes (cypresses & white statuary) on the island of Kerkyra, where, according to legend, Odysseus was beached by Poseidon-whipped waves after his release by Calypso. He there met Nausicaa, who took him to her father King Antinous, in whose court O. sported until sent home to Ithaca.

Glad to have read *The Odyssey*, I spent my time ashore walking on the wharf and some old fortifications on the seawall. Corfu seemed a classical backwater: the town hushed and peaceful, the harbor waters silky green, no breath of air. Back on the ship I communed with my journal: looking forward and back, mainly laments and introspection.

Yesterday I lost my good pen, broke my haze filter, my windshield came undone twice, the motor refused to start three times, & they bent my brake handle while loading the scooter on the ship. But we are safe in our deck quarters, & happier with the state of the trip. Hector says he may go on to Egypt with me.

So it appeared that our long colloquy on the beach at San Giorgio had borne fruit. But it had also prompted me to start making my own calculations, which seemed, in part, to point in a different direction.

Time to face some facts of this trip, of living, of my own being. Ever since the idea first hit me, I have wanted to go back to Spain & work on the guitar. I still want to see, experience, know, but only as an adjunct to something else. Sooner or later, I must satisfy that urge.

What I'm doing could hardly be called facing the facts of life, but it makes some of them clear. One is fortunate not to be hungry. I don't require much in the way of creature comforts: clean, warm clothes suffice, a sleeping bag is fine, I like doing my own cooking, etc. I can live on relatively little. I do need some livelihood. I will want money for a car, as well as for sustenance. I think I could be happiest as a writer or musician. I must know if this is so before I settle for less. I have come closest to self-fulfillment while writing & playing. I have more confidence in my musical ability than in any other. I could live as a moderately successful musician. Maybe a family could, if I taught. I must find out if I can improve as a writer & musician. If the answer is "yes," the way is plain & the only question is courage.

So I soul-searched that afternoon while dolphins curveted delightfully in the pellucid waters under our bow and we retraced Odysseus' route from Kerkyra to Ithaca. Wasn't the trip's purpose to find me a calling? Partly, yes, and that was necessarily self-centered. But it was also to meet other people and find out how they saw the world.

7:45 PM - Had a very enlightening conversation with Takis, a Greek civil engineering student. Although his English is weak, he has an inquisitive mind & a pleasing personality. He told me much about Greece, for instance that its politics & poverty are 2 "great" but "simple" problems, illustrated thus. "I have a big window, and before the window is a large stone that keeps the light from entering. You say, 'Why not move the stone & let the light in?' Ah yes, simple, but the stone is great. That is the problem."

He says that the Greek & western churches split in 313, then sought a doctrinal difference to validate the split. The Catholic church held that the Holy Spirit emanates from both Father & Son; the Orthodox Greek that it emanates only from God. He laughed, & so did I. T. considers Greece neither East nor West. Greek church music existed as melody before the church took it over; Gregorian chant grew out of western religion. Strains of Indian & Egyptian music are in it.

Takis' English must have been pretty good! I was learning to appreciate foreigners' achievements in my language; to ask myself, for example, if I could have expressed those ideas in any tongue other than English. (Apropos, this journal entry includes a Greek alphabet, with the names and sounds of the letters.)

Takis was reluctantly returning to university in Athens after a *Wanderjahr* spent mostly in Germany.

I felt "somewhere else" tonight as we entered the harbor at Ithaca. We slipped quickly through the narrow neck of white granite, against a hard wind, into the harbor, around which a tiny village clustered. We sidled gently against the shore, as Odysseus did 3000 years ago. On the way out, I saw a tiny, frail light flickering against the otherwise unrelieved blackness of a mountain: a lone shepherd, tending his flock. The chill I felt was not entirely from the cold -

The *Miaoulis* eased through the bottleneck, whose cliffs were suddenly very close, and entered the deep port and a strong sense of the Other. Whitewashed earthen houses crowded around the wharf, shadowy beyond its lights. The rest of the dark island was felt only where it blotted out the stars. Most of Ithaca's population walked down to the harbor for our call. It struck me that this was the kind of thing - perhaps *the* thing - I had come to see.

In the middle of that second night we called at Patras, a hazy dream of lights and voices; the fatigue of deck passage was taking its toll. But all that was forgotten in the morning as we swept through the narrow Corinth canal piercing the Peloponnesian isthmus and emerged into the blue, white-capped Bay of Piraeus. Raw, almost wintry gusts raked the ship, slicing through my layered shirts. Our approach to the Piraeus ("port") and Athens lay along a shockingly barren coast of grey and pale brown hills. It was difficult to imagine how anyone could scrape up a living here, much less create a magnificent culture. I did not realize how much the climate had changed since Pericles: those devastating centuries of deforestation and erosion. "You will not like Greece," Jeff Garibaldi had predicted. "I do not know why you want to go there. It is all rocks and hills and poverty."

As soon as the *Miaoulis* docked we had to face some of the old problems and I felt a twinge of nostalgia for the ship. It had been good to us, providing diversions, fresh scenes, and friends who traveled "our way" and shared useful information. We collected the Lambrettas, tied on our packs and went bumping over cobblestones toward the *Douane* building, chased by a pack of ragamuffins shouting at us in Greek and German. En route we stopped at a sidewalk café. The curious kids hung around the scooters, fingering them and the packs, despite our efforts to shoo them away. The proprietor, Stavros, who helped keep them off, spoke some Italian, so we were able to order coffee and bread. Hector and I had learned enough Italian to feed and house ourselves, ask directions and maintain our vehicles, but now had to make our way in a land whose language was a total mystery, so we welcomed Italian as an old friend. When the bill came it seemed high for *espresso* and *pane*, though, and we said so. Stavros looked hurt and mumbled something about *amerkani*, but named a lower figure that (he said) Germans paid! We agreed, and tipped him enough to come close to "the American price."

The City of Athena

After an easy passage through customs – while clearly not impressed by our vehicle documents, the agent accepted them with a shrug – we were soon on our way to "the cradle of democracy." Swirling along in commercial traffic on the broad boulevard that leads from Piraeus to Athens, I heard Hector honking and glanced back. He was pointing ahead and left. There the white buildings of the Acropolis ('the high city'), instantly recognizable, shone dully through a bluish haze, seeming to float disembodied above the still invisible modern town: sufficient reward for what we had been through so far. We gave it two thumbs-up.

Traffic in central Athens was as heavy as in Manhattan, and the driving was wilder. In a bookstore near the central plaza, I dove for a Greek phrase-book like a boy hitting the first lake of summer. We bought books on Greece, Istanbul, and Mediterranean history before heading for the Youth Hostel on the southeast slope of Mt. Lycabettus. The nearest campground was said to be well outside of town and probably closed for the winter, while the hostel was cheap (35 cents a night) and convenient to the city. Jim, Jerry and Charley were already there, and helped us find bunks in the crowded dormitories. The warden, who did not hide his dislike of Americans and English, did recommend a restaurant across the street and show us the *cold* showers. Our fellow hostellers included dozens of young people from various countries, traveling on the cheap, interested in art and history, happy to trade information: further evidence that we would not find ourselves as isolated as we had been led to believe in the distant USA.

In the afternoon of that first day we walked around our rather nondescript neighborhood, but the next day we spent reading - one might almost say cowering - at the hostel. Far too ignorant to pose as a student of Greece, I studied outlines of Greek history, art, and literature, and read biographies, as if cramming for an exam - which, in a way, I was. We also bought Youth Hostel International cards, valid the world over: in effect accepting the limitations of city camping on this trip. The brief entry in my journal is redolent of cultural shell-shock.

Oct. 27, Youth Hostel, Athens, GREECE - The language already a problem, & attempts to learn will probably be abortive.... Wonderful letter from Penny brightened up trip. Decided to stay in Youth Hostel - we enjoy the cosmopolitan company - & washed the salt off the scoots. Spending day reading before taking on the country tomorrow.

Penny's letter responding to my confession offered understanding and forgiveness. Hector, however, had a letter from Andrea that told how hurt Penny had been when she learned of my "shipboard romance." I knew that, of course, and deserved reproach, but resented being chastised by a third party. Maybe we all needed to learn more about how much of the truth to disclose to whom.

The next morning we took the scooters from the building entryway where they sat and puttered across town to the Acropolis. Knowing how often the place had been described, and fearing that my own reactions would sound banal, I did not write of the visit. A few washed-out slides show that it was a fine day; bright sunshine made the whiteness of the *Erectheum*, the Temple of Athena Nike and the *Propylaea* (entrance way) almost blinding. The Parthenon, seen across a field of rubble, somehow survived overexposure of both kinds - which, of course, is what it means to be "classic." Seeing the Theatre of Dionysus, where the plays of the great Greek dramatists were first presented, was a thrill. What touched me most, though, was not the great, wasted buildings, but a small sculpted head of Artemis (4th century BCE) in the little Acropolis museum. The face had the loveliest lips, human or artificial, I had ever seen. Whatever men have yearned for - in women, in corporal beauty - was in those full, shapely lips; Plato would have said that they touched the Form of Beauty. Guilt and absolution kept me from seeing them as Cleo's: they were the Ideal Young Mediterranean Woman's.

There were too few other visitors to figure prominently in my pictures, except for some young Greek soldiers in smart blue uniforms, clowning as they lean against one of the Parthenon's columns, who asked me to take and send them the photo. I couldn't tell them that it would be months before the slide was developed and months more before I saw it (we were mailing film back to the US for safekeeping). By then I had lost the address they scrawled on the torn corner of an envelope. Sorry, guys. That morning we also visited the Agora and the Areopagus hill, where Orestes took a close decision from the Furies; bought a postcard of the Theseum temple; and wrote a joint message to mail to Doc Heninger (*requiescat in pacem*), who had taught us some of the Greek classics in translation.

The next day we took on (so to speak) the National Archeological Museum, our first major collection of the trip, where I jotted down descriptions of and comments on some items. These notes, I hoped, would keep me "thinking articulately" during the visit, and provide a lasting record of what I might otherwise soon forget: a record on which I could draw in later museums. This quickly became a habit. I discovered that I could toss off generalizations about art history with frightening facility. "A little learning is a dangerous thing," warns Pope (a notorious killjoy); "Drink deep, or taste not the Pierian spring." Hey, we would go right by that on our way to Turkey!

Oct. 29, Athens Museum - Like the Acropolis, Egyptian influence. Large exhibit of Mycenean excavations (1500-1200 BC). Pieces of beaten copper, bronze & gold, daggers & jewelry from graves. They played "let's pretend" [with the dead] like the Egyptians.

Cycladic white marble figures, earth mothers (24-2200 BC) - elongated, flattened form, like African wood sculpture given Picasso by Matisse...Fragments of Mycenean pottery, designs of men, animals, & symbols like early American Indian...Beautiful & well-preserved wrought copper or gold necklaces (hexagonal flowers).

Statuary: copy of an Athena by Phidias...Praxiteles: torso of Aphrodite. A fine statue of a toga'ed young man, angry. Great bronze of Zeus or Poseidon, holding trident or thunderbolt; hollow eye sockets. Brilliant statue of Paris or an athlete with lifelike eyes.

By then I was feeling so full that I had to stop. The Athens Museum matched the wealth of any collection I had seen in

Paris, Rome or London, and its rarefied atmosphere of classicism, untainted by any later "decadence," was new to me. I saw for myself what I had read in books: the unashamed adoration of the human form, and of course subjects from classical (not Christian) mythology. If I could find time to come back after traveling more widely in Greece, I might appreciate it even more.

The Delphi Expedition

We rose at 6 the next morning, breakfasted on coffee and "a kind of shredded wheat biscuit stuffed with something chewy and soaked in honey" - my first *baklava* - at the pastry shop across the street, and were on our way by 8. Some Athenians walking on the *Iera Odos* (once a "Sacred Way," now a narrow cacophonous market street) that morning may have noticed an unusual apparition. Bumping slowly over the cobblestones, honking - well, squeaking - frequently, dodging carts and pedestrians every few seconds, came two Lambrettas driven by young men in garish red helmets. Olive-drab packs and miscellaneous equipment tied crudely to the luggage racks slipped a bit with each jolt. The leader, angular and bearded, wore khakis, a grey wool shirt, and paratrooper boots. On the rear scooter were a stocky driver in jeans, a bomber jacket and cowboy boots, and a grinning passenger (Charley from the *Miaoulis*). Any passerby aware that, over twenty centuries ago, chanting torchlit processions of initiates made their way along the *Iera Odos* from Athens to Eleusis at this season might have mistaken this for some kind of farcical re-enactment.

Halfway to Eleusis we stopped in the hamlet of Daphne to see an inconspicuous Byzantine monastery and church of whose mosaics Charley had heard at the hostel (inside tips, maps, brochures, travel companions, mechanical advice, folksongs and unedited ideas are free of charge at a youth hostel). From up in the dome a few faded mosaics - a stylized Christ *Pantocrator* ('ruler of all') giving the blessing, flanked by his prophets - gazed balefully from their golden realm at the littered and deserted floor. No other visitors and no clergy were in sight. In a side corridor we found a startling head of Christ in fresco, which did not look Byzantine at all. Our argument over whether it was neo-realistic, impressionistic or surrealistic lasted back out onto the road and endangered us for miles.

Once beyond the grimy commercial suburbs of Athens, the "way" broadened and became a gently sloping avenue beneath towering poplars. On the plain at its foot, near the coast, we found once-potent Eleusis, now reduced to a museum and a field of rubble in front of caves sacred to Demeter. Her daughter Persephone had been abducted by Hades, king of the underworld - whither the caves *might* lead. Eventually Demeter and Hades worked out a settlement whereby Persephone would spend six months aboveground, during which vegetation flourished, and six months below. This was a significant myth for us: Eleusis was about seasonal change; initiates walked here every autumn to ensure that Persephone, sunlight, and fertility would return. But I lacked the imagination, there in the shadow of a chemical factory, to summon up the prosperous temples of a powerful mystery cult that almost had Aeschylus (an initiate) executed for a dramatic indiscretion when it was flourishing, and provided stiff competition to St. Paul a few centuries later. If I had a few million I'd rebuild Eleusis.

At 10 AM we set out again, this time for Delphi. West of Eleusis the road crossed a spine of low mountains, and a stiff headwind sweeping down their slopes slowed our progress. Fighting to keep up speed, I maintained 2nd and 3rd gears, but Hector, with the extra weight, was often reduced to 1st, and in the half hour it took me to climb the hills he fell 10 minutes behind. At the top, worried about the strain on his motor, he apologetically put Charley off. "You're throwing me to the hitchhiking wolves?!" he joked, but a truck stopped as we were talking, and I negotiated a ride for him in French. Charley and his benefactors blatted off down the incline in a burst of blue exhaust. Thereafter we fared better, enjoying the colors and forms of the rolling countryside, and the smoothness of the scooters.

Where the western slope of the range meets the Boetian plain (see Europa and the Bull in Ovid's *Metamorphoses*) stands the village of Thebes, a relic of the city of Oedipus, Tireisias, Antigone, and other characters from history, myth, and literature. We had studied it in Comp Lit, and now, incredibly, were there...here! After refueling, we ate grapes amid laughing school-children near a ruin labeled "the palace of Oedipus" - and perhaps it was. The atmosphere was mellow: the good-humoured kids were a far cry from the jeering urchins of Naples or Piraeus, and the weather suggested *early* autumn; yellow leaves were just beginning to spiral. At Avellino the season had seemed perhaps three weeks later, imparting a sense of urgency.

Then west again, along the plain of Boetia, a narrow tube of fertility between low rocky hills. It was perfectly flat and four to six miles wide; roads, power lines, fields of cotton and rows of trees - mostly slender cypresses - all ran up and down it, never across. The character of the land, abrupt in its transitions between homogeneous and well-defined areas, was a constant source of interest. Gradually Mt. Parnassos - sacred to Apollo, home of the Muses - grew clearer, dominating the skyline. Its blues and purples harmonized with the green scrub and pastoral lawns on which sheep grazed, and complemented the ruddy soil in the foreground. The vividness of the colors in that pure atmosphere, the sheep-bells, the scent of vegetation and the rush of scenery made the climb a total sense experience as rich as rare. Once, as my tires bit into a tight outside curve, I looked up from the road and glimpsed the entire Boetian plain back to Thebes. Realizing that I could not have had the sensations of that moment in a car or on foot, I began to believe in the aesthetic value of scooter-riding with the fervor of a devotee at the Eleusinian mysteries. We stopped and made the Lambretti pose for formal portraits.

To our surprise there was a new youth hostel in Delphi. The only other guest was a rugged, heavily bearded USAF veteran whom we had met at the Athens hostel; he had shown me how to adjust the gap on my sparkplug so as to improve the starts of my machine. He called himself a "scooter bum," having logged about 12,000 miles on his old Lambretta since leaving the service in 1958. He was nursing a nasty abrasion on his hip from what he said was his first fall after all those miles, in some construction on the way from Athens. The scooter could not continue, so he sent it back to the city on a truck and hitchhiked to Delphi. When he described the scene of his spill I recalled the place: loose gravel and some oil on a curving grade (I *walked* my scooter over it on the way back). From this time I became apprehensive of falls and drove more cautiously, which, I would discover, did not necessarily mean more safely.

Oct. 30, Youth Hostel, Delphi - If the country around Mt. Parnassos is not the most beautiful I've ever seen, it comes close.

Only Switzerland & parts of the Rockies rival it. Can't begin to describe the variety, color, detail & form of the countryside we drove through coming from Athens (164 kms.). I was uplifted & happy. Mt. Parnassos loomed as a majestic challenge an hour before we began the ascent. Snow hangs in the upper gorges. It was a tough haul, but richly repaid by clear air & tremendous vistas. We'll stay over tomorrow.

Well might we devote a day to this historic and spectacular place! Delphi, like other hamlets along the road, was nothing itself, but location, location.... It has a precarious toehold among terraces on the steep brown flanks of Parnassos' southwestern shoulder. Too close in to see its peak, the cluster of faded, off-white houses hangs above a gorge, a river, and a plain of dark olive leaves a thousand feet below, far beyond which is the Gulf of Corinth and then the Peloponnesus. Every object and scene there gains from the drama of its setting. You can never take in the whole 360-degree pageant at once, but what you cannot see at any moment is still felt, the mind somehow bringing the unseen portion of the panorama to bear on what you *can* see. It is difficult for a toad or a twig to look other than beautiful when set at Delphi.

Oct. 31, a pine grove on a cliff overlooking the Delphic oracle - Amazing that I'm even here. It doesn't hurt to wonder "Why me," but the point is I am here, & my duty is to see, note, & observe.

A soft rain, falling from grey-white clouds sailing quietly through the passes, has cut down photographic possibilities & made it uncomfortable to be out. I'm sheltered here; Hector is taking pictures anyway. We were up at 6 & in a mountain meadow by sunrise to watch & photograph. Dawn was stormy but lovely.

Spread out below me are the Temple of Apollo with its attendant temples & treasuries. The Tholos & Temple of Athena are further down the slope. To my left, the theatre; above, the stadium.

Hector had us up and out before dawn, early rising being an article of faith with him. And it was worth the effort to be well above Delphi when the daily marvel occurred: the deep gorge, glistening forest, brown plain, wrinkled mountains and distant gleam of the sea, all created anew out of nothing by imperceptible degrees, tone by tone. Fiery triangles glowed between mountain passes and a low deck of cloud, sending oblique shafts to probe along the valley. When the light grew pale and white we came down to eat, leaving a shepherd we could not converse with scratching his head. Have aliens visited us? Ask him.

Later we roamed the venerable ruins surrounding the Oracle of Apollo, where a priestess once sat entranced over a smoking vent in the sanctuary while priests received anxious petitioners with rich offerings in the antechamber. It is sometimes called the world's first international intelligence system. The Delphic Oracle's motto, "Know Thyself," adopted by Socrates and deemed an appropriate challenge to the priests, petitioners, actors and athletes of ancient Delphi, certainly was so to us.

That afternoon we rode down to the broad plain below Delphi and found it a valley-sized olive orchard walled by mountains on three sides. Low earthen dikes (raising workers above the reddish soil) ran down the long rows, shimmering leaves gave glimpses of cloud-purpled hills, and a pleasant little road led nowhere that I knew of. We were blessed with mild weather, and I was happy to putter along at 25 mph through the orchard, or stop and lie under an olive tree. Hector wanted to go faster and left me behind: the first time I noticed this discrepancy in driving preferences.

In good weather, even 35 cents a night for the hostel seemed a waste, so we camped behind a small deserted chapel on a spur a mile or so east of Delphi. The tent was unnecessary, and would require drying time in the morning, so, parking the scooters six yards apart, we tied a rope between them, stretched the plastic tarp David had given me over that, and put air mattresses, sleeping bags, packs and ourselves under it. Another superb Delphi vista opened up ten feet from our shelter. Halloween was appropriately chilly and uncanny: lightning flashed and thunder muttered in storms that towered above smooth mountains far to the west, but overhead the myriad stars shone gloriously. Shepherds' fires winked in the dark hills, as on Ithaca. From time to time a dog barked somewhere below.

Nov. 1, Restaurant Delphi, 7:15 AM - A cool night & morning. We pitched camp behind the white church outside of town. Had to go to bed at 8 'cause it was dark, & I woke up at 12:30. Awake for 2-3 hrs., but slept the last 3. We were up at 6 in the half-light, broke camp with one eye on the sunrise, & were in town for breakfast at 7.

After consuming a good meal by local standards - egg, toast, warm milk - we took the road in perfect weather, but stopped half a dozen times the first hour to re-tie our packs and look back at Mt. Parnassos. Among other pictures, Hector snapped one of me and my scooter in front of the mountain. Wearing my grey wool shirt over a Windhome sweatshirt, and gloves, I look serious, focused. The scooters ran beautifully, and even with tiptoeing through the stretch of construction we made it back to Athens in under six hours: an exhilarating run. I told my journal that night that the trip was "picking up speed" and "acquiring a kaleidoscopic quality." Less than two weeks earlier we had been languishing in Naples, talking about quitting before we had started. That seemed worlds away and centuries ago; now nothing could have been further from my mind than abandoning our Odyssey on a Scooter.

That day we both ran out of gas (i.e. used up the fuel in the main tank and switched onto reserve) within 200 yards of each other. No harm was done - we filled up just down the road - but it set me to examining the numbers. It took 5 liters to cover the 170 kilometers from Delphi to Athens. Using rough equivalents and doing the math in my head, I reckoned that as almost 95 mpg: a level of performance that I thought we could count on. But I was doubly wrong. The correct figure was barely 80 mpg, and later, under adverse conditions and when there were no gas stations "just down the road," that would sink significantly.

On the morrow we investigated the costs of sailing to various islands, and gave – actually, sold - blood. Yes, there was a connection. At the hostel we heard that an Athens hospital would pay $10.75 for a pint of healthy blood: that was food and lodging for a week (I was too ignorant of economics to ponder the mechanics or ethics of exchange rates). When we learned that it would cover the cost of voyaging to Mykonos, Rhodes, and Crete, we volunteered for the needle. The idea of making our next move by sea was attractive; we also priced voyages to Istanbul ($24 return) and Alexandria ($43). We decided to tackle Mykonos first, though, after touring the Attic peninsula, which we did the next day. I had an upset stomach, but declined to connect that with selling blood.

Attica

Nov. 3, Temple of Poseidon, Sounion - Under drippy skies we drove this morning down to Sounion. Good roads & a pretty if deserted & slightly desolate coast. Near Athens, the features (flat, open land, "houses of leisure," sand & unused soil, scrub growth & pines) are similar to the Carolina coast. The differences are in the Mediterranean trees & shrubs. Wish I had some botany.

Farther south, the peninsula resembled coastal Maine and was almost unpopulated. Happiness, I thought, would be to build a cabin and live in one of those empty coves, where pale ochre rocks half-enclosed a jewel of jade water. The partly ruined temple celebrated by Byron ("Place me on Sunium's marbled steep") sits atop a cliff at the tip of the peninsula: an example of the classic Greek flair for dramatic architecture. Approached from the land, on their own level, its white Doric columns are less impressive than the green Aegean Sea they overlook, but from down below, the temple becomes a pearl against the blue sky, an Olympian crown to the precipice. And it *is* a Temple of Poseidon, intended to be viewed from the sea; the cape was difficult for ancient sailors to round, and they made sacrifices to the sea god while the temple was in sight. From below, the prospect justifies Byron's impressionistic image: a steep cliff "marbled" by the temple atop it. I could not find the initials he is said to have carved into one of the columns.

Before noon we left to drive up Attica's east or "Green Coast" to Laurion, whose silver mines were a vital source of Athenian wealth during the Persian Wars. Thence the road ran through low hills and past farms toward Athens: pleasant country at first, with fertile soil and seas of yellowing grapevines, then more barren. Twice we were caught in showers and brought out our bulky ponchos. We took shelter for awhile, but when it persisted we pushed on, laughing. I experimented with sitting on the *rear* seat and driving from there to ease the fanny fatigue. Not safe!

At a junction we turned east and drove out to Marathon. The countryside looked bleak; nothing was to be seen on the plain but a dirt mound amid olive orchards. I clambered dutifully to the top and tried to recite what I could remember of Byron's rhapsody -

The mountains look on Marathon
And Marathon looks on the sea;
And musing there an hour alone,
I dream'd that Greece might still be free;
For standing on the Persians' grave,
I could not deem myself a slave -

but my effort was undercut by the laughter of three peasant women picking olives nearby. It sounded derisive; perhaps they were laughing at me. Well, Greece *was* free, though poor, and why should they share my romanticizing of her past trials and glories? But did they even know what the mound was? Their ancestors probably laughed at Byron. Somewhat underwhelmed, we drove "home" in the rain, having to grit and bear it. The distance from Marathon to Athens was 42 kilometers: a heck of a run no matter how good the news. We both turned over 1500 kilometers that day; the scooters were officially broken in.

If the Athens hostel was home, its residents were our family. My favorite siblings were two Nordic blondes, as cool as they were beautiful, traveling together on an old German scooter. They raised the standard of male attire without even asking, visited several "important sights" a day and helped clean the hostel. I also liked Julius of Johannesburg, a hale-fellow-well-met with a guitar and a lot of folksongs; we traded back and forth one evening to mutual satisfaction. There was a bearded guy from Scarsdale who had left his damaged scooter in Saloniki on an aborted run from Istanbul, and had no plans. He warned that northern roads were bad. I distrusted Zane, an articulate Harvard grad with glittering eyes who stroked his Mephistophelean goatee and said he had just won a big graduate fellowship. The consensus was that he must be brilliant. He had a large retinue of female followers: sufficient reason for my dislike. And *Zane*?

Our autocratic *pater familias* was Dmitri "the warden," enigmatic and often hostile, a fitness buff who kept several guns in his room and seemed to be preparing to repel an American invasion. His latent enmity became open when he heard that several of us had sold our blood. To do so, he said, was robbing his impoverished motherland; he swore all one evening in German and Greek. Dmitri did a hundred push-ups and took a cold shower - the only kind available - every day (pride and hygiene forced me to follow suit). I wondered what he had done during the Nazi occupation, and what conclusions he had drawn from it.

Travel agencies were not created for travelers such as Hector and me; agents disliked our "How much can we see for how little?" approach. But they possessed information we needed, and through one of them we arranged to take the overnight boat to Mykonos, from which we could reach Delos, and perhaps Rhodes. The scooters would stay behind, to be serviced and stored by Lambretta. After lunch on the 4th we shouldered our packs and took the tram to Piraeus - making us appreciate what other hostelers did all the time and reminding us why we had bought scooters. At the port we had several hours to wait.

Nov. 4, a park in Piraeus, 2 PM - Aspects of Athenian life... kiosks are ubiquitous, selling chocolate, cigarettes, candy, chewing gum, magazines...Fewer people offering to "help" you [than in Italy], but everybody very curious & won't quit when we can't understand... Great numbers of men play with colored strings of beads; psychologists would call it "mass compulsive behavior"... The Greeks have an irritating negative facial gesture, but I like them better than Italians - less hostile, seemingly more honest.

When I first saw the "Mediterranean negative" – chin lifted, eyes rolled up, tongue clucked - in Athens, it looked so contemptuous that I took it as an insult. Later we learned to enjoy it, and would ask children questions designed to make them perform. "Worry beads" were another social custom that would follow us around The Sea.

Our economic life was now such a preoccupation that I took stock of my daily "average food expenditures" like a budget-conscious housewife, or an accountant's son:

<u>Breakfast</u>: generally 2 drachmas of bread, 2 for honey, 2 for butter, sometimes 3 for a honeyed roll or 2 for milk; sometimes a drach. of grapes. Avg: 7.5-8 ds., about 26 cents.

<u>Lunch</u>: Sometimes a dish of vegetables or meat (6-8 ds.); or else more bread (2 ds.) and fruit (2 ds.), + chocolate (3 ds.). Avg: close to 8 ds., about 27 cents. (In Naples we might spend 75c.)

Dinner: meat, bread & vegetable (15 ds.). Otherwise, it's a saslik (very good: meat, tomatoes, greenery & onions wrapped in a highly seasoned bread roll), 3.5 ds., + a pastry, 3-3.5 ds., fruit, 1-2 ds., & either chocolate (3 ds.) or ice cream (4 ds.). Avg: 14-15 ds.: 45-50 cents. The most I've spent on a full meal is 17.5 ds. (58 cents).

The grand total was ca. $1.10. I wished that it might be a dollar even - and so it soon became. Money was time; to stretch one was to stretch the other. If it costs $2 a day to live, then every $2 saved is another day somewhere. If I ate on the street instead of in a restaurant, passed up the honeyed roll or the dessert, I would soon save a dollar, then another. My weight began to drop, but physical condition was not yet a concern. We budgeted 50 cents a night each for lodging, and never exceeded that in Greece.

7:30 PM, aboard Pentelis - Deck passage - out on deck this time - will be cold.

I quickly staked my claim to a wooden-slatted park bench by spreading my sleeping bag on it. The bag was the object of much puzzlement; I had to explain its function to several Greeks. The phantasmagoric night left a mixed residue of sensations: noise, bright lights, vibration, seeping cold, and waking in the center of a circle of curious Greeks, to whom I must explain my presence in my 25 words of Greek or their 50 of English. Now they seemed as rude as Italians, and I sometimes lost patience with persistent ones; there were limits to this ambassadorial stuff! To them I would explain, with gestures, that Hector was a beatnik from Tennessee and I an existentialist from Connecticut. They would nod and say "*Ja*?" (They always thought we were Germans.) It seemed preferable to just repeating, "I don't understand. I'm sorry." Using interpreters, Italian, and some Greek, we called ourselves traveling students - not *toureestes*.

From time to time – and there was plenty of that! - I sat under a light next to a warm smokestack out of the wind and read, or wrote, or thought about a vocation:

Over half the cars in Athens are American. The Greeks either have a taste for the big car or import duties favor the U.S.... Was approached this afternoon in the park by a gross prostitute. Insisted on sitting on me & fingering my hair. She smelled. "You fahck? You fahck?" - "Selectively." I thought it was funny.

I want to write more than ever. The desire comes welling up, though devoid of specific ideas, & with it a small voice warning that my writing is bad. Yet the feeling for meaning and symbol is there.

Once I looked in on the quaint "heads," but decided to screw up my bladder to the sticking point rather than venture on them, and returned to my journal. It had been a day - and was a long night - of taking inventory.

Another difficulty...capturing the idea for a good story. I am too yoked to reality to move comfortably in realms of surrealism, etc. An action has not only its surface meaning but symbolic significance; I am aware of objective correlatives, multiple symbols, words as colors & sounds. But the techniques of non-objective literature are beyond me. My knowledge of mythology & the classics is also limited. Yet I improve in all these respects. This & the conviction that I have sensibility lead me on.

Ideas for stories are in my head, but none is burning to be written, in Blackburn's sense. I want to write an "island in the sun" story about the idyllic dreams of a young man or couple, which have a Tantalus-like quality. This story is hard to plan until my own attitude towards life has crystallized enough for me to know how to end it.

I still hope that my view of life firms up so that I can finish the island story. Dr. Blackburn, a fine man and an inspiring teacher, taught creative writing at Debrew. Over the years Mac Hyman, Bill Styron, Reynolds Price and Anne Tyler attended. In his class I finally found the people I was looking for, though not until my senior year. Meeting them sooner would have made a huge difference to me.

Mykonos and Delos

I had managed to fall asleep when the deck porter (who of course knew the destination of the foreign celebrities) tugged on my foot in the pitch blackness of early morning. "Mykonos! Mykonos!" he cried, pointing all around. Had we rammed into the middle of it? I stood up. Mykonos appeared as a half-circle of dim lights low on the dark water. Less dramatic but more open than Ithaca, it spread homely arms to the sea, and we had stopped within their parentheses, a quarter-mile from shore. I crammed things into my pack while he chanted distractedly - with true Greek feeling for the tragic limits of life - "No time. There is no time." Heavily laden and still groggy, I barely managed the awkward leap down into the motor launch, and had to be helped up onto the bleak and deserted quay. The few other debarkees disappeared into the tourist hotel and the *Pentelis* into the night in the opposite direction. Hector and I were alone on the broad concrete promenade.

A few *tabacs* and cafés were open for early-rising fishermen, and we had bitter Greek coffee at one of them. Its black-clad customers, reserved in speech and gesture, paid little attention to us as they drank coffee - or *ouzo*! - at small unpainted wooden tables and talked fishing. The proprietor polished his cups and watched us without expression. Hector smoked a rare cigarette and I tried to think. It was 4:15 AM, we were encumbered with packs and had no place to sleep. What to do until morning? We ate something, chewed gum for our awful mouths and walked to the hotel, where a light was still on. The tourists had all gone to bed. The gentle clerk - perhaps the owner - let us stash our packs in a dark nook of the lobby and we started walking, carrying only cameras.

Beyond the quay and the streetlights we took whatever way led upwards. Whitewashed houses gleamed on either side of the dark path: cobblestones, then dirt. The air was chilly but not cold. We climbed tacitly, the lights dropped behind, and the sky filled with stars. As we walked, joining a gravel road several yards wide that led inland between low stone walls, the blood warmed and spirits rose. Below us now, the silent white town dozed by the sea. On either side the land dropped away into a valley: barren soil, stone walls, white houses. Sheep bells tinkled nearby. In the east a serrated line of hills underscored the brightening horizon. A mile further, when rose and orange began to tint the clouds, we turned and followed the sun's color-awakening progress west. An old woman, seated between wicker baskets on a burro, passed by, nodding. Northwards, a hill, gnarled with age and erosion, became milk chocolate studded with white marshmallow homes. The air, preternaturally still and clear, seemed expectant; then the sun rose full, and the magic evaporated. We hurried back down to the port.

A big breakfast at the hotel earned storage space for our packs indefinitely, so we decided to explore the island further.

Retracing our morning steps, we hiked on for about six miles, until the Aegean reappeared beyond the island. Only one collection of whitewashed earthen houses qualified as a village, whose little store provided snacks and shelter from a brief shower. We were quite a sensation: Hector for his cowboy boots, I for my height. Forced to keep it simple, we exchanged professions of good will. When the shower passed, I rambled through a side valley while Hector explored an isolated beach. We met in a rocky gorge to climb back up a cow-path to the top. Most of the island was stony and barren, hardly arable; sheep-herding was its only "inland" industry, unless you count religion: we saw a good many of its 300 churches. Every building was white (it's the law). We reached town late, fetched our packs and toted them half a mile uphill to a small grassy flat we had noticed among the terraces, overlooking the town, the sea and other islands. Sheltered by the hillside, some prickly pear, and the ubiquitous stone walls, we pitched our tent at sunset.

Nov. 5, Mykonos town, 8:30 PM - Great day! Mykonos is picturesque & beautiful; we walked about 20 miles; tonight we met Jim & Jerry [from the Miaoulis], & Diana & some other girl from Debrew. We convinced the girls not to go back to Athens, but to stay here for awhile & ride around the Pelopponesus with us.

Though not yet familiar to tourists, Mykonos was already well known to young budget travelers, so it was natural for Jim and Jerry to turn up there. But that they should do so with two Debrew girls qualified as a coincidence, and we had a noisy reunion. We both knew Diana; she had been a class ahead of us, and knew Penny and Andrea. The "other girl from Debrew" was a nurse named Lu. Whereas Diana had been prominent on campus, a popular cheerleader and sorority girl, Lu had been obscure. "Oh, you wouldn't know me," she laughed. "I was nobody." I liked her at once. They had been on Mykonos for five days, but agreed to pass up the night boat to Piraeus, go back with us in a few days and make a scooter tour to Mycenae and Olympia. *We* decided to leave our campsite the next morning and move into the *pension* where they were all quartered.

Walking away from the harbor lights at midnight to our tent on the dark hillside I felt like a gypsy. Through the quiet came sounds of singing and dancing from town, softened by distance, the slosh of waves on a beach, and a goat's plaintive bell. Had we tented throughout our stay it would have been a different island for us, but when society called we did not resist. Once the morning dew dried, we struck the tent, packed up and descended to town.

The quay was rife with images asking to be photographed or remembered. A tan and white cat posed before hanging folds of brown fishing net, drying in the morning sun; a pelican - not just *any* pelican, but Petros, the town's mascot - perched on a red and blue dory. We crossed the peninsula on narrow streets, came out on the western side and soon found "our" *pension:* a ramshackle green frame house of two stories, resting on a white-washed earthen base. It faced the sea on a shallow bay; an open veranda, supported by slender wooden beams, hung over the clear water. Jerry's room, where we crashed, cost 45 cents a night, including use of the faded sofa and chairs on the balcony. Also rooming there were Dante, an American student; Stella, a shy English girl; Melody, also English, who looked like a raven-haired Brigitte Bardot; and her son, Sebastian. The husband/father had gone to Athens on the night boat with Jim to buy film for an "art movie" about Mykonos.

We set off on a side trip at once. A fishing boat would carry paying passengers the few miles over to the ancient sacred isle of Delos most mornings, returning in the afternoon. That allowed only four hours in the extensive ruins, however, so we decided to spend a night there.

Nov. 6, on Delos boat - One-stroke chug, pumping to Delos. No boat to Rhodes; plans must change. Will camp on D. with the girls; perhaps stay [on Mykonos] a few more days. Great island.

More story material. A "Cult of Relative Absolute" - satire on relative, subjectively determined values. Also, a young boy's truth-realization of Americans as seen by their coarse actions in a small Italian town.

My ideas for stories (as vague as my grasp of engines) are revealing. At Windhome I had tried to visualize myself at Barney's age, around 35. What appeared onscreen was a bearded outdoorsman, already noted for his precocious book *The Cult of Relative Absolute*, exposing that cult to the world. *Or* should it celebrate its arrival?! Well, maybe it was more feasible to write a story than the book. The people we had met were starting to shed new light on American *mores*, but my feelings about these fresh perspectives were also far from clear. Again, which side should I choose?

For some reason I did not mention the exquisite sixteen-year-old girl who stood up front, as silent as a bowsprit, oblivious to the effect as the wind pressed her pullover and sheath skirt against her body and made her hair stream back. Cleo's beauty had stunned me; now I wondered if she might be only an average young Mediterranean woman. Hector and I gaped while Di and Lu smiled. Who *was* she? A local, someone said: the daughter of one of the caretakers who lived on Delos. But I resisted prosaic explanations, regarding her as an avatar of Aphrodite: the olive-skinned peasant variety, not a pallid Botticelli aristocrat. On the island she disappeared into barren hills for the day and a half we stayed. Did she have a home there, or a shrine? If a perfect Venus de Delos in marble or porphyry is ever unearthed, I will know what we beheld.

Famous in myth as the floating island that Zeus chained so that Leto could give birth to Apollo and Artemis there, and in history as the seat of the Athenian confederacy, Delos proved to be a small, rocky, desolate island, deserted except for us and the caretakers. Acres of low ruins and rubble covered much of it. A few columns and lion statues had been set up, which made good pictures, but the effect was contrived, and jarred with the prevailing Ozymandian decay. A black horse grazed on the short grass before the Temple of Isis, where 2500 years ago Egyptian priests lent the prestige of their presence to the rising Aegean power. Elaborate mosaics in the remains of large villas represent a later era, when wealthy Romans turned Delos into a resort. We ambled among the porticoes of the supposed dwelling of Marcus Sextus, a 2nd century Greek merchant whose last voyage is celebrated in the book *The Cruise of the Dolphin*. And yet… I was having trouble staying focused.

Delos, noon - The island is wonderful for mythological associations & remains of antiquity, but I'm reaching the saturation point for ruins. I've never been happy sightseeing with other people, & had to split up from the others to get anything out of walking through temples, agora, etc. Even then I wasn't enthusiastic, & the Museum, which I walked through in 10 mins., was a total loss. It wasn't very good, anyway.

Don't know what I do want to see. Greece will chiefly be ruins. Turkey will be a change, but Egypt will be more [ruins]. I'll have to make adjustments & work up interest. I don't feel I'm putting enough in or getting enough out. The inside is pushing more than the outside. Affairs such as plans with Penny, choosing a vocation, etc., are more alive & real than ancient Greek culture.

This was a major reversal of my state of mind before the trip, but I was also reflecting Hector's continuing doubts about its value. He told me that his father had written, questioning his interest in "old rockpiles." Well, at least his father wrote him! But I wondered why he had told me that. Was it a warning, a harbinger of another crisis?

How do you reconcile the ancient Greeks' pious concern with their gods & their artistic interest in the human body? (Christian question!) Their gods were conceived in human form but endowed with human weaknesses: immortal yet fallible. Thus adoration of the human form might be only an extension of god-worship.

My exclamation is the important unfollowed lead here: what needs reconciling? If the question is pursued, the answer may lie in the differences between the concepts of afterlife – and the attitudes toward this world that flow from them - in ancient Greek religion and in Christianity.

We pitched the tent in a stone-walled field that served as the campground and next to it rigged the tarp over a rope as a shelter for us. I climbed Mt. Cynthus, the island's low summit (from which Jove watched the birth of his twins), in the last light, and drank in the dusk-softened panorama of classic ruins, mauve islands, and the calm, orange-splashed sea. The black horse was still, or again, grazing by a temple on an upper terrace. Di and Lu had undertaken to cook dinner on our capricious gas stove. They even found three wildflowers somewhere and put them on our rock-slab dinner table: a feminine touch long absent and highly appreciated. We ate by candlelight after dark and turned in early, but between giggling inter-tent pillow talk, sexual tension, and later the cold, I slept little.

Shortly before the boat arrived the next day, Hector and I had a memorable swim in the pellucid Aegean. The water was so clear that from the pier the blurred saffron gleam of boulders on the bottom seemed just beneath our feet, but Hector dove in, surfaced unhurt, and swam out with quick strokes. Reassured, I dove shallowly and kicked along underwater, scattering white-pearl bubbles in a sea of cool sapphire. A sailboat was anchored a few yards offshore. I swam down its anchor chain until my ears hurt; the bottom appeared as distant as ever. We splashed and washed in the chilly water until we heard the chug of the approaching boat. Except for two bored men at the museum, and the horse, we had had Delos to ourselves.

Nov. 8, the waterfront house, Mykonos - The charms of life here have a Siren-like quality which lulls one into insouciance. It has bothered us very little that there are no connections to Rhodes in the winter; we return tonight to Piraeus, starting around the Peloponnesus tomorrow. That will put us [back] in Athens about Friday & we will see about trips to Crete, Rhodes, & Istanbul.

I did not take my own image seriously enough: one of the Sirens' ploys is to make you forget your schedule. Nor had I learned the eastern fatalism that hedges all statements about the future with a provisional "God willing." Not that deities kept us from sailing that night, or the next; Mykonos was just too good to leave. Character is fate, too.

In the meantime, we are quite content. The camping on Delos was a great success, & the island's ruins were very much alive.

It is wonderful how creature comforts and two days' worth of hindsight could combine to throw a golden haze over the restless discontent I had felt while there. But which one was true, was *my* truth? Should I believe my on-the-spot reporting, or the later, sunnier version?

I was glad that no ship left last night for Piraeus: we had a chance to stay here (Jerry invited us to sleep in his room) & enjoy the company of Di & Lu, Jerry, & Sebastian & Melody. The island lends itself to artistic endeavor: photography, painting, the solitude & atmosphere to practice music & writing. Jerry said M. has a surrealistic quality: octopi hanging over clotheslines, the town pelican (who once caused the M. fleet to sail on Tinos) strutting around the waterfront, etc.

As we heard the story, Petros - who was considered a good-luck totem - either flew over to, or was abducted by fishermen from, the neighboring island of Tinos. Both versions agree that the entire fishing fleet of Mykonos then sailed across and demanded the return of their pelican, rather as the Greeks went to Troy for Helen. So epic and tragedy become farce in their modern reruns.

I worry that I'm with Americans & English too much. That would be against a First Principle. But those I'm with are interesting, adaptable & not obnoxious.

Ah, so if the Anglos were "interesting," it was okay to hang with them? Actually there was little alternative here. The islanders spoke a dialect unintelligible to me, and scarcely comprehended my phrase-book Greek. With our landlady and with restaurant-keepers I could transact simple business, but any real conversation had to be with the few English-speaking Greeks or "my own kind."

So we settled happily into our little community. Most mornings I awoke to a peculiar sound: "*whoosht*!" followed by "*splat*!" Venturing out, I found that a fisherman just in from the sea was tenderizing a small octopus or two by sweeping it in a vertical circle like a cricket bowler and flinging it down on the concrete footing beneath the veranda again and again. Then, still early in the morning, two of us would go to the nearby bakery for a round, one-kilo loaf of brown bread hot from the oven. While one trotted home, shifting the loaf from hand to hand to avoid burning his fingers, the other would buy honey and butter. Six or seven of us would draw up chairs around a circular table on the porch, put the loaf in the middle, draw knives and break bread together. Afterwards I would play with Sebastian, or read to him, translating from *Robin des Bois*. This helped Melody, who seemed depressed by the demands of motherhood, and caused the others to say that I would make a good father. It was rather enjoyable to help Melody.

Influenced by Hector's serious photographic sorties, I also made a point of taking pictures, and once or twice I even went shopping:

Mykonos has wonderful woven & knitted garments for reasonable prices. A wool sweater with a large collar may be had for $6.70. Diana has talked me into buying one for Penny. Can't decide between a blue or an olive pullover. Di says she'll deliver it personally.

In the early afternoon, several of us might have coffee at a table on the quay, Mykonos' social center, where we could linger, enjoy the breeze off the bay, and talk or not. If Melody was with us, we were sure to be joined by an elderly Greek aristocrat who was gently besieging the citadel of her fidelity. He might have sat for Lawrence Durrell as Capodoccia. As three of us generally escorted her, he would in time withdraw, resigned, his dignity still intact.

Usually we all ate dinner together at one of the seafood restaurants where you could point to your choice of dishes in a glass display case and fill up for 50 cents. Anytime after 8 the men would start dancing, alternating between the leaping *pidiktos*, the languishing *syrtos*, and ballroom dancing that required "our" women as partners. The dancers, with their bandannas and cocky berets, were artists whose intensity and pride of bearing rivaled those of an Andalusian gypsy. Late one evening, with the music and gaiety in full cry, a half-drunk dancer seized a small wooden table in his teeth, lifted it and whirled it about in slow circles for a good minute, never losing the rhythm of his dance, before setting it down exactly where it had stood. His friends then replaced their cups and glasses on it and went back to talking. The dancer spun into his chair and spat a little blood aside in the sawdust. Zorba, eat your heart out.

Nov. 9, the waterfront house - Another free night here on the floor; a grey early AM on the island, harbinger of winter. Book on the Byzantine Empire is good & I'm making progress.

I always feared when writing at Debrew that it was too Apollonian a process: I sat down, puzzled out a story & began. The approach was intellectual, emotions being only shadows in the characters. Now I seem to be starting to undergo an emotional crisis which I have suspected was necessary. Last night, having begun the "Italian boy" story, I was suddenly assailed with doubts, self-accusations, fragments of scenes, feelings of guilt. I walked in pain, as if giving birth. I was happy that it was there, yet knew that I could not yet let it forth. But it <u>will</u> come, I believe. In the meantime I had to write, & wrote a Dionysian something, useless in itself, neurotic, Freudian, tortured. Yet it was a wonderful release, & may serve as a trigger to a more useful creation. It was new for me - literary free association.

Whatever was brewing inside, the *Dionysian something* did not survive. It apparently did not occur to me that I might *be* an Apollonian, not a Dionysian, writer.

A pleasant day of reading, writing and swimming led into a beach party – meant as a send-off for us - in the cove beyond the windmills that night. We built a bonfire, cooked fish and potatoes, drank wine or *ouzo*, sang, and swam in the dark sea. Everyone was high and happy, though Di had too much *ouzo* and retired early.

Toward the end there were some bedroom irregularities, or at least unusual traffic. Di made a point of telling me one morning that she had *not* spent the night in Jerry's room, as if it were a point that needed to be made. "Di, I don't care," I said, embarrassed by this eruption of bourgeois morality. "Well, *I* care," she replied tartly. Later she remarked that he was not a man she would have dated in college, and that involvement with him was a sign of change and growth in the year since her graduation.

On our last morning we went swimming again and I lost my towel at the beach (no small matter when you carry only essentials, one of each). That afternoon someone borrowed the village carpenter's guitar for me. It was fun to play again, even on an unfamiliar instrument, but I was rusty, and soon tired of trying to solo under scrutiny. Melody (said to be an accomplished cellist) asked me not to attempt Bach unless I could do it well, so I scratched that entry.

Oh, and much more that went unrecorded…Sebastian, his towhead halo-bright in the sun, fishing in the cove by the house, or speaking Greek with the black-clad grandmother who sometimes cleaned fish there…a gathering on the porch when Melody remarked, "I like to keep my body warm," and Hector, looking far away, moaned appreciatively. We all laughed, and he came back to us. "Sorry, I was thinking of something else," he explained, and Melody said, "That's all right." *Very neat, Hector*, I thought. *I was thinking of something else, too…*Jerry making a precise freehand drawing of a teasel one day as we talked about modern art and our ambitions. "I know what you're about," I ventured to say. "'Western man is in search of a new synthesis'": a sentence lifted from Ernest Mundt's *Art, Form, and Civilization*.

Jerry glanced over at me for a moment. "Right," he said, and went on with the drawing. He came from somewhere around Pittsburgh and had been to Carnegie-Mellon. In a few days I had come to like and respect his quiet strength. Did he hope to make a living from art? I asked. "Oh, from commercial art, probably, yes," he said. "My own on the side, perhaps." It was Jerry who warned me, that last day, what Hector and I were about to undertake. "Do you understand who you're going to be traveling with?"

"Do you mean Di and Lu?"

"Your Di and Lu are Diana and Lucinda. Diana is Artemis, chaste huntress and goddess of the moon. Lucinda is 'the shining one,' another moon-goddess, who helps women in childbirth."

"Well, she *is* a nurse. And Di - Diana - *is* athletic."

"There you are. So watch your step."

"Gosh, I don't know, Jerry. I mean, they're nice-looking girls, but…goddesses?"

"It's not about beauty, man. The issue is the female principle. Think about it: the word *moon* is embedded in *month*. Do you know Latin?"

"Well, some."

"The Latin word for month is *mensis*. The Latin for monthly is *menstruus*. You see? It all hangs together, from the moon to the monthlies."

"Heavy! Any advice on how we should play it?"

He shook his head. "You have to work out some things, tactics, for yourself. Just be aware of underlying realities."

"That's gnomic! And what can we make of 'Jerry'? Are you a Jeremiah? A German? Or a flimsy builder?"

"There are several possibilities," he admitted with a slight smile. "But this isn't about me."

Nov. 10, aboard Pentelis - We wrote a grand farewell to Mykonos. Tonight we ate in a group at The Café, then had a chocolate at a wharfside table. Everyone - Dante & Stella, Melody & Sebastian, Di & Lu, Jerry, Hector & I - was in high spirits, warm with the sweet sadness of parting. Then the boat, & laughable confusion & hurried good-byes. Should have liked to meet Dennis & see what Melody loved. It shakes my values to see families like that. Such fine people, in personality, taste, manners, brains, yet M. looks loose & racy, to say the least. They weren't married until 4 years after Sebastian was born, & then 'just for his sake.'

The next 24 hours passed in a blur: a sleepless, cacophonous deck passage, arrival at Piraeus on a grey, drizzly dawn, a taxi for four to the hostel. We ate *baklava* and drank coffee until the hostel opened, then repacked to make two bags do for four people. From the Lambretta garage where they had been serviced we reclaimed the scooters, tied on, and headed into heavy downtown traffic. Diana went with Hector "to balance the loads" (she being heavier than Lu, he lighter than I). Driving a scooter again was fun, but carrying a passenger was new to me: the extra 110 pounds of flexible weight, which might influence the balance at unexpected moments, had to be taught neither to resist the lean nor to "help" it, but just to become part of the scooter. Somehow we survived Venizelou Street, Omonia Square and the *Iera Odos*. Then the road opened and Hector wanted to speed up: the scooters, past their break-in period, might now go as fast as they could. I felt wary about that, though, and let him go on ahead. We passed Daphne and Eleusis, bore left at the Delphi fork and headed across a rolling steppe that sloped down toward the Gulf of Corinth and the Peloponnese. The sky had cleared.

The Island of Pelops

A winding, hilly road led along the Gulf to the bridge over the Corinthian Canal - last seen from the *Miaoulis* - and the storied town of Corinth. Oedipus grew up there; one of its legendary kings was Sisyphus. In ancient times its industries, especially shipbuilding, made it such a wealthy commercial center that "Corinthian" became synonymous with luxury. After buying bread and cheese at a dark shop in the new town we spent an hour or two at Old Corinth, a few kilometers away. The extensive ruins, few of which were upright or impressive, displayed familiar forms: *propylaea*, *agora*, theatre, Temple of Apollo, shops and stalls. Generally similar to others we had seen, the fragments were, where standing, graceful, and the little museum had some good pieces of archaic and Hellenistic sculpture and pottery, radiating the subtle elegance of classical art. This was, after all, home ground for Corinthian columns, as well as for triremes and ill-fated royalty.

South of Corinth the road entered a more pastoral landscape: the hills and valleys of the northern Peloponnese. Through a notch in a ridge we descended onto the Plain of Argos - a region of variegated fields and slim cypresses not unlike Boetia - rejoicing to hear the song of the open road once more. Saving Mycenae and Nauplia for the morrow, we turned east towards

Epidaurus. Then, about ten miles into some rocky hills and an hour before sunset, Hector's scooter surprised us all by ceasing to sing the song. Evidently double loads and higher speeds came at a price.

Nov. 11, hotel in Lygourion - The excursion into the Peloponnese has begun. The scooters, double-loaded, ran well at 60-70 kph, but Hector's ran out of gas at 160 kms. I had to fetch some from a village 14 kms. away over darkening hills. It was an exciting episode as I lashed on the gas can & sped back - until the girls' luggage burst open on the rack & spewed film, hairbrushes, slips & assorted dainties over the road for 100 yds. A lady riding on a plodding donkey up ahead watched impassively, & I had to laugh.

I often wondered how we looked to the folks we passed, and would have been glad to peer into the mind of the black-clad peasant woman who observed this mishap. I stuffed everything back into the moon goddesses' packsack, retied, and raced back to where the others were waiting in the dusk. We poured in the gas, groped our way to Lygourion after dark, and negotiated beds and food in our broken Greek. We were out of the tourist orbit here, far from any English. Yet somehow I procured a can and gasoline from a humble household in a village whose name I never learned; once they comprehended my props and gestures, their generosity did the rest. And they understood "*Efkharisto*!"

The country around Argos was lovely - suggestive of Disney's illustrations for Beethoven's 6th [in Fantasia] - but around here it is again quite barren.

I wrote by candlelight at the dinner table, there being no electricity in Lygourion. The sun now set at six, and that was the end of good vision. Each room had two *basins* of water, but no taps or sink. The bright lights and cosmopolitan air of Athens seemed worlds away. Our phrase-book Greek, fairly useful in the larger towns, drew blank looks when we asked some street-idlers for information. We all walked through the dark streets, excited by the remoteness, and retired at nine. From our window at bedtime I could see only the dull gleam of starlit olive leaves on the surrounding hills.

At six AM the wan November sun looked ominously wintry. I dressed quickly in the chill. Out in the street the air was cold, crisp, and faintly pungent with leaf-smoke. Fields, yellow with dead stubble or plowed brown, steamed in the growing warmth. I spoke to three boys, who just stared; then to an old man, a Van Gogh-like figure, who stopped long enough to establish that I was an American student, shook hands gravely, and walked on. At a pump I drew icy water to wash my face. After all, it *was* good to be up early! We breakfasted at the "hotel" on hot milk and soft-boiled eggs before starting for Epidaurus.

Nov. 12, Epidaurus antiqua, 10 AM - The ruins of the Temple of Asclepius, the beautifully restored & acoustically perfect theatre, many ruins & a museum full of fine architecture & sculpture: I begin to understand the meaning of classical grace. Countryside very pretty.

Epidaurus (pronounced *Epidavros*, we discovered) was a pleasant surprise, though we had heard about the marvelous acoustics of the 4th century BCE theatre. When the only guide in sight struck a match down in the center of the orchestra circle, we heard it distinctly in the top row, far left, of the semi-circular auditorium, which can seat 14,000. The other ruins offered little else of interest, but the museum was excellent: elaborately carved bas-reliefs on pediments from the main temple, and a few good statues. The region was considered to have curative powers from an early date - rather as tubercular New Yorkers went to Saranac Lake later - so it was natural to say that the god of healing was born and could best be worshipped there.

As the charmed peace of early morning was dissipating, we cranked up and started west, back through Lygourion towards Nauplia or *Nafplion* (i.e. "naval station." We were learning how Greek pronunciation worked - "u" was sounded as "v" or "f" - and how corrupted the place names had become, mainly with Latin forms). In full daylight - and with plenty of gas - it was a joyful, mildly exhilarating ride. Nafplion, a port on the Gulf of Argolis, turned out to be a small, pretty town with a large public park and a Byzantine church among tall pines. That the town is named for a son of Poseidon and an Argonaut suggests its antiquity. In 1829 Greek guerrillas took it from the Turks and made it their first capital.

We could not pass up the two Venetian citadels - Palamede and *Akronafplion* ('high Nafplion') - on a mesa behind the city, though this involved a skidding climb up a muddy road under construction. It is now paved, but at least we had a sense of *earning* our panorama from the top: a 360-degree vista of mountains, sea, the plain stretching north toward Argos, the stone houses of Nafplion below our feet, and the tiny isle of *Bourzi* (with another Venetian fortress) out in the bay. Finding ourselves the only visitors, we spent a carefree midday ascending ramparts and descending into dungeons, taking pictures, and sunning on the rocks like lizards. I eyed the grey, bare mountains on the far side of the gulf apprehensively: they seemed to oppose our way to Olympia. Finally we descended the hill in a long slither and whirred off up the road to Tiryns and Argos. The names were resonant, but the minimal ruins there left too much to the imagination to compete with Epidavros.

After lunch we turned west toward the mountainous crest of the Peloponnese. It was a slow, often first-gear climb up steep grades and around hairpin curves, but often rewarding: the long ascent could open to sudden colossal sweeps of mountain-and-bay grandeur at any time. The weather was mild, the air invigorating. Halfway across we stopped to rest the scooters on a bleak patch of meadow. A sheepskin-cloaked shepherd materialized to beg a cigarette, which he obtained from nurse Lu. We exchanged formal pleasantries in Greek, shook hands and went our respective ways. Climbing on through subalpine landscapes, we crossed the pass and started our descent to *Tripolis* ('tri-city'). A smooth road ran straight down these gentler western slopes, and the day's excitement came to a head in an exhilarating 70 kph rush into the central valley.

Cruising the streets of Tripolis in search of lodging, we stopped in front of a small hotel. The proprietor came out to negotiate, and as we bargained the usual crowd gathered. The upshot was that we could save a drachma each by all staying in one room. While Hector and I consulted gingerly with our passengers - myself very mindful of what Jerry had said about their mythic identity - the gist of the situation became known to the kibitzers, who began laughing good-humoredly. It *was* funny, and soon we were all roaring, united momentarily by the imagined bedroom farce. With the goddesses' consent we took the room, but, wary of the fate of Actaeon, I hung the white tarp over a rope stretched the length of the chamber. We ate across the street at a cheap "walk-down" restaurant whose owner treated us to wine. Having spent about $2 that day, I wondered how else I could have received so much value for it. And the day's reality inevitably beggars my description.

Walking on the main plaza at dusk, I saw a Greek Orthodox funeral procession. Several great-bearded, black-robed patriarchs, some swinging censers, preceded the bier, and a crowd of weeping women followed, many of them chanting or ululating softly. Some of them may have been paid mourners, but at any rate this had been *some*body. It looked and felt like a manifestation of the collective unconscious, or a Greek chorus at the end of a tragedy. What Jung and Aeschylus had not prepared me for was the corpse itself, lying in state on a wooden slab. I had never before been so close to a dead man or seen him so fully. He seemed to be sleeping, and likely to awaken with the motion. I was too shaken to follow them. That night I slept poorly, alternately thinking and dreaming of black-robed Death or of the Shining Ones nearby.

Nov. 13, Olympia, noon - Again, traveling by scooter through scenery- & history-rich Greece produces so many impressions that I fall behind. Drove the 130 kms. from Tripolis, through mountains & rain, in under 4 hours. Were up at 5:30, on the road in semi-darkness at 7. The scoots ran well through a series of hard pulls under heavy loads. The country - first barren mts., then smaller mts. & deep gorges, finally rolling pastoral hills - was continually a source of interest & beauty, bathed in the yellow of autumn. The rain & clouds of early AM became the balmy Indian summer of midday. I had to go on gas reserve 16 kms. from Olympia. It was a suspense-packed ride & coast down to O., but we made it.

The Tripolis valley was pleasingly somber: mist-shrouded fields and cottages in muted hues extending to mountains whose tops were hidden in low clouds. There were no sounds, no signs of life. From the back seat, Diana kept me shivering with tales of sleeping in foggy fields in Yugoslavia and waking at dawn to the stares of black-clad farm workers. The land turned more barren, an unrelieved brown, as we ascended the first slopes. Valley fog gave way to real cloud, which proved to be very wet. We stopped long enough to don our ponchos and pressed on into an Arcadia the poets had not prepared us for; it was Jeff Garibaldi's "rocks and hills and poverty." After a pause to dry off in a small town on a cliffside, Hector's scooter would not kickstart: he had to push and compression-start it. The weather grew worse and the road steeper, but a moment came when I realized that this apparent "hostility of nature" exhilarated me. In time the grades and the weather became gentler, making the last miles down the valley into Olympia a visual feast, despite the concern over low fuel.

6 PM - The ruins of Olympia & its museum having been seen, we are tucked in a cheap hotel for the night. This is a great comfort, as we have clean rooms, reading light, & running water to solace us against cool winds and low clouds outside. I fear winter is near.

Inexplicably, I did not even mention seeing Praxiteles' statue of Hermes and the infant Dionysus – the concept, the composition, the spirit, the inherent brightness, the smooth marble curves of the only authenticated Praxiteles - in the museum, or walking around the original Olympic stadium! The next day gave us perfect, crisp fall weather, but the mechanical side of the trip fell to pieces.

Nov. 15, Tripolis, 6:30 AM - What a wild & trying day yesterday was! We got up at 5:30 in order to leave Olympia by 7, see Mycenae, & still get to Corinth by night. 50 kms. from O., my scooter kaputed. The motor died under a load, & repeated trials with 2 riders only produced more of the same.

We were sailing up a grade in third gear when the motor gasped and died. I slumped, horrified. Was it just hot and tired from the heavy load, or was there some deep, hidden cancer? Hector began shuttling the girls to our nearest haven, the mountain hamlet of *Stavrion*, while I re-checked everything. Fuel, sparkplug, mixture: all looked normal.

It would, however, take me up to Stavrion, where we spent 5½ hours getting various "mechanics" to try to fix it, & roaring off on false alarms.

Roaring off, and coasting back. Soon the whole village was involved, and very sympathetic. On one test run, I carried a big mechanic up a mountain grade as if it weren't there, but the motor died when I tried the same thing with Lu. That should have told us something, but we weren't listening on the right frequency. At length, a friendly truck driver offered to take us and the scooters to Tripolis, 85 kms. away over the mountains, *gratis*. We accepted gratefully, and most of the population of Stavrion lifted the Lambrettas aboard. It was a beautiful, rugged drive; to be able to watch the scenery was a boon, a silver lining, I told myself.

We were out in the open body of the truck, exposed to the wind & the wide sweep of scenery. The results were chilling & breathtaking.

In the highest mountains we slowed briefly to let a quiet peasant jump to the ground. He disappeared up a gully at a trot while we were saying *Addio*. One of our truck-mates pointed out the man's thatch hovel, high up on a barren ridge. Towards evening, in a village square, we acquired an impromptu passenger: a teenage boy, joy-riding to Tripolis. As if to remind us of what we missed by having our own transport, he sang Greek folk melodies in a haunting voice while we ran down the valley: a perfect accompaniment to the purified, scented air and failing light.

Arrived in Tripolis at 6 & in an hour the scooter's trouble had been diagnosed by a garage as "points" and "fixed." I hope so, but I'll have to see it first.

Nov. 15, Argos, 1 PM - I saw, all right. After running beautifully through the mountains, the motor died twice 10 kms. from Argos & again in town. Took it to a 'cycle garage; after 2 hours & great linguistic pains, the points were uncovered: they are burned and need replacing, but he thinks I can make Athens.

Wait a minute: they did the points in Tripolis! Why were they burned the next day? How often did they need replacing? They looked all right to me, but *something* was wrong. Not until later did I understand the truly sinister side of all this: that several young mechanics with dubious credentials and no idea of what was wrong had spent hours fiddling with my perfectly good engine. I was never convinced that it ran quite as well afterwards.

Nevertheless, we had an enjoyable two hours at the ruins of Mycenae - Agamemnon's castle overlooking the plain of Argos (where the *Orestia* opens) - that afternoon. As we walked about the palace, Tombs of the Nobles and Beehive Tombs, Di and Lu regaled us with artistic, archeological, and botanical lore - stuff "not in Will Durant," said Hector. Then we headed north for Corinth, following a bus full of laughing children for part of the way.

Corinth, 8 PM - We've made it thus far with no further scooter trouble, but I expect it at any moment & cannot relax & enjoy the driving. We've taken a room in an 18d. hotel, cheapest available, & will complete the drive to Athens in the morning.

There it was…another predictive statement without placating the playfulness of the gods! But speaking of relax and enjoy: we again shared a room, and though the tarp was duly stretched it was not an insuperable barrier.

Tonight is reciprocal backrub night - with appropriate noises of pleasure - & they do feel good. The girls have made the trip more fun, & their background reading has helped our study of Mycenae, Tiryns, & Olympia.

Note the quick, nervous turn from body to mind. In truth, we were in shoal waters if Jerry was right: anyone listening from outside the door would have thought we were having an orgy. Hector and Diana went for a - tactful? - walk after their duet while I administered to Lucinda. We had struck no sparks, really; still, as I kneaded and allowed myself to think about women for the first time in a while, I pondered my relationship to what Sophocles called a slavemaster and Kurt Weill *die sexuelle Hörigkeit*. Was this an opportunity or a set-up - a godsend, or a conspiracy to drag me down to animal realms? Was Lu really Circe? And what would constitute *laese majesté* in this case, anyway: hitting on the goddess, or neglecting her?

"Ow!" said the patroness of childbirth.

"Sorry, Lucinda. I was thinking of something else."

"Lucinda!" She laughed and turned her head. "Where did you get *that*? My name is Nancy Lou."

"Ah. I was misinformed." The others returned soon after, ending my reveries and missteps for now. Later, Diana found me doing sit-ups and offered a knowledgeable correction to ease the strain on my back.

"You studied phys ed, didn't you? I have *that* right?"

"Yes, it was my major. What do you mean, right?"

"Did it involve any bow-and-arrow stuff?"

"Yes, archery was one of my sports. Why?"

"Just curious, ma'am. There, is that better?"

The countryside was very attractive in Argolis & around Olympia, as well as in Arcadia. The Peloponnese (for the hero Pelops, father of Atreus) is generally more fertile than the mainland, but Arcadia was more rugged & barren than we had expected.

I won't forget - the little fellows who come onto deck passage at every stop while I'm sleeping, yelling, "Oristay le cumion?" ("Do you want some of this god-awful gummy candy?")

The next morning we left the Peloponnese and headed for Athens. When we arrived - after one more engine failure - I drove straight to the Lambretta dealership and asked the head man to fix it or make me an offer: I was ready to look for another mode of conveyance. But after listening to my story he told me at once what the trouble was.

Nov. 16, Athens, 8 PM - Back home, & the Great Mystery is solved. The scooter quit because Lu's poncho clogged the air scoop. It happened again today 28 kms. from Athens, & we let the girls hitchhike from there. I'm glad it's only that, but I had it all checked anyhow. All is well for 15 ds., except now the battery is shorting out.

When we met the girls afterwards I started the engine with the scooter on its stand, invited Lu to sit on the back seat and shove the extra material of her poncho under the front seat – *where the air intake was* - as usual, and watched her face while the engine choked and died. She blushed contritely, but I assured her that the problem was my ignorance. Still, it was sickening to think of the hours those 15-year old mechanics had spent probing the motor. Had they known the real problem all along?

Despite these troubles, on the Peloponnese I had begun to daydream about a *flying* motorscooter. At first these were just passing fancies of swooping through canyons or landing on islands, but then I started to wonder how it might be done. A propeller shaft with folded blades could emerge from under the luggage rack, stubby wings swing out from beneath the floorboards, a 5th gear position link the motor to the prop. With power-to-weight ratios, materials, and the question of balance I did not concern myself: let the aeronautical engineers earn their keep. I was a concept man (I'd just tell them where to put the air scoop). In reverie I leaned back, watched the road fall away below, climbed out over the Aegean, banked around the Temple of Sounion and made a neat two-point landing on the Athens highway. These fantasies recurred later apropos of other places. And why shouldn't our machines soar as high as our dreams? "What is now proved was once only imagined," wrote Blake.

Greek myth would supply the name: *Phaeton*, *Pegasus*, *Dedalus*, or *Icarus*, depending on how well it flew.

Hector and I agreed that the pace of the trip had become so fast that a layover day was in order before sailing to Crete. What a change from the early days! It meant giving up on Rhodes, but this way there would be time to read more about Crete and do it justice once there. We thus had a chance to catch up on hostel society. Zane was still around, stroking his goatee, mouthing off about personal and national sex habits, and making irksome efforts to seem piercingly bright. Julius, the folk singer, was back in town, and better company than Mephisto.

I found a guitar today, belonging to an English boy in my hostel room. It cost him $10 here. He & I, Julius, and 2 others sang folk songs for over an hour, a musical experience as interesting as when the Greek boys in the truck to Tripolis began singing their repertoire.

The Island of Minos

Nov. 17, aboard Kanaris, bound for Crete, 7 PM - Another deck passage, this time in the direction of ancient Minoan civilization. Once more we are in the midst of cramped people, bales of cargo, coils of hemp rope, live animals, pungent toilets, elderly women in black, soldiers galore, & "Oristay le cumion?" It's the most colorful, cheapest, most uncomfortable way I've ever traveled.

I spent hours playing the guitar in the hostel today. Mostly I just practiced or amused myself, but also did some group singing. It was fun, & the audience appreciative. I can't, however, take seriously the idea of myself as a career musician.

My family, friends, and teachers would doubtless be relieved to hear that, though surprised to learn that I was even considering such a course of life. Yet people with no more talent than I seemed to be making a living with just a voice and a guitar: look at the Kingston Trio! Before leaving college I had attended a recording session by a folk duo and helped arrange a chorus for them, complete with harmony. They wanted me to learn the banjo and join them. Another road not taken! Classical wasn't the only way to go.

Motley day. Up at 7, ate warm bread, butter & honey, read for awhile; then left my battery for recharging at the garage. An hour reading in the gardens near the Art Gallery. We met the girls at noon & drove them back to lunch. Spent the PM packing, storing the scooters behind the restaurant, & playing guitar. Bade farewell to the girls & a good YH crew at 4, hiked to Omonia Square & took the electric train (2 ds.) to Piraeus. Sailed at 6:30. A beautiful full moon has just risen above the hills & crystal-clear lights of Athens.

This lunar spectacle can hardly have been an accident. Despite my casual treatment here, we had an affectionate, hugs-and-kisses parting from the Shining Ones, who had added a lot to our recent travels. It was easy to feel sentimental about leaving them - and Julius and other friends at the hostel, whom we would probably never see again.

The folksongs being played on the mandolin by a soldier have a curiously East-West quality: very repetitive, with many runs, possessing the quasi-modal sounds of Spanish music, often sung antiphonally, the effect being East European & gypsy, yet with a relation to US country music in the rhythm & syncopation.

I remembered reading a story about young Bela Bartok awakening from a stupor in a Moroccan bar as a sailor intoned a melody that Bartok had heard in Spain, but that he knew came from Persia. His epiphany then - folk music as lines of force criss-crossing the earth, forming a network that recorded historical and ethnic movements - altered the direction of his career. Was he not on a *Wanderjahr*? Perhaps something similar would happen to me.

Nov. 18, Kanaris, off Crete, 8:30 AM - Docked for 2 hrs. in Canea, capital of Crete, this morning. Little to see except rocks, a port & a town, but we were able to get off & get breakfast. (On the loudspeaker, "Rudolph the Red-Nosed Reindeer" in Greek.)

Last night read Will Durant's section on Crete, which helped fill gaps in history, culture & art. Finished book on the Byzantine Empire yesterday. Spent ½ hour talking to a Greek soldier who spoke some English...very friendly. Although he wore 3 chevrons, his pay is only 100 ds./month [$3]; 50 & 70 go with the other 2. He was curious about soldiers' pay in the U.S.

We spent a lovely morning slicing through the pond-smooth, aquamarine Aegean along the north coast of Crete in mild sunny weather. Porpoises or dolphins occasionally curveted at the bow. Only a fringe of snow on the island's mountainous spine hinted at the lateness of the season.

Hotel Hellas, Heraklion, Crete - A little knowledge is a dangerous thing. I go around museums (the Archeological Mus. here this PM) spouting artistic hypotheses: "the swastika is a sun-image"; "Cretan decorative whorls are snake & fertility symbols"; "Cretan masks of beaten gold are forerunners of Gk. tragedy masks." A real academician would doubtless quiver with rage.

My half-remembered, half-created theories were so enjoyable that their soundness seemed beside the point. The Heraklion museum was, quite unexpectedly, one of the best we had seen; I took pages of notes on interesting or beautiful items in its large collection. Jars and libation vessels dated as early as 3500 BCE made all European art seem recent. Minoan art struck me as uniformly tasteful, and often appeared quite "modern." A graceful "leaves of grass" vase would have done credit to any contemporary atelier in Paris or Vermont. On a black steatite vase, a relief of marching musicians looked like a New Orleans wake. Fertility symbols were ubiquitous: bulls, snakes, bare-breasted earth goddesses. The museum expanded my horizon, revealing an advanced, many-faceted society of five millennia ago that had been wholly unknown to me two months earlier. In crafts, at least, the Minoans seemed to rival the ancient Greeks, and I could see parallels with Egyptian art. Like Bartok in his Moroccan bar, I had a powerful sense of cultural connections, which grew stronger the next day.

Nov. 19, Great Palace at Knossos, 9:30 AM - The grasp of dramatic presentation which Minoan civilization bequeathed to Greek architecture is manifest at Knossos. Doubtless the 2nd millenium BC Cretans built the palace on a hill for military considerations, but the architects knew how they could enhance such a location. Lesser buildings are on the slopes of the hill around the royal dwellings; entrance-ways are situated so as to direct the gaze toward the vista; everything builds up to the pieces de resistance: the great porticoes & frescoes, the central court, the rooms of state. You can't tell me that the Cretans didn't understand architectural psych & delay of reward!

Suddenly a lot that we had seen made a new kind of sense. The design of Greek theatres, the placement of the Holy of Holies in temples (Oracle of Apollo at Delphi), the situation of the Temple of Poseidon at Sounion, the processions of initiates to Eleusis and of athletes at Olympia: all exhibited this grasp of drama and controlled heightening of excitement. Had the Greeks been consciously extending a bequest from the Minoans, or did they work all this out for themselves? Perhaps it didn't matter, except to scholars.

The palace presents such myriad detail that description is impossible. Lintels & porticoes of light wood, & dark red columns with black trim are characteristic. The palace covers 20,000 square meters & is conjectured to have 1600 rooms, of which 800 have been excavated.

Later, Pensione Hellas - The "light wood" is in most cases concrete painted. Yet some of it is wood, or a veneer. Restorations can be confusing; wonder what they were trying to approximate?

I did not know then that Sir Arthur Evans's reconstruction of Knossos (ca. 1900) was quite controversial for its high degree of conjecture: some of what I had seen and admired was not 2100 BCE but 4000 years later. No wonder it seemed modern! So how much had he distorted the picture? It certainly wasn't *all* Evans; shortly after he began excavating, torrential rains threatened severe damage, but the ancient drainage system functioned well enough to carry off the water. Yet several famous frescoes, such as The Bull and The Prince, on display *in situ* turned out to be copies of heavily restored originals in the museum. Evidently the watchword was *caveat spectator*.

Palace was of such size that I would find a room or a whole suite that I hadn't seen in an area I thought I'd covered. They used split levels (5 or 6), bright colors on columns & murals, indoor baths & pools, & sunken courts. And the dates make your head whirl: what was old in western Europe seems nouveau fait in comparison.

Living in a breezy stone palace made a lot more sense in the subtropical Aegean than it did in England or France. The palace of Knossos may have been the origin of myths about the labyrinth (from *labros*, a double-headed axe, symbol of the House of Minos) that King Minos had Dedalus construct to imprison the Minotaur, hideous offspring of Queen Pasiphaë and a white bull. Later, Ariadne showed Theseus how to find his way in to kill the thing, and out. Dedalus and his son Icarus were held in the labyrinth until they learned to fly. So it was not surprising that I got lost at times.

Wandering thru corridors, I came on some familiar vases. Turning around, I said, "I've been here before" - & wondered if that is what we search for. Many of our actions seem to be based on this need: geographical (we find pleasure in familiar places), intellectual (we associate, correlate), psychological, emotional (choosing a lover who has much in common with us), social (cliques, clubs), spiritual (we seek a religion which accords with our preconceived notions of God).

It was becoming a habit to try to find large meanings in the daily minutiae of travel, but this passage would arouse scepticism in several disciplines - especially theology. Later I realized that exceptional people do find ways to overcome or sublimate this instinctive love of the familiar.

In Egypt, I think we will find the source of everything we've seen. In fact, the logical way to do the trip would have been Egypt, Crete, Greece, Istanbul.

Evidence of Egyptian influence on the Minoans and Greeks (which historians document from trade routes) was accumulating almost daily. The Athens Museum provided many examples (e.g. from Mycenae) of figures drawn in the ancient Egyptian way, each part of the body shown in its most distinctive profile, the hair falling in long rows of coils. Minoan pottery depicted hunts in papyrus marshes. Delos and Olympia had Temples of Isis, the Heraklion Museum a clay figurine dedicated to Isis or Serapis.

In our usual parsimonious fashion we walked to and from Knossos (7 kms. each way) on its free day, saving the 10-dr. entrance fee as well as bus fare. We did, however, take a bus 35 kms. east to Mallia and the ruins of another Minoan palace. Here the stones outlined floor plans but no one had restored the place, and I saw Evans's point; *my* imagination, at least, needed more prompting than low stone walls provided, there and at Tiryns. We slept in the adjacent olive orchard that night and walked up to a roadside restaurant for breakfast the next morning.

Nov. 20, Mallia, Crete, 9 AM - Having slept under the tarp, we await the bus to St. Nicholas. Just walked a mile down to the beach.

The coast of Crete is rocky & precipitous, with great peninsulas reaching out. Blue-green surf roared on a sandy beach, & 2 rock islands threw up showers of spray. Shafts of sunlight touched grey mountains thru low & turbulent clouds. I realized last night that the values of Galbraith's "affluent society," to which I glibly subscribed last fall, have come to mean less, & the older sustenance values (food, shelter, clothing) more, thru existentialist living.

It is unlikely that I had grasped either Galbraith's ideas or existentialism at that point, or had ever "subscribed" to the affluent society's creed; I was trying to heighten a contrast. What this meant was that I *wanted* to move away from the kind of life my parents lived in suburbia toward an existence that made minimal assumptions about values, took chances, and built up meaning inductively from experience.

At the shore I remembered some lines that Penny had sent me in Athens: "He stands on strands of foreign lands I do not know; / He walks and talks with ancient stocks of long ago." Now I was living them, life imitating art. If I had been one of those Georgian aristocrats who brought along a painter on his travels, I would have had this scene depicted. In the distance left, a grey rocky cape sweeping into the sea, half-circling a turbulent bay of jade waves, whitecapped. In the foreground, an arc of beach: dunes and scrub, windswept and littered with gifts of the sea. Middle foreground right, a gaunt figure, hands in pockets, shoulders hunched against the wind that ruffles his hair and shirt, watching the horizon for his ship to come in. With the addition of a sea-monster it could be passed off as The Fate of Hippolytus.

Nov. 22, Pension Hellas, Heraklion, 11 AM - Returned Friday night from Mallia & Gournia: neither place of much interest, but countryside beautiful & bus ride colorful. Were supposed to leave for Piraeus at 5 PM yesterday, but boat did not show. Will leave at 1 today, arrive 8:30 tomorrow, leave for Istanbul as soon as we can.

With each deck passage, the idea of *voyaging* to Istanbul sounded less attractive. Besides, the scooters might be useful up there. And if we sailed back to Athens in December, then what: a ship to Alexandria? Go home? No, we would try the drive - and maybe keep going.

The bus back to Heraclion reminded me of Jake's ride into the Spanish mountains in *The Sun Also Rises*. The roads were terrible, the peasants friendly (they seemed to like the Americans at the Air Force base). At one point the bus stopped in the massive, brutal, spectacular mountains; Hector and I followed others toward a white earthen building we took for a *pissoir.* It was a roadside shrine.

As penitents, then, we attended Sunday morning mass in Heraklion Cathedral. Its most striking features were an ornate marble altar screen with half-columns of green marble and a central partition of fabric, closing off the sanctuary; and the pulpit, which was built into a column and reached by interior stairs. The physical separation of male and female worshippers, and the loose structure of the service, surprised Protestant eyes. Celebration began at 8 AM and was still going strong when we left at 10:15. People came and went throughout, usually buying a votive candle (1 to 10 ds.) as they came in, placing it on a great candelabrum, kissing some of the hundreds of icons, then standing and crossing themselves. There were no pews, only a few stalls for early arrivals and the elderly. The mass had some impressive formal elements, including a resonant sermon by a tall, black-robed patriarch with a grey beard a foot long, and several fumigations from a pewter incense lamp exuding sweetly pungent white smoke, but most of the time the priests seemed to worship privately by the altar as the congregation watched, neither singing nor responding.

The choir consists of about ten men on each side. The music is sung by the choir & 2 priests, who have good voices. No accompaniment, but the pitch remains good. There is considerable antiphony, & solos against humming. The sound has a haunting quality, like Gregorian chant except for touches of Eastern mysticism.

Eastern mysticism? I tried to figure out what made the music sound exotic. It wasn't the unison singing, which was Gregorian, or the antiphony, which was Renaissance, or humming behind soloists. Then I realized that they were using *organon* (parallel octaves, 4ths or 5ths), a mediaeval style abandoned by Renaissance composers. So it wasn't really "Eastern" – though the Eastern Church might have *preserved* it - just Other, and old. Overall it was a pleasing sound, strange to my ear.

In the cathedral I saw two striking examples of piety…a young boy held up by his older brother to kiss a sacred picture above his head;

an old peasant woman in black crossing herself 5 times & each time bending down athletically to make the point on the floor. I left wondering what it was all about, & doubting it was worth it.

Despite almost an extra day given by the non-appearance of our ship, we only scratched the surface of Crete. Hagia Triada and Phaestos on the south side, Lasithi in the mountains, were sites we didn't even try to reach. This was part ignorance, part fatigue. And fear of the lateness of the season kept us from extending our stay: while Hades and Persephone were heading south for the winter, we would be heading for Istanbul: 1240 kms. northeast over mountains. I also missed the social and mythic dimension that the moon goddesses had given us; we were again men without women. Existence seemed a bit thin, and not as much fun. Still, we kept at it, doing what we could do.

The market street is full of color, & reminiscent of Casablanca: awnings, vitriolic language, pigs' heads & feet, carcasses, etc.

The ship arrived that afternoon and another deck passage began. Now it seemed less exotic, more of a grind; I did not even record the name of the ship. The only noteworthy occurrence thereon was meeting Savas, a young Greek soldier who played the guitar. He was on his way home to Thessalonika – *Saloniki*, he called it - and invited us to visit him there. He even wrote down the address, which I accepted so as not to offend him.

The Realm of Boreas

Nov. 23, Amfiklia, a restaurant, 8:30 PM - One moves to keep warm, & moves fast when it's very cold. Arriving at Piraeus around 7 after another stinking, colorful deck passage, we cleared our baggage from the hostel, got our scooters & my battery, hit the laundry, P.O., bank & Am. Express, & left Athens (I hope for good) at noon.

"I hope for good" is almost "God willing." Fatalism! The chilly, half-empty hostel offered no familiar faces; clearly winter was upon us. Squinting into a light rain, we drove out of Athens, past Daphne to Eleusis, and headed into the hills, where we were soon enveloped in dense, wet cloud. It was almost dark at 2 PM. Lights on! I waited for Hector at the pass, unable to see his headlight until he was within 100 feet. As he passed we honked, waved and laughed wildly in acknowledgment of our shared idiocy.

Drove under grey drizzly skies in increasingly cold weather all afternoon. After passing thru a thick icy cloud crossing the pass into Boetia, arrived at Thebes at 2:15 & stopped for tea.

Warmed slightly by the tea and cakes, we soon gunned away into the decaying afternoon. At *Livadia* the road forked momentously: left to Delphi, right to Istanbul. New ground! As dusk fell and the drizzle continued, we traversed the gloomy valley behind Parnassos, whose massive snowy flanks heaved up into low grey clouds and disappeared, looking as if they might rise forever. Villages were few and small: the first we tried had no inn at all, but around 5 we reached *Amfiklia* and found an unheated room.

We are 55 kms. from Lamia, 1st big milestone, but they may be icy ones. A cold drizzle has been coming down since 4, & the mountains which hem in the town - Parnassos & Kallidromon - are blanketed with snow a good way down. Our room is more than invigorating: it's cold. I fear we may have to drive thru snow tomorrow, which would do much to dampen & chill spirits. "At my back I always hear / Time's winged chariot hurrying near / A crunch of snow, the sighing wind, / The cry of winter, the autumn's end."

We arrived soaked, and it was difficult to dry off under those conditions (why poor Andrew Marvell had to pay for our discomfort remains a mystery). The bedding looked thin, so I inserted my sleeping bag between the sheets and wore most of my dry clothes into it, but still shivered fitfully during the night. I lay wondering – finally! - if we had just left it too late. How casually I had slighted the ancient stones of Mallia, dreaming in their *warm, dry* hillside meadows above the Aegean! And now this…we knew nothing about these villages, having no guidebook for this region. If we had had one, would they have been in it? These people had nothing; they were the poorest of the poor, out here on the back side, the hinder parts of shining Parnassos.

Nov. 24, a restaurant, Katerini, 7:30 PM - Safe, warm, full & dry again! We have come to value those states after today's drive. The same cold drizzle that plagued us yesterday made driving conditions poor from the time we left Amfiklia at 8 until Larisa, at about 2:30. By that time we were out of the mountains & on a fine new road built by NATO. In between, we fought the cold, the rain, 3 steep climbs thru snow-covered mountains, & roads that several times turned to slush or potholes at crucial turns or hills. I asked myself if I weren't crazy to be there. It was no weather for a scooter.

Once we stopped to evaluate the conditions and our prospects. The weather was dismal - rain and cold in the valleys, fog and snow in the mountains - and whenever the pavement gave out (usually on a descending curve) we had to fight to control incipient skids. A couple of pictures that day reveal hairpin curves on steep mountainsides with sparse vegetation, glimpsed through holes in the clouds. One shows me on my scooter in the roadside slush. Bearded, helmeted, in full-length poncho, gloves and paratrooper boots, I look serious, *engagé*. On the luggage rack, exposed to the elements, are the bulging pack, camera bag, tent, tarp, and canteen. The scooter is mud-spattered; fog hides everything but a steep bank patched with snow right behind me, and the next tricksy curve.

"What do you think, man?"

"Pretty bad! Can't get much worse, can it?"

"Can't it? (Pause.) Think we should give over?"

"You mean go back? Then what?"

"Don't know."

"Let's see how it looks around another curve or two. If it doesn't improve by the next pass, we'll see."

It generally *does* improve – at least psychologically - after the pass. To his credit, Hector encouraged me onward until it *did* look better ahead than behind, and by then neither of us wanted to go back through all the stuff we had already covered. So we kept on, taking the road not yet taken, taking what the trip had to offer.

Morale stayed high thanks to occasional valleys & straightaways that let us speed up, the gloomy beauty of the scenery, & stops for tea & warmth. We have now faced the works, except for bitter cold & snow on the road. The scooters, I must say, have some guts after all.

I dressed today in underwear, 2 prs. socks, boots, khakis, sailing shirt, wool shirt, sweater, sweat shirt, helmet & poncho. That's all... except gloves, & it was my hands that froze.

We think we can take cold weather? Today I was amazed to see, on barren slopes when it was coldest, the tiny tents of work gangs, & the clay & straw huts of shepherds living in the mud, wind & snow.

On a bleak brown-and-white steppe where it was snowing heavily, solitary shepherds wearing great fleecy ramskins stood by their flocks. They stared at us and we stared back. I felt somehow judged, seen through. We were mere passersby, dipping our toes in discomfort, playing briefly at what they lived.

In mid-afternoon, beyond Larisa, we descended through the famous Vale of Tempe, with Mt. Ossa to our right, onto the seacoast plain. With better weather and pavement, we hoped the crisis was over. Where the new road curved by the flanks of Mt. Olympus, we saw a guy pushing his Vespa the other way; Hector gallantly stopped to help. He was an American, bound for Athens, who had run out of gas three miles back. We fetched him some, talked briefly about our travels, then parted, wishing him Godspeed. At dusk the skies cleared and it grew colder; the pure white shoulder of Olympus flamed a frigid orange. We spent the night in muddy Katerini, lingering in its warm eatery.

Nov. 26, a restaurant in Komotini, evening - In Katerini we were up at 5:30, delighted to find clear tho' cold weather. Took the road at 7. There was sufficient light to see, but no color until 7:30. It was worth waiting, however, to see the first tints of rose touch the snow-crowned ramparts of Mt. Olympus & Pelion. The sun was a seething ball of fire coming from a blue sea.

Temperatures were close to freezing at first, numbing my fingers inside lined gloves, but with sunrise to starboard and the blushing ramparts of Olympus on our port quarter, I was in heaven. The going was good, despite an eerily bright ground-fog to a height of fifty feet or so. If the road would stay down by the warm sea, we might make it!

We raced the 60 miles to Thessalonica along the fertile plain, a semi-circular strip a few miles wide around the Gulf of Thessaly. Occasionally we brushed hills a few miles inland, which rose farther off into snowy mts. Once we passed plowed fields of dark brown, from which the sun's warmth drew vapors that obscured the way.

During my heroic-couplet period a few years later, this scene for some reason volunteered for dangerous service:

The fields of Thrace lie black beneath the sun.
Dark, fecund plots of teeming earth and dung
With steamy vapors fill the morning air,
And cart-ruts gleam with frosty diamonds rare. (etc.)

(Thrace actually lay a couple of days ahead, but it fit the meter better than the other candidates.) Now that we were approaching...this city, I hoped to resolve the confusion over its name. Most western maps gave it as Thessalonica or Thessaloniki, often with Salonica in parentheses. What I consistently heard Greeks say was "Saloniki," without the Thes-. When in Rome....

We reached Saloniki before 11; across the gulf Olympus remained dimly visible through the haze. The usual crowd gathered when we stopped near the railway station to reconnoiter. A man wanted us to visit him. We could not overcome his insistence, so I crammed him on the back of my scooter and, following his directions, plowed shakily through the muddy outskirts of town to his squalid house in a field. Poor, polite, and sad, he wanted to feed us. Communication was difficult, but we told him that we were going to stay with friends, and started back into town. He waved from his gate, reserved and enigmatic on a cold morning. I felt depressed: had we insulted him after all? Was this what it meant to reach out to the world?

Spent 4 hrs. sightseeing, visiting Byzantine churches - including St. Demetrius & St. Sophia - the White Tower, the waterfront, the old city walls, the Gate of Galerius & residential sections. About 3 we began hunting for the house of Savas Papadopoulous, the Greek soldier on the Heraklion-Piraeus boat. It was on a dirt street in a poor section of town. Only his Greek-speaking mother was at home, but English-speaking brother George soon showed up.

By then the entire neighborhood was curious about us, but again we could not understand each other. George, a thirtyish businessman, invited us in and, after we had talked for awhile, told us that Savas had not yet arrived; he was presumed to be on the way. Very embarrassed to be imposing on their obviously narrow circumstances, we tried to bow out, but Mama, who had been busy in the kitchen, brought in food for Savas's American friends, and George insisted that we stay the night. My heart sank, but it had become a question of honor for them: they would brook no denial. Besides, by now it was getting late to find an alternative, and we *had* hoped for a free night, hadn't we? So we accepted. A second brother, who spoke some German, showed up along with his "*Freund*." From the art on the walls, we learned that George was a cubist painter! It was he who ran the household.

Greek homes are not matriarchal: when I tried to help with dishes or fold a blanket, they all laughed. They retain the vision of America as a land of plenty & look down on Greece. Their hospitality was amazing. We drove the 2 boys around on our scooters for over an hour as reward; during a stop at a billiards room, I was robbed of my spare spark plug from the glove compartment.

Returning, we saw that there was no guest room or spare bed: they intended to displace someone for us. Agreeing that we had to draw the line there, we pulled technology on them, spreading air mattresses and sleeping bags on the living room floor. Though initially dismayed, they were delighted by the novelty of it and let us have our way in that regard. Exhausted by all the social interactions, cultural adjustments and linguistic efforts, I soon fell asleep.

In the morning they begged us not to leave, to wait for Savas; he was sure to arrive soon, maybe today, and would be very sad to miss his American friends. A health to Greek hospitality and the Papadopoulous family! They were desperately eager to industrialize and attain western prosperity. Their antique past, "the glory that was Greece," "the cradle of democracy" and all that, were nothing to them. What could we say: you're wrong? Your dreams will turn to ashes? Maybe they were right! Saloniki rubbed our noses firmly in "the real Greece," and reminded us in no uncertain terms that, while we could buy gas, order food and rent rooms, we hadn't learned enough Greek to have conversations. If it had not been for George, we would have been completely stymied.

Today we arose with the family at 8 &, after sincere farewells, took off at 10. We burned the road since, covering 260 kms. before camping near [Komotini] in a field at 4. The day's drive was mostly on good roads thru valleys or low hills. We were never more than a few miles from the sea on our right or the mts. on our left. The sun & warm weather were blessings, & most of the country was very pretty.

In fact this was one of our Great Days: crystalline skies, vaults of white clouds, a decent road wandering over varied countryside, bright in fall foliage. For me, Saloniki had left a residue of melancholy to be dissipated: the scooters were in their element and perfect for the purpose. Hector led at a good clip, and as I viewed his jaunty, rugged figure up ahead, urging his steed through Macedonia, he seemed cast in the heroic mold. Maybe I should write a book about him! Once we took a break by a wide, rushing stream in a pleasant valley; a shepherd immediately materialized from the bush to offer "old Greek coins" for sale. I refused politely, and we parted on good terms. Kavalla, an attractive little seaport near the site of the battle of Philippi, provided lunch. At the end of an hour's stay, its entire male population (it seemed) bid us *addio*. Pitching our tent in a bare field a few kilometers before Komotini, we drove into town for a hot Thanksgiving dinner. It was a big indulgence, for which we paid: locating the tent again in total darkness with only our feeble headlights required a long, anxious search.

"If our luck holds, we'll spend tomorrow night in Turkey," concludes the entry written in the warmth of Komotini's leading chowhouse. The next begins:

Nov. 27, pension in Orestias (Greece) - Our weather luck held, but our road luck ran out, so we spend one last night in Greece, at this village 26 kms. short of the Turkish border. The difficulty was about 45 miles of bad road between Alexandroupolis and here: partially unpaved, partially old pavement full of protruding rocks, washboards, & chuckholes. Even at that we might have made the border if we hadn't had to wait until 9:30 to leave because of a wet tent.

And why (having failed to put up our rainfly) did we have to wait two hours for the sun to dry the dew-drenched cotton? We were afraid of mildew. Ah nylon, where were you?

Once we pushed off, driving the back country was delightful - except for construction in barren mountains near the Mediterranean, and the almost savage curiosity we excited in every hamlet. Mistaking us for Germans, the urchins would run behind us, yapping "*Deutsch, Deutsch*" or "*Heil Hitler*!" And my motor suddenly died just outside Alexandroupolis, the last large town in Greece, where the road turned inland. It restarted readily but scared me, bringing back all the old Pelopponesian anxieties. Maybe just a bit of dirt in the fuel? Soon afterwards the road suddenly went bad. Hector topped a rise; his head snapped viciously and he gave an emphatic palms-down: *Take it easy*! For thirty hilly miles, "highway" was too good a word for what looked like a former or proposed cross-country route.

At 4:30, with the sun low, we pulled into Orestias, the last village before the border, set on bare rolling plains. It looked like western Kansas but it was Thrace, a region the ancient Athenians considered synonymous with madness. As we entered town, a lively fellow leaped out to block the road, waving a wad of bills and shouting, "You need Turkish money?" He was offering about 50% more Turkish *lire* for our dollars than the official government rate, which he made sound artificially low. Still in economy mode and unused to two-tiered currency systems, we did not understand that this was the black market. Hector bought $50 worth, which he split with me (a practice we had adopted to save our smaller-denomination travelers' checks). I thought so little of the matter that it is not mentioned in my journal, but we had naïvely lit a long fuse for ourselves.

At our *pension*, the boy who assisted the owner called Hector "Tony Curtis" and me "Rock Hudson." We ate a big dinner at another hot, smoky workman's restaurant and congratulated ourselves on having come this far.

The economy of the desolate, underpopulated and little-visited Thracian steppe seemed to consist mostly of sheep herding and vegetable farming. Teams of white oxen strained obliquely at their yokes to pull primitive wooden carts. The number of brick houses, even in small villages, surprised me; their roof tiles were shaped like small quonset huts. And the East was beginning.

Interesting - & entirely logical - that the closer we get to Turkey the more mosques appear in the villages. Their spires are striking - most are white - & are throwbacks to the days before the population exchange (1923). The further from the sea we travel, the more barren the hills become.

Our final day in Greece began early; we rolled out of the silent village about 6:30. It was a gloomy, drizzling morn, and the twelve miles to the border were accomplished on a dirt track, a "shortcut" that roamed over an utterly empty plain. Egdon Heath would be Elysium compared to that no-man's land, which belonged in an Edgar Allan Poe story. In a downpour, the track

- which was just a flattened portion of the plain – would soon become impassable, but we escaped with a heavy mist.

Greek police and customs were housed in three unheated buildings at the edge of the plain near a copse. The official exit procedures went smoothly and quickly. The rain increased, keeping the day dark, as we puttered off toward a faintly-lit cluster of grey shapes down the road. The Greek sentry raised his turnpike and nodded stolidly. After a month in Hellas - and a total contribution of $50 each to the economy - we were in Turkey.

...one civilization is ending and another beginning.

Claude Levi-Strauss

V. Dionysian Realms

Overland I went,
... and so, along all Asia's swarming littoral
of towered cities where Greeks and foreign nations,
mingling, live, my progress made.

Dionysus, in Euripides' *The Bacchae*

In the Name of Allah, the Compassionate, the Merciful.

Those who say, 'The Lord of Mercy has begotten a son,' preach a monstrous falsehood.... That they should ascribe a son to the Merciful, when it does not become him to beget one!

In the Name of Allah, the Compassionate, the Merciful.

Alif lam ra. These are the verses of the Glorious Book. We have revealed the Koran in the Arabic tongue so that you may understand it.

The Koran

I rolled into Turkey burdened by more than an awkward backpack. My education and culture, when they had not just ignored Asia, had handed me half-truths about it. What was insidious about this burden was its invisibility: like most westerners, I had imbibed a Greek perspective on the East with my mother's milk. For the ancient Greeks, easterners meant trouble. Persia sent her armies; Paris, who abducted Helen and caused the Trojan War, was from Asia Minor. Greece had some Asian gods, but gods of a particular stripe. Dionysus was the patron of fertile farmland, wine-making, tragedy, and orgies in which both his enemies and his devotees went mad and people were torn to bits. Orpheus, a wonderful singer and lyre-player whose music soothed wild beasts and savage breasts, was finally ripped apart in a Dionysian frenzy. These gods, who have intrigued modern intellectuals, were deities of passionate excess, of Thracian irrationality. Thus I saw myself as going from the land of Apollo, god of the sun, of reason, order and "fair boundaries," to that of his half-brother Dionysus, son of the moon, deity of mob violence.

But at least I knew *something* about the classical and biblical Near East, even if it was slanted. Not only Dionysus and Orpheus but "Homer" (and according to some sources Apollo himself) hailed from west Asia. So if, as Nietzsche and Stravinsky believed, the Apollonian and Dionysian components of art were equally vital, one needed Asia as much as Greece, itself partly Asian. Those equivocal, featureless borderlands in Thrace, which joined, separated, and blurred the divisions between western and eastern cultures, made a useful point, had I but grasped it.

Still, all that was *ancient* history, before the Turks. I knew more of Constantinople and the Byzantine Empire than I did of Istanbul or Turkey or Islam. What images did I have of them except as the enemy? "They" were, had been, *Saracens*, hostiles in the Crusades, *infidels* who finished off the Byzantine Empire and went around changing venerable names to outlandish ones. Later, as the Ottomans, they were *the sick man of Europe* from whom the modern Greeks had to win their independence; people who conducted massacres, butchered the British at Gallipoli and against whose empire Lawrence of Arabia fought. Greece was a fount of western civilization and still its eastern outpost; the Turks' language, religion, and culture had always been emphatically Other.

Such matters are in the mind of the beholder, of course, but they affected the way I perceived the next few months. As when excited in Casablanca, I seemed to sense subtler emanations in Turkey and the Levant. For a time I surrendered to them, as one must do to enter a hypnotic trance. Unusual dreams, repressed before they were understood, plagued and intrigued me. My conceptual processes ceased to operate in their usual way. I visualized myself moving along the perimeter of a great circle drawn around the Mediterranean, holding on tightly but only just, in danger of flying off into the lands beyond and simply disappearing, oblivious to all that "the west" represented. At times I felt a strange pressure in my head, like centrifugal force. With many eager glances at the roads leading east and through moments of psychic anarchy, I held on and careened 'round the corner, leaning into the turn.

*

Scenario: Rain, or heavy mist, obscuring a bare plain. Two low grey buildings, dimly lit on an early morning in late fall. A road. Two faint wobbly headlights probing the gloom, a mutter of engines, dark shapes materializing. They stop and fall silent before the house marked *Gumruk ve pasaport kontrolu*. Two silent, well-muffled drivers bear documentary gifts within to the bureaucracy, which is somnolent. But one guard is awake, and when the travelers wave their papers he grunts them to a seat and disappears.

"Well, okay, we're in Turkey."

"Um, we'll see about that."

The guard reappears, waves them to a room with an active, welcome potbellied stove and two more guards. Reserved nods of greeting, or at least acknowledgments of co-existence. Another grunt, another seat, but a key personage is evidently missing. Minutes pass in silence.

Enter stage left a dishevelled figure in a faded bathrobe. He squints darkly through long black hair at the applicants as he seats Himself at the desk and holds out his hand. Passports and other documents are hastily proffered.

"*Ameriki*?"

The visitors nod. "Yes, *ohi, si.*" The agent stamps, seals, writes, speaks - in English! "Write here" - he points to an open passport - "how much money…you have."

The travelers reach for their wallets and money belts to count, but Himself dismisses such nitpicking with an impatient wave. "No, no. *About*…how much?"

The submissive infidels consider, reckon, write. Silence.

"*Carnet*?"

Anxiously they point at the document in his hand, saying, "That's it." He grunts and frowns. Fog, almost as dark as night, has descended at the windows.

"*Carnet de passages en douanes*?"

"Yes, that's it! We used it in Italy and Greece."

The stamp is given: reluctantly, with a doubtful frown, but given. "O.K. Cigarettes…you?" The *Ameriki* sadly have none to offer. They receive their duly processed papers again. "O.K. You…can go."

"Thank you, sir." The foreigners depart, the whir of their machines quickly swallowed by the mist. His Fairly Highness exits to bed. The guards approach the stove bearing wood. The fog reigns, unchallenged. *Curtain.*

*

This is no country for old men – or anyone. The House of Usher might have stood behind those gallows-trees, though it has certainly sunk into the marsh by now. Still, what better place for a border than a region where no one lives, or wants to live? Cold and wet: maybe this town will have a warm place to eat. Paved road ahead. Uh-oh, cobblestones! Windshield's coming loose again. Hector must like jouncing, the pace he goes.

We rode off through bleak forests & swampland. The rain stopped, but dense cloud lay over black trees & desolate countryside. Passed a beautiful camping spot outside town. Approaching Edirne, had a glimpse of our first big mosque, its minarets rising from the [ground] fog. As I tried to cross a small bridge, a herd of oxen or water buffalo came from the other side, & I had to slip between two of the black monsters.

The muddy, single-lane humpback span feels *very* small; I'd stop after seeing the beasts if I could. One sideways swipe of their horns and something of mine gets punctured. Fortunately they are docile.

Grey, the dominant tone of the clouds and fog, harmonizes with Edirne's mud-slick pavements and somber stone façades. Except for Turkish lettering on the signs, this could be northern England at the same season. We park the scooters and enter the warmth of what looks like a tea shoppe. A pleasant, dignified waiter shows us to a dark wooden table by the large, many-paned front window. Tackling the new tongue with spirit - and using Greek to elucidate! - we order *chorba, omlet, ecmec* and *chai*, then settle back to watch the street scene. A peasant walks by carrying a metal basin full of stones on his shoulder. Stores are opening; people are buying, selling, talking and walking. Most men and women wear clothes of coarse, dark fabric, often threadbare. I enjoy soup, a large omelet, bread and tea for 20 cents at our Orestias exchange rate (about 30 cents if we were buying *lire* through a bank).

Too soon we are back out in the damp chill, kicking the scooters to life, off to find fuel. We decide to skip the great *Selimiye* mosque in favor of an earlier arrival in Istanbul, which is a long way off and has many mosques (true: but a mistake). After another linguistic struggle, we buy 5 litres of gas each, and the requisite oil to mix in, for about 40 cents: less than half the Greek price - but they don't have a "scooter pump" that *mixes* oil and gas (we pour in the oil first and the stream from the gas pump mixes it). Off the cobblestones and back on the road, we face east toward the bleak plains. Brown below, grey above, and a gusty, quartering headwind: no comfort here.

For 10 kms. east of Edirne, "no man's land." Then we passed - on asphalt roads in bad repair - into hills, which looked habitable or at least arable. The heaviest traffic was ox-team carts, loaded with straw or vegetables, & peasant families bundled in dark, warm clothes. The shepherds had whole animal skins over their backs to ward off the biting wind, which blew down from the Black Sea without respite.

The 230 kms. to Istanbul were a hard pull for the scooters, which ran at full throttle for almost 6 hours. The wind was against us, & we seemed to always be climbing long slopes in the steppe.

Our 150cc Lambrettas have to be nursed in these conditions. Approaching each hill I try to reach 75 kph, but most climbs reduce me to 45, where I have to downshift; then at the top it starts all over. Crouched behind the windshield, cursing and shivering, I am wholly involved in the problem. The road angles southeast from Edirne through Babaeski, Lüleburgaz and Çorlu, to the shore of Marmara Deniz and thence to Stamboul.

There were colorful breaks in the journey. One small town had an open-air market; colored awnings protected goods that ranged from livestock thru vegetables to fabrics. In several towns a military band was playing - some sort of festival day? - as if to salute us.

We play to this conceit, waving acknowledgments as people stare. We do not stop, however; "there will be markets in Istanbul." The plan is to eat lunch somewhere, but when a building that looks like a café appears on the left and I pull into the gravel turnout to wait, Hector shoots past, sailing to Byzantium, oblivious to my waves and yells. By the time I catch him it is too far to go back and too late to bother with lunch: a whiteness on the hills along the Sea of Marmara is announcing Istanbul, meeting-point of Europe and Asia. At 4 PM we ride in tandem along broad, empty boulevards where the city has begun to expand outside Constantine's walls. The magnificent wedding of sea, land, and sky suggests San Francisco with minarets; merely entering the broad gap in the 1600-year-old walls is like a formal ceremony, a passage to the past.

Stamboul

Nov. 29, [Konya Ugur Hotel] ISTANBUL, TURKEY - In 6 days we made it, & on the 7th day we rested! I'm really proud of our having conquered distance & the weather to that extent: Athens to Istanbul has a mellow sound.

It is a sprawling city whose distinguishing marks are its mosques & mixture of old with new. Went looking for Am. Express, but I ran out of gas first, so we settled for the Hotel Alp - one night of luxury at $1.40 each. The spacious room, good heat & lights, & warm tap water were great, & we washed ourselves & our clothes gratefully.

A nearby restaurant served an ample, almost genteel dinner for about 60 cents (the price of our Thanksgiving feast in Komotini). It was delightful to be in a metropolis again, ogling chic young women in high heels and good clothes, the likes of whom we had not seen since Athens, or even Naples. The *Alp* had no secure parking, but the Marine guards at the American Embassy - after some hesitation - let us stow our scooters inside their gates for the night. At 9:30, too tired to write, I fell into my comfortable bed.

Today we slept ourselves out & made a thorough search for a cheap hotel near the RR station. Finally came up with this for 6 lire (48 cents) each per night. We have a room about 16' x 7', cold running water & an adequate light. The only heat is downstairs in the office, which has a coal stove & free tea, where we're already well known.

The *Konya Ugur*, a few blocks south of the Galata Bridge, provided a congenial home throughout our time in the city. The "office" - also the owner's parlor, and the common room - was generally social: men would be gathered around a potbelly stove, and protocol dictated a small glass of tea for every arrival. As we came in the front door to a narrow, tiled corridor, a glance through the windowed upper half of the partition revealed if the parlor was "receiving." After a while the regulars would wave at us to come in. We decided to remain five or six days - or more, if the stove stayed hot and the tea kept flowing.

This afternoon we walked around downtown Istanbul for 3 hrs. There are quite a few large mosques, & their architecture intrigues me. A glimpse inside showed worshippers with no shoes doing obeisances on a carpet....Shoeshining must be an hereditary [occupation]. The shoeshine boxes are very ornate with carved or painted wood & brass fixtures....The military is everywhere, which makes me uncomfortable. Their trucks & jeeps overrun the roads; they overrun the streets.

The market is a smaller, slightly less intense replica of Casablanca's. Striped awnings make great halls out of 5 or 6 streets, & in that space there are hundreds, maybe thousands, of stands, stalls, & hawkers [selling] food of all sorts, cooked or raw, hardware ranging from knives to jewelry, clothing, silk scarves, gloves, wool socks, suitcases, every sort of shoe & boot, unclassifiable miscellany, & game tables. Immensely colorful & vivacious area -

This was the Egyptian Bazaar in the nearby part of the city that we explored first. In the smoky warmth of the parlor that evening I made friends with a drunken truck driver whose face and expressions reminded me of Ernie Kovacs. He had been a tank driver in Korea under McArthur and knew some English. The American soldiers he met there had sung the praises of life in the USA; his discontent and naiveté were pitiful. He wanted desperately to make enough money to leave Turkey and go to the States, where he would have friends, a warm home, and at least a visit to Susan Hayward. Someone had given him a cheesecake picture of her, inscribed "Come to my house," and he all but drooled at the thought. He was an interesting and likable tough guy for whom it was easy to feel sorry.

Nov. 30, a restaurant, Istanbul - Our early walk began at 7 AM & carried us thru a hazy series of suggestions & lines: prostitutes tugging at a sleeve; minarets rising missile-like; ferries & tugs racing thru the harbor & disappearing into the smoke; the orange sun rising to silhouette barges & masts. Thru all these we crossed the [Golden Horn] & climbed past another striking mosque, finally arriving at the Istanbul Hilton: incredibly lavish but handsome.

Our dawn walk, a sensory feast, yielded a poem and a picture of a scow and seagulls crossing in front of the rising sun; barred with cloud, it looks like a telephoto of Jupiter. Everything was strange, novel, exciting. Off a square up in the newer district near the Hilton we found a kind of drugstore, dark with mahogany-stained tables and booths, almost empty at 9 AM, which served breakfast. I settled down with orange juice, hot milk, soup and an omelet, feeling that it had already been quite a morning.

It occurred to me that day that our long conversations on the subject of what foods we liked and would eat upon our return *might* just qualify as a food fixation. Were we hungry, homesick for our favorite dishes, or both? I had noticed that I was visibly losing weight.

In the Blue Mosque, 3 PM - It is odd how religious preconceptions & the stereotype of the Turks as "barbarians" or "infidels" combine to suppress my response to the ornate delicacy & beauty of this building. Interesting, psychologically, how learning influences perception.

This, of course, is confused even for a stereotype. "Barbarians" was a Greek term for non-Greek-speakers; "infidels" was what early Muslims called Crusaders and other non-believers, who returned the favour. Then I tried to write my way through the prejudice.

Mosque gets its name from interior decorations: tiles & frescoes in blue geometric or floral patterns, ranging in close ranks over 4 immense columns, 4 pointed arches, quarter domes & walls. Pulpit [minbar] has small minaret as canopy, steps inside. Everywhere are Turkish characters: on framed signs, on circles, in bands around columns. Stained glass is in patterns, no portraits. Colors - wine, pale or deep green, yellow - are good. Worshippers enter in sandals, kneel on haunches & pray with uplifted palms or bowing, sometimes aloud, usually silently. No sign of clergy. Huge unadorned chandeliers (electric) hang from ceiling to within 7 feet of floor. There are (holy) water founts at each column.

Here I first saw calligraphy as an art form. Muslim artists, discouraged from depicting humans or animals that might be worshipped as idols, turned to geometry, plant life, and the letters of the Koran. (Ataturk, who ordered modern Turkey to use the Latin alphabet, would have frowned at my calling *Arabic* letters "Turkish characters.") Overall, the interior gave as august an idea of divine calm and majesty as any European cathedral I had seen. The essential effect of the building was to mute, restrain and filter the outside world so that only a pale, quiet version reached worshippers through colored windows and massive grey walls. Pigeons swooping from high up near the ceiling contributed to a strong sense of space, as if the dimly visible upper vaults reached almost to heaven itself. Outside, the low sun was softening the mosque's greys toward purple. I gave up trying to write about it and took a picture. The barren plains and steppes to the west seemed immeasurably far off now.

Dec. 1, Topkapi Palace - The collection of the Oriental Archeological Museum consists of stone reliefs & statues, statues & miniatures in bronze, hieroglyphic carving on stone, sarcophagi, & gate & door decorations from the Assyrian, Hittite, Egyptian, Aramaic, Sumerian & Arabic civilizations. Most of the art dates from 7th-10th cents. BC & is quite good, although not of Minoan quality.

Istanbul's chief museums are grouped in a small area of the old Ottoman palace grounds, so we also visited the (non-oriental) Archeological Museum that morning. Its collection came from further west - Phoenicia, Turkey, Greece - and a later period: mostly 200 BCE-200 CE. The humanistic treatment of gods and heroes showed Graeco-Roman influence, although the black sarcophagi from Sidon suggested that the Phoenicians also knew Egypt. The museum's prize was "the sarcophagus of Alexander the Great" (4th century BCE). Whether it depicts, or ever contained, the body of Alexander, it is impressive: 6 feet high, 8 feet long, 4 feet wide, and splendidly carved in relief. There were also sculpted saints, winged lions, and knights errant from the Middle Ages.

Between the museums was a statuary garden. A Roman torso of a pensive, perhaps melancholy young man suited my mood and the day. The quality of light that seemed to mold and express Istanbul at this season was most palpable here. An autumnal wistfulness permeated the sunshine that fell from high, washed, pale-blue skies upon the yellow leaves ("or few, or none") of poplars and birches, imparting a nostalgic tone to statues and minarets. The year was cool and dying. December first! A victory of cold over warm was impending, but for now they maintained a delicate balance. Here, where few travelers came yet, the late-season loneliness invading Italy and Greece felt keener, and ascendant. Time to turn south to warmer climes and a higher sun! Yet the weather remained fine throughout our stay: crisp, sunny, lightly hazy. What northern Greece had threatened did not materialize. "Go South" signals were clearly displayed, but no penalty was exacted for eking out these few precious days.

6 PM - Visited the Covered Bazaar today: fairly genteel shops & snack bars in a white tunnel. Small windows, high up along the arch's curve, let in smoky shafts of sunlight. We ate shish kebab and returned stares. An interesting place, but not so colorful as the narrow streets which surround it. Overarched with weatherbeaten awnings, these streets pulse with the life of dark shops & stalls. Blacksmiths ply their trade with foot-run bellows. Human pack animals wearing cushion-frames bear loads as big as themselves. Singers walk slowly down the street, carrying printed pages which give them the words to their strange chants.

These "chants" were intoned verses from *The Holy Koran*. From the Middle Ages to the 18th century, street singers held forth in European cities too, though *The Koran* was not part of their repertoire. The bazaar also reminded me that Istanbul was *a city of odors: the tang of different kinds of smoke, the aroma of bread (a yeasty smell you can almost bite), the clear scent of fruit stands, the pungent stink of horses & their leavings, the smell of iron & wood, hot & cold. You almost traverse the city by going from one to the next.*

The olfactory gamut inevitably brought up our leading preoccupation - but then so did much else:

The basic fact about the food is its cheapness. Most of it is no better than U.S. food. But how well the Turks (& Greeks) understand the subtlety which imagination can inject into the world of bread! Not only are the pastries delicious & varied, but honeyed bread rings, caraway seed rolls, sugared & fluffy popovers, & Italian sandwiches are only a few of the variations on the old theme of yeast.

Trying to live cheaply, one necessarily becomes an authority on the staff of life. Cosmopolitan Istanbul offered a wide selection of what the world's cultures have done with bread, showing us how narrow our American experience of it had been. Of course we were fresh from college, and neither of us had come of age in a major city.

The next morning we walked up the Old City's narrow streets to the Topkapi grounds again, this time to see the palace itself and nearby *Aya Sofia*. I spent three happy hours roaming and writing in the Topkapi - a far cry from the days when museums just tired and confused me. But this was not any museum. When the palace was examined after the fall of the Ottomans, the world's largest collection of Ming Dynasty pottery, a gift from China to the *Sublime Porte*, was found in the basement. It had not been opened.

Dec. 2, 9 PM - The Topkapi Palace was a real treasure chest. As residence for Ottoman monarchs from 1453 to the 19th century, it accumulated a lot of wealth. The oriental section is outstanding, but in the Treasury lies the heart. Thrones, sheaths, vases, jewelry cases, toilettes - everything which could be inset with precious stones has been, & the results are impressive, if not always tasteful. Tapestries & weapons were less artistic, but interesting.

Best of all was the collection of Chinese and Japanese porcelains, bronzes, and beaten gold, dating anywhere from the 6th century to the 18th. The porcelains were mostly blue figured on white, but some were white or gold on a blue deeper than Wedgwood's. Beside them, metalwork and porcelain *bric-à-brac* from Europe looked trivial or fussy.

Aya (or *Hagia*, or *Santa*, or *St.*) *Sofia*, a church or cathedral renovated as a mosque and now called a "museum," was another mixture of styles and times:

Built by Constantine, rebuilt by [Constantius], & finally constructed in its present form by Justinian, Aya Sofia (Holy Wisdom) shows the vicissitudes of its environs. Most striking are the almost garish intrusions of Islam: the church became a mosque in 1453. The pulpit [minbar] isn't bad, nor the chandeliers, but the huge circular plaques with [Arabic] characters are gaudy & out of place. Different sections of the marble & the mosaics show where the church was repaired after an earthquake in the 6th century, beat around by the Turks, & restored extensively since the Republic. The dome is 170' high, & the huge scale of everything gives rise to St. Peter-like illusions. Gold mosaic work is good; frescoes in yellow paint come off worse.

The "illusions" created by the huge pendentive dome made it difficult to estimate size; a plaque that *looked* portable turned out to be twice my height. If the interior was partly spoiled by dueling religions, the addition of minarets and a crescent ornament to the dome did not mar the outside; the proportions were intact, and if anything the tall, slender towers enhanced them. My favorite views of Aya Sofia were from the lanes ascending the hill, where you were too close to photograph or see it all at once.

After lunch we made a brief visit to *Yerebatan*, the huge underground cistern built by Justinian in case of a siege. Stone steps led down to a gloomy hall (140 yards long, said the guidebook); a forest of columns (336 of them, ditto) lost itself in the darkening distance. Clear water dripped from the ceiling and stood a foot deep on the floor.

That afternoon we walked eight miles and saw two other mosques. A few miles up the Golden Horn, beyond the city walls, stands the small, picturesque, and important *Eyup Sultan Camii* - the Turkish equivalent of Westminster Abbey. Eyup, a companion of the Prophet, is buried here, making it the fourth holiest place of pilgrimage (after Mecca, Medina, and Jerusalem) for Muslims; prayers uttered here are thought to have special powers. The Ottoman sultans received the sword of Osman at Eyup Camii, and many of them gave it rich gifts. Pigeons and storks paced the blue-tiled court as some Believers did reverence before a niche in the courtyard wall. Inside, the prayers seemed very intense: there was much scraping of foreheads on the floor, and two kneeling petitioners in the rear chanted their devotions in the modal scales of the East.

The Fatih Mosque, built by & named for the conqueror of C'nople, is big. We arrived in time for [sunset] prayer. A [muezzin] gave the weird call from a high parapet; worshippers streamed in, & we dared to follow. Some 200 men (women prayed in the rear) were aligned in rows at the end of the mosque by the big [mihrab]. A white-chapeau'd [imam] led everyone in what could pass for calisthenics: stand, kneel, bow to scrape forehead, up, bow, stand, etc. But there was nothing humorous about one of the most solemn religious rituals I've seen. In fact, nothing I know in religion matches the echoing pregnant silence which follows the [imam's] tortured wail of "Ah-laww."

There were terms that I didn't know or had wrong, and proceedings that I could not understand, yet this first exposure to formal Muslim worship moved me in ways I would have thought impossible, given that church services had not done so for years. No doubt novelty was part of the effect - the revelation of an ancient system of belief and worship - but the obvious depth of communal feeling, and the dignity of the ritual, also contributed.

Dec. 3, boat from Asiatic to European Istanbul, noon - 2 hrs. spent walking thru Cadacul [Kadlkoy], Asiatic Istanbul, this AM confirmed what we suspect[ed] from the absence of guidebook material: there wasn't much to see. The Crimean Memorial, Florence Nightingale Hospital, barracks & mosques were all passed virtually unnoticed; only the terminus of the Baghdad RR & the Great Mohammedan Cemetery produced faint stirrings of the imagination. Not even the thought "This is Asia" saved it from being what it was: a dingy urban area, commercial outlet of Istanbul to the East.

That other suburbs over there might be more attractive did not occur to us; we were willing to relegate the area to "doesn't-need-to-be-seen" status. The warmest, most memorable part of the morning occurred at 6:30 AM as our friend "Ernie Kovacs" (a "lovable & perhaps complicated lummox") led us to the ferry slip. In the street, he moved familiarly among knots of friendly Turks in the half-light of a misty dawn. They all seemed to know him, and he had a laughing word for each. In one group, he jocularly clapped two of them into a head-knocking collision with a light movement that bespoke great strength. At the slip he insisted on purchasing our tickets - to our dismay, bitterness against the poverty that kept him from America the Bountiful being his *idée fixe*. As we glided away he stood waving, one of our benefactors, then shoved hands in pockets, turned, and trudged back into the city.

That afternoon I sat on a park bench in the New City with my journal and caught up on a backlog of topics. One was the cult of Ataturk ("Father of the Turks"): Mustafa Kemal, Turkey's first president, whose pictures and busts were everywhere, he who emancipated Turkish women, adopted the western alphabet and turned Aya Sofia into a museum of the history of civilization. Another was the phenomenon of which Hector and I were part. In Istanbul we had found no youth hostel and seen no other young travelers, which made me more conscious of them.

There are a number of Americans, young ones, traveling as we are. They swell the ranks of other travelers - German, British, Australian, South African, Scandinavian - who have realized that the world is wide & ought to be moved around in. It's comforting that our wanderlust is not nearly so rare as wealthy Suburb or provincial Debrew would have had us believe. Take note, pale neighbors back home, & do not confuse security with Americanism, the "good life" with ignorance, or the neighborhood with the world!

We are part of an int'l camaraderie determined not to accept the conventional answers to "What is life?" & "What am I to do with it?" We are known by beards, packs, military surplus clothes, & sometimes scooters. We ain't pretty, but we're digging toward the roots of int'l understanding in a way gov'ts cannot: by proving that the basic human motivations are everywhere the same.

Our ranks include the Californian whose Vespa had run out of gas near Mt. Olympus; Jim, Jerry, & Charley; an ex-AF mechanic who'd been traveling for a year on his Lambretta; the guy who wrecked his scooter in Thessalonica; Julius from S. Africa & the folk-song collector from England; 4 girls from Australia; a 60-yr.-old laborer from Canada; Di & Lu; and us, of whom at least one is proud to be a member in good standing!

Although this is naïve, uncritical, and feisty, a too-ringing manifesto of a decentralized "movement" that had never been a secret in many countries, I can neither condemn nor suppress it. After all, this was the period of the Angry Young Man. Angry about what? In my case, about having led such a sheltered existence as never to have met a single student traveler who might have told me about the whole corps. Fifty years on, seeing other young folks go off on their travels, I still think that they - and all of us - are the better for their wanderings. International service organizations such as the Peace Corps and CUSO just organized what we were doing in makeshift fashion, harnessing that energy.

I'm as happy about the future of the trip as at any time since early last summer. Hector has expressed willingness to try for Central Africa by train if it's practicable. Nothing definite yet, but the possibility is again open. For the present, we will train on Sat. to Adana, drive into Syria, & sail from Latakia or Beirut for Alexandria. Found out today that a Russian boat goes from both ports around 12/19. Crazy!

Central Africa! Hadn't that hope been buried in Naples? But in the realm of Dionysus, many irrationalities – including rebirth – begin to seem possible. If we'd come this far.... We had visited two travel agencies to learn what options existed, and were aware of some openings to the south. That the idea of taking a *Russian* boat struck me as "crazy" is a footnote to the Cold War. In a bookstore that day I bought *Tarhan's Illustrated 6 Language Guide*, with "basic words and key phrases" in French, Spanish, Italian, German, Turkish and English, and drawings (of foods and objects) to which you could point when all languages failed: a useful resource and good entertainment at slack times.

Dec. 4 - Covered some pleasant country during a 110-km. scooter excursion this AM. At about 8:30 we wheeled out into the street, bumped over Galata Bridge, & headed up the Bosporus for the Black Sea. After running through quaint resort towns (on cobblestone or "smooth" brick), we turned inland & found better roads. The way runs thru a fertile valley between hills reminiscent of Westchester Co. around Chappaqua, then climbs said hills & drops down to the coast of the Black Sea at Kilyos, ca. 35 kms. north of Istanbul's fashionable Taxim [district].

La Mer Noire was placid: clear waters, unruffled by any breeze, lapping the beach as if they were lake waves. The Sea refused to give any objective correlative to the great Red mystery which borders its northern shore, but merely blended with the sky in hazy anonymity....

More Cold War thinking, with a tribute to the suggestive powers of color. Somehow I expected the *Black* Sea to be stormy or dark, providing a crude correlate of international communism. But it remained defiantly pretty - insisted on being a calm sea plied by a few fishing smacks. We gamboled on the beach and then whirred back to Stamboul, stopping once to photograph the countryside, which did feel like New England in early autumn.

We did not leave on Saturday after all. Hector was waiting on some film, so we had a final day of reading and revisiting sites in halcyon weather. I rode out to the place where we had entered Istanbul to photograph the boulevard and the walls. One slide shows three vehicles and three pedestrians along a half-mile stretch of road; a few locals stand by a stone parapet. It is a quiet scene, awaiting tourism. I also tried to capture the bazaar on slow color film, producing an *Etude noir*. That night we paid our bill and said goodbye to our friends at the Konya Ugur. They seemed sorry to see us depart, especially Ernie K., who doubtless wished that he too could just pick up and go when he had seen enough. I felt sad to be leaving the city's grey mosques, purplish haze and pungent streets, and apprehensive about what Asia Minor might throw at us.

The Orient Local

At 0530 Sunday Hector announces that it is time to rise and get to work: our train leaves from the far side of the Bosporus at 0840. We finish packing, wheel the scooters out into the false dawn, tie on, drive to the ferry slip, purchase tickets and board the ship. No problem: we know the system. By 0645 we are crossing the historic waterway on our clearest morning yet. Boat traffic darts chaotically about the harbor, gulls glide, a smoky pall makes impressionist paintings of bridges and mosques. On the Asian side, two minarets are silhouetted against the east's fiery red. This is something like an Eastern Adventure!

Then we notice that we are not heading for the Baghdad Railway station in *Haydarpasa*, but further north, to *Uskudar*.

Wrong ferry! That necessitates a crosstown dash of about three miles over wet trolley tracks and cobblestones, packs bouncing, behind windshields opaque from mud. When we reach the large, handsome station by the water, the local hustlers – or whatever they are - know what we want and expedite us as if the train were leaving soon. After wheeling the scooters into the baggage room and removing our packs, we are told that the fuel must be drained. So, back outside to pull off side panels and the fuel hose from the carburetor. Watching freeloaders crowd forward with bottles that plainly are not coming with us, I wonder if this is really about safety, or just a scam. The prospect of arriving in Adana with no fuel is unattractive, so we open our main-tank valves for them, but save the ¾ pint in reserve. They seem delighted to obtain a few liters from each of us. I try to explain that our fuel is a gas-oil mixture, but they probably know that: there are lots of two-stroke engines here.

Back inside, the station agent wants to weigh the scooters on his scale. It does not reach from wheel to wheel, however, and thus may damage their vulnerable undersides, especially the muffler, so I persuade him - in Turkish! - to accept the weight listed in my owner's manual. All arrangements being completed, he totals the expense: $20 apiece. "*Ogrenci*," I say (student). "Ah," he replies, and divides by two. For $10 each, we and our scooters can ride across Turkey for two days and a night, 3rd class. Of course we have no idea what "3rd class" means around here.

Now they say the train will not leave until about 10, so we eat breakfast at a nearby shop along the curving riverside street. Having no idea what food will be available on the train, I down a four-egg omelet and buy two hard-boiled eggs for the trip. If the eggs are binding, so much the better, probably: maybe I can last until Adana. Walking back we have time for a more leisurely look at Haydarpasa, but in the station they are now anxious to load the scooters on the train. This proves ticklish: it takes four or five of us to heft the 238-pound Lambrettas onto the shoulder-high floor of the baggage car. Feeling grateful, I tip the porters 5 *lire* (40 cents), which Hector considers excessive.

We must now find places in the 3rd class cars, already crammed to capacity; it is all we can do to force our way down the aisle with bulky packs. Every compartment is full, every seat taken. When I put my pack down, people have to step over it to get by me. Hector has disappeared in the crush. Everyone seems to know everyone else, and carries on ear-splitting conversations. Outside, a peasant woman in loose dark clothes squats on the platform breast-feeding a baby, surrounded by all but oblivious people. This I have not seen in North America, or even in Europe.

Mercifully, some of the more colorful and voluble characters in the car prove to be visitors. They depart in an orgy of cheek-kissing; a conductor trying to shoo them off is almost in tears. In their wake I find some aisle space for my pack in the next car and *leave* it there, consciously breaking rule #1. The tent and camera bag slide into a nook in one compartment of "my" car. The train starts to move with visitors still spilling off the steps to right and left, then running alongside; only the platform's end stops them. We emerge like a butterfly from the cocoon of well-wishers into the open sunshine of the yards. The conductor blows his nose loudly and starts collecting tickets.

Soon afterwards I am cordially invited to take an empty seat in the compartment by which I am standing. None of my new mates speaks anything but Turkish, so I amuse them by passing around the six-language phrase book, which quickly repays its purchase price. One of them points to the expression "This is my friend," and gives me a dazzling smile. All nod emphatically. Point made! I coach them to say it in English, and they enjoy my efforts to pronounce "*Arkadasimdir.*" We could go on like this for hours, which may prove useful. I start adding to my vocabulary-and-phrase list, begun at the Konya Ugur. The "conversation" consists chiefly of proper names - America, Ankara, Adana, Egypt, Eisenhower (*eem*, "good") - and nodding. By lunch-time we are such close friends that they offer me their bread and sardines. I cannot take outright gifts from these people, so we pool our supplies and have a feast.

An hour later the conductor appears, looking purposeful. It takes me some time to understand that he has moved Hector into an unused kitchenette in the 2nd class car just ahead, and wants to consolidate his "foreign problem" by putting me there, too. I try to resist - having begun amicably with these Turks, I don't want to leave, or arouse ill-feeling by accepting what sounds like a relatively plush deal - but am powerless against his importunities and the language barrier. My concerns prove groundless. I revisit my friends several times, and they always welcome me warmly. Nor is the tiny kitchenette that good a deal: curious

Turks are constantly pushing open the door (unless we jam it shut with our shovel) to view the foreigners. They are almost invariably friendly once contact is made, but all our attempts to communicate are repetitive and unsatisfying: a long series of retreats from zero. I *hate* understanding so little of the language; we *must* do better with Arabic.

Once I attempt to write something in my journal, but all I can manage that day is

Dec. 6, train to Adana, 3:30 PM - The sum of individual parts turns out to be greater than the whole!

The next morning I explain that "the whole" is our train trip to Adana, while the "parts" are "a very entertaining and colorful cross-section of Turkish life," but constant social interactions leave no time for scribbling. By then it is clear that public transport and your own are two different modes of life. You do meet The People this way!

We are fortunate to make friends with Çimlik, a Turkish-speaking Yugoslav who gets on our case. Having gleaned some basic information from us - American students riding to Egypt - he deals with all visitors throughout the afternoon and evening, ejects interlopers from the kitchenette and persuades the new conductor not to eject *us*. If we try to communicate more, it always ends in defeat. Çimlik clearly wants to tell us about the country we are traversing, which by evening has exchanged the verdure and fall colors of the coastal lowlands for a barren interior plateau. He helps me trace our route on my map. In little towns, white-veiled women sit by the windows of dark rooms, drawing back if they notice any observer. Hector or I gets off at each stop to buy bread ("*ekmek* checks by the yeast beast") or whatever food is being sold on the platform: none is available on the train. These treasures we share with Çimlik, who contributes sweet rolls, oranges, and cold chicken. Thus we establish communication based on food, his assistance of fellow foreigners, our needs, mutual good will, and the few words we have in common.

Night is an unpleasant dream-haze of glaring lights, cold drafts, sudden intrusions, nasty looks from the conductor, and dimly-lit platforms that appear for a moment and then recede into the void. At some point while I am asleep, Çimlik disappears - Hector thinks he was thrown out by the conductor - and we do not see him again. *Gule gule, Çimlik, ve tesekkur ederim*! Farewell, man, and many thanks.

As often as our whistle-stop local halts on this nearly 600-mile journey, it disgorges other passengers on the run amid desolate hills and wastes, many of them overnight. The conductor warns them a minute or two in advance, opens the door (admitting a blast of chill air) and lowers the steps. The train slows to a trundle and a single dark figure drops off the lowest step into total blackness. Seconds later, a few lights show briefly in the hills. The process is oddly familiar: our rescue truck in the central Peloponnese, depositing hardy, grizzled shepherds in the mountains.

By morning of the second day fatigue is taking its toll. Luckily the Turks have exhausted their curiosity, for we are too weary to be civil or alert. I study my phrase book, try to write, compare the landscape with the map. We crawl over hills and plains of varying fertility, seizing any excuse to stop. Some areas are plowed and look arable, though never rich. Slender white birches, pines, and scattered olive trees sometimes border the track or cluster about a few stark buildings. On sidings sit old European freight cars, chassis high above the wheels. A line of snowy mountains gradually climbs the horizon to block our way: the Taurus Range, from which Hittite tribes descended onto the Syrian plains. By early afternoon it forms an unbroken wall from south to east. At 3 PM (when a hostile conductor ejects us from the kitchenette) we begin a slow climb, and soon add a second engine. The air grows cool, and clearer; walls of granite and noisy white mountain streams come as a relief after the dull plateau. As dusk falls we are negotiating narrow high passes and throwing snowballs whenever we halt.

Dec. 7, on board - As Di & Lu said, 3rd class on Turkish trains is bad. Aisles are crowded with standees, & each compartment has its quota of 8. [Turks] are voluble & expressive, like Italians, & very warm & hospitable once you break through, e.g. the crew in my first compartment. On my last trip there was great name-exchanging, profession of close Turkish-American relations, & handshakes. Almost all the men wear mustaches. Cruelty: they kick dogs, throw orange peels at & steal from the kids who sell at each stop, etc.

(One book I had read on the region said that cruelty was a trait of "the Arab character." That bothered me; surely it was stereotyping? But now my own observation of Turks showed how easily one could fall into generalizing.)

After ejection from our refuge we plunge back into the social whirl of third class - as colorful, dirty, and manic as deck passage - where we quickly strike up scads of non-English-speaking acquaintances. Though tired from poor sleep and the strain of baffling attempts at conversation, I am glad to be out of the ghetto into which we were pushed and back among the people. Then, as darkness falls, musical instruments come out like nocturnal creatures.

A waft of percussion and woodwind music issues from the next compartment. I move into the corridor to look in its window, and my compartment-mates follow. Others come from throughout the car, crowding into the narrow space alongside the compartment or even into it, where, amidst eight Turks drinking yellow wine and smoking dark cigarettes, two swarthy, mustachioed peasants are playing a large bass drum and a double-reed snake charmer's pipe. As more passengers press toward the door, some to watch and some to dance (male couples) in slow gyrations, the wine takes hold, cigarette smoke eddies more thickly, and music swirls around us: Indian-sounding, but mixed with rhythms and improvised breaks redolent of jazz. The breathing technique of the piper is admirable; the nasal, piercing tone of his pipe never ceases until a song is finished, when it breaks off abruptly, in mid-line it seems to me. Always there ensues a moment of silence: no applause or commentary. Then quiet talk, growing louder, and wine makes the rounds, and cigarettes. But when another wailing, intricate piece begins, everyone stops to listen.

During the session an idiot boards the train at a tiny stop in the mountains: a boy with hideous sightless eyes, of whom the Turks seem roughly fond. They taunt him, push and pull at him as he presses blindly down the aisle, but he accepts all this with a placid smile, and later they laugh with him and make room. At the height of a tormented and wildly syncopated piece I see an extraordinary image reflected in the glass of the compartment door: behind me, standing on a chair, is the demented boy, face contorted in a fixed expression of pleasure, eyes rolling senselessly, making strange rhythmic noises with his twisted mouth.

After an hour or so the car quiets down. We have reached the south coastal plain, and most people become withdrawn and silent as they watch for the city lights. We all seem to have had enough of everything but rest.

Dec. 8, ADANA, Turkey, 8 AM - We pulled into Adana, a mild, palm-growing town & climate, at 7:30, took leave of our buddies & got the scooters. Mine had a flat, which I changed there. I'm now waiting for it to be fixed. Hector's had no gas, so we pushed 'em 2 kms. to a hotel, unloaded, & pushed to a garage for gas. We spent a comfortable night, & are preparing to head for the Syrian border -

a hundred and fifty miles away. After eleven hours of sound sleep, I finished tracing our route across Turkey on the map, whose network of red and yellow lines looked like varicose veins. From Stamboul we had gone east along the Sea of Marmara to Sapanca, where we turned south, then east, to Eskisehir; south again to Afyon, and southeast to Konya and Karaman, where the line bent northeast for awhile. Somewhere around Ulukisla the rails turned southeast to cross the Taurus and descend into Adana. The weather had held the whole way, having been mostly clear ever since Saloniki. Only one day in Istanbul was rainy and cool; some days were actually warm. Adana felt balmy; perhaps we had come south in time to avoid a severe winter. Evidently the trick was to stay near the Mediterranean.

Turning the Corner

Here beginneth the second of my journals, a school notebook purchased in Greece, with a cover drawing whose irony I did not then appreciate. A man is kneeling, eyes closed and arm upraised to shield himself from the glory of a heavenly figure at right; in the background, a servant tries to hold a terrified horse shying from the apparition. The Greek text reads, "Saul, Saul, why do you persecute me?" The man, later known as Paul, is having his "*quo vadis*?" moment on the road to Damascus; he has about as much idea of what he is getting into as I did. He was, by the way, "of Tarsus," i.e. from the Adana district. Grandmother Wade, watching my mother mark our route on a big map back home, was pleased to see that we were retracing Paul's missionary journeys. I never denied it.

An intensely blue sky, latticed with high tendrils of cloud, arched over Adana, whose whitewashed earthen buildings were blinding in the warm December sun. The train that we had boarded in cool grey Istanbul had disgorged us on a sun-blanched Mediterranean plain. I had become accustomed to feeling climate changes gradually, to working for them on the scooter. The train had largely insulated us against the elements, and I was (for the moment) glad to be again in the open where I might experience the world.

The hotel clerk sent me to an elderly mechanic who fixed my flat. Though we could scarcely communicate, he was civil and fair; toiling alone in one cluttered room, he took evident pride in his work. By the time I returned to the hotel, Hector was chafing to go. We tied on packs before a crowd assembled, apparently, by one of our friends from the train. He led them in cheers, communal handshaking and waving as we set off for our first full day of scooter travel since reaching Istanbul ten days earlier.

Dec. 8, hotel in ANTAKYA, Turkey, 7 PM - Very tired & would like to rest, but I'm already behind in my records, & much more tomorrow. We stand on the threshold of Syria & the Near East. Like the Hittites 3500 yrs. ago, we have come from the heights of the [Taurus] to the Syrian plain. On our right is the Mediterranean; on our left, rugged mountains hiding great plains; behind us Asia Minor; ahead, the Syrian border, 30 miles away.

Left Adana at 10:30 AM. Many trucks on the road, but no sooner had we got out of traffic & onto good asphalt than my motor started failing. I stopped, adjusted the mix, tightened the air vent, & in a few minutes it ran really well. Don't yet know the trouble.

Probably dirt in the fuel line (not surprising, after draining the main tank and running for awhile on the sediment-rich layer near the bottom), but the nasty sensation in the pit of my stomach when - with no one on the back seat, no poncho in the air scoop - the engine sputtered, choked, and died, would not go away. Less easily purged than a dirty plastic tube, it rode with me: a chronic unease about when the motor might quit next. It was hard to relax and enjoy the drive. Yet the familiar exhilaration was still there, too.

The road was excellent - much better than I expected - the weather clear & warm, the countryside exciting. We found ourselves crossing a wide plain [with] high mts. in the distance both north & south, &

an occasional sand-color ramparted castle on a rocky hill. These were intriguing, suggesting Arabs or desert feudal lords of centuries ago

- or the Crusades? Actually the principal castle on that stretch is neither Arab nor Crusader; it is a mediaeval Armenian fortress, *Yilan Kalesi* (Snake Castle), but what did we know of Armenia and Armenians? Nothing as yet. We stopped to photograph, but did not try to reach it; the open highway was beckoning. I opened the throttle and stretched up to catch the wind on my forehead. Hector, riding ahead, would look back occasionally, grin and give a thumbs-up. I even enjoyed the tang of diesel smoke as trucks and buses went by: a familiar part of our sensory environment ever since we started scootering in Italy.

We would see three or four hamlets at a time among green fields, out on the plain away from the paved road. Most consisted of a few dozen adobe houses, such as we had seen all across Turkey from the train, clustered around a tan minaret, the only structure of more than one story. From a distance these villages seemed picturesque, neat and clean, and we left it at that, running happily at up to 80 kph as the road bent south. Commercial traffic was constant, the whine of tires on pavement a song of travel.

About 12 we sighted the blue of the Mediterranean & knew we had turned our 2nd corner of it. Jagged, snow-capped [mountains] on our left sometimes sent probing fingers down to the sea for us to rise over. We ate a light lunch - feeling pressed by curious bystanders - in Iskenderun, then spent an hour toiling thru a range between us & Antakya. The steep slopes & a headwind made it a slow, 2nd-gear haul, but we coasted down the other side without engines. The road was full of tight but banked hairpins, quite dangerous.

In Greece we had picked up the bad habit - not yet paid for - of saving gas by coasting down mountains. On the descent I could see that the next plain stretched to hazy mountains on the horizon, probably in Syria. The last 40 kms. to Antakya lay across that plain: as attractive a landscape as I had traversed. In its dark soil grew a wide assortment of verdure, from slim poplars and other golden-leaved trees to cotton and deep grass of sherwood green.

Cattle, sheep & horses shared dirt roads with peasants in bright colors. The women prefer loose, baggy clothes in red, yellow, blue, green. Small villages of mud brick & clay tile roofs breathed blue smoke & were gone. Little hills jutted abruptly out of miles of flat ground. The road rose & fell through a leafy tunnel of yellow.

Behind us, north, the Amanus range that we had just crossed now rose almost halfway to the zenith, dominating the pastoral countryside. Gurney's *The Hittites* says, "Seen from the Syrian plains, these northern mountains form a mighty wall...which seemed...to divide the whole world east of the Mediterranean into 'inner' and 'outer' halves." We had no real guidebook here; it was histories that told us what we were seeing, what the Turkish place-names meant or hid. Iskenderun was Alexandretta, founded by Alexander the Great (Iskender=Alexander) after his victory over the Persians on the Plain of Issus, which we had raced over. Antakya had been the Antioch of the Gospels.

Antakya, which we reached at 3:30, is a pleasant town. It nests on the lower slopes of a mountain on the edge of the plain, & boasts Roman walls, a museum of Roman & Byzantine times, & the world's first Christian church. We quickly drew a crowd when we stopped in front of this hotel. It's like being in an automobile accident 5 or 6 times a day.

Unhappy image! I meant that we would suddenly be surrounded by strangers, attracted by our odd appearance and arcane operations. A quiet, pleasant man in his 30s who spoke some English helped us answer the onlookers' questions. We asked him if Syrian money or maps were available in town; he thought not, and we found none, nor a spare gas can. He brought a letter, written in French, for me to translate. This drew more kibitzers. What I told him in English he would translate into Turkish for the recipient and other listeners. The writer was a young Antakyan who was making good (he said) as a clerk in Paris - and proved it by writing in French, which his family and friends could not read. The crowd's reactions to the young prodigal's panygeric on his wages and bachelor's life would have gratified him. Hector walked off a few yards and took a picture of this scene; a couple of dozen rapt Turks are gathered around me, but several are staring at him. Later, at dusk, we took a walk along Antakya's smooth-worn old streets with our friend and another local gentleman.

To conserve the last of our Turkish money we took a single room for 6 *lire*, overlooking the storied River Orontes. It being my turn on the floor, I unrolled my bag and was soon dreaming about the open road - or rather of leaving it to soar over sands and seas, turning and banking in the widening gyre. I reveled to see minarets and castles fall away below, to probe narrow granite gorges and make giddy swoops at the surf. Even when awake I was often away in the sky, returning just in time to avoid an accident. Steep mountain roads were poor terrestrial substitutes for the vertical freedom I desired.

Rising at dawn, we strode from our room looking …unheroic. A corner café was open, and provided soft-boiled eggs (to be sucked from the shells like raw oysters) and warm goat's milk. Not bad, actually. Everything had to be done in Turkish; the proprietor and his wife seemed not to have served non-Turks before. They were so amateurishly eager that I wondered for a time if we had blundered into a private kitchen and they were just too polite (or unable) to disabuse us, but no - they understood bills. All was at length accomplished with elaborate ceremony, over-tipping, and professions of good will and undying friendship.

Back at the hotel we quickly packed, tied on and trundled away down nearly deserted stone streets in the half-light of 7 AM. Thanks to the advice our friend had given the night before we did not miss the ruined Christian church on the southern edge of town, said to have been established by St. Paul, and if so the oldest in the world. What remains are three unroofed walls of grey stone built against a sloping cliff that serves as the fourth. The massive wooden door was locked, but through the keyhole I saw that boulders and bushes ruled the interior; lichen and moss had colonized the walls. The scene was cheerless on a December dawn, suggesting the Celtic holy isles more than the coast of *Mare Nostrum*. The neglect of the site generated an air of futility and somber ruin; Turkey might be a secular, not a Muslim, state, but even less was it a Christian one.

Things Rather Fall Apart

High among the barren peaks south of Antakya, we snarl up the twisting road toward the border. Here it is full day, though still early; jumbled piles of mountains stretch as far as I can see under pale blue skies. Leading up a steep ascent on pebbly tarmac, I hit a straightaway near the top and twist in the saddle to check on Hector. He is nowhere in sight, which is unusual, so I turn and start back down. In a few minutes I meet him climbing the long grade. His trouser knees are torn and dirty; he is visibly shaken. We stop.

"What happened, man?"

"Took a spill on an oil slick."

"My God! I saw that. Didn't you see me wave?"

"Nope. Guess I was watching the road."

"What was it like?"

"It's a shaky feeling. I've still got butterflies. It was real quiet, lying on the road listening to your motor fade away."

"Are you hurt?"

"Just scraped knees and elbows."

"Let's have a look." I break out the first-aid kit for its virgin service. He has superficial abrasions on both knees and one elbow. I douse them with merthiolate and apply gauze patches and bandaids. His heavy khakis and windbreaker have limited the damage. "How's your head?"

"Helmet did its job. Look." There is a long whitish scrape mark on the left side.

"Feel like going on, or want to rest a while?"

"Let's get on to the border. I'll lead."

We resume the climb, taking it slowly, reach the top and start down. The road winds around uneven hills in a series of hairpin curves before dropping to the few houses of the frontier village in the valley. Trying to conserve my scanty gas supply, I shift into neutral and coast, as before. But suddenly, leaning into a curve, I see that I won't make it: I am pointing out of the road into a ravine. Touching the brake makes it worse. Instinct dumps the machine in a second, saving me a *bad* accident; I just lean in farther until the wheels slip out from under me on the pebbles. Where did I learn *that* move?! We smack onto the pavement: the Lambretta on its side, fenders crunching, motor screaming, I bouncing on my hip. Coming to my feet at once like a groggy boxer, I grab the handlebars of the scooter, whose wheels are over the edge of the curve, spinning in the air. It grates to a stop and I kill the engine. If we had gone into that ravine, the trip might have been over for both of us.

My heart is pounding and all my senses are hyperacute - to the ringing stillness of the mountain air, the numbness of my body, the whir of the still-gyrating wheels, the purr of Hector's scooter on the road below. I yell and wave. He looks up, sees me, slows, wheels his machine and climbs back up. By the time he arrives I have my Lambretta on its stand and am limping about, conscious of pain in my legs. We stare at each other.

"You didn't! You *did*. How are you?"

"About the same as you, I guess. Shaky."

"Talk about sharing the hardships of the road! Let's have a look. I think you got it a little worse."

My scrapes *are* more extensive. While we are picking the gravel out of my wounds, cleaning and bandaging, a truck stops and the men proffer assistance. We thank them in Turkish but wave them on; they cluck sympathetically as they drive away. We finish and prepare to try again. Kickstarting my scooter - it starts! - I climb stiffly into the saddle, remembering what that American vet in Athens told us: "There are only two kinds of scooter drivers: those who have fallen, and those who are about to."

"All right," says Hector, donning his helmet. "Let's see if we can make this damned town. You want to lead?"

"Hell of a day for second riders!" We drive into *Yayladagi* side by side. The day is still young, 10 AM, and we clear the first part of the exit process, the police, without difficulty. At Customs, however, the inspector demands that we hand over our wallets and money belts so that *he* can count our assets. Now our purchase of Turkish *lire* in Greece, Hector's splitting his with me, and the casualness of the official at Edirne ("*About* how much money?") combine to incriminate me: on paper I have spent nothing in Turkey, and my guesstimate ($885) proves to have been too low by $17. I also have a few Greek drachmas and some Belgian Congo francs that Penny gave me as a joke. They are confiscated and I am accused of not declaring them. The fine is the value of all undeclared currency plus triple that amount: in sum, $78. This seems astronomical, representing six weeks of travel in these countries for us. It takes three hours of arguing through a translator whose French is worse than mine even to establish this much, by which time I am enraged, and still unsure whether I have broken the law, fallen into a small-town scam, or both.

The day becomes a blur of wrangling. I change my mind several times about paying the fine as various officials soothe or infuriate me. If I pay, will the money go to an appeals court in Mersin? Maybe. If I don't, will *I* have to go to Mersin and await trial? Probably. Can I call my consulate? They wave at the ancient phone and laugh: Be our guest. The day has moments of absurdity that would be funny if they weren't so expensive. Once I agree to pay, I must be formally tried, so we all go into the little courtroom next door. The quiet, business-suited judge with whom we have conversed for hours now appears in red, white and purple robes. All stand! Every question that I have already answered is asked again, passing from "*le juge*" to the French translator to me and back. It is part Gilbert and Sullivan, part Kafka, part kangaroo court for speeders in small-town America. Predictably, I am found guilty and fined $78. They allow me to submit a letter in English and French giving my side of the story. Will it reach an appellate judge in Mersin? Maybe. I can also write my ambassador in Ankara.

Later that afternoon I am asked to serve as lawyer for an Australian student who is being prosecuted on a charge similar to mine but speaks no French. Aha: now the system that just busted me wants to use me! I probably can't cut a deal for myself, but at least I can enjoy the absurdity of *his* trial, and have at the system again. The procedure is the same, except that I have to turn each question into English for the defendant and his friends, and translate their responses back into French. Now I know the traps and what they are looking for, however, so when Bruce incriminates himself in English, my translations become very free. After all, it's just a game; if I burst into a patter song, an orchestra behind the walls will join in. The translator keeps nudging me: "*Tenez-vous droit pour son honneur!*" "*Ne souriez pas!*" Yeah, right, lotsa luck. You want *me* to respect *this* court?

In the end my eloquent pleas for Bruce's innocence, ignorance, and bad luck in losing his bank receipt when he was *robbed* (a nice touch, I still think) earn him a Not Guilty verdict. I wonder if this decision could be the judge's way of evincing sympathy for me, of making up. Still, victory in my first (and I hope last) gig as defense counsel in a Turkish court! My client is grateful and wishes he could help us; I assure him that he has provided the best, in fact the only good part of this day, and that my services are *pro bono*. Not the least of my pleasures is knowing that he is as "guilty" as I. Here's hoping that Mam'selle, who started teaching me French in ninth grade, and my other former French teachers, including Barney and Jean, would be pleased.

At last it is time to pay the fine. But when I see the avaricious inspector grabbing at my money, I suddenly know that it will never leave Yayladagi, and tremble with the effort of not belting him, rimless glasses and all. Two policemen are standing behind me, but I would get in one good punch. Luckily I recall what we have heard of Turkish prisons. I do get his name, never spoken or displayed, by asking a junior associate who looks sympathetic. He nods, and later hands me a folded slip of paper. On it is written, "Zeki Ozkurt." *Tesekkur ederim*, whoever you were. In olden times around here, knowing your enemy's name conferred power over him. Maybe it still does.

Darkness has fallen when we are finally free to leave. I am shaking with anger and fatigue; my knees are swollen and sore. We have no Turkish or Syrian money, or food, and have not eaten since breakfast. The plan is to drive the few miles to the Syrian border, camp there, and be ready when they open in the morning. With the aid of our feeble headlights and a half-moon, we trundle slowly along the dark road, climbing through wooded hills. The sky is clear; stars twinkle in the chill air. A mile and a half from Yayladagi I feel a sickly sponginess and wavering in the rear tire, ease to a stop, and dismount to look. Sure enough, completely flat. I just stand there, shivering and numb, until Hector's light reappears. In a moment he draws up, his headlight beam illumining the tableau starkly.

"What happened? Not another fall?!"

"Nope. Flat rear tire."

"No!" He slumps. "Want to change it?"

"Can't face it tonight. Too tired - cold - disgusted! In the morning - "

"Okay, we camp here." Rolling the scooters off the road, we pitch the tent in a small space among conifers. The night is cold and noisy: once it is wild pigs rooting around in the woods, later a canine howling farther off. When he heard where we were going, Ernie Kovacs said, "Watch out wild dogs in mountains. They eat animals, people, anything." Did he mean wolves? After 3 AM I sleep no more, but lie there hoping that was the worst day of the trip.

We rise at first light, Hector striking the tent while I change the tire; then drive off, still fasting. I, at least, am oblivious to the sunshine and crisp air. The Turkish border guard frowns over the crossings-out and contradictions in my passport - the product of yesterday's vacillations - and phones Yayladagi for instructions. I wonder if they will decide that the cow can be milked again this morning, but they want no more of me back there, and he waves us on. We nod equivocal farewells to Turkey. *Gule gule*, folks: is this how you want to be remembered?

A short distance up the road, a gate lifts to admit us to a wide clearing containing the Syrian border post. Again the police inspection is routine, but the customs inspector will not accept our Italian *triptiks* (which cost $11 each) as true *carnets de passage*: legal guarantees that we will not sell the scooters in a given country without paying duty. We have long worried about the validity of our documents, which raised eyebrows in Greece and Turkey. Now the line has been drawn: thus far but no farther. Discouraged and infuriated, I am shaking again; Hector stares out the window, his jaw clenched. But it doesn't matter how we *feel*: the scooters cannot pass. We could, they say, pay $35 each to customs in *Latakia* for a transit permit to Lebanon, but there might be more trouble there. In any case the Lambrettas have to stay here; we must hitchhike. And do many cars come through here? "No many." Communication is difficult: these are Arabic speakers, though they know some Turkish words, and the policeman has some English. We wait the morning out, penniless and hungry.

Dec. 10, Syrian customs at the Turkish border, 10:30 AM - Since I last wrote, the roof has collapsed on the trip and our morale. Until the sympathetic border policeman gave us a chunk of bread with cheese and marmalade and water a little while ago, we had not eaten since breakfast yesterday.... We are stuck at the border with no money, hoping for a ride to Latakia, a bus to Damascus, & a [carnet] there. I am hungry, tired, impatient, & doubtful about the future.

The hospitality of the police inspector was like an oasis; he treated us kindly when we most needed it, bridging the gap that had recently developed between us and officialdom, changing the dominant feeling from hostility to mere entrapment. As we ate ravenously, he expounded some of the region's modern history. On a map in his bare office he pointed to a piece of Turkey that bulges south into Syria. "That is *ours*," he said. "Those French… But someday" - and with cupped hand he swept the bulge into his lap. A fundamentalist's fervor gleamed in his eyes; this was not the man from whom to obtain a balanced view of Middle Eastern politics (it would be some time before I learned that he had a good case). Through it all he remained friendly, showing us a picture of his girlfriend in Latakia, and writing Hector a greeting for Andrea in beautiful Arabic flourishes. At least we hoped it was a greeting.

At 1 PM a car approached from Turkey: a Mercedes-Benz driven by a Harvard business student who was glad to help. Hardly able to believe this benign turn of fortune, we locked everything lockable on the Lambrettas - which we left with deep misgivings - and put our packs in his trunk. The policeman looked sorry to see us go; his three companions at the isolated post were crude men who seemed inferior to him socially and intellectually. He waved wistfully as the black sedan gunned away towards Latakia.

Our benefactor, Stephen, was eager and intelligent, but had difficulty staying on the road. Oops, he would say, as his tires ran off the edge of the pavement onto the rough shoulder again. His dogmatism and omniscience soon rubbed Hector the wrong way. I tried to act as a buffer. Stephen *did* know a lot, especially about the Crusades; from him I learned enough political and religious history to contribute substantially to my enjoyment of Syria. He just had no sensitivity, no awareness of how he came across. Traveling alone, he seemed nervous and unhappy (the classic Harvard student, I thought uncharitably). As we bounded along over the rough pavement at double the speed of the scooters in the superbly engineered Mercedes, discussing art and history, I saw how different the trip could have been, insulated from…everything out there. In less than an hour we broke out of the beautiful pine forests and began a descent to the plain, to Latakia and the sea.

We said goodbye to Stephen, cutting the cord to all this comfort, at a bank near some cheap-looking hotels. By late afternoon we had bought Syrian money - *legally*, at a bank! - procured a room, and eaten a good meal, which we defined as lunch, to be followed shortly by dinner. A faint-hope visit to the Customs House proved fruitless: they could not or would not furnish us with a *carnet;* we would have to go to Damascus and try there.

In Latakia we were able to use French at times. I felt grateful to the French Mandate, but disloyal to our police friend with his old map.

In the evening we walked around Latakia, sampling its neighborhoods. After our last few days, the nondescript seaport seemed a wonderworld of luxuries. The food was strange, almost exotic, with fragrant meats and sweet pastries hot from the deep-fat fryer. I had my first *kibbe*, and fried doughballs rolled in honey and cinnamon sugar. Bare electric lights burned garishly for no apparent purpose, as if they were loved for themselves. The stares made us feel deeply alien, but that was nothing new, and after all, we *were*. Men and boys held hands like European girls. When we asked our hotel manager about bus tickets, he found two lads to conduct us to the station. As soon as we were in the street my escort took my hand. I withdrew it instinctively with a shudder; *then* thought, there may be unknown codes here. Was this homosexuality? One of my books had warned about this, as well as cruelty. The boy seemed surprised and hurt, as if I had refused to shake his hand. I distracted him by asking about Arabic words, and he taught me to count to ten - knowledge that I soon used in buying bus tickets.

Dec. 11, Hotel El Arabi, DAMASCUS, SYRIA - Although the principal problems remain unsolved, our general situation & morale [are] much better. We left Latakia by bus at 7 AM today for Damascus, which we reached at 3. It is a modern, impressive city, & we are entrenched at this hotel for 2 L. (56 cents) a night, ready to try for [a carnet] tomorrow. Have just finished a therapeutic letter to the American consulate in Ankara about the mess in Turkey. I felt weak & sick until this PM, however, even with 8 hrs. sleep. Don't want to push my physical condition like that again.

A clear sky was diffusing grey light over the dirt parking lot as we boarded an old yellow bus (the kind I rode to school in the '40s) for *Damas* that morning. We put our packs with other luggage on a roof rack running the length of the battered warhorse, then took a seat together among other early arrivals, but signally failed to blend with them. As soon as the driver stepped aboard, he cast one glance over his passengers and motioned us to the seat just behind him: to keep an eye on us, or to give us a better view? He was a good-natured, darkly handsome young man, and his concern proved entirely benevolent; at the gas stop he gave me a piece of his big circular loaf of brown bread. *Shukran ektir*! This was out on the desert, due north of the great mountainous spine of Lebanon. The featureless plain of dirt and stones glared under the noon sun as I sat on a whitewashed boulder in the station's apron, eating my bread and looking up at the white massif etched on a blue sky. Meanwhile, the Mobil pumps were rotating their dials with Arabic numerals - which is how I learned them.

The ride was long, bumpy, sometimes dull yet never boring. There were the shifting landscapes...south of Latakia we followed the coast almost to the Lebanese border over a rolling, occasionally bleak plain, cultivated here and there with various crops. Long before we turned east, the ramparts of Mount Lebanon, a towering mass of blue-grey topped with pure white, appeared to hover some distance above an indistinct horizon. Inland, the country became more desolate and less populated. The road went through rocky, barren foothills, then turned south again over low hills undulating to an almost flat horizon. Once mountains shut off the Mediterranean influence, we were in dirt, then sand, desert: a gravel waste of stones, gritty dust and sand. A virtually uninhabited region, it needed only sand dunes to look like Hollywood's idea of "Arab-land." Other than a few villages with adobe houses, and a few camel caravans, the classic beasts of burden exuding their natural air of haughtiness and insouciance, we saw nothing.

And there was the acoustic and visual entertainment on the bus. Although I could not understand the conversation around me - we had outrun the Six-Language Phrase Book now and must start from scratch - Arabic was the most melodious tongue I had ever heard; its quasi-musical chanting and fluctuating intonations seemed to complement the fluid grace of the written alphabet. Equally impressive were the handsome, sensitive, alert faces of our fellow-passengers - of the men, anyway: the few women kept their faces mostly covered. Both main types of headdress - the white or multi-colored kerchiefs over the head and neck, held around the forehead by a headband, usually black; and the red fezzes with black tassels - were becoming. Now if they would just be reasonable about *carnets*....

When we reached Damascus the driver pointed us toward the city center, a mile away. It was the old pre-scooter days relived as we trudged heavy-laden into the metropolis, trying to imitate the swinging gait of the camels. Fortunately the first hotel we tried proved satisfactory - I was feeling woozy - and we took a third-floor room. Our window looked out over a small plaza and a busy boulevard, past minarets to barren cliffs walling the city on the north. Later I watched dusk settle over Damascus as a *muezzin* chanted the call to prayer from the balcony of the minaret across the square: *Allaaw-hu Akbar,* 'God is great.' But how could I, how can I, represent the length and heaviness of the "ll," the dark resonance of the "aa," or their effect on a newly-arrived infidel?

Damascus is a shock after the desert. Its plain is fairly fertile, watered by one small river supporting lots of trees, but that doesn't prepare you for a city which is large & modern, with broad, tree-lined thoroughfares, a large int'l trade fair, many good hotels, restaurants & shops, neon lights & French. I really like it. Old Damascus is spread along the slopes of a hill. Had my first Arabic lesson tonight from the friendly crowd here in the "chapter room." I'll learn it!

Of course that remained to be demonstrated: thus far my runs at Spanish, Italian, Greek and Turkish had fallen far short of the more bullish predictions.

Our chamber and a dozen or so others opened onto a large, carpeted common-room warmed by a pot-bellied stove near one end. In the evenings, most of the guests - several of them students - forsook their solitary quarters to form a sociable group near the stove, where we were in great demand. At first their desire for our presence felt intrusive; someone would knock softly on our door while we were reading or writing and request our company. But after one evening spent in this conclave I was happy to return: it was a free language-lesson and an ego-bath. There were always one or two English-speakers through whom the curiosity of the others was channeled to us. This could be exhausting when it was ten to one, though even then it was gratifying to have them hang eagerly on our every word. We had a double return to any remark inspiring amusement or appreciation: an immediate response from the English speaker(s), and a delayed one in translation. They asked good-naturedly about our trip, our reactions to Syria, and life in America. *Our* questions concerned language and politics, but it did not seem to be a political crowd - or else they did not feel comfortable discussing politics with us.

Dec. 12, El Arabi, 8:30 PM - A rag of bone, a hank of hair, a ray of hope. Spent a frustrating day hunting for the Motor Club, talking to customs, checking in with Security Police. All footwork & paperwork. Upshot: documents not valid; customs impotent; sharp man at motor club wiring ACI [Auto Club d'Italia] for a guarantee of responsibility for a carnet. Won't know until Monday. Tomorrow we see the city, equipped with a good map & a guidebook to Syria. Today had time to wash & shave.

The climate is excellent. Mornings & evenings cool, middays warm. Bare brown hill rears up behind the city, carrying some houses with it; its sandy color contrasts with the glowing blue of the sky.

The crowd here in the chapter room very friendly & eager tonight -

but *not* willing to state their opinion of the UAR (United Arab Republic: Syria and Egypt, 1958). When I asked them about the area around Iskenderun and Antakya, however, they spoke freely, taking the same line as the border policeman. Between the two wars, they said, the French handed over to Turkey part of their League of Nations mandate for Syria: Antioch, Alexandretta and vicinity. Their story was that the Turks took it over militarily, despite the verdict of a fact-finding commission against them. Syrian maps (except the one at the border post) still included the territory in Syria; Philip Hitti's book on Syria said that France ceded Alexandretta to Turkey in 1939 to secure its allegiance in the war. I wished I had known enough to ask the Turks for their side when we were there.

We had acquired a map of the Graeco-Roman world somewhere – from Will Durant or a fellow traveler - that gave the classical names of these lands. From *Italia* we had voyaged to *Achaia* and scootered up through *Macedonia* and *Thracia*. The Turkish train had skirted *Bithynia* and gone through *Galatia* to *Cilicia*. Lebanon would be *Phoenicia*. But this was Syria, then as now.

Most of our time in Damascus went down the bureaucratic drain; we haunted more offices than monuments of civilization, and the cloud of "our problem" louring overhead darkened our stay significantly. The next morning, though, while Hector was off photographing, I went to the famous old Ummayyad Mosque, learning that the ugliest of its three minarets was a Turkish addition to the original Arab work. Both the courtyard - a *pot pourri* of Greek and Roman columns, Byzantine mosaics and Islamic styles - and the mosque proper are on the grand scale; the interior, covered with (they say) 280 rugs large enough to be carpets, is probably a hundred yards by thirty. Shafts of sunlight, angling down steeply from high stained-glass windows, made the hundreds of glass chandeliers into so many prisms and created warm spectra on the carpets. Worship was quiet and solitary: here and there a man knelt on his haunches, praying softly or performing obeisances.

And here too was Stephen, peering into corners and being bright about entablatures and calligraphy. I was glad, as it gave me a second chance to thank him for his help, and for what he had taught us. He seemed pleased to hear this, and to see me; again I thought him lonely, and wondered if that worked for him. Stephen was (of course) staying at a good hotel, but admitted that it had nothing like the Arabi's common room. He sounded almost envious, and I invited him to drop by, but he never came.

I also went in the cloistered Mausoleum of Saladin, a pleasing and historic site, but was more interested in the old bazaar nearby, which spread over dozens of square blocks, some covered, some not. As in Casablanca and Istanbul, every kind of shop and craft was represented, making a scene rich with "color" - including filth and poverty. Two snobbish-looking camels arrived from the country under full loads and sashayed down the the Street called Straight, hardly glancing right or left, seeming to say, "I've been on straighter streets than *this*." What was significant about that morning, I thought, was that I was touring a strange city on my own, and quite enjoying it.

Dec. 14, Hotel el Arabi - Two more days have passed. Have to wait for the 4-7 PM hours of the Motor Club to see if our wire has been answered. At the [U.S Embassy] today, a knowledgeable woman helped us, but was at a loss how we could get a <u>*carnet*</u> *if ACI says "no." She's driving a gov't car to Aleppo in the AM, in which we may ride if our business is done. If we don't hear tonight, the situation will be up in the air; if we hear "no," best guess is we pay customs to get scooters thru Syria, ship them from Latakia to Naples, meet them there after Egypt. Did get my statement of the Turkish border mess "officialized" & mailed from the [Embassy].*

Yesterday we gave Damascus one of our walking tours, such as have previously been accorded Lisbon, Casablanca, Naples, & Istanbul. Climbed almost to the top of the habitations on the hill - one of the stiffest walks yet. Up there the houses are of dried earth, the roads steep, the paths dirt or gravel, & the view over the city impressive. Descending, found that the Trade Fair is closed, & settled for watching the U. of Syria soccer players work out.

The walk pointed the contrasts between the two Damascuses. In the hill-slum, dusty paths at right angles to ascending streets (that went right up the fall line) led along terraces to communal water pumps, apparently the only sources up there, where children with buckets were gathered. We tried to talk to them: unsuccessful, except to amuse them. Down in *la ville*, the French mandate years could be felt in the plane trees and Lombardy poplars planted along wide boulevards and in parks, where old men in black coats and red fezzes strolled, talking quietly.

There was a Cairo boy here last night, very friendly. He was smoking a cool contraption which could easily catch on as a social gambit in the States. I tried it, & it was good.

There follows a drawing of the onomatopoeic "hubbly-bubbly" or *nargulleh*: a circumspect way of smoking tobacco (or whatever, but tobacco was all I ever smelled there) through a sort of water filter. The smoke that emerged from the mouthpiece was milder than what I remembered of cigarette smoking. If I had had an entrepreneurial bone in my body, I would have put the trip on hold and arranged to export hubbly-bubblies to the U.S., where they were rare at the time. Another missed opportunity! My efforts to use the device caused general merriment.

His friend, an English-speaking Syrian, today took us to the U. of S. to attend his philosophy class. It was in Arabic, & I got nothing but "Mohammed" & "Allah" once or twice. All the students stood when the prof entered or left, there was an almost constant undercurrent of whispering, students came in quite late, the argument often grew heated, & the class lasted 1½ hours.

The lecture began at 8 AM. We three joined a stream of students moving through the morning haze toward a venerable group of buildings, pausing briefly to purchase breakfast, pen and paper. Arriving a few minutes early, we took seats on wooden benches with others. When I asked our friend the topic today, he said, "Islamic philosophers," mentioning some names unfamiliar to me. Afterwards we went out to colonnaded quadrangles and lawns among throngs of students acting much as they do everywhere; the hails and farewells, intense or trivial conversations, and last-minute errands en route to class could have occurred on any campus. I was mildly surprised to see Syrian girls in western dress among the throngs. Some of them came up to our guide and asked him about us with open curiosity. After a while we left him and walked home.

This experience, coming soon after our debacle at the Turkey-Syria border, re-opened the question of the value of our travels. One day I remarked that attending an Islamic philosophy class at the University of Damascus *sounded* exotic and made fine letter material, while the reality had been uninspiring, incomprehensible to us, and thus rather boring. I said this without ulterior motives; it was simply my response at the time. Big mistake! Hector seemed impressed, and grew thoughtful. Twice later he alluded to that morning, with his own coloring and emphasis. I felt that we were in a slack, troubled period between the pleasures of Greece and the excitement of Egypt; Hector, perhaps more candid, was acknowledging a more general dissatisfaction. For the moment the threat lay quiescent, but it was there, and within a month would resurface strongly.

In Italy I had noted the autumnal sereness of earth and sky, which, along with the paucity of tourists, gave me a *fin d'année* feeling: the natural year seemed spent. This sensation gained ground until Istanbul, yet now, at the approach of the solstice, I realized that it was gone. We had become used to being loners, to being stared at as isolated oddities. Moreover, in Syria the seasons (including the tourist season) were less marked and less influential on us. There was not that brooding period between climatic extremes that is the European and North American autumn. Where the sun burns more than the cold freezes, fall is less ominous. In fact we had now moved into the mild part of the Mideastern year that travelers prefer.

We did *not* receive a wire from the ACI that night, which left us angry, frustrated, and puzzled: should we wait longer, or accept the Embassy's proffered ride to Aleppo? Hector wanted to leave, to get out, and I felt sick and docile, so we went. It was a good move: Damascus had been mostly a bust, the very winter of our discontent. Since we had not expected to visit it, I had read nothing relevant, knew little about Arabs, Islam, Syria, or Damascus, and had forgotten most of the Biblical associations

I had ever known. It was annoying to be without the scooters and entangled in bureaucratic problems, but the trouble lay deeper. Intensely conscious that my ignorance had deprived me of rewards that Damascus could have given, I vowed - futilely, of course - that it would not happen again.

On the morning of the 15th we drove north with "knowledgeable" Miss Lueders and Albert, the Embassy's Armenian driver ("French citizen, Syrian, English, it doesn't matter: we are all Armenian"). Both were so generous that we quickly awarded them "Benefactor" status; and their manners seemed pleasantly familiar, *western*, after our recent social contacts. The drive was swift and comfortable, giving us a much-needed sense of momentum. Most of the route lay through semi-desert or low rocky hills like those seen on our way from Latakia. An occasional camel caravan gave picturesque relief to the monotonous horizon. We halted for coffee in Homs, where the estimable Miss L., bless her, bought a kilo of assorted cookies for the road.

Then on to Hama, where Albert insisted that we stop and see the ancient Roman *norias*. The what? "*Norias*," he said. "Don't you know? It's an English word." *Norias* (not in my dictionary, Albert) turned out to be surprisingly large, venerable, mossy, noisy black water-wheels, connected to aqueducts and still working. On the desert not far past Hama, close to the road, were several villages of "beehive houses": sand-colored adobe homes shaped like, well, beehives *maybe*, but more like rocket nose cones, pierced at regular intervals by poles, with vents near the top.

Things Also Come Together

A little before 3 we reached ancient Aleppo, set in a reasonably fertile plain and dominated by an acropolis-citadel, the scene of several stomach-turning blood baths. With a population of around 375,000, Aleppo was thought to be larger than Damascus, they told us. That surprised me: from up on the hill, Damas had looked larger than that. And how would they *know*, anyway? Could they take a reliable census? "You may be right about that," said Miss L. complacently. Both places claim to be the oldest continuously inhabited city in the world. We were there for so few daylight hours, though, with vital business to transact, that no sightseeing was possible, nor did we ever obtain a vista of Aleppo such as we had had in Damas. Albert treated us to a late but tasty shish kebab lunch in an Armenian restaurant – there was a large Armenian community - and found us a clean, cheap hotel.

Best of all, as soon as we walked into the *Touring Club de Syrie* and told them what we needed, they started writing up *carnets* for us. Too good to be true, of course; there had to be a catch. *Oui, mais…* could we just have our Consul sign guarantees of responsibility (which is what we had vainly asked ACI to do)? We walked quickly and anxiously to the Consulate, our last hope. This might well kill the deal: why should they go out on a limb for us? No one in the Damascus Embassy had offered that. We were shown into the Consul's office without delay; he didn't seem to have much business. A pleasant, greying man in late middle age, he spent a few minutes talking to us, then just… signed the guarantees. I watched, incredulous, as he did this enormous thing, and forgave his awful French. It struck me as a matter of class, of social standing: he sized us up and decided that we were good risks. Had we been scruffier, or exhibited worse manners, I suspect he would not have signed - and the rest of the trip would have been different, scooterless. We returned to the TCS with the guarantees, filled out forms giving information about the Lambrettas, paid $14 each, and left immensely relieved, clutching our *carnets* like the blue-chip stock certificates they were.

Dec. 16, Latakia, 8 PM - This morning Albert drove us to the Consulate, we said our goodbyes there, & drove with 3 Aleppo Consulate men to Latakia. "Group Leader" was Bill C, Princeton '53, whose Ivy League dress & argument for the Navy ("it teaches you to lead men") could soon have gotten on my nerves.

Our conversation focused on how the UAR experiment was progressing. Albert had been down on it, saying, "It hasn't worked. We were better off before." He thought that "the people" were against it. The Aleppo Consulate view (of both Syrians and Americans) was that "It is an alternative to Communism. Give it a chance." It felt good to be able to ask questions, trade views and debate in our native tongue after weeks of pidgin English. Less controversially, they told us some of the history of the "Crusader country" through which we were passing. We had seen a ruined Crusader castle on a hill south of Latakia, Miss L. had mentioned some strongly-built forts in central Syria, and the castles near Adana might have figured in the Crusades.

Thereafter we raced the sun. Arriving in Latakia a little after 1, we took a taxi, the only available means of transport to Kassab [the border post], at 1:30. For this we paid 90 cents each. Arrived at 2:45, impressed by the difficulty of the mt. road, the stiff wind, & the fact that less than 2 hrs. sun remained. We decided to try it, risking a night of having to camp in the mts. Had our [carnets] stamped by the grinning customs man, reclaimed our scooters & stored gear, tied on & left at 3:15.

Yes, the formerly dour *agent de douanes* lit up, transformed by the sight of our orange booklets. "Ah, *des carnets!*" he exclaimed, nodding vigorously. The police inspector, to whom we had entrusted our possessions, had kept them all safe. Full marks! A brief debate over whether to camp there, close to possible hospitality, or set off and risk being caught in the mountains again, was quickly resolved in favor of *doing something* after days of forced inactivity, though by then we had only an hour and a quarter of daylight left, and the taxi had taken that long. The scooters all but whinnied as we stroked them, purred that they were good Lambretti, and cinched their loads tight.

The sun was low & blinding, the road steep & treacherous, & I was still gun-shy after my accident. But we kept plugging & made surprisingly good time - 43 kms. the first hour.

On winding, precipitous roads in gusty winds, 27 mph was pretty good: not much slower than the taxi on the way up. We pressed, but cautiously, this being our first scooter ride since That Day. We had a losing streak to break. I kept my eyes on the road, despite one or two splendid peripheral glimpses of hills, plain, and glaring sea far below the dense pine forests of the mountains. There were even some decent camping spots up there if we needed them. But clear skies helped to prolong the daylight; we reached the coastal plain, ten miles from Latakia, with a quarter-hour of sun left and opened the throttles, grinning foolishly, feeling we had it made. A friendly motorcyclist escorted us in, yelling something in Arabic that he wanted us to understand. We never did, but rolled triumphantly into Latakia at 4:30.

"Tomorrow - Beirut!" I wrote in my journal, still tempting the gods with arrogant predictions. Being gods, of course, they could choose whether and when to punish presumption, whether to use a short leash or a long one - those being the only real choices, and not mine to make.

The next morning we followed the route our bus had taken for the first 50 kilometers south, along Mediterranean promontories and over stony, arid hills a few kilometers inland, where the glowing blues, mint-jelly greens and tan limestone of the coast narrowed to rock and soil colors: chocolate, rust, mauve, grey. A steady wind blew in our faces and a bright haze obscured Mount Lebanon. Hector had a motor failure in this hilly region. By the time I pulled up he had restarted it, and worked the throttle back and forth until the motor ran smoothly. Probably a little something in the gas line again, we said. We were getting used to such occurrences. But how did the dirt get in, and where did it go after it passed through the line?

When the road to Damascus swung east, we continued south onto "new" ground. The last 30 kilometers to the border were desertic: a dry, sandy plain near the coast, swept by strong winds blowing from the mountains to the sea. We fought a veritable dust storm, against which, at times, I could not maintain 4th gear. We had to lean into the wind, a technique that worked well except on the bridges that spanned a number of dry watercourses or *wadis*. Their low walls blocked enough of the wind so that the support on which I had been leaning was suddenly removed; the first time it happened I almost fell to my left, but uprighted myself after wavering. Three or four seconds later the bridge ended and the wind hit again, pushing me over to the right. Lean left! After the first bridge I could anticipate the effect and partly control it, though the wind was not constant. Altogether it was a desolate region, with only a few low green plants and the telephone poles breaking the surface of the flat. It looked like pictures I had seen of the North African coast road. Was this a foretaste?

The Syrian border post sat in the midst of this scene. I held my breath as a mustachioed official examined our *carnets*, but he passed them - and us - routinely. We allowed ourselves half-smiles of relief. A short distance further on, still in this wind-blasted desert, was the frontier of Lebanon, near the village of Arida (I wondered if the name was allegorical or just a happy accident).

Polite, English- and French-speaking customs men inspected the *carnet*, grinned at our apparel, and issued us entry visas for $3 apiece. Cleared for the Republic of Lebanon in short order, we grinned like idiots and exchanged a ritual victory handshake. It had been our easiest border crossing since Greece. The Trip was once more on the wing!

Dec. 17, Pension Australia, BEIRUT, LEBANON - Surprisingly few things went wrong on our first full day of traveling in a week, & we snarled into Beirut a little before 4 PM. The drive from Latakia ran the gamut of topographies. ... The windswept desert lasted only a few kms. past the border. Then suddenly we were sheltered by the coastal hills, which had just become visible; the road became excellent; verdure of every sort grew along the road; the wind abated. Thoroughly enjoying the warmth and the color of the countryside, we rolled into Tripoli, where we ate a good lunch.

We cautiously noted the eerie way that topography and climate seemed to reflect our elation, as if nature really did sympathize with human moods and use the "pathetic fallacy." The sheltering hills surely existed before our coming, yet they materialized from the haze just when we needed them, wanted them, were, perhaps, ready for them. It was, of course, much likelier that our feelings reflected the topography and climate, but that more prosaic interpretation could wait for a less ebullient day.

The unpretentious restaurant that we happened to choose proved to be a hangout of Tripoli's Armenian community, who were not reticent about sharing with us their aspirations of returning to their homeland in eastern Turkey, which had expelled them (those it did not massacre) from it. It was a vivacious, noisy, gala lunch. We left lamenting and lamented by half a dozen sworn comrades, blood brothers, and were escorted for several blocks by an enthusiastic squadron of runners.

From Tripoli to Beirut was a two-hour drive: two beautiful hours skirting the green hills of Lebanon on a smooth road, with a sort of small-scale Pacific coastline on our right. A warm sun was welcome on my face: it had been a while. Palm trees and palmettos, banana plants, various evergreens and deciduous trees, flowers of bright purple and red, and ten-foot-high stalks of pampas grass topped with white cylindrical blooms adorned the roadside. My scooter (still unnamed; Hector called his "the Far-Darter") hummed through lanes made into tunnels by overarching trees and across promontories through veils of spindrift. It was simply a great day and a great place to be out on a scooter, and we had nearly missed it altogether.

> *In the Name of Allah, the Compassionate, the Merciful*
>
> Have We not lifted up your heart and relieved you of the burden which weighed down your back?
>
> Every hardship is followed by ease.
>
> 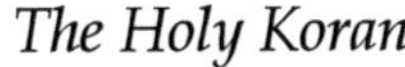
> *The Holy Koran*

16. On Galata Bridge, Istanbul, Turkey, at dawn

17. Riding for a fall in south Turkey (Winter Wright)

18. Beirut and the Mediterranean from Mount Lebanon

19. Hector and a Roman cornice, Baalbek

20. The ruins, village, and harbor at Byblos

21. Beirut and Mt. Sannine from at sea

VI. *La Dolce Vita*: Christmas in Beirut

> The way was broad and the going was good.
> They gazed at the mountain of cedars, the
> dwelling-place of gods and throne of Ishtar.
>
> *The Epic of Gilgamesh*

Gilgamesh and Enkidu walked west from Mesopotamia to "the country where the cedar is cut" in order to slay Humbaba, the guardian of the forest. Our goal was less ambitious and bloody. Driving south toward Beirut, leading - for the moment - charmed lives, we did not plan to linger there: a Russian ship would be leaving for Egypt, our major goal now, in two days, which sounded about right. We skirted a large bay, passing the gala opening of a swank casino, lush banana plantations, and the famous ruins of ancient Byblos. Two new mosques, built of tawny stone in a squared-off style, had minarets with broad facets that looked clumsy after Istanbul. At the southern end of the bay, Beirut (like Tripoli) occupied a long peninsula between the sea and green foothills, which here rose steadily to the high, snow-capped ridges of Mount Lebanon.

Dec. 17, Pension Australia, BEIRUT, LEBANON - It is difficult to know what Beirut is all about. It is big - took 15 mins. from the outskirts to the waterfront - [with] modern stores. There seems to be as much French & English as Arabic [spoken] downtown, & an occasional minaret looks out of place. We spent our only daylight hour in Cook's, checking boat schedules.

Compared with Damascus and other recently-visited cities, Beirut looked sleek, wealthy, European: more Mediterranean than Middle Eastern. A friendly, helpful agent at Thomas Cook's recommended a *pension* in the central *Bourj* district. There, as in Damascus, we had an upstairs room opening onto a large hall, which served as our *salon*.

The mental block vs. Israel [is] almost paranoid: the name is scratched out on magazines, no info in the travel agencies, etc. A bank clerk in Latakia started holding forth on the Negro problem in America, & I had to remind him that nearly every country has some race problem -

What could I have meant?! That Israelis were the Arab world's African-Americans? Which country did I think had a "race problem" with Jews? I was abysmally ignorant on this issue, despite (or because of) being a fairly regular reader of *TIME* and *The New York Times*.

Future uncertain. Russian boat leaves 18th instead of 19th, which is too soon. We probably take one the 21st or 26th. If the latter, we'd have time for Jordan & Jerusalem. Looks like no mail for Xmas.

Hector said tonight that if we can't drive across N. Africa, he'll take a boat to Italy. I would like to drive it: if that's not possible, I'll ship on to Morocco or Spain alone.

Behind such reports on travel plans lay hours of reading, information-seeking, and discussion. We still lived by our founding principle: that we were two independent travelers, making choices no farther in advance than necessary. When I asked Hector in Athens where he might go after Istanbul, he replied, "I don't know yet. I'll see how I feel." That became our stock response to any query about the future. "If we know exactly where we're going next, and when, why not quit kidding ourselves? We're tourists," he said. "Why have scooters and backpacks and grubby clothes if we can't go where we like when we like?" Many times we almost split up (never in rancor), but always in the crucible of debate one was persuaded. There were difficulties, of course - the future was always uncertain, every opinion and alleged fact was cross-examined, daily diplomacy was required - but we would have had it no other way. Freedom and independence were worth much more than their price.

What makes this particular report noteworthy is that the idea of heading south from Egypt to Central Africa – still alive in Istanbul in early December – seems to have given way to that of crossing North Africa.

Dec. 19, Pension Australia, 1:15 AM - A strange & varied day. Found that tonight's Russian boat would [overcharge] for the scooters, decided to leave the 26th. Delivered the scooters to be [serviced]. Discovered from the [Embassy] that getting into Israeli Jerusalem is difficult, sometimes impossible, takes time & red tape. Not being in a mood for such, we will skip Jerusalem & settle for quieter holidays here, with side-trips to Baalbek & perhaps down the coast.

Writing after one in the morning was strange! We did not know, nor did the US Embassy point out, that the major Christian sites were in Jordanian *East* Jerusalem, not on the Israeli side. Innocents abroad, we shied from illusory difficulties, ignorant of the real ones. We (and the Embassy) had no idea how long and arduous this trip would have been on scooters: winter conditions inland, mountain passes, a stony desert in rain or snow - probably two or three days each way. If we *had* gone to Jerusalem despite all this, it is impossible to say how the trip and our lives might have been affected. The landscapes, or the Holy City itself, could have struck us; and from Amman, roads led east to resonant destinations: Baghdad, Iran, India. But our time was limited, and the centripetal pull of the Mediterranean world was stronger at that time. More roads not taken.

Laurent, our friend from T. Cook, is the latest of our Great Benefactors. He is also a singer of concert stature, a friend, & a quick discerner of our fatigued state of mind. He took us to a rehearsal of Xmas music, to dinner & a movie tonight, & has invited us to move to his house for an indefinite stay. Dazed & grateful, we've accepted all this, as well as tickets to an operetta he's appearing in.

At the rehearsal, Hector and I sat in the darkened nave of a Maronite church while Laurent's choir sang from the loft. (Maronites are a Lebanese branch of Roman Catholicism, named for St. Maron.) When they began to perform *Cantique de Noel* and the clear tones of the solo rang out, we were startled to recognize our friend's voice. The dapper little travel agent was also a trained and powerful tenor.

Met another of the int'l camaraderie staying here, a 33-year old American with a high-school education, traveling alone. He's been gone for 3 yrs. on this jaunt, working here & there, pushing on, low on money, very friendly. A nice guy, to whom it was easy to talk. He's feeling pressed to call it quits. He corroborated my guess that teaching is the best profession to enable one to travel. He spoke highly of Australia's standard of living, & of their need for teachers.

I found Stan interesting at first, and his relaxed manners wore well. It was a couple of days before I realized that - considering his experiences - he was actually rather dull, which was food for thought. The personal benefits of all this travel were *not* given or automatic; they depended on what you carried with you. His prospects for finding happiness and/or prosperity in America after years abroad looked dim to me. Also staying at the *pension* was a young Australian woman, flying from London to Sydney - with stopovers, obviously. Jeanette, who had been teaching in Canada and Athens for two years, went out of her way to find us some addresses of North African youth hostels.

Then there was the strange interweaving of my moodiness & memories of Penny, making the day sometimes grey but often rose. This afternoon I became very dispirited & restless. Xmas decorations had a lot to do with it, & hurrying shoppers; perhaps I am a little fatigued of traveling & need some home life; or I just need Penny.

Beirut was a feast of social warmth, nostalgia, and Yuletide cheer between stretches of relatively ascetic and outer-directed travel through alien scenes. Homesickness had not appeared until now – among familiar carols, strings of colored lights, and throngs bearing gifts. Laurent said, "Christmas is better in a Christian city," meaning Beirut; but it was also more poignant, and repressed longings surfaced. In Beirut, for the first time since Greece, I let other humans - absent or present - lay claims on me. This was bittersweet, reminding me of all I was missing on this trip. Long, deep, soulful conversations about life and love, for example, such as I had had with Phillip: Hector and I did not communicate like that. At the Catholic services to which Laurent took us, with music flooding over me, I would look at the icon of the Virgin Mary and see Penny. This mixed adoration, both intimate and reverent, seemed entirely appropriate and satisfying - though I knew it would appall Penny.

That morning we visited Lebanon's National Museum, the locus of archeological interest in Beirut. It was quite new and well laid-out, but after Athens and Istanbul the contents seemed slight. Enough Neolithic pottery already! Stone slabs bearing some of the earliest Phoenician alphabetic inscriptions, bas-reliefs, treasures from the royal tombs at Byblos - including attractive bronze figurines with gold-leaf decoration - and massive sarcophagi formed the bulk of the collection. Except where touched by Egyptian influence, most of the work struck me as journeyman in quality, without individuality or any salient characteristic. I wondered if the virtues of Phoenician and Mesopotamian art were simply not on my wave length, and looked forward to Egypt more than ever.

At midday we moved to Laurent's apartment building - not "house" - halfway across town to the south, in the *Achrafiyeh* district. My first impressions of Beirut had by then been largely confirmed:

The buildings are new & modern, with apt. houses in pastel colors & rounded balconies. Downtown shops are well equipped, & many people speak French & English as well as Arabic. It's a rare conversation that's not at least bilingual. B. is wealthy: many American & [new] cars, few beggars & no slums [seen] yet. One or two mosques date to the Crusades, & the Museum has objects from 2000 BC; otherwise the city is devoid of historical interest. It is nevertheless pleasant.

Those who had warned that Beirut lacked the antiquities of other Levantine cities were basically right, then. What they did not know (but Laurent did) was that Beirut *at Christmas* would evoke memories and associations that those other places could not, opening doors to Christmases past. Nor had they mentioned that Beirut would have on display more attractive women than any city since Naples. Watching men and boys hold hands, walk arm in arm and confide like lovers, I wondered where a different concept of masculinity ended and homosexuality began in these lands. We read, and were told, that this behavior had to do with females being withdrawn into *purdah*. Yet looking around we saw few veils, and lots of high heels and well-packaged figures that came equipped with hands to be held.

Dec. 20, chez Laurent, 9:30 PM - Our threesome walked today through the campus of the American University, which is very attractive with its palms & Stanfordian architecture, & along the surf-spattered coast to Pigeon Rocks, where great yellow rocks jut 100 feet above white water.

This walk, which introduced me to the American University of Beirut, was more important than I realized then. I did not exclaim, "Eureka! I will prepare myself to come back here and teach," but the seed was planted. It was just the sort of discovery that a *Wanderjahr* is supposed to produce.

Went this AM to a rehearsal of The Cupid & the Cutlet, as I'm to prompt Monday. Although the operetta is nothing & most of the talent mediocre, it was fun to be again on the fringes of show biz. I was amazed by the trilingual ease of the conversation.

The operetta was a bit of Italian fluff in which Laurent had a leading role. As in most of my brushes with the stage, I occupied a marginal "friend-of-a-performer" niche.

I've sung in concerts before with little preparation, but today took the cake. L. put me in the choir at a convent where he was soloing on "Holy Night." I walked onstage with hardly a prior glance at the music, & read, bluffed, mouthed & bellowed my way thru the program. It was fun to sing again, esp. Xmas music.

An amazing development: L. has decided that I have a good voice & musical talent; not only is he encouraging me to study piano & voice, but speaks of helping me financially & [with] influence. It's something to think about.

I thought about it a good deal over the next few months. Laurent might have little money or influence to offer, and none that I would take, but that wasn't the point. Not since Greece had serious cogitation about a career occupied my mind; I was shocked to think how much time - time that was supposed to produce a decision - had slipped by without any discernible progress. Thus when an answer, however improbable, was proposed, it was relief and gratitude that opened the door, rather than critical judgment. Since nothing seemed to be happening inside me, I was ripe for an implant, and the idea of a musical career simmered on one burner or another for the rest of the trip.

On the 21st Hector and I used my scooter to fetch the Christmas tree that Laurent had picked out. Hector sat in back, supporting the 8-foot pine vertically. We were quite a sensation, cruising through central Beirut with our coniferous hazard to overhead wires. I took the long way home to avoid the city center, but got lost and went through most of the downtown anyway.

We rode out to the Foret des Pins behind the Museum & walked around. It's pastorally pretty, but not yet landscaped. Walked again around the AUB, tasting the college flavor, ogling the Milk Bar & peeping in the busy hospital. [That] night I went with L. to the performance of his operetta at Beirut College for Women. No prompting was needed, & neither was I.

Baalbek

Laurent insisted - with the full authority of Thomas Cook - that we go see *Baalbek* ("Lebanon's most interesting ruin"). Having grown soft in four sybaritic days, we were slow to swing back into our saddles, and puttered out of Beirut at the leisurely hour of 9 AM, packs and all, planning to camp somewhere and give Laurent a rest. Their weight helped to make the ascent of the foothills a tough haul, though from their pine-forested upper reaches we had vistas of Beirut's white tongue lapping at the Mediterranean. Then came our real challenge: the grades of the main range. The tangible, yard-by-yard sense of gain when climbing mountains on the scooter had not lost its appeal for me. Each bush or boulder passed, each hairpin ascended, felt like an inchworm-like extension of self, and a victory.

Dec. 22, chez Laurent, 6:30 PM - Just back from an exciting, cold, & worthwhile day trekking to & from Baalbek. The road climbs sharply up the mts. behind Beirut, drops into a narrow valley separating the Lebanese from the anti-Lebanese range which borders Syria, & then runs north for 40 kms. across a rolling colorful plain to Baalbek. The ruins of the great temples are the most immense & impressive I've seen anywhere, including Greece.

Approaching the modern village, we wondered if a couple of small outlying ruins could be the famous site. But in a few more minutes, half a dozen 70-foot granite columns, topped by a massive, ornate cornice, rose behind the villagers' humble houses, and we knew that we had found the ruins of Roman Baalbek.

The Temple of Bacchus is in good condition, the Propylaea & Cour des Autels fairly so, & there is enough left of the Temple of Jupiter to overwhelm you. The scale is gigantic, the stone-cutting sometimes delicate; the total impact - with a backdrop of snowy mountains - dramatic almost to the point of awe. The history of Baalbek - from Biblical legends (Cain, Solomon, Abraham) to Roman construction - is interesting, & adds meaning to the buildings. Much of the stone came from Egypt, as far south as Aswan. Very enjoyable.

We had the site almost to ourselves, but restoration and excavation were still proceeding, so it would probably be a greater tourist attraction in the future. In one photograph, Hector stands before a fallen piece of cornice; it is on the ground, but he still has to look *up* to the lion's-head waterspout. Another shows grey clouds hiding the mountain tops where the cedars once were, and fresh snow powdering brown hills below the overcast. As we prowled the ruins, dark clouds blew in, preparing an ambush.

The trip back must have been received by the gods as payment against some debt. My scooter, burning too much gas, ran onto reserve 15 kms. from Baalbek. I had fits getting it started. Then I ran out entirely in 10 more kms., which really bothered me. Fortunately there was a station only 2 kms. away.

Pushing my clumsy load along, I had ample time to reflect on a) the complete idiocy of not filling up in Baalbek; b) what might have increased my fuel consumption so sharply right after a service; c) the chances of having any major engine problem repaired around here; and d) the awkwardness that this sort of performance could create in Africa. The plains that had seemed "colorful" in the morning looked bleak and inhospitable under louring clouds. A fresh wind sprang up - from ahead, of course. When I pulled back out on the road after refueling, the darkening air was filled with a fine, hardly palpable mist; as we climbed away from the somber plains, this "dampening on" became a drizzle, and we stopped to put on our ponchos.

The difficult haul over the mountains, about the steepest we've faced, was done in a cold, hard rain. I had more power & cutting-out troubles. I'm afraid there is something badly wrong.

Several times, on hills that Hector was taking in second or third gear, my motor felt and sounded as if it were dying until I downshifted to first. Was EE 1068 rotten inside? A premature dusk descended on the desolate heights about four. I switched on my headlight through the highest stretch, where damp cloud-tendrils blew across frosty subalpine barrens. It looked a lot like the Greek mountains in November. My damp shivers shook the Lambretta.

But all troubles were rectified by a few minutes' vision of impressionistic paradise as we descended the seaward side & broke out of the clouds. Through the rain-smeared windshield I saw the grey blanket tear & lift, revealing a deep gorge & fertile valley to my right, catching the low rays of the sun on red roofs, a thick rainbow standing up from its fields; the golden-yellow glow of the muffled sun filled the sky to my left. One huge purple cloud to the south was edged with burning orange; Beirut was revealed on its promontory, touched with white light; 10,000 feet above the city, a billowy cumulus was etched white against a patch of blue sky. It was pure nature touched by pure art, & worth all hardships just to be part of it.

Not until I noted the date did the full meaning of this expedition strike me: this had been our solstitial observance. Baalbek, like the solstice, was all about the sun. Baal, a Canaanite deity, held the title *Lord of the Sun*; the Greek name for Baalbek was *Heliopolis*, "Sun City." He was also Lord of its opposite, the storm, of the weather generally, and of the seasons, which made him the god of fertility/ infertility (his worship included an annual death-and-resurrection cycle). The Romans connected him with both Jupiter, their top thunderer, and Bacchus, god of the harvest, which was why they had the biggest temples at Baalbek. Baal was also *Lord of High Places*, so we should have expected a display of his powers on Mount Lebanon.

After all our packing, the inclement weather chased us back to Laurent's warm, dry apartment that night. We had seen no campgrounds or signs to them, and flinched from free-camping up near the pass in freezing rain. "Fortunately he really seems to like us," we told each other, and made our peace with staying until we sailed.

We've been having an on-&-off conversation with L. about politics. Net impressions: Arabs are treacherous & self-interested, nowhere to be trusted; Moslems here are anti-American & anti-Christian, feelings which were fanned by the 1958 crisis involving the Marines; the Americans made great mistakes by going against the British & French in Suez & doing what they did here; ex-Pres. Chamoun was a shrewd man whom we should have left in power, & he is now climbing back to the top with a new political party; Lebanon is more than ½ Christian.

I took this as "the Lebanese view" of Mideast politics, but Laurent was exercising the host's privilege of indoctrinating visitors; it was years before I realized the extent of his Maronite bias. Arabs, of course, had no monopoly on treachery or self-interest. And who *were* "Arabs"? Was he not one? By Arabs he meant Muslims, not Christians. Did Muslims' "anti-Christian feelings" perhaps mirror the anti-Muslim feelings he displayed? What the U.S. did in 1958, I learned, was to help uphold the Lebanese constitution, which forbid the president from succeeding himself. And while Lebanon was "more than half-Christian" (Maronites, Greek Orthodox, Roman Catholic, etc.) *when the last census was taken*, that was in the 1930s; the Maronite-dominated government had not held one since. By 1959 no one knew what the proportions in the demographic mix were, but it was widely believed that the Muslim component was increasing. If *they* had a majority now, the assumptions on which the constitution was based - according to which it delegated offices and power - were obsolete: it would have to be changed and the Maronites would lose control.

Byblos

The next morning I took my scooter back to the Lambretta workshop - the first we had seen since Istanbul - and ordered a proper tune-up. They installed new points ("*trés avancé*") and tinkered with the carburetor. Then we headed north along the new highway toward Byblos. Now my *maquina* was running fine - on the flat at least, and the next mountain was a long way off. We were humming along the expressway at 80 kph when two motorcycle cops waved us over. Big fellows, for Lebanese, handsome and formidable to behold, with well-padded leather jackets, helmets and dark glasses: the Marlon Brando-CHiPs look. Scooters weren't allowed on the freeway, they said. Sorry, we didn't know, was the obvious reply: there had been no sign. Then it came out that we were Americans, and that one of them had worked in Chicago for awhile, and that seemed to make a difference in the regulations. Okay, said Chicago, you can use the highway: just be sure to come back before 4 o'clock, when we go off duty. "Yes, *sir*!" Handshakes all around, great waving, and we separated, having learned something about the administration of law and order in Lebanon.

Byblos (in Greek, *Gebal* in Hebrew, *Jbail* in Arabic) dates from before 3000 BCE; some ancients thought it the world's oldest city. Around eighteen civilizations have dwelt there, including Stone Age, Neolithic, Egyptian, Phoenician, Hyksos, Assyrian, Babylonian, Greek, Roman, Byzantine, Turk, and Arab. The French excavation's trenches ran right to the edge of modern houses. Phoenician merchants exported cedars from Byblos to Egypt and imported papyrus, which they sold around the Mediterranean. *Biblion* became the Greek word for book (and the root of "Bible"). Baal was worshipped there, as was *Baalat Gebal*, "The Lady of Byblos." The Egyptians identified them with their gods Osiris and Isis, saying that the former's coffin was washed up at Byblos and found by the latter. For myth and history in Lebanon, you go to Byblos and Baalbek.

Some of this we knew as we explored the site, which was a rather unkempt clutter of broken sarcophagi, fallen columns and orphaned capitals, interspersed with oleanders and other native shrubs and wildflowers in bloom.

Most imposing is the 12th century Crusader castle, which has been used by successive occupations, & bears scars. There is a rusty cannon ball in one wall, fired by the British. The chief historical interest of B. is the finding there of the Sarcophagus of Ahiram, which bore the first traces we have of the Phoenician alphabet. Ahiram, a Phoenician king, died in the 11th century BC, & his sarcophagus is in the Beirut Museum. Other remains at B. are more sarcophagi, Assyrian & Persian foundations, Roman columns, & various walls.

There was also a well-preserved miniature Roman theatre that looked as if it might have been for children: five tiers of stone seats in a half-circle around the little orchestra, facing a stage raised perhaps three feet above the ground. If you lost interest in the play, you could just gaze at the Mediterranean a few hundred yards behind the actors. Nearby was an equally cozy little harbor, still used by fishermen, which probably explained why Byblos had always been a popular place to settle: there are not many such snug havens along this leeward coast.

Driving back from B. along the wonderfully green & pleasant coastline, we took off up a steep winding road into the mts. at Jounie. It didn't go into the hills, just climbed right up the face of them; rose serpent-like thru glinting forests of pine, coming out in a few mins. at "Une des plus belles vues du monde" near the imposing church school de Notre Dame. The view was as advertised, esp. with the sun coming into the sea behind Beirut.

It had not taken long to find a mountain after all! We raced up around the curves with exuberant whoops and motors at high rpm; then descended at a more restrained pace and whirred back into the city without misadventure, ahead of our own personal police deadline.

Yuletide

Christmas Day was to be a gala affair. In the morning we made preparations for Laurent's *soirée*. While Hector was off dining with an old friend (his former camp counselor) from Tennessee and his Lebanese wife, I spent a halcyon hour on the sunny balcony writing, and hoping that the sweater from Mykonos had reached Penny.

Christmas Day - We are still enjoying the semi-fanatical hospitality of Laurent. Helped decorate the Xmas tree yesterday, went to 2 church services last night. A few gaily wrapped packages lie under the tree. One is a Gilbert & Sullivan score book to L. from [us]; one a bar of chocolate to Hector. I feel grateful for the privilege of having any Xmas at all. At the same time, I feel keenly the incompleteness of spending it away from love, friends, home.

Reviewing what 1959 had meant, I counted my blessings and gave thanks for "a good year - in many respects the happiest & most fruitful of my life." My college career had ended successfully, and I had made some progress as a writer and musician, composing an essay and a piece of music that both won prizes. And it had brought me Penny.

It was the Windhome year, when I rediscovered nature & the value of silence. And it is the year when my convictions about the nature of travel, about a young man's choice of career, about learning the ways of the world, go from the blueprint into the action stage.

Our lives in Beirut had now become quite social, and sometimes educational. Staying with Laurent naturally involved us with his friends – whom I took to represent the Francophile, "Arab-free," Maronite Christian center - while Sara, a young Beiruti whom Hector had met on the *Conte Biancamano* and who had insisted that he look her up, tried to draw us into her circle. Its chief members were her girl-friends Samia (known as Sambo) and Sevin, both of whom spoke English and were better company than Sara.

Poor Sara: we all dislike her. She is something of an enigma, intentionally, I think...terribly sensitive, as petulant & unstable as a child, transparent & vulnerable in her moods. She borders on an hysterical personality.

Sara usually fixed me up with Samia. After a party I drove her home on my scooter, and she invited me up for a nightcap. When I hesitated, she said, "Oh, come on. My husband does not come for an hour, and it will be so boring": my first intimation that she was married. I pleaded a headache, but was grateful for the lesson in Beiruti *mores*.

One day Sara conducted us to *Le Petit Versailles*, a small replica of the real one. Some of the ornate reproductions from Versailles were exquisite, but the larger question of what this piece of *ancien régime* elegance was doing in the modern Middle East never came up in that company. It was, you might say, the *cloisonné* elephant in the room.

With both Sara and Laurent planning our time, a conflict of recreation directors threatened to develop, so we decided to introduce them to each other and ask them to mesh their activities. This worked, yet the social whirl soon palled. As overdue as I was for co-ed diversion, mere partying seemed superficial and dull after months of intense educational travel. I might have felt differently if the young women had been attractive or interesting, but they seemed only well-dressed, well-made-up, and expensively perfumed. Were we not their Christmas playthings? Our hosts could have spared most of their trouble; I preferred political discussions to being "entertained."

Laurent's Christmas party began at 5 PM. Sara, her two friends, two other young women, and two young men we had met before arrived in quick succession. We talked, danced, and overdosed on tea and pastries. At about 7:30, when it broke up – the guests had other parties to attend - Hector, Laurent, his niece and I scootered to the Bristol Hotel, which to my amazement had a small circular skating rink, and rented skates. The ice was rough and my skates were dull, but I had a good time, despite taking a glorious fall while skating backwards. Laurent's niece seemed to regard it as a special performance for her benefit. "*Joyeux Noël, mademoiselle,*" I said.

*

Fair weather blessed our day of departure. The sky was luminous, glowing azure behind Mt. Sannine, the snowy ridge that backdrops Beirut. Laurent and his friend Enrico treated us to ice cream and orange juice at a restaurant overlooking the sea at Pigeon Rocks. Our waitress was a young German who was traveling *counter*clockwise around the Mediterranean on a motorcycle and thus knew the route we might take. "What's it like?" we asked. "How are the roads? Is there gas? Can we do it?"

"*Ja, warum nicht?*" she shrugged. (She did *not* say, "*Dumkopf*! You vill be facing headvinds!") We purchased our tickets on the *Achilleus* ($25 each: two weeks in Greece!), negotiated customs, and boarded, all under the supervision, and sometimes the financing, of Laurent. The goodbyes were effusive on our side, surprisingly low-key and subdued on his. I wondered if we had been important to him, at least as a diversion, or had disappointed him. Would he miss us?

When we sailed at four, he and Enrico were still on the pier. Laurent looked rather forlorn, and I felt an unexpected twinge to be leaving. "Quite a little guy," said Hector, as we leaned on the railing and watched him across a widening gulf. The ship backed in a half-circle and gathered way: west, then south. For an hour we had splendid panoramas of the aureate city under its snow-capped mountains as the sun descended. This was how Phoenician sailors saw the coast, and the view for which they named it *lubnan*: "of a milky whiteness." The eastern sky was pale, the sea dark. At dusk I came inside to write a *post mortem*.

Dec. 26, aboard Achilleus bound for Port Said, 8 PM - Lebanon & the Near East lie behind, & we enter an exciting stage of the trip: Egypt, southwesternmost prong of the ancient W. Asian cultures, the "anvil of civilization," & chief object of my fantasy for months. We will be at Port Said in the morning, & hope to drive along the canal to Suez, thence to Cairo. It is - at last - Africa.

Deck class is almost genteel: we are no more than a dozen passengers in a fairly large, clean, & airtight room; a good commissary & a well-lighted dining room adjoin; smells are nil.

What could they possibly mean by "deck class," anyway? Warm, clean, odorless, colorless, it had nothing in common with Greek deck *passages*. Thinking back to our companions on those, I knew they would join in my laughter. Deck class, indeed. Perhaps the designers had lived privileged existences under the Czars. All we lacked were beds.

I've been reading Durant's pages on Egypt, trying to jog my emotions with anticipation. I'm not capable of it anymore, except in brief flashes.

I wondered if apathy was related to general health. My physical condition - underweight, undernourished, weak from bouts of illness, penny-pinching and a third-world diet - was poor, my resistance low; cuts and scratches healed slowly. Ribs were a prominent feature of my torso. It was difficult to find nutritious food that was cheap enough to fill up on, and discouraging to be losing weight on the same diet that sufficed Hector. Good food might be even harder to locate in Egypt, while poor and dubious fare would in all likelihood be generally available for a song.

I was still trying to make sense of Beirut. What *was* it, really? What did it think it was doing? The parts of its society we had seen were very Christian, yet it was the capital of an eclectic, multi-faith country

set in the midst of Arab & Jewish lands. No wonder it's cosmopolitan. The use of languages is a measure of the social order: Arabic in the lower, less-educated classes; French is the salon society language; English is useful & commercial. There turned out to be a large number of beggars, but the city is, in the main, prosperous.

The people are hospitable: exhibit A was Laurent. We owe him 6 nights of lodging, 8 meals, 10 taxi rides, 2 movies, a Xmas party, 2 hot showers, 1 shoe polishing, 4 sock darnings, much laundry, 1 shoe repair, 2 facial massages, 1 stud & tie-clip set, a box of chocolates, 5 boxes of cheese, 2 loaves raisin bread, a 10-liter water bag, a box of Tide, a 5% discount on our boat tickets, & much musical encouragement & morale-building. He's done much to convince me of the advisability of a musical career. I'm ready to travel some more.

In two paragraphs I had written myself from apathy to enthusiasm. But…shoe-polishing, sock-darning and facial massages? I drew no inferences from them, or his apparent lack of a girlfriend. It did not occur to me at the time that Laurent might be gay, and that that might be the source of his interest in us. We thought of him as an artist. The "taxi" rides were in *services,* Mercedes-Benzes that shuttled back and forth along set routes and picked up as many passengers as they could hold for 25 *piastres* (8 cents) a head: my first glimpse of this splendid system.

Hector's friend Leo, resident in Egypt by way of Harvard, is a wealth of information. I met him today - a common-sensical person. He says that the roads from Alexandria to Tunis are passably good, & gas plentiful. I'm ready to try it.

Leo's friends, I later discovered, did not consider him a "common-sensical person"; what I picked up on was his good will and "wealth of information." He knew the area well, spoke Arabic, was working for the UN in the Egyptian Delta, and wanted us to visit him there. He would be, in fact, our next Great Benefactor, and for once we had met him ahead of time, before we had left our last one. Maybe we were finally getting the hang of this business.

I spread my sleeping bag on one of the padded bench seats and settled down for a good rest; entering Egypt might be an ordeal. The classical hero's enemies tried to catch him when he was sick, tired, injured, or off guard. It might work the same for us; the readiness is all. Wooing sleep, I mused on how we had spent our time and how it might have been different. Had we stayed on in the Pension Australia we would probably have seen more of the country. We had not made the easy run down the coast to Sidon and Tyre, nor up to the River of Adonis "where the names of famous men are written." We had not even tried to reach the cedars, now reduced to a couple of pockets in the mountains; the Ottoman Turks had felled them to burn in their locomotives on the Lawrence-doomed Hejaz railway, and now goats devoured the seedlings. Unlike our hard-traveling, must-cover routes, these were side trips, options, and we had a tendency to pass them up.

Yet Beirut without Laurent would have been much poorer, and was in any case unimaginable now. All told, Lebanon had been as welcoming a haven as we could have wished for our Christmas; Baalbek alone, I thought, was worth the stayover. The thrumming of the *Achilleus'* engines down below gradually mingled with the mythic churning of my mind. Was that a waft of perfume from fragrant trees ashore? Let Achilles bear me away from Phoenicia to the land of Isis and Osiris, where the cedars had gone!

> Thy lips, O spouse, drop as the honeycomb:
> honey and milk are under thy tongue;
> and the smell of thy garments is like the smell
> of Lebanon.
>
> *The Song of Solomon*

VII: Gifts of the Nile

Was ich besitze, seh ich wie im Weiten,
Und was verschwand, wird mir zu Wirklichkeiten.

Goethe

(What I possess, I see as if at a distance,
And what vanishes, seems to me Reality.)

The bench seat and lounge provided a comfortable night's sleep, but I became restless at 4:30, rose and went outside. It was still pitch black (a week past the solstice, we had light from about 6 until 5) except ahead, where Port Saïd glowed on the southern horizon. The soft slap of waves was audible over the engines' dead-slow beat. Gaza lay low and invisible to the east, but the hush and prescient brooding darkness lent themselves to thoughts of the tormented Strip. The "inscape" of the hour seemed Gazan, without any visual correlate. As it was unpleasant to see nothing and be vaguely uneasy, I went back to "bed."

Dec. 27, Youth Hostel, ISMAILIA, EGYPT, 9 PM - Made it to Egypt, our 3rd corner of the Mediterranean. Dawn revealed the busy shipping traffic of Port Saïd. Long breakwaters reach out into the sea to start the [Suez] Canal. It is a well-equipped, modern port; freighters of every flag & description were in the harbor.

We were still a mile or so from the quays at first light, but already the flat, sand-colored shore partially enclosed us in long arms. Port Saïd barely broke the skyline, except where cranes and masts created an ebony filigree above the docks. The Canal was said to be bringing in 30 million Egyptian pounds a year: not bad for a poor country. To our right, west, the coast stretched toward Alexandria, merging gradually with a bleached sea and sky. On our left was the emptiness of eastern Egypt. Why did it seem ominous? We didn't intend to cross *that.* I must be in the grip of romantic fantasies. Small customs and baggage boats began homing in on the *Achilleus* like hungry predators.

We spent an hour on the boat plus 3 hours on shore clearing police & customs. Total cost, about $5 each. I won't dwell on it: it was the old stuff.

By 10 AM we were standing with our scooters in downtown Port Saïd, duly certified for travel in Egypt. The interval had smacked of earlier bureaucratic encounters, and I was relieved to come off so lightly and cheaply. Various "agents," speaking some broken English, had put themselves forward, each insisting that we would need *him* to survive the "formalities." We chose one, or were awarded to him, and he took us through the procedures, eventually naming his price, over which we haggled. The details of this little comedy, played out on the docks and in the offices of Saïd, are unimportant, but it was wonderful how *baksheesh* – our money, distributed by him - could smooth the roughest path. In the end there was a marriage of convenience between Extortion and Bribery.

Free at last, we drove around the city for an hour. It is very modern, spacious, generally clean, & growing. Minarets have squared corners, & are often of light brown stone, tasteful & suited to the countryside. Along the sea-front boulevard, single dwellings & apartment houses are springing up, sharp in greys & whites, with balconies. This is the area bombed in 1956 by the British & French, & all rebuilt since.

Wonderful how a little bombing opens up a neighborhood, making it "spacious" enough for "very modern" buildings and giving it a certain macabre interest! (An old Baedeker says flatly, "The town of Port Saïd is uninteresting; the traveler may take the first train to Cairo.") Most of it appeared to postdate the building of the Suez Canal. The unweathered sandstone would have been more attractive had the light facades not reflected an unrelenting sun, strengthening the aura of hot dry sandiness prevalent even on December 27th. It was somehow comforting - like running into an old friend abroad - to learn that the ancient city in these parts was *Baal-Zephon*: the Old Guy's writ ran here, too.

Phoenician merchants brought the cedars, and religion follows commerce, says Durant.

After a pick-up lunch (long on carbohydrates as usual) we began our Egyptian travels, unpromisingly enough, by traversing industrial and military zones.

At about 2 we started south along the Canal Road, for which we had obtained permission. Near the city on the south was a heavily built-up area with RR freight yards, unloading facilities & piers, & much barbed wire.

The road crossed a small, concrete-paved tributary canal - where policemen at a guardhouse inspected our papers - then passed into fertile country bordering the Suez Canal's west bank. The landscape, vastly different from what we had been seeing and thus of interest, left a welter of sense impressions too numerous to absorb: the visual counterpart of hearing music from an unfamiliar culture for the first time. I could not tell whether the visual edges were harder or softer than usual, but everything looked strange.

Palms waved overhead, high grass with white cylinders on the end edged the road; groves of trees occasionally appeared along the [way]. Saïd is out on a peninsula, so we had open water on both sides for awhile.

I know now that those were royal palms and pampas grass, and that the water belonged to the swamps and ponds of Lake Menzaleh, part of the delta of the Nile and site of two of its seven mouths, but I cannot *feel* them as I did that day. Unfamilar dark-leafed trees clustered in tight defensive formations against the hostile elements. Bit by bit the scene grew more arid as the lakes fell behind.

Then we settled into open country, increasingly desert, & roared at 70-75 kph [alongside] the 150-yd. wide canal. It is only one-way, except at one point, & the ships go in caravans.

In a side-by-side, full-throttle test on the empty road, my scooter, running better since the tune-up in Beirut (and I was losing weight), edged slowly ahead of Hector's at 50 mph.

Villages were few and small; the dark pavement ran straight as a ruler beside calm blue water. Once I stopped to take a picture of the Canal, and while on the embankment noticed a patrolling soldier not far off. I pointed to my camera, then to the Canal, and made an interrogative gesture. Silly me. He shook his head and wagged his finger sternly. I stalked back to my scooter, madder but wiser, drove half a mile south and took a photograph.

A few diaphanous veils of rain now hung down to the sandy plain; we hummed through one without slowing. It was still sprinkling lightly as we stopped at a police checkpoint in the waste, wet and laughing. The officers caught the spirit, so our minutes there were warm with the transient fellowship of the road. Then off again, whirring over steamy pavement, pouring it on across the flat expanse, sniffing the heady perfume of parched land and hot asphalt freshened by rain, reveling in the alternation of void space with short bursts of verdure - until the Ismailia Canal branched off west across the desert toward Cairo. *West*! How long had it been? Had we then reached our farthest east? Already? I thought.

Ismailia, which we [reached] at 4, is a town of 120,000 [with] a series of beautiful parks which must equal Central Park in size, & exceed it in beauty. They are complete with tall palms, red & purple flowers, soft dirt & pine-needle paths, & exotic bird calls reminiscent of "Green Mansions."

The film, that is. Those rain-sweetened parks, "lovely, dark, and deep" in the cloudy twilight, spread from the banks of the canal toward the low buildings and damp streets of the town. During a search for the youth hostel, Hector suddenly cut in front of me to make a U-turn; caught by surprise, I hit the brakes and went down in a moment. Number two! I was up immediately, running the Lambretta, which was suddenly *beside* me, to a stop. It was a cool move, actually: like bouncing up after a slide in baseball. A small crowd gathered. Hector was solicitous and apologetic, but I had been following him too closely. Damage was minimal: the left side of the kneeguard was slightly bent but easily straightened, and my pack barely torn. Though shaken, I was unhurt; even my rear end, numb from smacking the pavement once, seemed none the worse for it. An old man in the crowd gave us directions to the hostel.

Ismailia gave us a cross-section of Egyptian life under the old and new regimes. We splurged at a hotel restaurant (soup, salad, steak, vegetables, fruit: 70 cents) to celebrate entering Africa and our first day in the #1 country on both our lists from the beginning. The Greek *maître d'hotel*, obviously pleased to have foreign guests, stayed at our table talking for half an hour, mostly lamenting the good old days under the British when Ismailia was a lively cosmopolitan city of 200,000. In seven years of Egyptian home rule, he said, it had lost 80,000 people, mostly non-Arabs, and was slowly dying. Gesturing around the dark, nearly-empty dining room, he said forlornly, "Now, it is not so good for us." An invitation to identify with that "us" was implicit. His grey suit and the restaurant's musty white curtains had a quiet, fading gentility. He spoke Greek, English, French, German, and Arabic: "I have needed them all."

We returned to the hostel after dark. The nervous warden at once sent us over to the local police, escorted by his "boy." Neither of them could or would tell us why, so our scurry across the dark square toward the lights of the station was suspenseful. But a gendarme welcomed us with quiet amity; he only wanted to check and stamp our passports. Remembering the same ritual in Syria - the other half of the U.A.R. – we relaxed. All was well. Stamp, stamp. Shake hands. Get out of there. We walked back to the hostel, where we were the only guests.

Later that evening the factotum brought ten or twelve local students, teen-age boys, into our dormitory. I was reading; Hector was already in bed. Looking up and seeing the swarthy throng push noisily through the doorway, I had a momentary qualm - what now? - but it was just friendly curiosity, which, while somewhat obtrusive, was harmless. Having heard that two Americans were in town, they wanted to shake hands and take pictures. The first was accomplished *con gusto*, Hector receiving in bed. He tried to demur at the photography, but they insisted, so he arose, pulled on his pants amid yelps of laughter, and they took their pictures. Good will abounded, and they departed after another orgy of handshaking. I gave one of them my address for a copy of the picture, but the mails have been slow.

In half an hour they were back with their teacher, who spoke English. He found me reading in the main room & welcomed me cordially to Egypt while his charges shushed each other at the door. They wanted to know why I had come to Egypt & how I liked it. I made my reply carefully, & he seemed satisfied. More good wishes, & they left.

A few minutes later four men drifted in, sat down, & struck up a conversation. Two were chemists working at "the lab" and teachers; the other two seemed connected with the hostel.

They were as disciplined as the boys had been unruly, but had not come to banter compliments. "Why is there so much anti-U.A.R. propaganda in the American press?" they asked. "Why are they so pro-Israel?" The game was on. "We sympathize with Jewish suffering during the war," I said. "But why take that out on the *Arabs*?" they countered. I was already out of my depth, knowing Mideast politics only through mainstream US print media, which they had read more carefully and critically than I. "Why didn't the U.S. support Egypt in 1956?" "It did!" I sputtered, but they thought otherwise. "Your papers are controlled by Jews," said another. I denied that, realizing at the same instant that I knew nothing about it. My defense was energetic but ill-informed and wholly inadequate; my visitors seemed to have a lifetime supply of grievances.

Hard-pressed, I tried a counter-offensive: by accepting Russian help on the Aswan High Dam, weren't they risking economic dependence and political infiltration? They smiled, allowed that to be a risk, and promised to be careful. At last we agreed on something: the inaptness of John Foster Dulles to his office. They closed on an amicable note, expressing respect for and confidence in Americans. I tried to pick up that tune, eulogizing their pre-colonial past and hoping that they would regain that glory. When they left at 11 I was bathed in sweat, having been made painfully aware of my ignorance. As an ambassador, I felt sadly *manqué*: more chastened than innocent. Vowing to learn more and do better next time, I went to bed. It had been a long day.

On Monday - aka Mail Day - we rose at 7, heated milk (using Laurent's Sterno-like solid-fuel tablets) in our room, and used it to wash down some cheese. The hostel boy came sniffing around, but we said we smelled nothing, so he shrugged and went away. And I had once been a judge on a student court! Breakfast over, we tied our packs on the scooters, which had spent the night in a glassed-in rear vestibule, away from curious crowds. I had taken the rare opportunity of having a workshop to clean and gap my spark plug – which it usually needed after a full day's run - and adjust the mixture (still set for Mount Lebanon) to sea level. By the time we finished, paid our bill, and rolled the machines outside, the sun was highlighting the foliage of the palms, and Ismailia's birds and children were audibly abroad. It was eight-thirty.

The parks between broad empty streets and the canal looked pleasantly cool and fresh, but once the narrow channel left Ismailia and started west it was crossing desert. The road (and railroad) hugged the bank, so *we* were never quite in the waste; still, it was Out There - beyond the verdure, half a mile from the canal - gleaming a tawny Old Ivory, scarcely distinguishable from the whitish sky except where darkened by cloud shadows. The *fellahin*'s toehold was small, then, but the narrow strip of green was a delight, more precious for its tenuousness. Big lateen-rigged *dhows* – one mast forward, two booms and a tattered white triangular sail - plied a waterway flanked by earthen embankments and clumps of lush grass. Eucalyptus trees lined much of the road and overhung the water in places. Sometimes a small plain opened out where a palm or two stood guard over a cultivated field.

Villages with mud houses appeared at intervals, & an occasional minaret reflected the desert color, gleamed a moment in the water & was gone. Snooty camels trod the high path opposite. Gradually we came into the delta of the Nile, & the swath of green widened out to as far as the eye could see. Hut villages in palm groves were on all sides, & the countryside [was] a deep green as we advanced on Cairo.

Its desert passage just a memory, the asphalt ribbon unrolled smoothly through tree-tunnels, curved among huts, faces, and palm fronds, then straightened again alongside the life-giving water. Sunlight poured through a thin overcast. When we stopped for gas at an unsigned station, olive-skinned villagers crowded close: silent, curious yet fearful; when I said "*Marhaba*!" to a little boy he jumped back. The flies were thick and cheeky. There was little dust in the air, but underfoot the soil was soft and sensuously smooth to the touch, like fine sand. In the palm groves bordering the canal, the dank earth teemed with generative vitality. Robed and turbaned Arabs moved slowly or stood immobile among stately trees in the forest-park, like figures in a nineteenth-century engraving of "Exotic Egypt." We were probably as close to Egypt's *élan vital*, the eternal present of the peasants, I thought, as we were likely to come.

The road became straight, flat and smooth. We drove fast - too fast to take in the life around us. Obsessed by the desire to reach Cairo and collect our mail, we sailed through villages almost as quickly as we covered the open stretches in between. To pass the copious unfathomable green Egypt of the Nile Delta at that rate was profane, though it would have been naïve to imagine that we could "take in" the countryside at half the speed, or by halting: we would always be aliens there. So we raced on, reached the broad boulevards of Cairo before lunch and homed in on American Express, near the spacious *Place de la Liberation.* There were Christmas cards and checks from our families, but

the prize, of course, was 10 delicious letters from Penny. Can hardly describe how I felt during the 2 hours I was poring thru them…I had been so starved.

My last mail had come to Athens over a month before. We located the Garden City youth hostel in a quiet, European-looking neighborhood and found space on the second floor. Late that afternoon, lying on my cot in the large dormitory, oblivious to everyone, reading all Penny's letters twice until darkness fell, I was transported, a wanderer given a vision of home, and dozed off wondering tritely how I could be so lucky. My trip was well funded again; the checks more than offset the Turkish loss. Yet if, as Penny wrote, the answers to many of our questions "lie within ourselves & each other," I needed to review exactly what I was doing, and why.

Later there were more questions. Hector and I had taken an afternoon walk - down the Nile, across the Lower Island to Cairo University, through the lush Botanical Garden and back via the Upper Island - during which he met a young Egyptian who invited him out to dinner. The invitation included me, and there would be girls. I was not interested and pleaded fatigue; Hector went alone. He was sitting on his bed, head down, when I returned after a late dinner. Clearly something was wrong.

I sat down opposite him. "Hi. What's the matter?"

He looked up glumly. "Well…I've had it with the trip. I want to start home - right away."

I inhaled deeply, held it for a moment. This was not the day to ask *me* to construct a new and profound defence of the trip! "Okay. Why?"

"Well, my letters…" He paused.

"I *knew* it. I wish...," but choked on my gall.

"It's not *just* that. I can't see the *value* to any more travel. I want to go back and start *doing* something."

Oh no, I thought, I've seen this movie, but he looked so unhappy that I tried to empathize. "When will you go?"

"Drive to Alex in the morning and take a ship from there."

"Without seeing Egypt?!" I was incredulous, even indignant.

"Yes...I think so. I'm just not interested. But where does this leave you?"

He spoke so apologetically that I wanted to reassure him. "Well, I guess...go on as we planned."

"See Egypt...drive the desert by yourself?"

"I guess so, sure...or whatever seems workable" - trying for a brave, quiet pathos. He grimaced. "Anything I can say to change your mind?"

"I don't know. Probably not."

That was a ray, I thought, and wondered if there was something else. "Why don't you sleep on it? We'll talk in the morning," I suggested, trying to keep my voice calm.

"Okay, fair enough. Good night."

The next morning, as we walked downtown to look for breakfast, Hector said, "Well, I guess I'm all right."

"What?!"

"All right about the trip, I mean." And with an embarrassed laugh he told me what had happened the evening before. The Egyptian had taken him to a good restaurant. There were no girls, for which he apologized. His host insisted on ordering an expensive dinner: several courses, dessert and coffee. Toward the end he excused himself to make a phone call, or go to the men's, and didn't come back. Hector was stuck with the bill. The oldest one in the book, but not a book we had read.

"A con man, Hector! I wish I'd come: maybe with two we'd have foxed him. How much did you lose?"

He swallowed. "About forty dollars."

I was shocked: that was about half my Turkish fine... over three weeks' expenses in Greece. "That's brutal - but don't let him cost you the trip, too."

Hector admitted that the scam had depressed him, and, together with his letters, had just been too much at once. But in the light of morning things looked better, and now he was ready to go on.

That's fine for him, but his lack of enthusiasm hurts the trip: he says he's not enjoying it, doesn't think we can camp, so we don't, etc. His doubts cause me doubt, when I think the stronger course is to let reasoning wait. It is difficult to know the dimensions of the values involved. What constitutes a "worthwhile experience"? Is it enough to absorb, or must I be giving, too? I don't know, but I will go on.

I lay on my cot re-reading that paragraph. Where was this coming from? It was like automatic writing. I had not realized that I had been harboring resentments. Did this go back to Italy? Or maybe even to his stepping back last summer? The way I had jumped at his mentioning his letters as a reason…had I not felt myself waver the previous afternoon when reading Penny's? Evidently I had some repair work to do. This should not fester.

In any case, that cloud too seemed to blow over; we went to the Museum together that afternoon. *The* museum.

Dec. 29, Cairo Museum, Egypt, cultural focal-point of the trip, for which we've been prepared by books & examples of Egyptian culture in every country we've visited. Egypt is the basis of them all; farther back than this you don't go. The Egyptian Museum, showplace of the land's antiquities, [is] a large, domed, off-yellow stone building on the main (Liberation) square.

Having set the scene, I took a deep breath and started walking. If I had learned anything about taking in museums on our trip, this was the time and place to use it.

Old Kingdom rooms…steles, sarcophagi, statues & mastabas (ca. 2900-3000 BC), chiefly from Giza & Sakkara. …lifelike, touched with humor & humanism, & noble…hieroglyphics much like American Indian picture-writing…in a line of figures, a woman sniffs a papyrus plant…. Pink granite columns, flowering at the top into intricate papyrus leaves… Stele of a royal favorite known as "The Bitch." …The statues: poses are formal, stereotyped. Common one is wife with arm about husband's waist. Men are powerful, women of more modest dimensions. Some look ready to bust out laughing.

Mastabas are ancient Egyptian tombs or "death houses," usually with sloping sides and a flat roof. The collection was arranged chronologically so that one could follow the evolution of the arts – which sounds heavy, but the wit and charm of the artists lightened many of the exhibits.

Middle Kingdom - gaily painted stelae...impressive small sphinxes... New Kingdom...large granite statues of scribes, kings, gods, bulls... some from Karnak...sphinxes & lions' heads in black & brown marble. Several erected by or of Queen-King Hatshepsut. Represented as a man. A transvestite? ...Real prizes from Aknaten's reign...a wooden coffin, shaped to the body, inlaid with colored glass & painted - from Valley of Kings at Thebes...a tremendous falcon & king in black granite.

After two hours we could absorb no more and walked back to the hostel, but the museum was still churning away inside me, and I was too excited to stop writing about it.

The Egyptians had reason to worship the sun, & perhaps invented the "sun image." My search for it on steles & mastabas was often rewarded. During the period of "heresy" under Ahknaten, they worshipped Aten-the-Sun.

We were standing in front of the museum when it opened the next morning. As usual, we split up ("two independent travelers"), Hector branching off with a "See you later." A history major, he was in his element and apparently enjoying himself. I picked up where I had left off the previous day, in the New Kingdom rooms.

...shaped & carved granite sarcophagi - deep repose. Finds from Luxor - Emphasis on function: a statue, carving or inscription is [also] an offering table, door jamb or basin. Their art was tied up with their daily lives. It is not 'art for art's sake,' but for users' sake.

A modern music course at Debrew had acquainted me with the notion that one culture's utilitarian crafts could become another culture's art. Most rooms were crammed with small *objets d'art*, but something of interest almost always emerged from the mass of detail.

Graeco-Roman room: Memorial stelae to a bull-god (remember Crete) said to be born of a virgin heifer. Greek-influenced Head of Serapis: classical & very good...monuments from the Meroitic civilization of the Nubian tribes of Sudan. Ethnologically, the beginning of Africa.

...the scale becomes almost too great with vast numbers of statues, some 30' tall, in a sun-flooded hall, around the balconies of which

lie uncounted relics - statues, steles, vases, etc. You mount with awe to the limestone colossus of Amenophis III & wife. Granite statue of goddess Sekhmet: woman's body & lion's head. …on floor, an immense pavement of painted plaster…Much wildlife: geese, grasses.

"Almost too great" for what? To enjoy? To learn from? No: to describe, inventory, record with pen. Faced with this *embarras de riches*, I felt a strong need to order it somehow, to make it mine. An obscure feeling that this was a college final exam kept recurring. Was I now an educated man? Had I learned and retained enough to help on this field trip?

The prize Mummy Room: skull from 1849 BC… Gory one of Sitkamose, wife of Ahmose, much scraggly hair & buckteeth. Rameses V (1161 BC) looks like a boy I knew at Exeter.

Tremendous mass of dates, names, places, & mythology involved in appreciating the history of this country. Intend to plow back into Cottrell's Anvil of Civilization on the train

- the train to Luxor. In Beirut, Hector's hometown friend and mentor Leo had suggested that we go at once (while he was still in Lebanon) to Upper Egypt, heart of the country's antiquarian interest, and that we take the train, since the road was long and dusty and the rail fare cheap. At the railroad terminal I had found that this was true: $2.60 (3rd class) for the overnight, 450-mile ride. By the time we returned, Leo would be in Cairo to show us around.

…beautiful wood carving of a corpse couchant, hands crossed, face serene, falcons spreading protective wings. Huge gold couches, supported by golden animals - but time to go.

No one has told the Egyptians that it's almost January. It was a good 80° our first PM in Cairo, & almost as high each PM since.

Upper Egypt

That afternoon we stored the scooters in a courtyard behind the hostel – said to be secure - shouldered our packs and set out for the railroad station. We had been in Cairo only two and a bit days, spent mostly at The Museum, but would return, *enshallah*.

Our train was scheduled to leave at 4 PM. As we waited on the hot, crowded platform, an Egyptian Air Force cadet named Samir befriended us, saving places when the train arrived (he dove in through an open window) and later pointing out spots of interest. During the two daylight hours of the trip we had several glimpses of pyramids to the west, beyond palm groves: *Saqqara* and then *Dashur*. I hadn't known there were so many south of *Giza*. At twilight, Samir, who looked very young for military service – but then cadets *are* young! - announced that he was getting off. We thanked him for his help and exchanged addresses.

Nightfall, and the loss of our only English-speaking acquaintance, forced us to turn to ourselves and our immediate surroundings for amusement.

The train, tho' full, was not overflowing, & cleaner than the Turkish train. Our fellow-passengers soon changed that, however, with orange peels, eggshells, [chewed] sugar cane, spit, etc. A carload of students from Assiut, encamped about three cars back, discovered us

several hours after dark, and what had been a rather quiet and monotonous trip swiftly became surreal. Nothing would do but that we pay a social call on their car. We were afraid to leave our packs unguarded, so

they brought us each in turn back to their fold for a round of noise, adulation, & curiosity. It was interesting, & lots of fun. My "turn" lasted 45 minutes. Upon entering the car, I was given a standing cheering ovation

- my first and last (so far). Giving the Eisenhower wave redoubled the noise, I noted for future reference. I was gently but firmly pushed into a seat,

surrounded, & bombarded with questions. In a moment, however, a teacher came to rescue me, taking me back to a seat with himself & another teacher. Still I was pelted with questions, many repetitious. All of them spoke some English. I was sung to, fed, laughed over.... Only one touchy subject came up: Little Rock & integration, with a coal-black Negro by my side.

I was in diplomatic straits, basically agreeing with their accusations and ashamed of my country's record in that area, yet finding their view of race relations in America simplistic. I tried to explain that we hate most those whom we have wronged most, but that did not cross the language barrier. Subtleties and balanced exposition being out of the question, then, I sketched a somewhat optimistic picture of progress on civil rights and tried to change the subject.

Then a boy sitting behind me pulled me around by the shoulder, &, his face half a foot from mine, bellowed over the din, "Do you love Jesus?" I was about to yell, "Yes, Lord!"

but thought better of it: the boy was probably Muslim, and unused to jocular irony or revivalist jokes. Unsure what rules governed religious discussion there, I avoided any credo, asking him why he would question me about my beliefs, and confusing him with abstractions (such as "religion") when he just wanted to know if I was a Christian. Finally I shook fifty or so hands and went back to our car.

Hector and I took turns climbing up onto the overhead luggage rack and curling up in an empty space, or stretching out over our packs: the only way to sleep. In between such naps I got Arabic lessons, ate hard-boiled eggs, and drank glasses of hot tea peddled by the *chai* man. The night passed slowly. The train, much quieter after the students got off at *Assiut*, grew quite cold; I walked up and down the aisle a lot, muttering, "Deserts!" It was definitely good to see Luxor in the clear dawn. We walked west down the main street and watched the sun turn the columns of the Temple of Luxor to rose - until the first breakfast place opened.

Jan. 1, 1960, Victoria "Hotel," LUXOR, 5 PM - ...Arabs: the Egyptian version does not present itself as admirable. Poverty puts them in a debasing condition which all but rules out dignity. The children seem always to be begging or taunting, stealing or pushing for a shoeshine. And they are universally dirty. It's all too bad.

Egyptians are an ethnological melting pot. Skin pigments range from black to light bronze. Features may be Arab, Negroid, or Western. The prevalent dress is a robe, falling to the ankles, usually with vertical stripes of red, blue, or green against the white of the cotton. Some substitute pajamas. White turbans are common.

After sleeping out the morning of the 31st at the hotel, we spent that afternoon and all of New Year's Day at various monuments and tombs. My journals for the next few days chronicle visits to antiquities on both sides of the Nile. I applauded the color and vivacity of the art, criticized the worship of bigness, exclaimed over the recurrence of symbols. Overwhelmed by the volume of new information, I tried to set it all down, to assist my sievelike memory and preserve both facts and commentary.

In the town of Luxor proper there remains only the temple built by Amenhotep III, Horemheb, & Rameses II, noted for papyrus-bud columns. These are impressive, as are huge statues of Ramses II (177 children), but the chief interest lay in the multitude of reliefs. Some (protected from the weather) retain their bright paint, & [bas-relief inscriptions] are a common denominator of every antiquity on the east & west banks of the Nile. Scenes from everyday life, scenes of battle, hieroglyphics, & the worship of the gods are depicted, & the life imparted everywhere by the artists over 3000 years ago is a wonder.

Later we walked two miles north to Karnak, the other point of interest on the east bank, beset by children begging for *baksheesh* (gifts) throughout the dusty, palm-dotted village beside the ruins. We knew what to look for: the Avenue of the Rams, the Hypostyle Hall, and the Obelisk of Hatshepsut. Some of the rams had been decapitated or wasted, but they still made an impressive avenue. The Hypostyle ("columns within") Hall in the Temple of Ammon was said to be the world's largest: fifty thousand square feet, with 134 columns of both the spreading lotus-blossom and tight papyrus-bud designs.

Many capitals and some lower parts of columns retain brightly painted designs. The total effect is surprisingly harmonious - at once immense & artistic, a difficult combination. To the rear stands the graceful obelisk, quarried from Aswan red granite, ferried, carved, polished & erected in 7 months: 97' high, a single piece of stone covered with hieroglyphics.

Both hall and obelisk were in good repair and are still marvels, but neither was the high point of my visit. That came, as it often does, from an unexpected direction: a minor temple, slighted by Baedeker, a hundred yards north of the Temple of Ammon.

One of the most provocative sights was in the small Temple of Ptah. Karnak covers 600 acres, was worked on by many Pharaohs over 1200 years, & it is easy to bog down. The poetic impact of this

Temple was thus welcome. You approach thru several chambers & portals, the walls being carved & painted. Inside, a headless statue in brown granite of the god Ptah sits under a small square hole in the ceiling. On one day of the year, the sun passes exactly overhead & illuminates him brightly.

That day is, of course, the summer solstice. Even at the opposite end of the year, with the main door closed, a faint shaft caught some highlights in the granite, and Ptah seemed to preside at the bottom of an eerie luminous pool. His headlessness was a major part of the effect. (This is the deity hailed in *Aïda* as "*Immensa Phtha!*") As my eyes adapted to the gloom, I saw another door leading to an inner chamber, which surprised me, since I had already seen the god for whom the temple is named.

To the right is a smaller chapel containing a black granite statue of Sekhmet - the goddess with the cat's head. The hole in the roof admits the direct rays of the moon on one night of the year. What astronomers! With the door closed, this feline statue, inscrutable & sinister, seems not so much to reflect the overhead light as to emit a faint glow from within. The effect with the moon must be gigantic. She seems the personification of the eternal feminine. The natives won't go near her, & if I lived here I damn well wouldn't either.

And on what night of the year does the moon light up Sekhmet? The winter solstice would be a good guess. With the door closed, the room was a Stygian black; for a moment I could see nothing. Then, peering, I just made her out - and took a step back. From the leonine head a thick mane fell onto her breasts. One hand stretched toward me, one leg reached forward to take a step. She was darkness visible, black on black, and my profanity was an invocation. How could you *not* worship? I re-opened the door quickly, admitting daylight. That she would turn up in my dreams, poised to take that step, was a foregone conclusion.

On New Year's Day we paid the few cents necessary to procure places in one of the graceful *feluccas* that sail the Nile, and so got across to Thebes.

On the western bank, in the ancient City of the Dead, lies a vast array of archeological finds. The famed Ramesseum had little to show except the grandeur of enormity, & some good relief carvings.

I wondered if it could have been the Ramesseum that "a traveller from an antique land" described to Percy Shelley, who later sat down and wrote "Ozymandias." The upper half of a statue of Ramses lay on its back in the dirt; perhaps it was the missing part from the poem's "Two vast and trunkless legs of stone"! Hector stood beside the torso, his hand resting on its shoulder like a benign mosquito.

The Valley of Tombs of the Kings & Temple of Hatshepsut...hold their own with their counterparts across the Nile. The former are the rock-cut burial [caves] of nearly every Pharaoh. Along the corridors & in the chambers are numberless reliefs, often still painted.

Amazed by the high quality of the craftsmanship, and charmed by the stylized reality of the scenes, I felt that the bas-reliefs and inscriptions, not the pharaohs' golden or ivory trinkets, were the real treasures of the necropolis.

There is so much of the people's life in these - religious practices, work, wars, play - that I felt very close to the ancient Egyptians. Large numbers of gods appear, & we learned to recognize the manifestations of many. A recurrent scene is of Pharaoh sacrificing to or being embraced by deities. In the hieroglyphics I could pick out letters & symbols: the scarab-beetle (resurrected soul); the sun disk (life, power, fertility); the life & sex symbol [ankh]; & others. Fascinating, these folk-myths, the imagination-play of the people.

There was also the serrated line that represented water, i.e. *Nilus*, the Nile, and became our letter "N." Some of my favorite professors (and *their* favorite authors) would, I guessed, be much taken with these inscriptions - and probably had been.

Also of interest: the gold-covered mummiform coffin of Tuthankamen in its floodlit chamber; the sarcophagus of Amenhotep II at the end of a long line of decorated chambers; & Queen Hatshepsut's colonnaded temple [set] against sandy cliffs under blue sky.

The coffin of Tuthankamen that I considered "also of interest" was subsequently removed to the Cairo Museum and later sent abroad to international acclaim. It made a famously splendid cover for *National Geographic.*

The sites on the west bank were too numerous and far-flung for walking, so we joined forces with several other guests at "the Victoria" and hired a taxi, or rather a series of taxis, to move between them more efficiently.

Visited the Tombs of the Nobles, relatively of small interest. They are right in a village, & were spoiled by the constant begging of urchins. The Colossi of Memnon, in a field beside the road, are ruined as to detail, & recommended chiefly by their size (ca. 70 feet).

Hmmm...perhaps the Colossi, though not exactly trunkless, were the origin of Shelley's Ozymandias? Or there might be several candidates. According to ancient legend, these statues emitted musical tones when the sunrise touched them. Sometimes, I thought, looking at the worn old stones, you're better off settling for the legend. But my cavalier dismissal smacked of fatigue: it was time to ride back to the Nile, sail over and find repose in the City of the Living.

Jan. 2, Luxor, 7 PM - Walked out to Karnak again, & thoroughly enjoyed a 2 hour ramble. Re-covered much of Thursday's ground. A nostalgic return visit to the temple of Ptah & Sekhmet, where I was again struck by the   of the black statue.

I considered a number of nouns for the gap - power, *élan*, *enargeia* - but none seemed strong enough; a blank would have to do. Wandering among the remains of an ancient civilization's great art, I kept asking myself what *my* artistic philosophy was, or if I had one. What is the purpose of art? What part of us does it come from? Do such questions have single answers? Are my responses those of an artist, or an appreciator of art? Is it possible or permissible to work at art without an aesthetic philosophy? I thanked the old Egyptians for raising these questions, but had to admit that my own answers were still embryonic.

My stroll to the Temple of Mut & its Sacred Lake [revealed] nothing but broken statues & low ruined walls. Some Arab boys kept me company all the way, asking for "bak-sheesh." I am occasionally touched by this, but can't support 'em by myself. I grow daily more callous toward begging.

For the first time on the trip, it became difficult to feel charitable toward the natives: just where charity was most needed! In Egypt we were obvious affluents - our pose of genteel poverty, at best a relative truth or useful fiction, was just a lie here - and the universal cry for alms was distressing. "How best to help?" now became a daily dilemma. Every solution had its critics. Torn between *laissez-faire* liberalism ("begging is our worst problem - don't give"), cultural relativism ("do you really think Western affluence represents a step forward for these people?"), and the scorn heaped on any attempt to "take up the white man's burden," I groped for a tenable relationship to these people, whose unwashed bodies and seeming indolence grated on me even as their indigence appealed to my compassion.

How had they, how had things, come to this pass? Will Durant put forward a climatological explanation in *Our Oriental Heritage*:

...along [this] sandy belt across two continents civilization once built its seat and now is gone, driven away, as the ice receded, by increasing heat and decreasing rain.

Ah, but were *all* countries in the same climatic boat equally "de-civilized"? That would require observation and study. Other writers presented other theories, mostly racial - the Arab strain introduced in the 7th century was inferior to the ancient Egyptian line – or political: centuries of colonial rule had beggared and debased the people. But whatever explanation you tried, the fact of social-economic decline just sat there, like a great boulder (as Takis had said of Greek poverty on the *Miaoulis)*, defying you to move it.

Remained in the room this afternoon, reading & washing. I ain't feeling too good - lightheaded & sore throat.

This was also a region where unfamiliar diseases against which I had no immunity were endemic. My malaise, unlike earlier ones, refused to be shaken off in a couple of days.

Jan. 4, some Filthy Hole in Aswan, 11 AM - Despite much rest & little food since Jan. 2, I am sicker than ever: diarrhea, light-headed, often bordering on nausea, & very weak. I'm being made to learn the hard way the value of some elemental comforts - health, cleanliness, good food, someone to look after me when I'm sick.

I had to stay in from the day's excursion. Friends from the Cairo hostel arranged a boat trip. I should be out in this fine weather seeing Aswan Dam, Elephantine Island, Temple of Isis at Philae & the granite quarry. Instead I lie on this dirty mattress, uncomfortable, angry, wondering what my trouble is, in an 8-bed room whose inhabitants spit on the floor, blow their noses in the lavatory, stare at me for 15 solid minutes & turn on lights in the middle of the night.

Lying there feeling sorry for myself, knowing that months of scrimping on meals must have lowered my resistance, I had no patience with the lower-class Egyptians among whom I was living. Why were half of them still sitting on their cots at midday, looking at me? Were they sick, too, or just idle? During the long, hot, tiring train ride from Luxor to Aswan the previous day, it seemed that a whole carload of open-mouthed, sleepy-eyed peasants would stare at us for minutes at a time. It looked so *stupid* (i.e. "stupefied") that I could hardly believe my eyes, and returning the stares had no visible effect. Yet those who sat near enough to converse with us had been friendly.

Once our train stopped on a dusty siding next to a slatted boxcar full of sugarcane. In two seconds an Arab was leaning out every window on that side, his feet anchored by another man, hauling in sugarcane stalks hand over fist. When we started again a minute later our aisles were several inches deep in the stuff. During the feeding frenzy that followed, I was persuaded to try the cane, despite my misgivings about its cleanliness. My obvious surprise at discovering that the chewed fibers had to be spat out after the sugar had been extracted was good for a laugh. So there had been some light moments, but also the dirt, the staring, the complete absence of privacy and sanitation.

This morning I was walking back from breakfast (ate at the Grand Hotel to get some good food; the Arab waiters looked archly at my clothes), when a Jeep containing 4 Arabs ran over a large black dog. They neither slowed, swerved, nor honked: just crushed it & sped on. The dog lay twitching & yelping in the street for a minute, then relaxed & died. A truckload of Arabs slowed down to pass him, & a few smiled. I almost vomited. Life here must be very cheap.

Was this an example of why some visitors condemned Arabs as cruel? Of course the episode provided no evidence that *human* life was cheaper here than elsewhere: only that the attitudes underlying the formation of the SPCA had not yet developed. Here, dogs were not pets but feral creatures, often roaming in packs, considered low life-forms and assumed to be disease-bearing. Whether the foundations of this view were religious or social, it existed - and not only in Arab countries, it turned out. I had some idea of my own culture's beliefs, but not of the global picture.

Aswan was astir with preparations for Pres. Nasser's imminent visit; he was scheduled to arrive the following week to declare that *work* on the High Dam had officially begun! With gaudy banners spanning the streets,

wooden platforms going up, the youth league marching with rifles in the street, the loudspeaker of a minaret nearby has been playing military marches, political news & recorded cheering for 2 hours. It went on at 5 AM with the call to prayer. Nasser-worship is even more prevalent here than Ataturk-worship in Turkey. His handsome face is inescapable on wall posters, framed photographs & paintings in stores, in magazines & newspapers, & in busts of various dimensions & materials. Nationalistic fools.

At times it seemed that mechanization and brainwashing were the main lessons that the Land of the Pharaohs had learned from western governments (though the great figures of the Old Kingdom might have recognized the techniques as well as the motivation). To me, this fervent worship of "the glorious leader" seemed wasteful, naïve, crude, dangerous - the patriotism of a psychotic child.

I roused myself to write some postcards and letters. Since receiving mail in Cairo, I had become preoccupied with thoughts of home, which appeared to glow brightly on my mental horizon.

Last night I dreamed, for the 3rd time on the trip, that I had gone home; & for the 1st time it wasn't a nightmare. It scared me, though, that where Penny should have been, there was an unfamiliar face. I'm glad that we shall be turning west in another week.

My unconscious was checking in. Enough of being alien, dirty, hungry, sick! In myth, epic, anthropology and history, heroes who descended to the underworld *came back*, and the death of the king/god at the end of the solar year heralded the (re) appearance of the once and future lord. Let darksome Dionysus die with the old year, then, and Apollo govern the new as the sun returned!

On and on I wrote, more and more wildly. The fever must have been strong in me, the illness at its peak, but I felt the need to work through this crisis of irresolution. Between fitful, tossing dozes on the sweaty cot, I seemed to be transcribing a revelation, imparted through the agency of my affliction. Possessed, prophetic - a new Muhammed! - I wrote whatever flickered across my brain-screen, raving about the need to *make those decisions*. I would…get married, I would…become a musician, as Laurent had urged, but first…I would, I would…fly for five splendid years with the Air Force! Or maybe with the Marines! After months of sporadic worry, I had transcended uncertainty and was ready to complete my Life Plan.

Most of the decisions made that febrile day were later thrown out on sober re-examination, but making them cleared the air and my mind. I began to regard these large questions as answered, settled, and to focus on external things again. Even when my resolutions were revised, I believed that I was doing what I had come to do, and felt easier within myself. Thus the second half of the psychic trip differed substantially from the first.

Jan. 5, Aswan, 4 PM - Due to my health misadventures, Aswan has been a disappointment. I missed seeing Elephantine & Kitchener's Islands yesterday, as well as the Early Tombs. I rested the whole day, & felt well enough this AM to go along in the group car to the granite quarry & the dams. There was little to see at the first: a colorless, rocky hill lying in the desert a few kms. out of town, distinguished chiefly by a 75%-quarried obelisk in it.

The granite for many of the ancient monuments of Upper and Lower Egypt came from this quarry. A more barren, wind-blasted, lunar setting for an important site can hardly be imagined. The sand dunes of Hollywood's deserts would look sensual and posh beside that stony waste.

The Aswan Dam, tho' significant & useful for Egypt, looked like most dams. The High Dam is all site & plans & hope. Sounds like a tremendous project, but there ain't much to see.

The most interesting part of that visit was meeting one of the Russian engineers. His "handler" and the Egyptians showing us around chuckled with delight in bringing the Cold War antagonists together. The engineer was a young man, not over thirty, who stood about six-four, with an imposing build and handshake, but spoke only through an interpreter, even to the Arabs. Our brief conversation was innocuous enough, and not unfriendly.

That afternoon, in a verdant park with a vista of the Nile, I looked out from benches underneath shade trees to a dazzling, sun-bleached landscape of cliff and rock and river-channel. All the forms were tortured, bizarre: bulbous white rocks bathed in mid-river like albino hippopotami; jagged caves pocked chalky cliffs. It could have been an illustration for *A Passage to India*. Even the river lost its usual serene unity of form to perplex itself in irregular channels. Here was an objective correlative of my illness: the right place to be sick and faint! Inner and outer corresponded weirdly, with incoherence as the Lowest Common Denominator. Nightmare City, and I was the mayor. A neatly-dressed young Egyptian, a student-teacher, sat down to talk, eager to exchange world-views. His was not insightful, however, and mine was Not at Home. He seemed as bogged down in education methodology courses as his American counterparts. For a few minutes we talked to some giggling girls, classmates of his, but I soon tired of this and dragged "home" to pack and lie down.

As the sun descended we walked to the station under full packs. My steps were shaky; Hector, already worried about my condition, had to catch me twice as I staggered and reeled on broken pavement. "Man," he said, "maybe you're the one who should be heading home." He looked and sounded half-serious, a mirror for me.

"No, I'd rather die here," I heard my voice reply, sounding as if it were coming down a long resonant hall from somewhere else.

Throngs of Arabs were already on the platform. When two of them met, they generally wound up and threw handshakes like right hooks. *Whack*! Then they exchanged a couple of words and moved on, apparently just casual acquaintances: it was like saying "Hi!" in America. As the train rolled in, the crowd pressed toward the tracks. An unusually modern car trundled by slowly, its windows open. Hector threw his pack in and dove after it. Then he took mine and helped me through the window. By the time the train stopped we were occupying facing seats, our packs alongside us as "pillows." Surprisingly, the train did not fill up, and our posh arrangement was never challenged. We settled down for the long haul north to Cairo.

Lower Egypt

Jan. 6, Youth Hostel, Cairo, 5 PM - Back "home" tired in body & mind after almost 20 hrs. on 3rd class carriages coming from Aswan. Maybe 2 hrs. sleep. Just waiting for Hector to get back with the mail before sacking. My health - fortunately - held out.

I.e., I was not quite prostrate, managing to carry my pack from the station. Hector soon arrived with a letter from Penny, which I read happily in the twilight and then slept for 13 hours. A general turmoil roused the dormitory the next morning: forty Egyptian boys from military schools, in town to pay homage to Nasser, were clamoring for beds. In a burst of international good will, the management asked all non-Egyptians to leave. Amid grumbling from displaced *franji,* we packed up and drove to Cairo's other hostel: a weather-beaten old three-deck stern-wheeler tied up to the west bank of the Nile. It was dumpy and cramped, with awful squatty potties, but picturesque enough to have served as a stage set for *Death on the Nile,* which was its nickname. Several of our friends from the Garden City hostel came over, too.

Leo had now returned from spending Christmas with his family in Beirut to his UNESCO post in the Delta farmland north of Cairo. At noon on the 7th he swooped down on us, obviously determined to earn his GB (Great Benefactor) merit badge. A veritable hurricane of hospitality, he had the same effect on my journal-keeping as a trainload of curious Turks. I managed to start one entry the next day -

Jan. 8, Cairo, noon - We are being entertained, edified, & squired around by Leo, Hector's friend, & I'm not going to have much time to write

- but that was it for the next 24 hours. Articulate, well-informed and solicitous, Leo was eager to show us Cairo. He did that, yet he also depressed me. His fluent Arabic, knowledge of Mideast culture and contacts with Arab intellectuals gave him an *entrée* to Egypt that showed how superficial everything we had hitherto seen, learned, and done really was. But I kept that feeling to myself, even to some extent *from* myself. He wanted to enrich our stay and share his knowledge, for which I was grateful; at every meal we picked his brain on Islamic history, Egyptian socialism,

Turkish calligraphy.... Leo evidently enjoyed our curiosity, and encouraged it; most Americans don't ask the right questions, he said. We had lots of questions, and if anyone could tell us which were the right ones it was Leo.

For three days he drove us around from breakfast until bedtime. One afternoon we "did" mediaeval Cairo: the city walls dating from *Salah-el-Din* (Saladin, 12th century); a 14th century patrician's house with steam baths, tile walling, and *jalousie* windows (wooden latticework through which the women could look onto an inner courtyard); and the aqueduct and citadel from Crusader times. Another day it was the suburbs: Helwan, with its mineral baths, on the south ("Cairo's Suburb"), and to the north Heliopolis, which boasted handsome boulevards, ornate Indian houses, and Egypt's military academy. Traffic jams and festooned arches showed that we had just missed seeing Nasser and King Mohammed V of Morocco. In between excursions we obtained visas for Libya ($2 each, 3 hours' work), and ate ice cream at glitzy Groppi's.

One night he took us to "Sahara City," a nightclub in a huge tent on the desert west of Cairo. En route we drove past the pyramids, vast black triangles in the moonlight. Eating squab and watching belly dancers, I saw that I had been missing some vital aspects of Middle Eastern life. There were also African dancers, and then the star turn: a Whirling Dervish (Leo explained that *Darwish* founded a branch of Turkish Islam that induced religious trances by spinning). In a floor-length grey robe and wizard's hat that made his whole figure conical, he folded his arms and spun slowly, gravely, without apparent effort, in epicycles, small circles that gradually described a large one, rotating around moving centers as he revolved around his own. It was eerie, yet less surreal than the grand finale in which all the performers and many of the audience danced in bizarre pairings - dervish and matron, belly dancer and businessman - for fifteen hypnotic minutes. Two women had fits (Leo said that their husbands had to grant them whatever they asked in that condition). Then the music stopped and everyone went limp. We drove home in a daze past the pyramids. Our bill, said Leo, was $6.

Jan. 9, on the deck of the paddle-wheel hostel in warm sun (about 70°) - The last few days Leo has not only been very generous & showed us much of Cairo, but has impressed me greatly. He is working on a

Ph.D. from Harvard. His field is Islamic culture, suiting him admirably for UN literacy work here & in Jordan. Intelligent, sensitive, & practical, he has added to my awareness of Egypt & life by his perceptive, frank talk. Our topics have included politics, sex, religion, Communism, meaning in one's work, raising children, & life in Egypt. He is a Quaker & conscientious objector.

The only depressant has been my health: never recovered from my Upper Egypt disease. Still have terrible diarrhea, constant stomach discomfort, & little strength. Hector & I are going with Leo to his home today to relax & see UNESCO before returning to Cairo.

I passed up a tour of the American University of Cairo and a reception for some itinerant students because, despite long daytime naps, I remained lethargic. The over-the-counter anti-diarrhea pills from home were making no headway against my enervating intestinal malaise and its revolting gas, so the idea of going to Leo's and consulting a doctor there made sense. It was easy to identify with the hundreds of robed men we saw sleeping on grassy places around the city. Leo said they had *bilharzia*, caused by a parasitic worm that lives in muddy, stagnant canal water (he himself had contracted it from tainted bath water when he first arrived). It was likely that some of those sleepy-eyed men in hotels and on trains in Upper Egypt had been supporting long *bilharzia* worms, he said.

The evening before our departure we tried to see the Leningrad Ballet, but they were sold out, so we settled for *Ask Any Girl*, with Shirley McLaine. The next morning I bought a large book on Spain and jotted down some tidbits from Leo's discourses.

Jan 7th was Coptic Xmas. The Copts are [a] Xian sect dating from when Alexandria was a great Xian city. 12.5% of Egypt & 25% of Cairo is Xian. There is a synagogue in Cairo, which Nasser has attended. "Nasser is too good for Egypt: he is very honest & insists on [honesty] around him. The mass of the people drag down the enlightened few & render his task all but impossible." "You can't believe the filth & poverty of the villages. Most farmers eat 2 small loaves of bread & a handful of beans a day; meat twice a year. Flies suck the liquid from children's eyes. The average wage is 20 cents a day." "The Russians have Egypt under their economic thumb."

I had never met anyone who was so inexhaustibly and exhaustingly instructive, whose conversation was a bravura lecture. Books about Egypt paled by comparison with his unceasing flow, which was lively and up-to-date. It was the nearest thing to being on-line in 1960; Leo foreshadowed Google. Like a web search, though, he was unedited, and *we* could certainly not catch him up. That these were only one man's views ("the world according to Leo") I was dimly aware - they needed checking - but for now it seemed enough to try to absorb what he had to give.

Jan. 10, UNESCO Fundamental Education Center, Egypt, 4 PM - Leaving Cairo yesterday around 4, we drove for 2 hours through the lush Delta in Leo's car to here. At the splitting of the Nile into its two main branches is a large & beautiful park, some 10 miles square. Its beauty is comparable to Ismailia['s]: poinsettias, pansies, other flowers, shade trees & long, dark paths.

We picked up much Egyptiana from Leo. The usual peasant fuel is dried animal dung. They raise pigeons (for food) in beehive-like houses. When the canals are full,, farmers over-irrigate their land, fear[ing] dry spells. The High Dam will make possible a 20% production increase. Nasser has brought fresh drinking water to 400 villages. But the women won't let their husbands drink it because they think that "empty" water produces impotence (Nile water=fertility). They also believe that marijuana delays male sexual climax & increases female pleasure, so they'll go hungry to buy it for hubby.

UNESCO's Arab States Fundamental Education Centre was housed in a dozen or more tawny, almost-new block-buildings amid green fields near the village of Minoufia. Staffed by Ph.D.'s, many of them Arabs, the Centre was training young Egyptians to educate the *fellaheen* in health, sanitation, agriculture, literacy (Leo's field) and "modern life." Eighty-five resident students chosen by the governments could use the art department, library, school, hospital, agricultural experiment station, and audio-visual facility. There was also an outdoor basketball court (I was too weak to play, but Hector showed the self-proclaimed local "champion" a few things about cutting and driving, Tennessee-style). Leo welcomed us to his comfortable apartment, and we settled down to a deluxe regime of hot baths, good sleep, good food, and tours around the Centre to meet his colleagues, many of whom took a surprisingly respectful interest in our travels.

Our few days at the Centre were quiet, pleasant, edifying, and therapeutic. Mornings I awoke to a world of mists, eucalyptus foliage, perhaps a white- or black-robed figure leading a burro past, with emerald fields and a palm tree at the limit of vision; later, as the fog lifted, the trees and buildings of the next farm appeared. Leo arranged for me to see a doctor, who said that I probably had amoebic dysentery and prescribed some powders. In 24 hours I began to feel better. Evenings we listened to a hi-fi in the next apartment, while its owners reminisced about previous UN assignments in Thailand and India. Most of my time was spent talking to the Arab trainees and staff about the make-up, abilities, and tensions of

the "Arab world." Many of the key positions here are held by Palestinians, Arab occupants of the lands which pre-existed Israel. They suffered terribly at the hands of Jews, yet seem the most moderate and clear-headed about solving the problem. Palestinians are looked upon as the Germans of the Middle East: industrious, responsible, clever, practical. Most of my informants seem to believe in "cultural characteristics"; people, they [think], have been indelibly marked by their country, climate, & historical background.

Egyptians and Syrians, they said, lacked initiative, being lazy and emotionally immature. Then the same people would argue that, because the Palestinians and Sudanese were among the most responsible Arabs, there was a correlation between *British* colonial rule - emphasizing dignity and respect for law - and progressiveness. Why weren't the Egyptians more advanced and responsible, then? Well, they admitted, the correlation isn't *perfect*; it needs congenial material. These were important conversations for me, marking the first time I had heard of Palestinians. TIME and *The New York Times* had left me so ignorant of them that I had to construct my own definition of who they were. Leo's wife, it turned out, was a Palestinian whose family had lost everything in the expulsion of 1948.

Leo believed that it was helpful for Arabs to see the two of them together in their apartment, treating each other as equals. Their own social backgrounds, he said, excluded women from full participation, and rendered them curious and a little giggly when faced with this (western) phenomenon. His words made me observe the Centre's society more closely. After a while I noticed the slight nervous shift that occurred anytime a woman entered the room: a phenomenon I associated with adolescent boys from all-male prep schools. Here it took the form of veiled references to infidelity, jokes or anecdotes with a sexual undertone, and an increase of silliness and forced laughter. There seemed to be an awareness of sexual possibilities that required sublimation or release in conversation.

Often, though, the talk was of history and culture: areas where they had much to teach and I to learn.

Our venture across North Africa takes on new coherence...it follows the thrust westwards of Islam. I hope that we can find evidence of this movement all along the Barbary Coast, as well as traces in Spain. "Moorish" was a Spanish term meaning "Moslem." The Moors were mostly North Africans & a few Arabians, carrying the sword of Islam against infidel Spain (711 AD).

Once, Egypt had been the place from which to jump off for East Africa, but inquiries in Cairo had turned up nothing that we were willing to pay (or wait) for at this point, halfway through our money and time. I would soon have to notify Debrew and my draft board that I was not returning to college, and then the countdown would start. We also asked Leo about budget travel to Nairobi with scooters. He shook his head. Something Leo didn't know! Darkest Africa took on new meaning. Even the idea of seeing Abu Simbel was scrapped when we found that you had to take a Nile steamer toward Wadi Halfa in the Sudan, get off at the ruin and wait several days for the steamer to return; by then we were too impatient to abide a delay of that magnitude. So now, by default, we were back to the plan of riding to Alexandria, then west toward the setting sun, toward home.

Leo offered us his car if we would leave for a few days while he caught up on work. Deal! We drove to Cairo, resumed our residence at Death-on-the-Nile, reclaimed our scooters, and split up for some individual sightseeing.

After two false leads I found the Coptic Museum. Not large or spectacular, but interesting. Most of the exhibits were carved stone pediments & capitals; there were also frescoes, pulpits, icons, & a beautiful 3-tiered golden crown. Many were from Saqqara, a Coptic center. There was a good deal of persecution during their early history.

18th century icons, decorated with gold, were reminiscent of Greek Orthodoxy. Here & in the Coptic church I saw earlier the paintings were concerned with Christ, the Last Supper, the Pieta & saints.

My next stop lay within the walls of the medieval citadel. The Mosque of Mohammed Ali (the 19th century Egyptian nationalist) resembles Turkey's mosques, but is perhaps even more beautiful. Passing worshippers performing ablutions at fountains in the courtyard, I left my shoes at the door and went inside. The prohibition on depicting the human form was absolutely respected; the only decorations were large plaques covered with Arabic script: virtually abstract designs (Leo said that calligraphers would rearrange letters for artistic effect). The stained-glass windows were semi-circular or rectangular swatches of color. The mosque's best-known feature is four great columns of alabaster, which is partially translucent (it is also called the Alabaster Mosque). The flame of the custodian's match, viewed through a few inches of stone at a corner, had a halo of delicate white and rose-brown tints. The larger of the two *minbars* (their design possibly based on Coptic pulpits), some 30 feet high, was ornately decorated with gold plate hammered into floral and geometric patterns.

I ran my hand over the cold surface; a deep voice intoned the first syllable of the numbing "Ahl-law." The reverberation was so quick & deep that I couldn't tell when the voice stopped, & the echoes rolled on undiminished until I was almost afraid.

Outside, the yellow sun-disk was settling into brown haze. A few minarets and a ruinous aqueduct rose above the sprawl of nondescript buildings below. After exploring the Citadel's walls and photographing a couple of friendly young Egyptian men who wanted to pose with the mosque as a backdrop, I scootered up a blacktop road that led east onto yellow cliffs, a stark formation dominated by gigantic boulders. On top was merely a collection of restaurants and nightclubs, but the view was impressive. This was said to be "the coming suburb."

On the 14th of January we rose at 5:30 (following a noisy night at the hostel), claimed our scooters from the garage across the street and rolled off toward Giza in the false dawn. A shivering gas stop at an early-bird station was quickly dispatched. As we approached the pyramids along a four-lane highway it was still only half light; ground fog lay all around us and enveloped the trees.

The dark bulks of the two larger pyramids (Cheops & Chephren) materialized suddenly from the cold air above the trees. In a few minutes we were walking around the noseless, enigmatic Sphinx. The area was deserted: it was only 6:30. At about 7 the fiery ball of Sun blazed up thru the haze to give a goal to the Sphinx's eyes & cast shadows. I was surprised & sad to see that the great figure has crumbled badly, some facial features being almost obliterated.

Yet the features (said to be those of the Pharaoh Chephren) retain their power by concentrating so fixedly on Elsewhere, some unknown realm or galaxy east of the dawn. Napoleon is said to have had one of his cannon shoot off its nose when he was unable to solve "the riddle of the Sphinx": one megalomaniac piqued at another. Stone crumbles, but Ego is eternal. The long shadows of dawn began to give character to the immense masses.

We walked to the Great Pyramid & watched the diagonal line of 3 progressively smaller pyramids march into the haze. It is big - 481 feet. Seeing no one around & the pyramid just <u>*there,*</u> *we started climbing. It's a hard but not dangerous climb, taking about 20 minutes. 2/3 of the way up we met an American, Terry, who had slept on top.*

Caught off guard, I asked foolishly, "What are you doing?"

"Junior year at the Sorbonne," he said with a slight smile.

I was stunned, having aspired to do that myself. "Don't tell me: the lectures were boring?"

"You got it. And in French!"

"The nerve!" We laughed. He had with him a bag of oranges and a copy of *Look Homeward, Angel.* Really it was too much: what could I say? Clearly one-upped, we bid him good morning and kept climbing. From the summit the whole area - pyramids, excavations, "solar boats," mastabas - was laid out as clearly as in one of Baedeker's plans, and our mount's shadow was most impressive. We photographed the next pyramid, but the dawn glow had become the glare of broad daylight, so we descended the great blocks, joined up with Terry and went inside the pyramid. Long, low, sometimes steep passageways, garishly lighted by neon, led to the central burial crypt, not recommended for claustrophobics. Back outside, dodging would-be guides, camel-drivers and watchmen, we escaped into Giza for breakfast, glad to have missed the tourist hours.

Thirty minutes later we set out for Saqqara, 25 kilometers south over back roads. On his second seat Hector carried Terry, excited both about the scooter ride and a chance to see the Step Pyramid.

Due to road repairs, we had to scooter dustily along a canal-side dike which bordered a mud-house village. Thence followed 3 miles of freshly-tarred slop, more dirt, & 7 miles of semi-pavement, semi-dirt in bad repair. It was fun. We were in the middle of farmland, puttering past road gangs & villages, occasionally rewarded with glimps[es] of pyramids on our right, seemingly close in the desert air. Finally spotted Zoser's Step Pyramid & turned off. Found the ruins of Saqqara on the edge of the desert, quieter & more isolated than Giza, luminous in the rarefied air, & very interesting.

Approached the Pyramid thru an entrance colonnade, which imitated in stone the mud palaces of the time. The Pyramid, 271' high, is the oldest stone building in the world: 2780 BC.

Dazzled by the blinding yellow-white tones everywhere and the crumbling perfection of the pyramid, I wondered if architecture had really progressed since the days of its builder Imhotep, traditionally the first architect. I walked around it to the western wall of the necropolis. The desert stretched to the horizon in bare immobile waves, a thing of great plainness, power, and – somehow - beauty.

We spent 3 or 4 happy hours poking around the sculpted & painted interiors of a smaller pyramid & numerous "mastabas," rock-cut tombs, scootering thru fine loose sand from site to site, & winding up with the impressive Serapheum - Tomb of the 24 Sacred Bulls: a long underground corridor with large crypts along the sides, containing huge granite sarcophagi in which embalmed bulls were interred. A real feat to get them down there! The sculpted art maintained a high quality, never later than 6th dynasty. The life, realism, humor, & technical skill of the artists were reminiscent of Luxor.

On the way back I stopped for a young Egyptian hitchhiker who was standing by the road near Saqqara, waving at every vehicle that passed, and, as a joke, at us. "*Al Qahirah*?" (Cairo?) I asked.

"*Aywa!*" (You bet!) he replied with a surprised grin.

"*Tfuddal*" (Please), I said, pointing to the second seat. He jumped on with alacrity and proved the perfect passenger, asking only the few questions I could understand and comprehending my answers, then settling back to enjoy the ride. The four of us returned to Cairo on the main road, highly pleased with how the day had turned out.

It was some time before I grasped the meaning of pyramids; that was *Traumwerk*. As in dreams of Sekhmet, there was no "action": I was simply made to look at the object until I realized that it was there to be understood. The pyramids, rising from square, solid bases to point at something far beyond our world, were relatively easy, whereas Sekhmet.... While some call her a goddess of war, I came to believe that her sculptors and worshippers knew no more of her meaning than I did; she stands for a dark side and mysteries we will never solve.

That evening Hector and I drove Leo's car back to Minoufia, arriving (predictably) in time for dinner. Our departure now being imminent, our friends at the Centre gave us a going-away party at which I became better acquainted with several of them, especially Ali Osman. "Allah!" he exclaimed when I described Sekhmet's temple at Karnak. "This fellow is a poet!" I took it *cum grano salis*.

The Arab intellectuals at the Centre are really down on Egyptians. They feel that they haven't the spirit, intelligence, or drive equal to their task. They ***are*** *immature.*

I, at least, had not earned the right to make any such remark. A little learning is a dangerous thing! The next morning Hector and I returned to Cairo with Im Sahid, another of the ASFEC staff. King Mohammed V of Morocco was still in town, and his cavalcade with Nasser brought out jubilant crowds along their route; public buildings, including museums, and most stores were closed. We decided to stay another day before hitting the road.

Whenever we stayed in a hostel, friendly travelers would share information with us. This was again true in Cairo, whose hostels brimmed with diverse characters from many lands; it was easy to skip the city's night life in favor of talking with them, swapping adventures. Two Germans who had just crossed North Africa on motorcycles told of all-day sandstorms, engine failures and mid-desert repairs, warning that the wind would be against us. One gave me his Automobile Club of Egypt map of "The Road of North Africa Coast." It showed every town, village or watering hole between Alexandria and Casablanca, the distances between them, and the cumulative distance from Alexandria. He had marked every place where he had bought or seen gas, and drawn a little sketch map of how to find the hostel outside Tunis. The map included the Mediterranean's northern shore, so it showed our entire trip thus far. Of all the useful things I was ever given or told on the youth-travel circuit, this must rank at the top. *Vielen dank'!*

A South African who had just hitchhiked from Johannesburg in two months for about $75 showed me that our original plan, East Africa and all, had been feasible. We needed merely to have come to Egypt and started: somehow, anyhow! It would have been a different trip, of course - no scooters, no Greece, no Beirut - and who can say which itinerary would have been more valuable to us in the long run? But we could have done what others were doing: hitchhike, take trains, boats or buses, even join tours. Our American sources had simply been ignorant, or timid; had we defied them and plunged ahead into our imaginings, we might have succeeded. Now too much time and money were gone to think of starting south; we had cast our die. It was a hard lesson painfully learned: *Don't trust what you're told at home about conditions abroad unless your source has been there recently, traveling in your style.* As if to drive the point home, on our last day at the Garden City hostel we watched a young American couple set off for East Africa on their 200 cc German scooter. My heart sank, my stomach ached, my teeth ground. *Argh*!

Not to idealize the hostel crowd, I quite disliked a young Jordanian who was traveling around the world on handouts. "*You* pay from your pocket," he explained, in a tone of patient condescension such as you might use with someone thought to be developmentally retarded. "But everywhere *I* am given money," he added loftily.

"How do you get it? Why do they give?"

He looked astonished. "But, I ask! I say I am poor student, I want to see your country, will you give me little money? Now I wait to see Gen. Nasser. It takes several weeks, but I am sure he will give me some money."

Yes, I'll bet you're a good beggar, a real lickboot, I thought, right up there with Uriah Heep. He had a groveling voice, but I noted that he had not come far from Jordan yet. With any luck Nasser would see him as I did. Leo said that student beggars who thought the world owed them a passage were all too common and he despised them, but I met only Uriah. I wondered uneasily if he might be closer to the traditional student of the *Wanderjahre* than any of us - *if* he had a craft other than wheedling.

Most of the hostelers, though, seemed fairly bright, often eager and energetic, sometimes sensitive or altruistic. On the whole I thought them a cut above most of my classmates at college, which probably meant that travel of this kind selected for qualities that I valued. Among them were a good many Americans, their backgrounds frequently similar to mine. As in Greece, I felt that we had come upon a proto-youth movement, though "movement" connotes organization, while this energy, welling up from far-flung sources, was restless and undirected. When Kennedy came up with the idea of the Peace Corps a year or so later, I said, "*Voila*!" We were, I think, looking for the Corps before it was formed, searching for meaningful international work, wanting a role in a larger play.

At the hostel I executed a project conceived on the *Achilleus*. We had seen several travelers who advertised their rambles with lists or maps on their baggage or vehicles. It was a good conversation-starter, and the piece of fabric that hung down from our scooter windshields over the handlebars, headlight and front panel provided an excellent space, so one evening I brought that assembly indoors, borrowed a black crayon from an artistic young woman, and drew a rough graphic of our travels on the heavy-duty material, using the German's North Africa map as a model. The headlight cut-out served as the Mediterranean. From Napoli at the noon position, the line slanted down to Athens, up to Istanbul, down to Beirut at 3 o'clock and Cairo at 5. It looked smart! Yet this was a curious moment for a peripatetic psyche, at once proud, and tiring, of his travels as he approached the blankest and perhaps most arduous space on the map.

On our last day in Cairo I revisited The Museum; then ate lunch at a restaurant to which Leo had taken us, where we became hooked on *muhalabieh*, a delicious milk-and-rice custard. I also mailed a letter to Debrew, announcing that I would not be attending second-semester courses (starting in two weeks) after all. My draft board would have to be notified next. Leo was in town again, being beneficent and taking pictures of us to be sent home. In one, I sit on my scooter, seemingly relaxed and healthy; in the other I stand with my pack on, appearing gaunt. Hector looks rugged, handsome, cool. Marlon and Skinny! Leo wrote my parents that I spoke Arabic as well as he did: this because I had asked a waiter for "*Myuh, menfudlak*" (water, please). Protective to the last, he escorted us to the start of the Alexandria highway in his car as we left town.

Jan. 18, Youth Hostel, ALEXANDRIA, 10 PM - Left Cairo on Jan. 17, 11:30 AM, after breakfast, courtesy of Leo, at the Hilton. He & Ali Ohsman saw us off. We cruised the 225 kms. over good autostrada in 4 hrs. 15 mins. The country was flat, fertile, covered almost endlessly with green, well irrigated, & dull after a while.

Yes, even fields of world-famous Egyptian cotton will eventually pall. This was the best time we had ever made over such a long stretch. As I followed Hector along the broad pavement at 70 kph, a motorcycle drew alongside and matched my pace. I glanced over. The mustachioed driver grinned from under his old British Army helmet. "PassPORT?" he shouted.

"Yes," I yelled back, "I have one. Do you want it?"

"No." He shook his head emphatically. "But you have all your papers?" I could not make out the expression behind the dark goggles. What was he, highway police? There was a sheathed carbine beside his fuel tank.

"I have all the right papers," I bellowed, trying to sound confident. "Do you need to see them?"

"No, it is all right," he replied, curving his cycle to within a foot of my leg. "But you stop and have tea with my friends and I?"

Ah, another friend! "Where is your tea?" I asked, playing for time.

He jerked a mittened thumb back over his shoulder. "Five, ten kilometers."

Ah, a way out. I said Thank you, but we must reach Alexandria before dark, and suggested that he ask Hector. With a cheerful nod he twisted his throttle and made up the 20-yard gap in a couple of noisy seconds. Soon he was in earnest conversation with the startled Hector, who, however, remained visibly negative for as long as necessary. At last the cyclist peeled away from him, spurting on up the road and out of sight. Hector twisted to look back at me, put his index finger to his helmet just at the ear and gave it a sharp turn. *Pazzo*, crazy. In a few minutes we passed one of the many guardhouses and there was our buddy, chatting with his mates. He gave us a casual wave, which we returned diplomatically, leaving our throttles at full.

The approach to Alexandria passed through vast palm groves and among shallow brown lagoons for a few minutes, a glimpse of an exotic, nineteenth-century Egypt that soon gave way to the bustling streets and European commercial façades of a modern Mediterranean metropolis. We must have gone by some outlying branches of Lake Mareotis (*Mariout*), but, not yet having discovered *The Alexandria Quartet*, whose 3rd volume had been published in the U.S. in 1959, I saw only some brackish pools. We generally notice little in transit, but must put down roots someplace in order to know it. I was conscious then - and much more so when I read Durrell later - that most of Alexandria, like the rest of Egypt, was eluding me most of the time. The learning involved in travel, if it is to be of lasting value, must somehow become attached to self, which takes time and/or intensity of experience.

We cruised down the Corni[che] & out to Ras-el-Tin the first evening. Today we went to Montaza Palace. The gardens were extensive & pleasant. The palace was a little too Baroque, but opulent and luxurious. This PM we visited Pompey's Pillar & its catacombs, plus the Roman catacombs nearby. Latter quite interesting for the mix of Roman with ancient Egyptian styles in the statuary & symbolism. Much difficulty finding these sites in the midst of slums.

Another book we could have used was E. M. Forster's *Alexandria: A History and a Guide* (1922), not yet available in paperback. It wasn't the history we needed (having Will Durant) as much as the guide. We knew about the city's associations with Alexander the Great, Cleopatra and other Ptolemies, Caesar and Antony; about the great *Pharos* (lighthouse) and library, both wonders of the ancient world long since destroyed; about Napoleon's and Nelson's visits. But we did *not* know, for instance, that Ras-el-Tin "is not ugly, as palaces go," or that Montaza, the old Khedival summer resort restored by King Fouad, was built to please an Austrian mistress. Forster could have helped us sort out the chaotic ruins around Pompey's Pillar, where the second great

Alexandrian library stood. We just had to muddle along with our eyes and scraps of local information.

Jan. 19, YH, Alex., 5:30 PM - We left the scooters at the "Lambretta agency" this morning with many instructions & misgivings. If the mechanic doesn't know what he's doing, we may pay for it out in the Libyan desert somewhere!

We were shocked to learn that Alexandria's "Lambretta agency" had no mechanical relations with Italy; there were neither spare parts nor a certified mechanic. The thorough inspection and overhaul we had envisioned as a necessary and inspiring prelude to our desert venture shrank to a routine oil change and grease job - and even for that *we* had to show *them* the lubrication diagram in the owner's manual. The cold feeling in the pit of my stomach must have engendered the dream in which I ask a veteran of the coastal road if we can make it. He smiles and shrugs. "Oh yeah, you'll make it," he replies. "You'll have trouble, I don't know what, or where, but you'll make it somehow." At the end I realize that this tepidly reassuring fellow is myself.

The Graeco-Roman museum was as good as advertised. Rediscovered Roman statuary, which, when good, rivals Greek. Several works (2 heads of Serapis, black granite of Apis) depicted gods; the best (sneering youth, reclining & soulless old man) caught real insights into human nature. The mixed god-systems of the Roman-Egyptian period (ca. 200 BC-200 AD) are very confused & confusing.

Forster warns that this museum is "not of the first order," gives a "false impression" of Hellenistic society, and should not be visited until one knows something about the ancient city; its mummies "have the air of being here because not good enough for Cairo." Unaware of how bad the collection was, I quite enjoyed it, though it obviously dated from a period when artists were more interested in recording decadence than in idealizing humanity. The finds from the temple of *Petesouchos*, the crocodile god of the Fayyum oasis, particularly interested me, as did the religious art in general. Serapion turned out to be an excellent example of pagan syncretism: his original name combined that of Egypt's chief god, Osiris (whom the Greeks identified with Dionysus), with that of Apis, the bull-god.

During the walk to Ras-el-Tin, we shopped extensively. I bought some sunglasses with specially-made sidepieces for $5, a new journal for 16 cents, & we combined on a specially-soldered funnel for 20 cents.

We were "girding for desert travel." The "sidepieces" or wings on my glasses were meant to turn them into goggles – none having been seen in stores - and keep blowing sand out of my eyes. The long-necked funnel would enable us to pour in extra fuel on the long stretches between gas pumps (the filler cap was down in a narrow gap between the two seats and ordinary funnels would not reach it). An old man with one eye, so abject that he refused a proffered tip as somehow undeserved or immoral, did the soldering. The meekness of his spirit was piteous as he accepted 10 piastres for his funnel and a quarter-hour's labor. Or perhaps I misread him, and he felt ashamed of or demeaned by doing business with infidel foreigners.

Ras-el-Tin, built c. 1810 by Mohammed Ali as main Alexandria residence of the Kings, sits on a promontory jutting northwest, surrounded by Navy installations. Here Farouk abdicated in '52. The magnificence & tasteful beauty of R.-el-T.'s interior rival Versailles. Delicately inlaid wood floors & cabinets of mahogany & ebony are everywhere; large rooms & ornate chandeliers are the rule; decorations of gilded metal & gold, & panels of satin adorn the walls. The total effect is more splendid & more harmonious than the somewhat gawky, on & off styling of Montaza.

A summer residence, Ras-el-Tin had some cold drafts in January, one of which was the certainty that it was an example of the spoilt regal cream that once sat atop the milk of the *fellaheen*. It was not difficult to imagine either the horror with which Egypt's liberals and revolutionaries must have regarded the palace, or the disgust that the kings, lounging among these splendid Gallic luxuries, would have felt for the squalor of peasant life. As in Beirut's *Le Petit Versailles*, I found myself asking, *What's it doing here?*

The Corniche extends a good 7 miles, & white, modern, typically French buildings line it for most of its length. Near Qait Bey, however, there are cheaper, almost garish apartment houses: the wash-in-the-windows set.

The "battered and neglected little peninsula" where they hung their wash was, however, "perhaps the most interesting spot in Alexandria," according to Forster, "for here, rising to an incredible height, once stood the Pharos Lighthouse, the wonder of the world. Contrary to general belief, some fragments of the Pharos still remain." Not knowing this, I may have kicked aside some venerable relic and thought it just a dirty stone. But did the Pharos factor really make the *present* peninsula any more interesting?

The glories of ancient Alexandria had flown, and the city Durrell created was not visible to us, yet we had some enjoyable times there. George, a businessman in his forties, saw us at the Lambretta garage and promptly invited us to dinner. Still wary after Hector's mishap in Cairo, we hesitated, but when he said that we would dine *chez lui* with his bride of four months and his niece, we accepted. George proved so hospitable, scrupulous, and respectable that we soon grew ashamed of our suspicions. He fed us sumptuously, showed slides of their wedding trip to East Africa (!), and inquired politely about our travels. His wife Ginnie, her alarmingly good figure poured into a basic black dress and opera hose, disturbed us all evening; the chic and sexy had come to seem phenomena of the past or distant future. George's niece Cecile was a sweet young thing of 14 who attended an Alexandrian girls' school. She dressed much like her aunt, making it clear that she too would have good lines: I marveled again at the early bloom of Mediterranean women. Cecile attached herself to us charmingly, offering to show us around town. We found that we had no prior engagements.

Cecile proved a good guide and competent back-seat rider on a scooter tour of the city. I could not decide which was more delightful: having her ride on Hector's scooter, where I could admire her demure side-saddle perch, or on mine, where she would clasp me as lightly at the waist as my first partner in dance class. In a few years she would make some lucky young Greek fellow happy. "What man can hope for a guard against the Daughters of Time?" asked an Arab poet of old. George and Ginnie, whose hospitality was bounteous, showed us their beach cottage in the suburbs at midday, and that evening we ate dinner with some older friends of theirs, business people who could talk intelligently of Egyptian and world affairs. These were people that Durrell would have known.

Alexandria being an international city, national allegiances seemed less important. George, whose last name was Greek, looked surprised when I asked whether he considered himself Egyptian (perhaps he wondered whether I might be CIA after all). "No," he said after a pause, "I am an Alexandrian, and that is different. My family is Greek, my friends are mostly Europeans, my business acquaintances are Germans, English, and Arabs. To live in Alexandria is to be from no one nation, but from all nations." He identified most with a Mediterranean business community, and, like most of its Alexandrian members whom I met, spoke Arabic, English, French, Greek, German and Italian.

George, Ginnie, and Cecile had no social competition from the sparsely populated Youth Hostel, but it did provide a sprinkling of national types. We ate several meals with a slender, intense, bespectacled young German who had not relinquished "*Deutschland über alles*" merely because the Nazis had failed; Nietzsche and Hitler were his mentors. He could not contain his racist crowing, nor did Hector try to conceal his dislike of the young *Übermensch*. I thought several times they would come to blows. Yet the fellow kept returning to us, as if he wanted something.

On the 21st of January, having made all the attainable preparations that either of us could think of, and said goodbye to our friends, we set about trying to stow or tie water bags, spare cans of gas and oil, and the funnel in or on the scooters along with our usual loads. It was just as well that we had to wait for the banks to open, because for a long while it seemed impossible to find secure places for all these items, which dangled unstably from handlebars, pack or windshield, or competed for space on the floorboards with brake pedal and feet. Yet this was all stuff we would need. How *had* our predecessors managed? (Answer: on motorcycles with large saddlebags or panniers.)

Eventually we set off, stopping at the bank. Hector went inside to purchase enough money to get us to the border while I stayed at the curb with the absurdly overloaded scooters. After a few moments a sleek-looking man in his forties, wearing a grey business suit and the ubiquitous sunglasses of the Near East, approached me. "Ho, ho, where are you going on *those*?" he asked in distinct, accented English, pointing to the Lambrettas.

"Ho ho, west across the desert," I replied.

He looked at me sharply. "I hope you know how to take them apart and put them together in the dark, then."

"Oh yes, sure," I said, as casually as possible, but was rattled enough to add inanely, "Why do you say that?"

He shrugged, smiled enigmatically, and moved away to stand and talk with some other men leaning against the wall of the bank. They all began scrutinizing me. And what arcane force sent *you*, I wondered, to stage this Kafkaesque anxiety scene, or oriental fable, or waking nightmare? I was glad when Hector returned, and started to tell him about the episode, but when I glanced at the wall again my gnomic interrogator had disappeared. Hector looked at me, a bit sharply, I thought. "So, we go?" he asked, as if that were now a point to be discussed.

"*Yallah*, we go." In a few minutes we were bumping through the western fringes of the city, over railroad tracks and cobblestones well designed to destabilize shaky loads. It was 11 AM as we rolled into open farming country - the last of the Delta verdure, gift of the Nile - and sped up. West, not south: I felt a final burst of regret at this definitive turning away from the old dream of black Africa. Well, it might be an adventure worth having anyway. "Cairo to Casablanca" had a nice ring.

... like a man prepared, like a brave man,
bid farewell to her, to Alexandria who is departing.
Above all, do not delude yourself, do not say that it is a dream,
... bid farewell to her, to Alexandria whom you are losing.

C. P. Cavafy

22. Lateen-rig sailboat, Ismailiya canal, Egypt

23. Avenue of the Rams, Karnak

24. Hector and the fallen Ramses II, Thebes

25. One of Cairo's youth hostels ("Death on the Nile")

26. Farmland at Minoufia in the Egyptian Delta

27. Chephren Pyramid, Giza, from the Great Pyramid

28. The Shell station, El Alamein (Winter Wright)

29. An equipment check in the Western Desert (Winter Wright)

30. Camping in the Siwa Oasis

31. Tea in the desert: the search for twigs

32. First night in Libya: the bombed house

33. A stop to swim: the Cyrenaica coast, Libya

34. Camping in the ruins at Cyrene

35. “Stripped for desert travel”

36. The Marble Arch, Libya

37. The Roman theatre, Leptis Magna

VIII. Headwinds

We created man to try him with afflictions.

The Koran

Conditions are not bad at first. The jarring exit from Alexandria loosens our loads enough that we have to stop and re-tie some items, yet the road is decent, the sun warm, the headwind moderate. Our Desert Campaign is under way, and the scale is African - 3000 kilometers to Tunis, 5000 to Morocco – even if it's not the Africa we sought. Never mind! Stop kvetching! There are still traces of vegetation (tall grass, palms, scrub brush) and some farming, with camels pulling plows or ponderously circumambulating wells, raising water buckets corkscrew-fashion. The road stays near the Mediterranean, which is milky green or aqua close to shore, deep blue flecked with white further out. We begin to bounce sharply over little sandspits jutting across the road; within minutes I have to call another halt and try to secure the can of gas better.

About 50 kilometers west of Alexandria we enter a more desertic region, barren except for low bushes - like mesquite or greasewood - and the wind freshens into a significant opponent. Chilled, I am thanking the Creator for the boon of a smooth road when I come over one of a series of low crests and run onto rough, mottled pavement with a tooth-rattling jolt. All right for You! Nor does the road improve; this third-class patchment becomes the new standard. Was it *ever* resurfaced after the war and all those tanks? Travel at over 50 kph is uncomfortable, though Hector drops back to say that it is no worse at 60, then bounces on ahead. Ten kilometers along this new surface the 2-liter fuel can falls off and springs a leak. I pour the contents into my gas tank (noting that the fuel level there appears lower than it should be) and throw the can into the desert. Anyway, onward, as Mort Sahl used to say.

At *El Alamein* (104 kms.) we reach famous, one might say hallowed, ground. Neither of us is really a war buff - which is strange, since it was the great global paroxysm of our childhoods - but we know that this was the scene of epic tank battles in 1942 - Rommel the Desert Fox and his Afrika Korps against Monty and the 8th Army - and the closest that the Nazis came to Alexandria. We stop at the quiet, impressive British cemetery, where neat rows of white wooden crosses stretch for acres. Leo said that we would see relics of the war, but nothing has prepared me for this moving, silent witness. What greater waste could there be than dying in or over this empty land? For the second time in Egypt, "Ozymandias" volunteers for service:

"Look on my works, ye Mighty, and despair!"
...Round the decay
...boundless and bare
The lone and level sands stretch far away.

Hector and I walk about there for an inexplicably long time in the wan sun, comfortless wind, and blowing dust tendrils without saying anything. I had uncles in this war, albeit in the Pacific. On up the road a bit, we visit the big white Italian memorial, where the dead rest in crypts.

We also discuss our options after Hector discovers a leak in *his* spare gas can, empties what remains into his tank and tosses away the container to join other rusting scrap in the long-suffering desert. At least we're reducing our loads, but are using so much gas bucking the wind that neither of us is likely to have enough to make the next town, *Mersa Matruh*, still 186 kms. away (Rommel, always short of fuel for his panzers, might have sympathized). Should we return to Alexandria, try again another day, or take a ship along the coast? Maybe our Lambrettas just aren't up to the job, westbound; all the riders we've met came from the west (of course), *with* the prevailing winds.

But wait: why *isn't* there gas here at this storied place, the first stop of any kind west of Alex? Looking closely at our map, we see that the *X* for El Alamein is not exactly at the place-dot, as in most other locations, but slightly west. Hmm...we *could* drive a bit farther, on hope, faith, or spec, and see what turns up. After all, Hector says bitterly, we don't need gas to go *east*: the wind will take care of that.

Jan. 21, police station, El Dab'a, Egypt, 5 PM - We're on our way across North Africa. Didn't leave Alex until 11 AM, due to having to wait for banking hours & tying on gas cans & water bags. After several false starts, hit the road with this arrangement: each carrying a spare ½ liter of oil in the glove compartment [and] one spare gallon of gas lashed on, Hector carrying 2 qts. gas in the canteen, me carrying the water bag with 3 liters water, & a 2-liter can of fuel.

...At Alamein we considered going back, but were too stubborn & proud to quit. Three kms. further we found gas & some food.

Pride is doubtless a major ingredient in our refusal to give up. What, limp back to Alex with our taillights between our legs and risk running into George? Or Cecile! So, score one for the cardinal sin, plus some faith and recklessness. No pump or logo identifies the stone-and-mortar blockhouse as a gas station, but it is *exactly* where the map indicates, and the red lettering on its whitewash arouses our interest. We stop, and our inquiry is richly rewarded with fuel (in cans) and bread. Hector snaps a picture of me and the building's two denizens standing by EE 1068. They look bemused but pleased with our road show; my grin reflects our improved prospects. On the wall behind us are painted the Arabic letters *shin-lam*: Sh-L. Shell.

We pushed on 37 more kms. to this station amid sandy wastes, & decided to spend the night. The soldier police are very pleasant; have given us cots inside. We have come 162 kms. from Alex, are 128 from Matruh (next gas), & 2773 from Tunis. Our longest stretch sans gas should be 286 kms.

I squint to write by lamplight in the adobe general store/ café across the road from the bare police bungalow after our meal of bread, canned sardines and tea. With no electricity, just the glare of lanterns surrounded by flickering shadows and then blackness (Plato's cave!), I have no difficulty in feeling night as a Hostile Entity. A few army barracks up a side road are the only other signs of human occupancy. Why someone put a checkpoint just here, in all these empty miles, is a mystery, but here it is, so you stop, produce passport, visa and *carnet*, and they inspect the sticker on the windshield and whatever else takes their fancy. Thus it is in a police state, where army and police fuse into one ubiquitous brown uniform throughout the country and are hard to tell apart (hence my term "soldier police"). We are the center of attention in this little enclave, but communication is difficult. Despite my vows and Leo's endorsement, I have *not* become fluent in Arabic, which has a tedious habit of varying in vocabulary and pronunciation from one country or region to another.

Pleasantly surprised that we have managed to cover a hundred miles in a short first day with the ungainly new arrangement on the Lambrettas, I draw a diagram for posterity: green water bag hanging down the front panel, gas can on the floorboards, food-and-camera bag on top of the pack, poncho and new funnel shoved under the tie ropes. (Not shown: anything that fell off and was thrown away.) During a month of touring Egypt, mostly by train or car, I almost forgot the exhilaration of actually setting off cross-country on the scooter, yet here it is again, rather like a taste of good champagne; under my grumbling and worry I am hugely excited to be embarked on this adventure. My mental focus has narrowed and intensified: overcome today's problems, cross another stretch of desert.

I have begun to wonder what "desert" means, though. Raised on Hollywood's barren sand dunes and Death Valley, I could hardly accept the first miles outside the Delta as "real" desert. Even here in this generally desolate waste there are clumps of grass and low bushes that look like sagebrush. We call it "scrub" or "coastal" desert.

Jan. 22, MATRUH, Egypt, 7:30 PM - Have reached first checkpoint - 290 kms. from Alex., 2645 from Tunis - & are in a hotel. The drive today was 128 kms. - 4 hrs. - over bad roads in barren country. Tomorrow we will try to hitch a ride to the Siwa oasis, 300 kms. south. Last night someone stole my sweater, causing great consternation. This morning a kind, English-speaking sergeant-major gave me a military sweater.

When we return to our bunks after dinner, my pack lies open and clothes are strewn on the cot. My only sweater is gone: a significant loss, especially on January mornings in the desert. The base commander initiates an inquiry that generates many phone calls, much charging about in the night, and eventually the news that a young soldier who went to Alexandria on leave soon after our arrival is the prime suspect. He cannot be reached now, but will return in three days, and then I will have satisfaction. Appalled to have set in motion the wheels of military justice toward some poor kid (and not about to hang around for three days), I explain that I just need a sweater for warmth, whereupon the sar-major sends to the warehouse for a coarse-woven, olive-drab Egyptian Army pullover, with holes at the shoulders for epaulets. As with the hubbly-bubbly in Damascus, my entrepreneurial flame flickers briefly (Ivy Leaguers would go for these) and expires, but I treasure the sweater - as I hope the private does mine.

Here ends my second journal - the one featuring Paul's epiphany - which saw me from his church in Antioch/ Antakya through our first falls and subsequent descent into bureaucratic hell to the sandy streets of Mersa Matruh in the Western Desert: Land of the Dead, realm of Osiris. Its successor, ready and waiting, has a windmill embossed on its dark brown cover. Maybe it will last me all the way to the land of Don Quixote.

Siwa: in the tracks of Alexander

The side trip to Siwa could have been one of our most glorious escapades (or complete debacles) had we done as we wished and ridden the scooters there. Leo had recommended the place, and Hector thought that a trip there, photographed by him and written up by me, could be turned into a saleable article that would help defray our expenses. We had seen such a piece in an issue of *LIFE* magazine at Minoufia, and were ready to believe that we might strike an equally rich vein ("Young Daredevils Reach Ancient Oasis on Motor Scooters"). Anyway, Siwa sounded interesting. A date-palm oasis 300 kilometers down in the desert, it *had* to be "exotic," perhaps "romantic," and Alexander the Great had made it "historic" by marching there to worship at the shrine of Jupiter Ammon (324 BCE). It was said to have some ancient relics, and had even figured in the desert skirmishes of 1942.

"But," warned the man at Mersa Matruh's gas station, "you have to know the way! After the paved road ends, there is nothing - only desert, and tracks going every way: some to Siwa, some to Libya, some to Fayyum, some to little settlements, some back to the coast! How do you know? You don't want to be lost in the desert."

He was right about that. We looked at each other doubtfully, wishing we had questioned Leo more closely. Our map showed a dotted line, a track, heading SSW to Siwa, but we had no compass, and found none for sale there. But hey, what if we just followed a truck?

"Maybe you cannot keep up, he go too fast, or you have to stop for some reason. Pour gas…flat tire?"

"Well…" No doubt we pursued the scheme less tenaciously because we were already tired of riding on rough surfaces, and the way would be long, the days short, the nights cold, and gas tight. "Will there be fuel at Siwa?"

"Maybe, if you can find it."

We frowned, shook our heads, put the scooters in storage, and for a few pieces of silver bought places on a supply truck heading for Siwa the next day. And when the pavement ended, and we saw *telephone poles* marching straight across the desert, heedless of the many curving tracks, to Siwa, and were angry - were *they* "nothing?" - whom could we blame but ourselves? Why hadn't we just driven to the end of the road and taken it from there? We had already forgotten the north-south travelers in Cairo; we did not *deserve* to strike it rich. How long, O Lord, until we learn to follow our star? Yet the road taken was memorable.

Jan. 25, SIWA Oasis, 9 AM - Left Matruh at 2 PM on the 23rd for a ride which will always be with me. About 16 people of all sizes, personalities, & [both] sexes crammed into the open back of a diesel truck in the space not occupied by empty [oil drums]. Hector & I were the object of all curiosity & humor, & for the first 5 hrs. the resultant mirth, songs, & faux pas made the time pass quickly.

We stopped once so that passengers could fan out and gather firewood – i.e. twigs - which were then bundled and lashed to the chassis for later use. Where the pavement ended, halfway to Siwa, there was an earthen roadhouse that sold big rounds of *hob's* (bread), canned food, and cookies. We crouched Arab-style with the others around a fire on the floor of the back room, eating bread and cheese and sipping from glasses of hot, sweet tea as they made their rounds. The room was a manger; the turbaned figures squatting in the straw made it a Biblical scene, except for the small gas stove that warmed the tea. Hector observed that we could certainly have driven this far, though we would not have been part of our little Siwan society that way.

At about 7:30 PM, the paved road gave way to a rutted desert track, with an increased strain on derrieres. The extreme simplicity of the Arabs, their ability to laugh 100 times at the same joke ("Shoocron! Ha, ha!" "Berberico! Ho, ho!"), and their lack of consideration for feelings, finally wore on my nerves & I grew short-tempered toward morning. Nevertheless, the trip produced some wonderful moments.

We traded songs - everyone clapping rhythmically to "Old Time Religion" ("It was good enough for Allah") - and stopped for tea around a campfire on the desert at midnight. The truck's headlights stabbed the void as I walked a big circle around our "camp" to get warm and loosen up. Rarely have I felt so isolated as in the chill blackness on the far side of the truck, where I heard the babble of voices but could not see the firelight. The remaining hours were mostly miserable. The cold became sharp enough (and I was wearing *everything*) that sleep was nearly impossible, although at times I managed to achieve a sort of dozing stupor. Once I started from a dream about falling into a toilet to find that I was slipping down into a stack of tires.

We arrived at Siwa's palm groves at 4:30 AM. Our buddy Samir negotiated to install us in the plain but comfortable rest house and get us out of the 30-p. fee. We got up at noon, walked into town & ate [a] breakfast of hot Arab bread. After looking around the ruins of old (Roman) Siwa for awhile, we hiked back to the rest house, got our packs & left them at the police station.

Ancient Siwa looked as if it had been bombed, but we were told that occasional hard rains gave it that appearance. The "Government Guest House" was a sad operation: sitting off by itself outside of town, empty, it brought to mind pictures of public housing on vacant lots in Eastern Europe, or a film of a Kafka novel. With no food, no running water, just bare concrete with minimal furnishings, staffed only by a semi-demented caretaker, it seemed a parable of the problems of state-sponsored tourist facilities in developing countries. The fee was waived that night because it was nearly morning, but the idea of paying 30 piastres to stay there - a mile from town - the next night when we could camp just about anywhere seemed absurd.

On our way to the police station we met a natty and high-spirited Samir, who squired us around all afternoon. "Siwa bad, all bad," he said, shaking his head gravely. Why? Poverty? Vice?

He would not elaborate. Maybe he felt ashamed of it, or perhaps it occurred to him that badmouthing your home town to foreigners was not a good idea in a police state. Together we drank tea, played a game like checkers, and bought some Siwa dates: 5 cents a pound and very tasty. Samir walked us to the fringes of the village (population estimates ranged from 600 to 5000), to the cemetery, to the drinking pool, fringed by sand and palms, and to the top of a hill in the center of town.

From there, we had a tremendous sunset view of the entire oasis, reaching the sand-lapped edges of the desert. [Siwa], 57 feet below sea level, is in a saucer-like depression surrounded almost completely by low, irregular hills, ridges or mesas. The palms, springs, & sand make it almost a stereotype oasis. But no camels.

Even camelless, Siwa struck me as just about perfect. Absurdly picturesque with its palm groves and robed natives footing it softly in the sand, it was quite unlike any other place I had ever stayed. Yet the outside world was reaching into Siwa. Samir and two other students on the truck, one a girl, went to school in Alexandria; they spoke a little English and French, and probably brought in a few novel ideas along with some infidel words.

Told that we couldn't sleep at the police station, we pitched camp under a palm tree across the street. It was one of our best nights of camping: well-pitched tent, not too cold, good location. We ate a tent dinner of a can of mackerel, an orange, & some dates. I slept pretty well, & we arose at 7.

After photographing our tent in the palm orchard - planted in rows and cultivated – we broke camp and moved over to the police post to await a ride north. A truck, first rumored to be departing the previous night at 10 PM, then "perhaps" around 4 AM, was now considered likely to go at "10, or 12, or 4." Evidently such things could not be hurried or anticipated. Having some discretionary time, I wrote up my journal, noticing that it was exactly four months since we had sailed from New York.

Samir arrived to collect us for another excursion. When I said that we had to stay and be ready for a truck, he seemed puzzled; everyone in town will know when it is going, he said, and we can see it from far away. The police agreed, so we returned with him to ancient Siwa - a hill outside of town – explored caves, took pictures, examined old carvings and hieroglyphics. Still no truck, so we turned social and were lionized at several domestic teas (the salty water tasted better in that form). The female student whom we had met on the truck - her name sounded like Festa - proved very amiable, inviting us home to meet her family. They received us calmly, nor did I find anything strange about them or their household. Sitting on mattresses or hassocks placed on carpets covering the earthen floor of the sun-dried house, lifting glasses of tea from low tray-tables, I wondered at my lack of wonder. My freshness must have staled: I was taking too much for granted.

Jan. 26, Matruh, Egypt, 9 PM - Back from Siwa. If the ride down was memorable, the return was an ordeal. After several false alarms, we left at 11 PM, in all cold weather garb, on top of a load of barrels. It was cold, cold, cold as I curled up in a 2' x 4' space on top of 2 drums. The wind & leaking oil kept comfort to a minimum.

Palm oil, presumably - definitely not petroleum. Towards dawn I raised up on a sore elbow and for the first time saw no telephone poles. The horizon was absolutely featureless. From the shouting in the cab, the arms stuck out both windows, pointing east and west, and the way the truck was turning right and left, I gathered that we were lost. But it didn't seem to be my problem at that point, so I curled up again and had my best sleep of the night, nearly an hour. When I woke again it was 6 A.M., the sun was rising and the phone lines were in sight. I "got up." Grim-visaged Hector also appeared from his perch.

In a few minutes we stopped, collected such twigs as the waste afforded, and re-enacted the ritual of tea in the desert. A venerable blue teapot was placed amid our burning "bush." As the water began to boil, the driver threw in some tea leaves. A minute later he snatched it from the flames - with some laughter over burnt fingers (no hot-pan lifter, of course) - and filled a sherry glass with steaming tea. When the first drinker finished, the same glass was refilled for the next, and so on until all had drunk or the tea was gone. Obviously this was not an entirely sanitary procedure, and I did not want another dose of dysentery, but for the moment the precious revivifying warmth overrode my caution. Maybe the scalding would suffice. Under the circumstances, it was not surprising that we dispensed with the traditional three cups per guest, each cup sweeter than the last.

Our driver and three fellow-passengers accepted us stolidly, almost without remark. We helped gather wood, shared the tea and the cold with them. Solid, lower-class draymen, they knew that we were Americans, but lived so far from The World as not to think that we should therefore be rich or fat or somewhere else on a tour. Perhaps they had heard of us at Siwa or Matruh. Months later, when a German with whom I hitchhiked told me sternly that I *could not be* an American because no Americans traveled this way, I remembered these men with gratitude.

At the roadhouse where the pavement began, we halted for two hours to await the return of some friends of the driver: shepherds with whom he had a luncheon date. After walking around for awhile, I stretched out on the tarpaulin-covered barrels atop the truck to bask in the weak sun, warming my heels. It was past noon when we started again.

The ride was slow: we arrived here after 18 hrs. at 5 PM. Now we are strapping on saddlebags & girding loins for a one-day stand to Sallum (230 kms.) & the border. The pressure is on to make it before our money runs out; somehow I'm very apprehensive.

Just why my nervous system chose this moment to flinch is not clear: perhaps a combination of worries about money, about mechanical breakdown in the desert, or about running out of gas. I might have taken heart from having found a half-decent pair of military-surplus saddlebags (for which I had been looking) in Mersa Matruh. Costing 80 cents, they eased our baggage problem somewhat. Even so, I had moved far enough into a realm of free-floating fear, adrenaline, and fatalism to inscribe in my journal an address to which it should be sent if found.

Jan. 28, DERNA, LIBYA, 9 PM - Don't know what to make of the last 2 days as regards my premonitions - they've been a mixture of near-calamities & achievements. Left Matruh 8 AM yesterday. Saddlebags worked well. Ran smoothly for over 100 kms. through rolling & then flat desert; then, in a series of hills, I had several motor failures. Motor would drop revs in 4th gear as [I] climbed a hill. I nursed each along by dropping into 2nd, finally it cured itself.

Clear exposition was one casualty of the desert crossing. *Of course* I lost rpm on hills and had to downshift: every scooter driver does! Yet this drop was abrupt and excessive, given the grades and the negligible headwind that morning. It was Mount

Lebanon all over again - but where was the mechanic who would set the engine to rights this time: Benghazi? Tripoli? Tunis? It sickened me to think of those boy mechanics in the Peloponnese tinkering with the motor, though I myself - cleaner and gapper of sparkplugs, adjuster of the carburetor's fuel/air mixture - might be implicated by now. Was this just bits of sand and dirt passing through the fuel line? Or the ghost of Lucinda, stuffing her poncho, or toga, in the air scoop?

At the Egyptian border post in the village of Sallum it took a while to clear police and customs. The inspector kept inventing charges - departure tax, visa tax, scooter tax - until I caught on and handed over the little Egyptian money I had left, telling him that this was all. He smiled condescendingly, took it, and waved us on through his currency filter. The last of the $50 that had carried me through Egypt thus departed in classic Middle Eastern fashion. *Now*, I thought, we're committed. We're not going back to *that*.

The Kingdom of Libya

In 1960 Libya had not yet acquired a revolutionary leader or an attitude. Still ruled by a king, exhibiting lots of Italian influence left over from decades of colonial dominance, allowing foreign companies to drill for oil down in the desert, quietly tolerating British and American military bases, Libya remained in effect an occupied country. Much of it was empty; parts were beautiful and historically interesting. I knew little about it, though, as we left Sallum and climbed a steep bluff to the Libyan frontier town, Capuzzo, which sounded mighty Italianate for the Arab world. The Mediterranean down in the half-moon bay at the western limit of Egypt was a lucid, vibrant blue, and the line of dark cliffs curling around from the southeast gave the land more character than we had seen since Lebanon.

It took under an hour to get through police, customs, & immigration in Capuzzo, which looks like a Kansas wheat town, complete with one water-tower, set in a perfectly flat scrub plain. Hector changed a little money, & we gassed up & moved on.

A friendly German tourist, heading east in a Mercedes with his family, filled us in on some places to watch for on the coast just ahead, including possible overnight havens. We noted - not for the first time – that both the best and the worst travelers tended to come from Germany.

We drove 15 kms. to a sheltering valley he mentioned, arriving a few minutes before sunset. Saw four bombed-out concrete dwellings a few hundred yards off the road to our right, &, finding they were deserted, put up for the night.

The choice was easy, the nearest hotel being far away, and night driving not an option. We wouldn't even need to pitch the tent. "It shall be no offence for you to seek shelter in empty dwellings," says *The Koran*. I tied a line across an empty window casement and hung up my damp laundry from Matruh. We lit a couple of Laurent's solid-fuel tablets, warmed a can of "mackerel pike" and ate some sweet Siwa dates, washing them down with water: "the only drink for a wise man," wrote Thoreau, and T. E. Lawrence agreed.

Then we had a look around. Judging from barricades of rusted jerry cans, bullet holes in almost every surface, and crushed roofs and walls, an obscure little fight took place there during the war, just 18 years earlier; the defenders must have been besieged and shelled. As a place to die, it didn't have much on El Alamein. After dark we went exploring by flashlight. A cave in a nearby cliff opened into a large, man-made vault - rather like Mycenae's beehive tombs - that could have been a bomb shelter/command post. 1942 seemed very close that evening. I slept well until a damp chill moved in after midnight.

Up at 7 in the cold, breakfast of corned beef hash & water, on the road at 8:30. Within 10 minutes I had 2 engine failures on hills. Changed the spark plug, richened the mixture: it seemed to help. On across the desert to Tobruk. On our left: brown, low-lying hills, creased with dark ravines. On our right the blue Med, 2 or 3 miles away. Perfect weather.

Just before Tobruk, we saw a Vespa coming from the west and stopped to talk. The driver identified himself as a student from Cincinnati, doing his junior year abroad, but denied any knowledge of Pyramid Terry. We traded information ("scoop") about the road in each direction, wished each other well, and went our ways.

Tobruk, set on a narrow peninsula, was clean, white, attractive. We bought Libyan money, ate lunch & got gas. Was sorry to leave a pleasant town so quickly, but we wanted to get to Derna.

"Pleasant" was not enough. We knew that Tobruk had been a strategic port, hotly contested during the war, but did not know anyone who had fought there, or want to visit another war memorial. And it was far too early to stop.

We pushed on at 1:30. By our usual reckoning I should have had enough gas for the hundred miles to Derna, so did not fill the spare can. Big mistake! Headwinds (and perhaps grit in the engine) were rewriting the tables: I went on reserve 46 kms. before Derna. Ten minutes earlier, the left clamp of my windshield had broken going over a bump, and I was holding it together to ease the strain on the right one. My reserve gas ran out on a barren steppe 28 kms. short of Derna. Dusk was falling, few vehicles were passing, and Hector was also low on gas. We flagged down a truck, but they had only diesel. Then a carload of Englishmen - two RAF officers from Tobruk and an Anglican clergyman - laboriously drained a liter and a half from their tank for me. It was the man of the (soiled) cloth - a true Christian! - who did the dirty work under the car. We thanked them fervently but quickly and continued west.

As we came down the hills above Derna - spectacularly situated - I felt embattled. I was holding the left side of the windshield. The right post slipped off. My pack was falling & I was low on gas. At a Shell station I remedied everything but the cracked clamp, now being welded.

With the crooked windshield angling wind into my face, impeding vision, and having to be held, I was hard put to negotiate the descending curves with one hand. These were classic conditions for an accident, but it was not my time.

We are now in a 20 piastre (60 cent) hotel - good room & lights, large clean bath, excellent supply store next door. I'll fulfill a long-standing ambition by having Corn Flakes for breakfast!

It had come to this: a tough day on the road, all my culinary deprivation and an obvious need to regain strength after the bout of dysentery, a decent array of imported goods in the general store, and what I wanted was a box of toasted cereal from the Kellogg's people. It was a form of homesickness, of nostalgia for childhood breakfasts.

Most of the desert along this stretch is fairly attractive - low scrub brush, flowers of feathery white & others like unopened jonquils, patches of grass, & occasional trees. And the plain is never devoid of some sign of life: a cluster of huts, a shepherd & his flock, some Bedouin tents on the horizon, a herd of camels, etc. Mementos of the war [are] numerous: rusted tanks, piles of old gas cans.

I had not expected to see so many relics of the war, nor so much life in the desert. Remembering the blankness of the Siwa road, however, I guessed that most signs of human and botanical activity would fade out a few miles south of the coastal highway, and true desert take over.

Derna, our first urban stopover in Libya, was an attractive collection of light-colored cubes perched between steep green hills and the wine-dark sea. Night fell soon after our arrival, but in the morning (after the big Corn Flakes breakfast) we glimpsed its mingling of houses and shops while fetching my windshield from the welder. It looked like a place one could live, and the stock in the general store showed that it was part of the Mediterranean commercial world. We took advantage of that, buying as much food for the road as packs and saddlebags could carry.

Getting underway in late morning, we drove at a leisurely pace along the green, rocky coast of *Cyrenaica* – the Graeco-Roman name for eastern Libya – which vied with the Amalfi drive and coastal Maine in beauty, but was more accessible. Surely it would be a big tourist center someday; we were lucky to see it in "before" condition. The road was well-engineered, the sea colors irresistible. We parked on a bluff, descended a goat path, skinny-dipped in the clear aquajade waters lapping a sandy beach, and dried off in the sun. The smooth bottom shelved gently to underwater rocks just offshore: a skindiver's paradise. I wished for a mask and snorkel, but not much else. Only one car passed during this half-hour idyll, and we paid it no heed.

Further on, I stopped to photograph the white houses and minaret of *El Gubba*, a village set amid thorny bushes, stones, and a few trees on a slope above the sea, which had paled to a robin's-egg blue. We reached *Cyrene* – once the eponymous capital of the district - at four PM, having taken five hours to cover the day's 25 miles. For a few cents the guard let us camp in the ruins, near the Temple of Jupiter. To the north, a broad green plain, cut by gorges, slanted to the Mediterranean, a thousand feet below in the distance. The desert was elsewhere, all but forgotten.

Jan. 29, CYRENE, Libya, 6 PM - The spread of the Greeks & Hellenistic culture through colonization is well-known. But the clearest evidence I've seen is here, where the ruins of a large ancient Greek town cover two hills & the notch between (where we camp). The remains lie around, under, & between the houses of the present village. There are all the features of a Greek city: agora, amphitheatre, acropolis, temples & fountains & baths to Apollo & Artemis. Romans & Byzantines colonized here later, but the essential spirit is Greek.

We had read somewhere that Athens was once the only Greek city larger than Cyrene. In places an old wall or corridor disappeared right into a hillside. Clearly there was more - perhaps much more - excavating to be done, but we saw no sign that anyone was doing it.

Today was an excellent day for a travel-weary traveler. Now the sun is setting over the sea, & the cold seeps in.

Time to start dinner. We cooked on a low stone wall at the mouth of a cave, and, after clean-up, left our dishes and pot on the wall to dry. By then it was dark, so we turned in. It had been one of our Great Days, I thought, snuggling down in my bag, and quickly fell asleep. Some time later I was either awakened, or dreamt that I was awakened, by Hector, hissing, "Sst! Hear that?"

"Hmm? Hey…what?"

"Listen! Something's rattling the pans."

I listen. That *might* be a distant clink. "Small aminal? Animal. Or the guard."

"Or a thief. I'm going out. You can come if you want." He starts getting out of his bag.

Knowing how dreams work, I'm not about to fall for that move: if I go with him I wake up, and it's cold, and I can't get back to sleep. Hector leaves the tent, and later I hear him calling: "Okay, dad, I know you're in there!" I giggle and relax;

the dialogue is really bad in this one. Later I wake up - or dream I wake up - and Hector is crawling back in. "So, what's up? Anybody there?"

"Didn't see him. Probably scared him off. Don't worry about it, man."

"It's only a dream," I say, and open my eyes on the morning. When I told Hector what I remembered, he said it had been real. I apologized for having missed the drama, and was relieved to find the cook kit intact.

We roamed around the silent ruins for an hour before breakfast, taking pictures by the early light and briefly disturbing a camel who was grazing on some spiky-leafed wildflowers with saffron blossoms. Two peasant women, their faces bare, sat talking in a white colonnade that cast strong shadows against the back wall of the agora.

When we had eaten, struck the damp tent, packed up and were tying on, I had a sudden inspiration. Curved packframe on luggage rack, slick metal to slick metal, had *never* been a stable proposition. What if I turned the pack over, putting the soft side down? Would the metal edges of the spare wheel cut the fabric? Would things fall out? I decided to experiment. It worked like a charm: tying the pack on was easier; bumps only settled it deeper into the open center of the spare; nothing fell out. To have solved that 5000 kilometer, four-month problem was a joy, a relief, a godsend. But why hadn't I thought to try it the first day?! And why *had* I today? The readiness is all.

Jan. 30, BENGHAZI, Libya, 9 PM - The first leg of the trans-North Africa haul, 1140 kms., is complete. We rolled into the port of Benghazi about 4:30, a run of 225 kms.: 5½ hours from Cyrene. The early part carried us thru the Cyrenaica highlands: wooded hills, patches of farmland, precipitous canyons & rural valleys. The country folk dress in very colorful costume: reds & blues for the kids, quilted shawls & serape-like blankets, black trousers & colored headdress for the men.

Few women were visible along the road. We enjoyed a sylvan lunch stop, consuming culinary delights from Derna in a pine forest on a slope overlooking the highway, where our patient steeds awaited us.

About 110 kms. before Benghazi, we dropped onto a fertile plain, good farmland, squeezed between inland plateau & coastal hills. Then up again thru the curves & drops of hills bordering the sea, & down to the lovely Med. The final 70 kms. were along the coastal plain, broken only by palms, & the gradually receding dark-ravined escarpment to the left. The road was bad, likewise sun & wind, & it was a tired pair that squeaked thru sand, mud huts & waving palms to enter Benghazi after another hour & a quarter.

We laid over the next day in Benghazi, which struck me as a dull, motley excuse for a city. The prominent foreign colony - Italian, British, American - seemed to live more apart from the natives than their counterparts in Alexandria, and their demand for imported goods caused higher prices than in Egypt: 60 cents a night for a grimy room in a *pension*, about twice that per day for a little food. Most goods were more expensive than the Levantine norm. "It's a colonized country," I wrote. "But it's a young, growing country, potentially rich in oil. So far I like it." Benghazi, however, was Libya at its least attractive: a shoddy veneer of European civilization stuck onto a sleepy Arab town, with neither culture showing to advantage. In Casablanca, at least the veneer had been chic; in Benghazi, it was peeling. What the Italian conquest of Libya had achieved, beyond building the coast road and a twin-domed cathedral in Benghazi, I could not see. Nothing in the city foretold its emergence as a centre of resistance to a despot fifty years later.

Such goods and services as it provided, though, we consumed. In the absence of a Lambretta shop, I had the Vespa people look at my carburetor; they charged me nothing, which was fair, since they did nothing. I wrote my draft board that I would *not* be starting school next month after all. The envelope dropped through the Airmail slit in the PTT building with a fateful swish. We mailed film home, bought a box of Corn Flakes, looked at stoves and saddlebags, bought a spare gas can. Clothes were washed and sewn. It was a standard layover day.

For some reason February 1st emerged as one of my favorite days on the trip, along with many more pleasant, and in some ways its emotional center. Apparently I had come for the adversity.

Feb. 1, [near] Marble Arch, Libya, 7 PM - I cannot find a single adjective for today; its events seemed to reach deep into my spirit. We are comfortably & warmly settled in a trailer lent by the commander of this [-], at which we arrived about 6 PM. On route to such comfort we had to undergo considerable trials.

We rose at 6:15, ate our 2nd consecutive Corn Flake breakfast, tied on & left our hotel at 7:30. By 8 we were gassed up & outside Benghazi on the highway.

This time we fill every available gas container, knowing that long empty stretches lie ahead. The road leaves Benghazi, as it came into it, heading almost due south: skirting the Gulf of Sirte, a place of evil repute for ill winds and shifting sands since Homer (Odysseus and his men may have been shipwrecked here). *Syrtis Major* - Big Sandy Bay - is a deep indentation into Africa, the place where the Mediterranean comes closest to the Sahara, and the heat exchange, aka wind, is (to put it mildly) significant.

The sun isn't up until 7:30 these days, & was still low enough for it to be quite cold. We ran smoothly on generally good roads for over an hour, through two small towns, the latter of which had gas.

It is not marked as a fuel stop on the map we were given in Cairo, and we think we have enough gas, and are in a hurry, so we sail right on through. Slow learners! But we don't have to pay - this time. Soon I smell the freshness of rain: a dark cloud is approaching from our left or desert side, moving west on its way to the sea. It passes in front of us, however, leaving the pavement just noticeably streaked and its smell sweetened by moisture. The sun comes out again.

But it shone thru a bright haze, light brown, of windblown sand which hung in the air all around for 15° above the horizon. About 70 kms. from Benghazi, the wind began, suddenly, rising in the space of a kilometer from nothing to full velocity. It was mostly free of sand, but blew from our right & from ahead. And it did not just blow, it raked us: only with difficulty could I maintain 60 kms./hr.

Mid-level cloud coming from the east, surface wind from the west and south: we must be close to what meteorologists call a wind shear. The scooter handles like a small boat when wind and tide are opposed. The westerly weaves a moving curtain of sand across the road and the Lambrettas rock wildly in its gusts: the worst conditions since El Alamein. An onshore wind like this could have driven Odysseus' ships aground. No one ever called *me* a "man skilled in all ways of contending," but I battle on, looking for my Homeric epithet. How about *Wind Rider*?

One post of Hector's windshield breaks, and he cannot hold it manually. We stop, remove the windshield and tie it to the newly-exposed top- or frame-side of my pack, where it nestles as if this had been planned from the first. *Now* I understand the importance of the new system! Then he removes a side panel, pulls out his battery - which has not worked for some time - pronounces it useless and throws it over his shoulder into the uncomplaining desert with heroic insouciance. "Stripping for desert travel," says Hector, breaker of scooters.

We passed regions of real desert: flat wastes of sand in every direction, broken only by little hummocks of scrub, populated only by herds of camels & a few solitary roadside workmen, shoveling in the wind

or sheltering behind low dunes. As we approach, they raise two fingers to the mouth in a narrow 'V' = "Got a smoke?" We make gestures of apology *en passant*; some of them smile and wave. What a job Libya's Federal Roads Department has with this long, vital, weather-beaten highway! Between any two towns, someone is shoveling, and FRD buildings are a welcome sight on isolated stretches. But keeping the road clear of sand is a Sisyphean task, and these windswept solipsists seem allegories of futility. Each man is alone with his shovel; there are no groups.

Later we passed into a region of hills, accompanied only by power lines (not even a RR), the wind, & shifting sands. Outside Jedabia, I ran on reserve. When I filled up, it had taken an appalling 8 liters for 160 kms., or 50 miles a gallon. So I still have my problems.

But it would tax our fuel capacity even at "normal" consumption (which I still think of as the 80 mpg we enjoyed in Greece) to cover some of the dry stretches on this road. At the new rate, my range, even with extra fuel, is 160 miles; according to the map, there is a gap of 180 miles between gas stations up ahead. I hope it is wrong, or that the headwinds will abate, or that Hector, still getting 60 mpg, can make it across and bail me out. As we lunch on bread, hardboiled eggs and coffee in a roadside café at Jedabia, we discuss how to carry more gas. The scooters already look like Hong Kong junks. Maybe in our mouths? It could double as mouthwash! Don't make me laugh! Turning back is no longer discussed. We'd rather push.

The truck stop looks like a place you might see in Nevada; big trans-Africa diesel semi-trailers sit all around the café on a field of gravel like hungry condors. But there is no tough-talking waitress, and the piped music doesn't swing, though it wails. So far the road has passed through or close by every town, and our map shows it passing through Jedabia (which the world will know, half a century later, as the battleground of Ajadabia). Yet there is no sign of a town here, at least not through the sandy, cloudy, opaque haze that passes for an atmosphere.

Before noon we drive on, bending southwest.

20 kms. after we left Jedabia I was having such trouble staying in 4th [gear] against the wind that I took [my windshield] off & added it to the pile. It helped, & by leaning forward almost parallel to the road, over the speedometer, I could make 60 kph or more, except up hills.

The windshield has been acting as a reverse sail, giving the headwind more purchase, and having to cruise in 3rd gear would be fatal to gas consumption. "Stripped for desert travel," both machines look sleeker, and two nested windshields tie as easily as one onto my pack frame. Hector takes the waterbag to balance the weights. Once underway, I rest my chin on the speedometer and hold onto the windshield posts, still upright on the handlebars. The throttle does not need to be held in position. The road is just a yard beneath my eyes, and it is like being sandblasted, but

what a sensation! The unbroken sweep of the headwind, plus my own 35 mph, flattened my glasses against my nose, deafened my ears; particles of sand made my face tingle; I was giddy from the swift unwinding of the road & the expanding rush of scenery. Hector's scooter still ran better, & he passed me

on a slight upgrade. For the rest of the day it takes full throttle just to keep him in sight. Both scooters are running faster and quieter with the new profile, though. In a

dark haze of floating sand, we labored through a weird countryside of white & brown dunes, startled camels bolting from the roadside, knots of huddled Bedouin staring from behind scrub bushes, & a wan sun working against huge white clouds & haze. By the time we reached the seaside haven of El Agheila, I knew once & for all that the core of myself was not ideals & intellectual life but instinct

& survival. I knew fear; my greatest desire was to assuage that fear. My deepest worry was the mechanical welfare of my scooter: with its soundness assured I could have been completely happy in the battle against the elements. We are as abstruse as our environments permit.

Now, in my comfortable study, this passage seems overwrought and would be easy to mock. Yet the knowledge I felt emanating from that day's struggle is proof against elderly scepticism. My present surroundings permit me to be more "abstruse," but do not expose that "core."

At *El Agheila* - near the bottom of the Gulf of Sirte's southerly indentation - we have another coffee and refuel. There's no light, two-stroke oil here (or anywhere since Alexandria), and we long ago used up our half-litre "emergency" cans. *North Africa is an emergency!* Oh, for the gas-oil pumps of long-ago Europe, where you just told the attendant 4%, 5%, or 6% mixture (though he often knew it already)! We have to use automobile crankcase oil, which, being heavier and not meant for ignition, is doubtless helping to foul our engines. If it comes in a can, at least we know the viscosity, but we use only a bit of a can per fill-up, and then how to store it? A bottle is best, if the cap fits. Often, though, it has been decanted into a random container, and looks used, pre-owned, recycled.

They find us a strainer for the gas and dirty oil, but blowing sand is everywhere: drifting into the gas tanks as we fill them, thence into fuel lines, carburetor, and cylinder; fine grains cling to the oily mesh of the strainer as I bring it away. Neither scooter will kick-start. I push Hector until his catches, and off he goes. Mine I start by running it along, pounding hard until I have 8 mph or so, shifting into first and releasing the clutch. As it kicks over I jump onto the seat and open the throttle. The engine catches at once; I roll off westward in pursuit of far-darting Hector. The afternoon is looking wilder than the morning.

Constant full throttle against the wind, tendrils of sand snaking across the road to drag at me, endless patterns of hills & dunes, greys & browns, dark light & light dark. I was a threatened animal. At 5:30, from 9 kms. away, I sighted the towering Marble Arch, marking the divide between Cyrenaica & Tripolitana. It's quite impressive, rising from the flat desert.

Mussolini's monument, desert tan on a white base at the boundary between Libya's ancient provinces, looks like the work of someone drunk on the grandeur that was Rome. The arch itself, 50 or 60 feet high but only the width of the road, is encased in a trapezoid topped by rabbit ears over a hundred feet up. All around, the lone and level sands stretch far away, broken only by a couple of radio masts and grazing burros: another Ozymandias, this time Italian. "Look on my works, ye mighty, and despair!" Up close the arch seems garish and ugly, yet it is a welcome landmark for which I feel only affection. Eyeing the cozy barracks nearby, we ask the guard who checks our papers where we might find shelter for the night. "*Non qui!*" he says hastily. One of our languages! *"Ma a 20 kilometri, ch'e un campo di Americani."* An American camp? He doesn't say anything else, but obviously considers us *their* problem. We may have just enough light to bridge the gap and find out who they are.

That little race against the sun was a pip: the first 15 kms. against the stiffest wind yet & a veritable sandstorm, the last 5 against the blinding sting of rain.

In *The Koran*, the Divine Messenger asks Mohammed, "Are you confident that He who is in heaven will not let loose on you a sandy whirlwind?" NO SIR!! Ten minutes before sunset I make out - through smears of dust and rain on my sunglasses - some tall antennae and squat buildings to our right. We turn up a track toward a small guardhouse. A sign there declares this to be an American ***** ***** base, which seems unlikely, as do most things that night, but the guards' uniforms and accents lend the idea some credibility, so we play along. A moment's uncertainty passes quickly: one look convinces them that we need shelter, and after a short phone call we are admitted. An orderly escorts us to the base commandant, a brisk, efficient man in early middle age who, after a few minutes' conversation, invites us to spend the night. I am reminded of the consul in Aleppo, and again suspect that class and manners are our *entrée* here. Which is just fine with us tonight, thanks.

We were hospitably received at this …station, & the sun set quietly & beautifully. We covered 374 kms. [today] - a new record.

Tough kilometers, into the wind on sub-par machines. We leave them in a dry, clean, well-organized maintenance shed as big as a hangar and take our packs to a cozy trailer. A shower, a hot dinner, a movie, and a good night's sleep follow in due course, my sense of having wandered into an unreal world increasing with each free, improbable boon. We and the men are equally curious about each other. Munching snacks in the rec room after the movie, narrating our adventures and bathing in their interest, I make one false step: "So, what are you guys doing here?" Silence and faces fall. A snap freeze. After a pause, one of them says, "Well, that's not something we can talk about." Aha! Right. Should have known. As we were! They probably wouldn't take us for spies, but they might suspect us of being US intelligence agents, CIA or CIC, looking for weak links, security risks. I suppose that they are doing communications and electronic monitoring, but keep my guesses to myself and go back to enjoying the unlooked-for sanctuary and slice of home. Weariness comes soon, though, closely followed by oblivion. It has been an amazingly long day.

Feb. 2, BUERAT, Libya, 7:30 PM - After a comfortable, well-fed night at the ...station & a hard day on the road, my theme again is simple values & essential comforts. What could be more important than good food, shelter against wind & cold & rain, a warm place to sleep & go to the bathroom? The rest is frosting.

*The ***** treated us magnificently. We had free access to the canteen. I dozed through the movie in order to be available for food, & was amply rewarded (coffee, fruit, sandwiches, pineapple & orange juice, milk & cookies). This morning we were fed breakfast & left with a handout: candy bars, sandwiches, breakfast cereals & sugar.*

Let the dietary emphasis here stand as a monument to the times. Several days' worth of breakfasts and lunches fill our saddlebags and a smaller pouch that dangles inside my handlebars; apparently they aren't afraid that we will report these freebies to Langley, or wherever. After breakfast we call on the C.O. to thank him for his hospitality. He is gracious, terming us "no trouble" and a good "morale boost" for the men. "They can use some diversion," he admits. For the first time I see that "shrewd" is another of his qualities. We linger a bit in his hut, not all that eager to depart; only the obvious boredom of most of the men and their open envy of our freedom make leaving bearable.

Eventually we do wheel out onto the highway - exchanging warm/dull/secure for cold/exciting/uncertain - and resume our progress, west-northwest now, angling away from the Sahara, toward Tripoli. When I look back after a kilometer, the place has disappeared as completely as Brigadoon, or the fellow outside the bank in Alexandria. Oh, probably just down in a dell - *that's where they always put communications posts, right?* I have been very discreet, but can now reveal it to be a Coast Guard station, presumably part of a postwar treaty. This was considered enemy - Italian - territory, and they lost. Too bad for the Libyans, who traded one occupation for another.

The morning was alternately clear & tempestuous. Running near the white-flecked green & blue of the Med, we pushed thru two wind-driven rain squalls.

Watching dark clouds and their trailing curtains of grey sweep toward us over the long roll of the plain, I find myself imagining the horror of desert battlegrounds, especially for individuals and vehicles under aerial attack with no place to hide. The use of aircraft to bombard surface targets began in 1911 – just eight years after the Wright brothers' first flight – when the Italians tried it out in Libya. We halt to don our ponchos, but find that stopping is wetter than riding. Let's see: maybe we should stop *before* the rain arrives! After each shower the air has a fine washed clarity, and the scent of the earth is almost worth the damp and chill.

In some respects, days on the desert tend to blur and run together; the topography, the weather, and our dilemmas having a certain sameness, several episodes might have occurred almost anywhere in Libya. Take the Damaged Bridge. Many of the countless spans across *wadis* (seasonal washes) were in poor repair: sooner or later one was bound to be *hors de combat*. So maybe that day, maybe the next or the previous one, we come to a bridge that is closed. One car sits at each end. A crew is examining the supports and a section of pavement and railing that has fallen away. We ask a guard how long the repair might take, but his answer is predictable: "*Bukrah*," which, we have learned, doubles as "tomorrow" and "the future." "*Mumkin al-yom?*" (Possible today?) A shrug. "*Mumkin*." Hector and I look down into the gulch that has to be crossed. It is perhaps 25 feet deep, with fairly steep sides and a rivulet at the bottom.

"What do you think? *Mumkin*?"

"Maybe. Let's try it. Waiting's no good."

We take Hector's first. Fearing that a kickstart might be difficult down in the little stream, he starts it, stands alongside, shifts into first and slowly lets out the clutch while keeping the handbrake on. No throttle! I hang onto the luggage rack from behind, doing my imitation of an anchor. Thus we slither down the slope to the streamlet, and reverse the forces: Hector lets go of the brake and opens the throttle while I push from behind. The Lambretta claws its way up the hill to the far side, spattering me only moderately. It worked! There are smiles and some applause from the spectators. Then we go back and repeat the operation for mine. We could have help by now, but don't need it. Within ten minutes we are on our way again.

We both ran out of gas near a town that wasn't there [except on the map], & were lucky to have to backtrack only 20 kms. for gas.

It takes some of our spare fuel to return to a station that we saw but passed up "because there's gas up ahead." Caught napping after our night of luxury at Brigadoon - *was that its true purpose?* - we haven't even noticed that this is the longest stretch without gas noted on the German's map, and are saved only by our extra fuel, and a source that he missed. This fuel scare, like earlier ones, shows how thin our margins are. We will not, in these peaceful days and with some traffic passing, perish; the stakes are merely discomfort, inconvenience, and delay: an hour, in this case, and 20 kilometers turned into 60.

Then on to Serte. The desert, all fine sand & green-topped hummocks, looked healthier after the rain. But it got boring. We ate a sandy lunch near a bridge 75 kms. from Serte, & reached it a little before 3. It was a small, white seaside town, where we gassed up & enjoyed the green trees along the highway.

In time, the world will know that Muammar Gaddafi was born here, or rather in a Bedouin tent nearby. He would have been 17 at the time, and probably off at school in Misurata, so he is not likely to have seen us that day.

The afternoon continues windy and chill. Desperately bored, I start timing the kilometer posts, trying to reach the next one in under a minute, but cannot get more than 60 kph out of the scooter. They seem to be counting down to insanity – mine - so I make myself desist and think instead about good times with Penny. We have an anniversary coming up on the 4th, as do Hector and Andrea. If we reach Tripoli by then, maybe we should wire them – something.

Then another long, dull stretch thru the most barren desert yet to this tiny truck stop where there is no gas, no inn, no electricity (can't even remember when the power lines stopped), but a bare room in the police station for us. It is welcome, a positive delight to be out of the night cold & the rain.

The police, though unfriendly or reserved, let us have a room on whose concrete floor we park the scooters and lay our sleeping bags. They seem to disapprove of our presence, and perhaps want to keep us under surveillance. From the crest of a bare hill behind the station, the wind-blown Mediterranean looks grey-green. At sunset we walk down to the wave-battered shore and through the village. Isolation, desolation, barrenness: *Buerat el Hsun* defines them. Such life as it has transpires in a dozen tiny, whitish mud-and-plaster huts near the road, where robed and turbaned figures move like shadow puppets in flickering rooms. We stare, they stare back, and there is no recognition; the sense of alienation is as powerful as the familiarity of the night before. Writing my journal by candlelight at a table in the hall outside our room, I wonder if the police are protecting us. By 8:30 I am too fatigued to do anything but crawl into my bag.

Feb. 3, HOMS, Libya, 9 PM - A tough day, spent mostly making tracks, leaves us both tired. We left Buerat at 8:30, & the 48 km. ride to the next gas at a crossroads was intensely cold. I was really miserable.

Without a windshield I find no defence against the cold, even wearing *all* my clothes and the poncho. Somehow it will seep in: up the legs, down the neck, along the wrists. I need down, and a real windbreaker. Hector, with his bomber jacket, seems marginally better off. The "crossroads" is a junction with a road that heads straight into the Sahara, going farther south than Siwa. We don't even notice.

We had hot tea & cookies there, worth waiting for. Then we pushed on, into a steady headwind, across bleak rolling desert. The desert in this stretch did not have the scrub-topped hummocks which often characterize it; neither was it flat. Grey clouds blew small sandstorms in our faces & added rain 13 kms. from Misurat.

Already dressed for rain, we press on as fast as possible through the blinding, drenching spray. My scooter has been running very weakly, only 50-60 kph wide open, but the headwind eases slightly – even swings around and tries to become a tailwind - as the storm hits, enabling me to reach 70. Hector's still runs a few kph faster in any situation, and it annoys us both that he keeps having to wait for me. Well, I'm taller and heavier. Or I *was* heavier.

The shower stopped as we entered town at 1:30. …20 kms. before Misurat, trees appeared by the road, & power lines took up the march. Misurat itself was quite nice, medium-sized, & surrounded by verdant fields & palm groves.

Verdant fields! We have seen nothing like them since the environs of Benghazi. The road to Misurata runs almost due north; we are climbing out of the baneful Gulf of Sirte, with its dip away from the main body of the temperate Mediterranean toward the Sahara's extremes. Through the Gulf the two were once connected.

Waiting for the bank to open, we ate a good hot meal. By this time of the day we were already tired, cold, wet, & sore. Riding with no windshield can be brutal.

No one suggests putting them back on, however: slower would not be acceptable. As soon as the bank re-opens after siesta, we cash travelers' checks and refuel. To our astonishment, the station has a pump with *mixed gas and oil* - as if we were coming back into European orbit. It is some comfort to think of the right stuff flowing through the system again, but is it too late? Chipping the carbon crust off our spark plugs has been getting harder and harder.

Half a century later, Misurata or Miserat made the evening news as a long-suffering battleground between pro- and anti-Gaddafi forces. If the teen-age Muammar saw us pass through that day he left no written record, fulminating against foreign pollution.

Left for Homs at 3. The road wound thru attractive countryside: rolling fields, shade trees, tall palms & [palmettos], flocks of sheep, yellow & purple flowers. After Zleiten, continuous glades of stately palms, which overlooked farmer's huts & rural peace. Stopped briefly at Leptis Magna, 3 kms. before Homs, then went into town to a hotel (it's cold & raining).

We paid 30 piastres (90 cents) for our room. "Prices here are really high," I groused, and "impair our enjoyment of the country." The trouble with traveling on the cheap is just this impairment. You get used to low prices, come to think of them as your due, and when you no longer find them, resent the higher rates as gouging. We had just had two free nights and had not paid anything since Benghazi.

We balked at unreasonable prices in 2 restaurants, & were ready to eat bread before finding Lumbarton House, a canteen for Scots. A kind old Scottish lady there served up a good meal of egg roll, peas, tomatoes, tea & jelly donuts for 9 ps. (27 cents).

Back on our feet! She explained that a British tank regiment was based nearby, which probably accounted for both Lumbarton House and the prevalent high prices. Another foreign military presence…were there any benefits in it for Libya, or was this still a punitive occupation? I also wondered what might have brought our grandmotherly hostess out here, but she was not garrulous, and our time was limited.

The next morning we spent three hours among the sprawling ruins of Leptis Magna, taking pictures in good weather. A huge site, not yet developed for tourists, it was historically and archeologically interesting, and beautiful in places. Much Roman pomp and love of majestic scale were on display, but a number of marble columns with ornate acanthus capitals, still in fine condition, had an Hellenic beauty. Some were atop the theatre, whose curving rows seemed to imitate the Mediterranean swells rolling toward shore. Though the theatre, market, and "New Forum" were obvious points of interest, I was most struck by the small, square Temple of Poseidon, off by itself at the end of a promontory. Inside, a flight of steps led down to wet stones. At the bottom I heard a roar, looked up, saw white water rushing toward me, and jumped back. The wave died at my feet, but the effect of the funneled noise and water had been frightening. What a brilliant, subtle tribute to the sea god! For a moment I felt, was made to feel, his power.

There were no guards or guides at Leptis Magna, no entrance fee, not a single other visitor that morning. A few hundred yards south of the site you were in semi-desert, with the odd palm tree and a couple of girls tending a flock of sheep, who were trying to cadge a meal from the stubble. From there the ancient structures, already blending with the sand and stones of the plain, looked like an old print of classical ruins in the Mideast, with its sepia-toned sense of melancholy and departed grandeur. Despite the air of decay, it was something to have come across the desert and found Leptis waiting in quiet repose.

Back in Homs, we ate a good 50-cent lunch of sausage, eggs, spam roll, orangeade, jelly donuts, & chocolate. Shoved off at 12:30 for Tripoli. Both scooters ran raggedy at first, but smoothed out [later].

"Raggedy": sounding ragged, I suppose, congested. Hector stopped once to clean his spark plug and said that he "might not make it to Tripoli," which was not his style at all. Finally his was running as badly as mine. The countryside was green and hilly for awhile, later flattening into a fertile coastal plain sprinkled with agricultural and animal experiment stations among private farms. Palms, shade trees, hedges and flowers pleased a traveler weary of desert austerity.

Feb. 5, TRIPOLI, Libya, 4 PM - Just when we seemed doomed to disappointment & expense in this high-priced city, the Marines came thru. After we exhausted our potential contacts and were turned away from Wheelus AFB, I got hold of Bill Kramer, a friendly, sensible Marine at the Embassy. He arranged for us to stay here at the two-story villa occupied by four Marines. Very comfortable & we have kitchen privileges.

Someone at Brigadoon Base had suggested that if we dropped the name of a certain officer at the huge American Air Force base outside Tripoli we would be invited to stay there, but it didn't fly; we never got past the gate. Pricing a couple of hotels in the city was enough to send us to the Embassy. I relished the irony of calling on the Corps whose anthem begins by hailing their service "From the halls of Montezuma to the shores of Tripoli." *Semper fi*!

We've completed the 2nd leg of the Big Trek (I hope the worst is behind us) & stand ready to move for Tunis, 800 kms. distant.

We're 1030 kms. from Benghazi, 2173 from Alexandria, & 7630 from Naples. The scooters are in the Lambretta shop for a long list of repairs which will require 2 or 3 days.

Making this appointment was our first act upon entering Tripoli. Our second was to locate the PTT (post, telephone, telegraph) and send a wire to our ladies. The word limit at the economy rate was ten, including the signature. Eight words in which to sum up our lives, to connect the key events of the present and past! After some thought, we sent:

DESERT SANDS, LAMBRETTA NEURALGIA
FEBRUARY FOURTH, SWEET NOSTALGIA

That should hold 'em! Let Ogden Nash turn in his grave. *Then* we went looking for a place to stay.

Had soup & fried egg sandwiches here last night, courtesy of the Marines. This AM we delivered the scooters & walked around Tripoli. Aside from the curving, palm-shaded beachfront boulevard & a Barbary castle there, the city seems to offer little of interest.

Of course this was a hasty, guidebook-less judgment. We knew that this was the old Barbary Coast (whose pirates brought the Marines), that "Barbary" was a corruption of *Berber* (a tribe and a language), and that there were once three Greek cities (*Tripolis*) here. Even so, there didn't seem to be much for a tourist to *see*. Oh, for a Baedeker!

Americans, British, Italians, & Western influence are in evidence everywhere, perhaps a partial explanation of anti-Western sentiment. Shopping section well-equipped but expensive.

Even then foreigners could sense danger in Libya; the continent was throwing off colonialism on both sides of the Sahara. Along the Med, Egypt, Morocco and Tunisia had already achieved some degree of independence, and it looked as if Algeria was heading down the same path.

We settled down to wait for the shop to finish servicing our scooters. A letter from Leo came to American Express containing snapshots of us. He wrote that a package of home-baked Christmas cookies from Penny was in the Cairo post office, which would neither give it to him nor forward it to us. *Cookies*? Hey, back to Cairo! Then, once we had photographed the old fort, some Italian monuments by the sea, the *duomo*, the odd minaret and picturesque well beneath royal palms, we just hung out at the Marines' villa, tasting the good life of the foreign elite, which I quite liked.

Feb. 7, Tripoli, 2 PM - Spent morning reading, listening to music on radio & phonograph, sprawling on the floor with tea & jelly rolls. This served to confirm some ideas about those pleasures for which I'll work. I could have used classical music, Segovia, or folk music, a text on Buddhism or a short story. In vignettes such as this I am drawn to a vision of domestic life. I'm sure it will come to fruition too seldom, yet it is what I crave. And I became restless, even homesick, for Penny, for Phillip, for Dr. Blackburn, for Friends & the Arts.

This too is part of "wandering"; such times may have been as formative as many a scootered mile and prowled ruin on my *Wanderjahr*. Education is about how we'll spend our money as well as how we'll earn it. I was figuring out what kind of life I wanted to lead, and the line between self-discovery and self-development is faint at 22.

Picked up our scooters last night. Mine seems improved in clutch & engine. Verdict was much carbon crust in cylinder, sand & water in carburetor. No wonder! Cost: $9.75.

This service - expensive for its place and time - had turned up nothing unexpected, and could not really be tested until we hit the road again. There was more desert to come, and miles to go before we slept. Still, it ought to help.

At Bill Graham's apparently sincere suggestion, we decided to stay over a day & leave tomorrow. The Marines don't need the beds, & we're buying our own food.

Neither of us liked Tripoli or was playing the tourist, so this layover day *after* our scooters' reappearance was an admission that we preferred domestic comfort to the call of the road. But in truth that was no longer news: by this time we had sated our travel-hunger, and would seize almost any pretext for a rest day.

Spent time yesterday washing, exercising, & reading. Completed the last 2 TIMEs, & read William Inge's "A Loss of Roses" in Esquire. Not very good, but interesting as a reverse apron-strings plot. A kind of inverted Look Homeward, Angel.

Kind of. This self-indulgent but restorative period ended the next morning as we reattached our windshields, said grateful goodbyes and headed west again. The country beyond Tripoli was much like that immediately east: flat farmland, occasional orchards, lanes (shaded by sycamores, palms, and evergreens) leading off to houses and farm buildings. Most of the soil looked reasonably fertile; patches of bare clay alternated with luxuriant grasses, trees, and cultivated fields. Desert took over again 80 kms. west of Tripoli. Our ride was, in retrospect, ominously smooth.

Feb. 8, Tripoli, Libya, 8 PM - Ah, frustrations! Wilt thou never cease? Again the spectre of bureaucracy reared its head today, & sent us scampering back to Tripoli from the border post. Seems we were supposed to register with the Police within 3 days after entering Libya, but no one told us.

At least no one that we understood. We might have suspected that Libya would have such a regulation, since Egypt did. As in Ismailia, our hotel-keeper in Derna (or the one in Benghazi) should have sent us to the police.

There was - naturally - "nothing" that could be done by the Deltas at the border, so we trekked back 114 kms., registered, cashed more money, and came back here for one more night. Gives me a chance to eat well & finish Brave New World.

Though I treated our late registration as a farce, we were lucky not to be burned for this offense, the government having been unaware of our subversive whereabouts for nine days over the allotted period. A relaxed immigration officer in Tripoli dismissed our peccadillo with a smile and a flourish of his pen, after which the Marines graciously accepted another night of civvy intrusion.

I had thought that this trip was teaching me a measure of self-control. One brief flare of anger today & I was all right. I'm learning to accept the unavoidable when it's only halfway down my throat. Hardly minded the ride back.

With the exception of one motor failure this morning, my scooter ran much better - smoother & stronger against the wind. But gas consumption is still high.

Our little *marche arrière* did give us a chance to have a closer look at the seafront castle that is Tripoli's principal attraction, and central to its history. It was as if a day of scooter travel had stirred up the touring juices.

Hector & I poked around the passageways & ramparts for over an hour, & thoroughly enjoyed it. It's a fortress, defended the city during the Barbary wars around 1800, & thus presumably fired on American frigates. Corridors twist & multiply off each other interminably, emerge into surprise gardens where fountains play on colorful Islamic tiles. Three gazelle occupy a small enclosure perched over the street which passes under the castle.

We treated ourselves to a lavish final dinner and breakfast, bid the Marines farewell - Hey, this time we really, really go! - and sallied forth in full regalia to try again. By now we had heard good things of the Roman ruins at *Sabratha* (skipped on the 8th), so we stopped there.

It was originally, with Leptis Magna & Oea (Tripoli), an important Phoenician trading post, but the chief remnants are Roman: a fine 3-tiered theatre with marble columns, & an extensive forum. The walls, of sandstone, brick, or limestone, were once faced with Italian marble.

The theatre was definitely worth a visit. Some columns were still standing on each of the three tiers at the back of the stage, which was being given modern planking. A frieze depicting noblemen, soldiers, etc., covered the three-foot- high wall that lifted the stage above the back of the orchestra. The building stood by the sea; a grove of young trees had been planted on the landward side. There was also a Byzantine basilica built by the long arm of Justinian, reaching out from Constantinople. Its excellent mosaic floors had been moved to the small museum.

At that point, the repulse at the border the previous day seemed to have had a good issue.

Both scooters were running nicely as we roared on to Zwara. I came into town at 70 & slowed to 60. It wasn't enough. I saw the goat 50 yards away, & knew he'd cross in front of me. He did.

There was a herd of them to the right of the road at the near edge of the dusty village, but this black one had a restless look, and at the wrong moment he started across the road. As I swerved left to pass in front of him he sped up, with a sure instinct for a disastrous trajectory. All I had heard of foreign drivers becoming mired in third-world lawsuits flashed through my mind, and hitting him would have thrown me flying. I *had* to miss him. Applying the brakes, I tried to cut back to the right, behind him, but he slowed down to stay in front of me. When my lean became too steep I lost control, came off the Lambretta doing 40 or 50 kph, somersaulted twice - I can still see the scooter one bounce behind me on each moving rotation - and just managed to roll out of the way of the sliding, screaming machine. Then I was lying in the sand beside the road. Hector ran up to turn off my engine. Some alarmed locals who had seen my spill also came rushing over.

It was my most frightening accident. Net damage: broken headlight, bent left front of scooter, twisted windshield frame, scraped pack, broken tent pole; two cut knees (one pretty gory), left sneaker chopped up, jammed left thumb, scraped hips [and elbows]. All in all, however, I was pretty lucky; I was going too fast….

Indeed. But again my helmet, which was deeply scratched, saved my head, and somehow I had broken nothing. One of the villagers kept murmuring about Allah, though whether He was being credited with saving my life or felling an infidel, or simply acknowledged as the Author of all, I could not make out. Now it seemed *less* fortunate that Libyan customs - just down the road at the western edge of Zuara - had sent us back the day before.

Half an hour later, with me "all patched up," we pulled into customs & completed formalities. We then sat down on a nearby sand dune & ate lunch - hardboiled eggs, bread, biscuits.

The officials, who remembered us, seemed glad that we had cleared our names and could be passed routinely. At lunch I applied antiseptic cream and gauze pads to my wounds, which were stiffening. Why did I have difficulty crossing eastern frontiers without drama of some kind?

After spending our last Libyan money on gas & food, we set out across the last 50 kms. of Libyan desert. It was broken by hummocks, scrub brush, & pine thickets.

National boundaries, in that part of the world at least, tend to lie in complete wastes, so even the brush and pines had mostly vanished from the flat sandy plain by the time we sighted the Tunisian border post in the distance. Vaguely aware that I was in a state of mild shock, trying not to think about the parallels with our exit from Turkey, I hoped to make a fresh start up there.

> The House of Supposition -
> The Glimmering Frontier that
> Skirts the Acres of Perhaps -
> To Me - shows insecure -
>
> - Emily Dickinson

IX. Tunisia and the Inn of Pines

> *...plus je réfléchissais et plus de choses méconnues et oubliées je sortais de ma mémoire. J'ai compris alors qu'un homme qui n'aurait vécu qu'un seul jour pourrait sans peine vivre cent ans dans une prison. Il aurait assez de souvenirs pour ne pas s'ennuyer.*
>
> Albert Camus, *L'Étranger*

In crossing the frontier, we were not only moving closer to Europe, but passing from Italian to French political influence; from a territory whose colonizer was now a defeated Axis power, to one colonized and then given independence by a (post-Vichy) ally. Tunisia was more developed, more progressive: a republic with a president and an elected parliament. The cultural air was different, nature was kindlier, and the standard of living was higher - none of which was obvious at the border.

Feb. 10, EL DJEM, TUNISIA, 6 PM - A great deal has happened in the last two days!... At the border, we acquired an emergency passenger: a 23 yr. old French boy whose Libyan visa had expired before he tried to enter.

Antoine had to hitchhike back to Tunisia, his ride having proceeded into Libya that morning without him. He was stuck in no man's land, like some character in a play by Beckett or Pinter. A dramatic refugee! With sympathy born of our own marooning at the Syrian frontier,

Hector got him on his scooter, & we split up his luggage. Seven kilometres later, I had a flat. Hobbling around painfully, unloading gads of luggage, it took me 40 mins. to fix.

The baggage came off because you had to lay the Lambretta down on its side to change a rear tire. There was no one around to hear me groan as I *knelt* on bloody knees; Hector had not seen me stop, and returned as I was finishing. Together we drove on to the small Tunisian border post. It awakened unpleasant echoes of the Turkish-Syrian frontier, where misfortunes came in triplicate: a fall, a flat, a bureaucrat. But we had already paid homage to bureaucracy in Libya, and Tunisia blessed us with a very helpful official, so we continued northwest across the rolling, green-flecked desert to Ben Gardane and completed the entrance formalities there. An American tourist, a schoolteacher who saw my torn, blood-stained sleeves and pants, tried to find a doctor for me, but he was out and we wouldn't wait.

We decided to scurry for the cover of Medenine, a larger town 76 kms. away. We only had 1¼ hrs. till dark it was one of those races against the sun which dooms you to a cold night on the desert if anything goes wrong

- it being understood that driving after dark was a fool's errand. Just what we proposed to do with Antoine if we *were* benighted - ours being a two-man tent - I don't recall. With little headwind and my scooter running better, I drove faster than at any time since the Egyptian Delta, 70-75 kph. Short memory! But the desert was goatless.

We made it by 10 mins. The desert, tho' still sparse, was hilly enough to have character, & greener than western Libya. We found a hotel room for 3 for 500 francs ($1.25). I changed the bloody dressing on my knee, & we ate dinner in the room.

It had been a grueling 280 kms. from Tripoli. We scanted Medenine (though its cave dwellings sounded interesting) that evening and the next morning, but I did find out more about Antoine, a student-teacher who

had been working in Tunisia (Isle of Djerba) for some time, & was down on Arabs. He was a semi-intellectual, a philosophical pessimist, an existentialist, & a free talker - interesting as a change from Hector, but I found him shallow in some respects.

Probably I meant "pseudo-intellectual": a "wannabe." In any case he was the nearest thing to an egghead we had met since the Cairo Youth Hostel. Antoine was thoughtful, had done some reading and had ideas, but – as far as I could tell across the language barrier - his opinions often ranged far beyond his experience and powers of reasoned argument, so I was glad when he decided to hitchhike from there. Djerba would have made a logical side trip had we been less fatigued, and I less bloody. Some think it sat for the Land of the Lotus Eaters in the *Odyssey*.

This morning we left Medenine before 9 & ran a rapid 76 kms. across steep brown hills & valleys to Gabés. We were cutting all the time toward the coast; the land was a rolling but progressively flatter plain, cut by ranges of barren hills & low mountains.

Gabés, an oasis-seaport ringed by palm groves, was a welcome haven. We cashed travelers' cheques, bought gas & oil, fixed my tire & Hector's windshield, & ate. Gas is expensive - c. 80 cents/gal. - but prices otherwise are reasonable. However, I'm only getting 22 kms./liter. At noon we left small, pleasant Gabés & started a 136 km. haul to Sfax.

That we had left the flat tire and broken windshield until then to be repaired suggests rushed, casual - some might say careless - or confident drivers. (Of course we now knew that windshields were a luxury option, and did still have one good spare tire between us.) But the low mileage - 52 mpg - shocked me…again. If I had known that figure in Egypt, would I even have started?

The road, which had angled northwest since the border, curved around the deepest western bight of the Gulf of Sirte and pointed north*east* toward Sfax. As in Libya, we kept to the coastal road, leaving the hinterland untouched; without a guidebook to suggest interesting diversions, we homed in on our chief goal, Tunis. This empty, agricultural stretch, almost devoid of towns, still looked more Mediterranean and less Saharan than any place we had seen for ten days.

The countryside, a rolling & windswept plateau, was the most pleasant scenery since the Cyrenaica coast. Olive groves in abundance; palms, cacti, sycamores & pines along the road: a blessed greenness began to pervade the land. I've never adequately appreciated it. Just before Sfax, trees with white blossoms, & others with pink.

Fruit trees! Probably almonds or cherries or both. After all, February is Mediterranean spring. The "sycamores" were likely poplars. Large, well-equipped Sfax exuded French commercial civilization and felt as "Mediterranean" as Beirut. Signs on the tall white buildings were in French, with or without an Arabic equivalent; European goods and services were generally available. We found mixed gas and good, cheap food with no trouble. Old citadel walls enclosed an Arab *kasbah*. Several brilliantly white mosques with rectangular minarets - the Tunisian style - served to dress up the city, but we were not in a touring mood.

The 40 miles to El Djem & its Roman Coliseum were pure pleasure. The roads were excellent, as they have been almost everywhere in Tunisia. We actually had a tailwind, & ran 70-80 kph with no trouble. The landscape was the most picturesque yet in Tunisia: gentle hills seemed clothed in one continuous olive grove; leaves glinted in the sun; the brown earth looked healthy. There was spaciousness & sweep to the land, missed since northern Greece. Green Tunisia - I like it.

The remark about "spaciousness" sounds odd coming from one who has been in the desert for three weeks. I was probably responding to the vistas afforded by hilltops; flat land, however spacious, has a short visual horizon. Still, Turkey and Mt. Lebanon had offered views with "sweep." The landscape's human touches were really its great attractions after the Libyan waste.

Gauging progress toward *El Djem* is easy. Miles before the low village appears, a huge coliseum, like Rome's but more nearly intact, climbs above the horizon, unlikely but undeniable. The only hotel being closed for the winter, we applied to the police, and, as in Buerat, were allowed to spend the night on the concrete floor of an empty room. My wounds, rubbed open during the day and festering, kept me awake unless I lay on my back, a position that did not help keep the cold at bay, or deal with a hot, spicy dinner soup to which my stomach had taken a dislike.

It was not, then, a restful night, but morning brought compensations. At the market stalls on the main square we put together the most satisfying non-American breakfast I had ever encountered: pieces of kneaded dough deep-fat fried to a crisp and eaten snapping hot (5 cents) from one vendor; hard-boiled eggs, a juicy orange, and coffee from another. Good food! Low prices! Then we *spent an hour clambering around the not-too-ruined Roman Coliseum, which rears sandstone walls above the white Arab dwellings as startlingly as a sea monster surfacing. Crumbled stairways, fallen bleachers, great holes in the ramps, & lichen growing along walls which once resounded to crowd noises all contribute to a fine effect of futile grandeur grown musty.*

Said to have been the third largest such structure in the vast Empire, it hosted gladiatorial combats and a full array of "games" in its day, including Christians versus lions, so it was not only "grandeur" that had passed away. An emotionally complex atmosphere hung over the place, and a power resided, as if there really were giants in the earth once - nasty fellows, some of them, but formidable. From a few miles out on the plain only the coliseum remained visible, monstrous against a leaden sky, while its crouching attendants blended obsequiously with the horizon. Newer and living, but incomparably less, they made the coliseum look mighty in its mossy death.

It took just over an hour to drive seventy-odd kilometers of pleasant green hill country to Sousse. The landscape seemed to be growing: hills became higher and steeper, intervening valleys wider, the horizon farther. Crossing a plain, I saw a long climb ahead; at full throttle I hit 85 kph (listed in the manual as top speed) at its base and rode clear to the summit in 4th gear. What a kick! My joy was not only in the speed, but in the evidence that EE 1068 was back in form. And if we had a little tailwind, we had earned it.

Sousse ("Souse" on our Egyptian map)

turned out to be chiefly a commercial port, pop. 48,000, French-influenced & possessed of a fine corniche, but otherwise undistinguished. Skies were grey & the weather cool. Noticed more rectangular Tunisian [minarets] & a prominent Christian church.

Be it known, however, that Sousse was founded by the Phoenicians before Carthage, that it has a museum, a mediaeval monastery-fortress, catacombs, important mosques, interesting old gates and battlements, etc., and that some Tunisians go there to vacation. Sousse was yet another place that we treated shabbily, ignoring or denigrating its attractions, as we tended to do whenever we were determined to keep on going. There is a price to be paid for "covering ground."

Making good time, we roared up the eastern coastal plain, hemmed in by hills on our left. Took time for one 10-mile detour to see Hammamet, a renowned beach resort with a fine vista of the Gulf of Hammamet, & also a typical Arab village.

Hardly! The bleak sky was an inducement to finish the day's run and find shelter, but someone - probably Antoine - had told us about Hammamet's white houses and fine beaches, though not about its extensive orange and lemon groves, cypresses, date palms and bougainvillea, or the bright unknown birds flashing among them. It had a history at least as old as the Romans - of course *they* would find it! In the 1920s Hammamet was frequented by the likes of André Gide, Paul Klee and Frank Lloyd Wright. Military types were not immune to its charms; the French Foreign Legion had a garrison there, and Rommel a temporary headquarters. The Hachette *Guide Bleue* gushes that Tunisia would not be Tunisia without this "earthly paradise," evocative of "tropical Edens." While eating lunch by the shore we were the objects of intense curiosity, as if foreign visitors were not then common. Or perhaps they came as respectable tourists, wearing decent clothes and traveling in cars or buses; having lived in my scootering outfit for so long, I was apt to forget how it looked. After lunch we

crossed a few hills & then were on the windblown strip of plain that skirts the Gulf of Tunis. Progressively higher & handsomer mountains kept us company, overlooking a fertile plain of olive groves & cacti. Countryside very pastoral & attractive.

It reminded me of Lebanon, albeit with lesser mountains. Some side roads or lanes were muddy quagmires from recent rains. Strong gusts of wind, hitting broadside, nearly blew us over, a phenomenon that now seemed more laughable than intimidating. Such is the psychological effect of familiarity, and being near to a goal in "friendly," settled country. The desert is partly a state of mind.

At Bourdj Cedria we turned right at the [railroad] station (as directed in Cairo) & quickly found Auberge-des-Pins in a pine grove, 100 yds. from a swimming beach. In the summer it must be much sought-after: 25 cents a day for resort surroundings is good anywhere.

In summer, of course, it probably cost more. We found the Inn of Pines from the sketch drawn on his/our map by the German cyclist at the Garden City youth hostel, much more, it seemed, than a month ago and three thousand kilometers east. We might miss it, he had warned: right at the Bir El Bey sign, right again on the frontage road, then left on the next side road and follow its S-hook toward the sea. And there it was! Two dormitories, a recreation building, and the warden's house: a satisfying goal - for that leg, at least.

We could not bear to stop just eight miles short of Tunis, so after securing beds and stowing luggage we drove on into the city, arriving about three. First stop was the French Embassy, where visas for Algeria were obtained, though Leo and others had warned that political tensions there might make entry problematical. And then what?! Sail somewhere. The embassy was closed for the day, but

American Express divulged glorious letters, & ship information: Sicily each Wednesday, nothing to Spain or Morocco. We booked passage for safety, got maps & gas, & returned to the hostel. The warden, an ex-cuisinier from Paris [he said], fixed an excellent meal of hot soup, bread, lettuce salad, omelette, & macaroni, plus delicious sweet biscuits, all for 45 cents.

Clearly, after three weeks of beating into the wind, we had landed on our feet. We seemed to be the only guests, which might explain the warmth of the warden's welcome. I concluded the evening with a gory hour of pulling the dressings off my torn-up knees, bathing the cuts and applying fresh gauze pads. Infection looked minimal, though walking remained stiff and painful. I went to bed with the worse of the two out in the air, having been too tired to chronicle our achievement that night.

Feb. 12, TUNIS, Tunisia, 12 noon - Arrivés, mon Dieu! Hier! Deux mille neuf cents trente-cinq kilomètres d'Alexandrie (3333 sur mon speedomètre), nous avons entré dans la ville française & moderne de Tunis. J'en suis fier.

So much for French practice, which I badly needed after months of wrestling with Italian, Greek, Turkish and Arabic. What would Mam'selle say? *Ah Reeshar, Reeshar, tiens, tiens*! Back in ninth grade she had taught us to conjugate *entrer* with *être.* French (good or bad) should be helpful from Tunisia westward. I was rusty, but pride in having driven more than halfway from Egypt to Morocco took precedence over grammatical considerations that day. It was like the feeling of reaching Istanbul from Athens – times three.

Derailed

"Reculer pour mieux sauter," runs a French saying: "Recoil in order to jump better." Yes, but…jump *where*? Our first choice was still to drive to Morocco, completing the "North African traverse," cross to Spain and circle the Mediterranean: that would be something! The problem - and great attraction - was Algeria, where we could choose between a coastal highway with Roman ruins, a couple of mountain routes through cork forest, or southern roads to towns such as *Ghardaïa* and *Laghouat* on the northern fringes of the Sahara. *The Sahara*! If there was a word or place with more imaginative resonance I couldn't think of it. But were they going to allow us to cross Algeria? And since ships went north, not west, from here, there was no alternative to the land route.

The three French protectorates in North Africa were evolving quite differently. In Tunisia, Habib Bourguiba and his Destour Party had led the country to independence in 1956; it had become a Republic, with Bourguiba - a sort of Tunisian Ataturk, whose picture hung in most shops, hotels, and homes - as president (1957). Its Constitution was less than a year old when we arrived. Tunisia was peaceful, as was Morocco, a more or less autonomous monarchy, but Algeria, largest and richest of the three, and closest to France, remained uneasily tied to the "mother country," aka the colonial oppressor. Algerians were divided along ethnic and religious lines on whether they should separate from France, and, if so, on what terms. French Catholic settlers (*pieds noirs*) tended to want close ties, native Arabs (mostly Muslims) a complete break. In France, Gen. de Gaulle, who had come to power in 1958, favored peaceful self-determination for Algeria, but he was up against both an Arab National Liberation Front (FLN) and rabidly anti-separation colonists, some of them war veterans whom he had helped settle in North Africa.

In January 1960, while we were in Egypt, whatever consensus may have existed among Algerians came apart. Many settlers felt that de Gaulle was selling them out, and the FLN had never trusted him. Various factions took to the streets; there ensued incidents that the French press called *la semaine des barricades* and English-language sources The Paratroop Rebellion, of which we had read - with growing unease - in Tripoli. Sporadic acts of violence, some random, some targeted, occurred throughout the country. This was the drama to which we were seeking admission. As we dressed, ate breakfast at the *Auberge des Pins* and prepared to go into Tunis, we reminded each other that part of what had attracted us to Africa was its exciting sense of political upheaval, of new polities emerging from the old. We had hoped to see the labor up close or visit the baby, though, not be kept away from the hospital. Ironic, wasn't it?

Feb. 12, Tunis, 12 noon - We drove into town on Hector's scooter this AM, & the French [embassy] confirmed in no uncertain terms the "no" to Algeria I'd been expecting. That made it definite that our next move is up into Italy to spend some time with Parry, with perhaps a 3-man trip to Spain in the offing.

Pow! Just like that - on with the trip! *Le Roi est mort; vive le Roi!* The French official explained that an American motorcyclist had been killed by rebels in the hills the previous week, and the U.S. embassy had begged the French - *un peu hystériquement,* his smile suggested - not to let any others in. *Qu'est-ce qu'on peut faire*? More well-meant American caution of the kind we had struggled to escape at home, but could not elude here. There would be no Roman coast, no mountains or cork forests, no Sahara for us. We would sail to Italy and drive up to Verona, where Hector's brother Parry was stationed. He had invited us to visit, and Hector wanted to go. So once again we would have to settle for Plan B, or, really, Plan C. Was it just bad luck, or something about us, that kept sinking Plan A?

I went through the motions of a layover day - "*bought writing paper...visited the P.O.; walked around the Frenchified, antiseptic, orderly Medina*" - in a state of dazed bewilderment. We were *not* going to ride west into (more) glorious adventures and the unknown dangers of the *Maghreb* after all, but sit here for five days, awaiting the next ship to Italy and its much-visited sites, which well-off Americans showed their children on summer holidays. It was undeniably a come-down, the breaking-off short of an obscure desire that lived deep inside. Over the next few days of hanging around Tunis, I spent, perhaps, too much time reviewing what had happened, what had *passed on*.

Our desert trek was over, then; a phase of the trip had ended. But why did this often-miserable stretch make all the rest seem only preparation, and our European future anti-climactic? I remembered hours of inescapable cold, the gritty taste of sand, long boring reaches of empty desert when my sand-clogged engine pumped feebly and the speedometer needle rose or fell with the land's slight roll. Strong images remained: wind-whipped Mediterranean shallows seen through a whitish haze of spindrift and dust; the desert's forms, studies in brown, grey, grey-green and off-white, shifting as we passed; and sand-tendrils, visible tokens of the wind, advance scouts of the desert, threatening that frail link between communities, sliding obliquely across the road to slow our progress.

The constant rush of wind on the days we ran without windshields, sandy rain on my face, embattled emergency stops when we had to shout over the wind, the Marble Arch bizarrely astride an invisible border, solitary shovelers staring at us: these would surface unbidden. I could summon up Siwa's palms, the coast at Derna, the ruins of Cyrene and Leptis Magna, the Scottish canteen, the warm feeling when we achieved some respite or interim goal - the good times - but what had gone deepest was discomfort, near-calamities, trouble, isolation. For me this was new light on nostalgia. Had Nansen, Amundsen, Scott and Shackleton come to *enjoy* the prolonged misery of the polar wastes, deriving from the experience the satisfaction appropriate to it? Did the neurons preserve pain better than they did pleasure? What a travel agency could be founded on that premise! After Great Pain a Far-out Feeling Comes Co. But maybe Outward Bound had already cornered that market.

These quasi-masochistic feelings were difficult to grasp, so I tried to analyze my reactions to the desert, which took some time. Its prime appeal had been emptiness: we had met three other itinerant foreigners between Alexandria and Tunis: one for each thousand kilometers. Well, we had wanted to escape tourism! It also had an aspect of danger, not the mortal threat of the jungle or the poles, but the riskiness of all remote regions if things go wrong or you foul up. Knowing that Libya was a place family and friends would advise against made me perversely glad to have crossed it; that the desert was uncomfortable made it the completer break with my past, the less like home. And the unique sense experience of desert travel compensated for every misery – at least in retrospect. Now I had really been through something worth going through, a thing beyond the ken (or desire) of middle-class America. As my "resolutions at Aswan" seemed to have fulfilled one goal of the trip, so the desert trek fulfilled another.

Meanwhile I rested, read, wrote, and recuperated at the *Auberge des Pins* between day trips. The balmy weather allowed me to hit the beach in swimming trunks, exposing my wounds to air and salt water. There I caught up on correspondence, and scribbled retrospective essays on what we had seen of North Africa.

Libya is a confused, western-Arab pot pourri, potentially rich in both trouble & oil. If the oil money now beginning to flow in southern Libya (into American & British pockets) doesn't wind up in local hands, I foresee trouble. Already there is bad feeling galore due to western military encroachment.

My main sources were the Marines and an American petroleum engineer we had met who shook his head over what he and his company were getting away with. "If they ever find out," he laughed, "I'd hate to be here!" Muammar Gaddafi may have been watching their activities by then.

Purdah was more widely observed in Libya than in Egypt. The women in Tripoli's streets had their robes gathered about their faces, so that only one eye peered out. Many of them had a mark, generally a circle, painted in the centre of their forehead, similar to the Hindu custom. In western Libya the white robe of coarse, heavy weave replaced the brightly colored fabrics of the eastern region as the most characteristic garb.

Whenever I looked up from a page, my eye rested on verdure and pastel hues. Besides clumps of beach grass such as grow on Cape Cod, there were dark green bushes, like gorse, and pale green cactus of the kind known variously as *maguey*, the century plant, or *agave*. Agave is a Greek name: the Theban Maenad who killed her son Pentheus, a Dionysus-denier, in a frenzy. These stories had a way of following one around, but what did the old girl want here? Had I been slighting some deity? My Bacchic side, no doubt. To the northwest, Tunis appeared as a white line bordering its blue bay; northeast, Cape Bon showed a purplish-green over lighter blue-green water. In 1943, the last of the Afrika Corps was trapped on the cape and surrendered *en masse*, so this was an appropriate place to conclude our history lesson in the desert campaign.

Green Tunisia, olive groves shimmering silver & green in the sun, rolling plains, soft green hills & far-off mountains, wide Mediterranean bays - it has a quiet natural beauty that is little known outside, but charming to me after the flat, sand-blasted vastness of western Egypt & central Libya.

So, despite my feelings about the power of the desert, I found Tunisia's "quiet natural beauty" "charming." That may be a lower order of attraction – its pastoral plains did not call up the adrenaline - but they came as a relief. We cannot always live in the austere; it is too demanding, and gives only an ascetic pleasure at the time.

Tunis is as French as a city outside of France could be. You see it in the way the women look & dress (legs!), in French signs everywhere, French spoken in the shops. They did well, les français: the town is clean & attractive, has good streets, plenty of trees & space.

In giving the French credit for the beauties of Tunis I was on boggy ground. My knowledge of France was limited to a few glamour spots; I knew nothing of its dark side - nor what might have been done here without their intervention.

The camels! Funny, ubiquitous, they have been given a variety of uses across North Africa. In Egypt they were mostly for transport, but in the desert they appeared pulling primitive plows. In Libya this practice became widespread, & peasants also had them raising water by turning wooden gears [over wells] (a job done by oxen in Greece, Turkey, & the Middle East). All of these uses are in Tunisia, along with the burden of hauling wagons in yoke. Adaptable beasts, but nasty when they spit [food] from one of those four stomachs.

Our Tunisian interlude gave us time to meditate on our lives and this enterprise. Now that we were no longer straining for a goal, but lazing at the *Auberge* or doing easy day trips, minds that had been focused on covering the next stretch grew more broadly reflective. Folk wisdom connects idleness with the devil, and fresh disquiets *did* surface that week, putting me in a more independent frame of mind and renewing some old doubts.

Feb. 13, Auberge des Pins, 5 PM - In the course of a day-off mostly spent around here, I've been reading Walk the Wide World *[by] Donald Knies, a California boy who hitchhiked over Europe, N. Africa & the East. Although it's badly written & eventually dull, he puts me to shame in certain ways. He has an eye for visual detail & an ear for foreign words, which I lack. The form is superficial; the ideas [are] commonplace. Yet he has the knack of discerning & remembering the unique & curious: an art I need to learn.*

The more I thought about Knies's book the more it bothered me. If his flaws were so obvious, if I could write rings around him, then how exactly did he "put me to shame"? The only answer evident to me was that he had found better ways of mining material from some of the places we had been than I had: that he was a better traveler.

His mode of travel - hitchhiking alone - has caused me to question my own. He seems to make contact with interesting people frequently: am I setting myself apart from the natives with my scooter & helmet? Am I hurrying through too much, to keep up with Hector & get my mail? Am I submerging my individuality by not traveling alone? Perhaps "yes" in every case; I may have to try it solo after Italy.

Perhaps? If Knies was right, I had made a radical error in conceiving the trip: there should have been no entangling alliance, no isolating vehicle. In a sense, I was no longer the person who had designed this journey to suit his 1959 ideas, aversions, and knowledge; *he* had acted reasonably given the data he had, and with due regard to his ignorance, prudence, and self-doubt. It was a forgivable sort of mistake - that of a past self with regard to the present - but one that had to be lived with nonetheless.

Walk the Wide World coaxed some of my ambivalence from its subliminal haunts. With amazement I found myself writing - after all the talk of consensual planning - that I was "hurrying too much" and "submerging" myself, and pointing a finger at Hector. The train of thought that started rolling that day did not have visible consequences for another month; in Tunisia I was just seeing my limitations as a traveler at every turn.

We have missed some good spots on the way up: Isle of Djerba, Kairouan, & Monastire should all have been seen, it turns out.

This was more than a bit disingenuous. The German in Cairo had sketched in a side trip to Kairouan on the map he gave me, and Antoine had told us about Djerba, but we had looked neither to the left nor to the right. Even now it would have been possible to drive to Kairouan or Monastir, but neither of us suggested leaving our pleasant digs and facing the road again. Color us fatigable.

The warden, a genuinely pleasant Tunisian Arab, is desperately eager to pick up English. He pestered us both last night so much to pronounce words for him that I agreed to spend an hour with him after dinner tonight, working on English.

Aha! Here was a case in point, practically a Don Knies character handed to me on a platter: a local who had (may have) cooked in Paris and was almost pathetically anxious to better himself by learning English, which we could teach him. Trying to see him as Knies would have, I realized that "pestered" was a false note. How and when had I become so self-absorbed as to resent friendly advances from the natives? The English lessons were expiatory.

Today went well. Spent the morning writing, exercising, reading, & tinkering with my scooter (I've been offered $150 for it).

And here, on cue, came an offer of relief from the burden of my isolating machine! Wherever this offer came from, however – presumably someone I met on a run into Tunis - it sounded low, and where would selling have left me? Taking the boat to Sicily with Hector, but then scooterless. Besides, I had grown fond of my mistake, if such it was, and headed off for a half-day outing on the Lambretta.

About noon I hopped aboard & putted off in search of pleasant countryside, photos, food & adventure. First went to a small Arab village (Soliman) about 5 miles away. I admired its minarets & white buildings against blue hills when we came in the other day; today I documented this photographically.

The turnoff to Soliman was back up the highway to the south. A few kilometers of pock-marked road led across fields to a cluster of white cubic buildings and three sandstone minarets, quite unlike the French-colonial style in our neighborhood. Close to the main road, prevented only by that little distance from becoming another exurb of Tunis, Soliman remained a quiet, relatively isolated Muslim community. It reminded me of a Turkish village outside of Adana that we had not had time to visit.

Though I left the Lambretta outside of town, hoping to be less conspicuous as a pedestrian, a crowd of urchins tagged along. Blinding whitewashed façades and deep shadows within doors made Soliman a study in black and white: a Cartier-Bresson village. Searching for a store I peered into dark doorways until I saw goods for sale, rather than hearthfires and huddled figures. In shops that I entered on some pretext, they treated me with a mixture of deference and suspicion that well expressed their provinciality and my strangeness. Beyond the poorer houses was the cemetery, its gravestones long white polished rectangles about six inches high; some of them had periscope-like protuberances at one end. They lay in an unkempt tract of wild grasses and uprooted agaves. We're a long way from Forest Lawn, Toto! By now I had entirely circumambulated the village and returned to the scooter, still with my *entourage*.

On the main road, I gave one of 3 little boys a 200-yd. scooter ride. He was very nervous - I'm sure he did it just to show his buddies - & was smiling & relieved when I let him off. Bought a pick-up lunch in Hamman-Lif, just up the road, & went on towards Tunis. After shooting photos

of my first-ever Norfolk pines, I turned left up a side road into the hills. Leaving the scooter in a small olive grove, I went off to eat lunch, but halfway through heard some curious noises from the direction of the Lambretta and returned to investigate.

A bunch of recessed schoolboys came chorusing across the fields. As they marched in ragged single file, the leader kept chanting a word - something like "marrhabah" - & the ragamuffin legion replied with a set refrain. It was like Hugo's djinns. Of a sudden there was a profound silence: they had discovered my scooter. When I arrived, they were seated demurely beside it, as if posed for a group portrait.

Dressed in cotton shirts, dark trousers, and jackets or sweaters, they all wore the red *tarbous*. My arrival did not disturb them, but when I pulled out my camera all hell broke loose and they fled in seeming panic. I snapped a picture as they scattered: a rear view of a mad scramble such as the last day of Pompeii might have seen. Their one-legged proctor, an older student wearing a robe, crutched across the plowed clods as fast as any of them. Some looked back from the safety of the nearest tree. Only one kid stood his ground and openly laughed at me: the Eternal Urchin, a triumph of mischief over superstition.

After walking about in the verdant hills for awhile, I drove back to the Inn of Pines. My knee was feeling better, my limp had almost disappeared, and my scooter was fully restored to favor.

Tunisia was another country for which I had not prepared, but the few scraps of history and legend we knew - Hannibal, Dido and Aeneas - pointed to Carthage. Now a quiet, upper-middle class suburb on the north side of Tunis, it was an easy day trip; we doubled up on my scooter. Our only trouble was finding, and appreciating, the sparse ruins. The rivalry between Rome and Carthage led to three wars, and Cato the Censor kept saying, "*Carthago delenda est*": Carthage must be deleted, destroyed, eradicated. When the Roman Senate decreed, Leave no stone atop another and salt the earth, it was not meant metaphorically. Though Carthage was restored under Julius Caesar and became a Roman colony, the remains were underwhelming.

Ruins are scattered about inconspicuously, difficult to find & unimpressive. Rome worked thoroughly. Best remaining are the Baths of Antonin & Punic Necropolis, & the Amphitheatre of the Martyrs. A white Episcopal church on a hill is the village's most prominent landmark. It was difficult even to bring Hannibal to mind. Question: what is "Punic"?

Thought you'd never ask. "Punic" derives from a Latin word that comes from the Greek word for Phoenicia, which is where Dido and her fellow colonizers originated, she being a princess of Tyre. That was in Virgil's *Aeneid*, but there was more to the story, at least for us. I had begun to realize that Phoenicia, i.e. Lebanon, might be the imaginative nexus of our travels. King Minos of Crete was the son of Zeus and Europa, another princess of Tyre, whose brother Cadmus founded Thebes, where Agave came from. Actually the plot was even thicker, because "Dido" was originally the name of a Phoenician *goddess*, probably a moon-goddess, and only later that of a Tyrian princess. Oh Diana!

Though we found hardly any physical artifacts worthy of all this mythological wealth - the remains were late Roman, and only just rated some token photography - the vista of the Gulf and Cape Bon (dull green underlying bluish purple) was worth the trip. Carthage, while it lasted, had a fine harbor and a glorious view.

Feb. 15, Tunis (Amer. Cultural Center), 5 PM - Today, on Hector's scooter, we drove to Bizerte & Menzel Bourgiba. The countryside afforded more pleasure than the towns, which are stock French commercial-Arab. From Tunis to Bizerte was alternate hill-valley all the way. The valley floors were carpeted with deep grass or flowers of white & yellow. Seen from above, it could have been light snow. Cattle & sheep grazed, peasants dug & plowed, villages flashed by.

The novelty here - for me - was riding as a "pillion" (back-seat) passenger. Physically it was not as much fun as driving, but there were compensations: I was able to observe the passing landscape more carefully, and could even jot notes and draw a map in my journal en route.

Bizerte lies at the seaward end of a large lake surrounded by a plain, then by hills. The natural contours are clearly visible, towns can be seen & identified from miles away; there is an aura of abundant space. In this way, the paysage is very pleasing. Neither town seemed to offer much except stores, restaurants, & docks.

As with Sousse on the way up, it was easier to slight Bizerte than to find what it had to offer: mosques, a *casbah*, a regional arts museum, something of the old port. Menzel Bourguiba, however, *was* just an arsenal-and-factory town. A canal between the *Lac du Bizerte* and the sea gave the lake the aspect of a lagoon. Circling it, we reached Tunis in time for more touring and a read at the Cultural Center.

Have been browsing the city. The large Catholic cathedral (most impressive religious edifice I've seen in Tunis) has a good mosaic on the main facade, an opulent interior, & ratings of local films on the bulletin board. Around the corner, the smaller, more austere Greek Orthodox church smelt of incense & had the usual preponderance of icons. But a wonderful stillness inside - a deep, quiet Christian pool.

Wandered again thru the Medina. There was much life there tonight. The souks were all lighted, selling jewelry, metalwork, tapestries & fabrics, hats, shoes, paintings & other merchandise. My earlier impression was strengthened: the French have been there. There are street signs, blue-smocked salesgirls, occasional cash registers. Fruit & meat stalls mingle with restaurants. No feeling that if you take a side street you might meet a bad end - as in Casablanca.

The French had been in Casablanca, too, of course, but either they interfered less with the native institutions there, or the Tunisians were more amenable to European ideas of orderly merchandising than the Moroccans.

Almost bumped into a purdahed [veiled] woman in a dark covered street there - immediately was writing a story. Suppose her blind or diseased - stumbling, pushed by the throng. I am sorry, want to help. She stumbles before me; I inadvertently knock her down. She cries out. My helping hand & apologetic words are not understood; she spits. I hurry away into the crowd.

I later wrote and published this ill-advised sketch, savaged by its only reviewer: a real-world cold shower for the aspiring young writer. Some ideas are better left alone until you understand enough to do them justice.

The USIS American Cultural Center's reading room was not only a welcome haven after our trans-desert haul, but also a vision of the good life, and its resemblance to a college library did not escape me. Eight months earlier, I had been a burnt-out B.A. for whom further study held no appeal. Now I noted with interest that reading and writing in this quiet room among others thus employed was satisfying and strongly attractive. Perhaps I had learned something important, to be filed under "Investigate Further."

That night after dinner, Hector and I had, if not quite an argument, then at least a bull session that underscored some of our divergences, in a way and to a degree that rarely happened. The next morning after he went off to Tunis, I sat down to compose a treatise on *Us*, warts and all.

We are very different & don't understand one another. Perhaps it is well that I will soon have a chance to break off & travel alone, before any friction might set in. Not that I dismiss or disapprove [of] Hector. He has many traits which I like & respect: common sense, conscientiousness, seriousness, intelligence, honesty & good manners.

But what? Well, there was "a vague something" that he had - or didn't have – that made it "difficult for me to commune with him." That was vague enough, to be sure, and I had trouble pinning it down. Either he lacked an "esthetic or spiritual" side, or he wanted to keep it to himself. So? Surely he had a right to select which thoughts and feelings he would share. Come on: what had happened?

Last night, when we wandered from discussion of our present weariness & restlessness into our most personal conversation yet, I understood more about the gap. I was talking - too ringingly - about hopes for My Work: mentioning "fulfillment," "essences," & "soul." Hector suddenly said, quite pointedly (& I believe with the force of accumulated irritation), that he "didn't know anything" about "souls & essences & fulfillment," didn't know if souls existed, & didn't expect that much from his work. He expects to enjoy it, to profit from it, & to wonder & worry if it's right - no more.

What really interested Hector was photography - he was a great admirer of Ansel Adams - but he doubted that he could make a living or support a family as a photographer. His plan was (after military service) to get a job, any job, to bring in the needful, and have photography as a hobby. *That* was where he would live, not in his gainful employment. Today this sounds reasonable, but in 1960 it shocked me that Hector did not intend to invest his best talents and highest ideals in his *work*. "Challenged by inference," I tried to define the terms he had questioned, elaborate on them, and rephrase my credo.

After these brief and uneloquent statements of belief, we both lapsed into more compromising & less honest noises, & went to bed. But things were in the open.

I can see Hector's side of this exchange more clearly now, and sympathize with his flash of annoyance at my pretension ("too ringingly"). Having heard it before, probably, he wanted to give me something other than a consent-giving silence, so he staked out his own territory. There was, then, communication, though not communion, our outlooks being fundamentally different.

As if to dramatize these contrasts, Hector left this morning for a day reading at the A.C.C., because "I can't stand to sit around here with nothing to do." To me, such a day as this is fraught with possibilities for self-entertainment. There's my journal, stories to ponder, Spanish & Italian to study, exercises to do, things to tinker with - all this if the weather is bad. If it clears, a scooter ride or hiking. Or I could just go lie on the beach & meditate on life, love, souls. In other words, today, like all days, has too few hours. Hector's desire to keep up with the world is admirable; yet I prefer to detain it.

I saw that "detain" wasn't quite right, but the idea of exchanging our piney idyll for the bustle of downtown Tunis, even at the quiet ACC, did not appeal to me. Go read newspapers and magazines? Let the world go its way! Later I found my meaning, better expressed, in *Walden*:

> I delight to come to my bearings, …not live in this restless, nervous, bustling, trivial … Century, but stand or sit thoughtfully while it goes by. What are men celebrating? They are all on a committee of arrangements, and hourly expect a speech from somebody.

Nearby is the famous passage about hearing a "different drummer" and stepping to another music. That was it, really: Hector and I were listening to different drummers, mine being the less worldly. Each of us was practicing Emersonian self-reliance, trusting ourselves, "vibrating to that iron string," yet two selves and two strings would not always be in unison. Goethe also spoke for me: *"Was ich besitze, seh ich wie im Weiten, / Und was verschwand, wird mir zu Wirklichkeiten."* The particular formulation is interesting: "What I possess, I see as if at a distance, and what disappears becomes my reality." Not that I actually possessed much just then, but trace memories of Greece, Egypt, and the desert often filled my mind.

In the Time book section, two scenes touched me strongly. One was that of old Bernard Berenson, marooned in an Italian villa during the war, reading aloud with his companions day after day, taking perceptive notes. Equally compelling was BB's observation that "leisure, even when badly used, is often creative," while the driven person is seldom so. I agree, & want my leisure to use!

The other portrait was of an elderly English novelist, spending quiet years in her dark, old-fashioned, high-ceilinged home, writing in longhand at a mahogany desk her novels & stories. What an enviable pastime; God, how I crave some situation like that.

I noticed how similar Berenson and Ivy Compton-Burnett were, and how privileged, but didn't yet think to ask what dues they had paid for their late-life creative leisure, or how the public regarded their work. They might be seen by most as hopeless dodderers, living in a sort of *ancien-régime* bubble, irrelevant to the modern world.

At lunchtime the skies cleared and I set off on a long walk through the hills. The topography was gentle but invigorating, the scale pleasingly small. Canyons opened out into fertile, carefully farmed valleys; ridges a few hundred feet high divided these into discrete little communities. In mid-afternoon I re-victualled from a store in one of them and climbed to a convenient eyrie from which I could survey the world below and think about our present condition. It seemed that the wind had dropped and we were becalmed, breeding discontent, as in Naples – although in truth there was wind here for the taking: we had let the sheets go, choosing to drift. But were we really unhappy with this interlude? I, at least, was enjoying it, and learning about myself. Dusk found me still up there, scribbling ideas for child and adult education in my journal. I scrambled down in the dark and barely made dinner at the hostel. Hector seemed glum after his day in town. My appetite was enormous, I was aglow from my walk and in some vague way felt vindicated. Nothing to do, forsooth!

The next day we left Africa. When I said farewell to the chef, sorry to part with him, the regret seemed mutual. In Tunis, once we had done our errands, I strolled through the city's main park and read in the Cultural Center. At boarding time, riding my scooter too casually up a gangplank leading to the hold, I almost lost it into the harbor; Hector had to assist me. We then dragged the two machines aboard while amused dockhands watched. Shades of Ischia four months earlier, when we were young! But we had grown more callous in the meantime: I shook it off, reminding myself that loading procedures on Italian ships were quite clearly *designed* to make you hire help.

Feb. 17, aboard Lazio, bound for Palermo, 6 PM - All formalities went smoothly today as we put our scooters & selves aboard the clean, modern Lazio for an overnight 3rd class run to Palermo. We arrived in town at 9, completed business with customs, Am. Express & the bank, & had the middle of the day to read, eat, & kill. We left at 4:30. Our dormitory has c. 115 beds, but who cares?

Yeah, grizzled veterans of Greek deck passages were not to be fazed by a large dormitory: what mattered was that one of those beds was *yours*. I located a vacant bench seat by a table where I could finish writing up Tunis.

Hiked into the hills yesterday for 4 hours. Touched at Potinville - a strange place where upper-middle class homes & gardens were only yards from mining shacks of corrugated iron & brush - where I bought some lunch. Climbed ½way up a hill & ate, ascended to the summit, surveyed my domain for awhile, & down.

Potinville's total lack of zoning (as I understood it) seemed bizarre: gracious homes sat cheek-by-jowl with shanties. I wondered whether mineral wealth had been discovered in a previously residential area, the wealthy had inexplicably adopted an old mining site, or it was just a company town. There was nothing to show which stratum had been imposed on the other. At the time I had seen nothing like it, though Potinvilles are not uncommon in the third world. Acapulco gives some idea of the effects.

Belvedere Park in Tunis is a verdant hill covering several acres. It affords ample space & trails for the itinerant, games & swan ponds for the juvenile, & good vistas of the city for the sensual.

Both times I visited it was being well used: dozens of Tunisian families, hundreds of people, some in eastern dress, some in western, were strolling, standing, or sitting on the grass, though they had no blankets or picnic baskets. "*Shameena al hawa*," the Arabs say: "We sniffed the breeze." It was pleasant to go, to have gone, among them, observing their leisure hours and having them pay no attention to me, almost as if they thought that I belonged there.

And it felt good to be on the ship, going back to Europe after three months in Asia and Africa. The sea was smooth, the lounge crowded and lively, and a dining room with Italian food would open in half an hour. I spent a long time on the afterdeck watching Africa recede. Dusk began to obscure the hills of Tunisia in our wake and settle over the grey swells of the Mediterranean: sky and sea meeting in peace. Recalling how Aeneas left Carthage, also for Sicily, with the flames of Dido's funeral pyre visible astern, I was happy to have no such burden on my conscience; the warden would recover, and might even continue his English studies. Still recovering myself - from my Libyan wounds, the loss of the desert, and the disappointment of being denied Algeria - I planned to eat well, go to bed early and sleep soundly. When I woke up, the *Lazio* would have returned us to Italia, and we would take it from there, as we always did.

> Is man to attain all that he desires?
> It is Allah who ordains the present and the hereafter.
>
> *The Koran*

38. Roman coliseum in El Djem, Tunisia

39. Schoolboys flee the camera outside Tunis

40. Greek temple at Agrigento, Sicily, Italy

41. A south Sicilian hill-town

42. Greek temple, Paestum, near Salerno

43. Three ages: the Forum, Rome

X. Closing the Circles: Italian Spring

Could any soil
Be more agreeable to me, or any
Where I would rather moor these tired ships,
Than Sicily?

Virgil, *The Aeneid*
(trans. Robert Fitzgerald)

The sea-path between North Africa and Sicily was well-worn: before Aeneas there had been Odysseus, after him came the navies of the Punic Wars, much later the Barbary corsairs, and in our lifetimes the Axis and Allied armies. My feelings about making this move were radically mixed: Italy would be familiar, and easier ground linguistically and logistically, than what we had been on or had hoped to cover; but it was, again, not our first choice, and the idea of becoming just another American tourist in Europe rankled. Was he who had braved shifting sands and camel spit to be seen wandering around St. Peter's, next to Joe and Adela with their Fodor guide and SAS bag? Must the veteran of Baalbek and the bazaars of Istanbul bandy words with pert guides, or he who had seen Sekhmet and planned to write for *National Geographic* display ignorance in the Pitti Palace? Were Italian *pensiones* fit resting-places for an intrepid tent-camper of Greek islands and palm oases?

In a word, *Yes*, but the pill was bitter. I was like an engineer who enters a railyard with his own ideas about a terminus, only to realize that the switches are being thrown elsewhere. Clearly our destiny had *not* been to see East Africa or traverse North Africa, but to retrace Paul's missionary journeys and the Mediterranean campaign. On the bright side, I told myself, southwest Italy, below Naples, was an unknown, and might be less touristy.

Returning to Italy, I wondered if journal-keeping was still worthwhile. Why bother describing famous sites that Dante, Goethe, Stendhal, Ruskin, Browning, Pound, etc. had already described? Ah, came the prompt answer, but those worthies could say nothing about *my* trip, the psychic voyage that proceeds in Italy as well as in Libya. *That* was my province; on that *I* was the sole expert. Write on!

Feb. 18, PALERMO, SICILY, YH at Sferracavallo, 9:30 PM - Our ship raised Sicily in the half-light at 6:30 on a mild morning. Weather here quite warm. Meals on ship small & disappointing. Coast of Sicily very precipitous, alternately mountain & bay. Mt. Pellegrino above Palermo imposing, was admired by Goethe.

The *Lazio*'s lackluster cuisine was a useful reminder that the business of tourism is to sell attractive packages, not to worry about what's inside. In this case I had salivated at the *idea* of an Italian kitchen in vain. Nature, however, did not disappoint; Sicily, Dante's "beautiful Trinacria" (triangle), was another island-mountain rising from the sea, as spectacular as its distant relations the Azores.

First day in Palermo was busy. Found more of interest than expected; my own reactions surprisingly fresh. Besides the Cathedral & Palatine Chapel, enjoyed St. John of the Hermits (red domes, relics of 11th c. mosque, a quiet cloister), the Porto Nuovo, the Quattuor Canti (a busy intersection with a fountain at each corner), & a L.50 ice cream cone.

In fact, most of my reservations about Italy were forgotten at our first stop; in the Palatine Chapel I scribbled notes as enthusiastically as on my first day abroad. And what was attractive there proved characteristic of Sicily: the visible blending (or juxtaposition) of the various cultures that had ruled or influenced Trinacria. This was not the mainstream tourist Italy I had seen in Rome and Florence: Roman, or Roman Catholic and Renaissance. Southern Italy was full of Mediterranean and mediaeval flavors, with traces of the Crusades and Muslim civilization.

[The Palatine Chapel is] *Roman in* [its] *basilical form, Islamic in the architecture of ceilings (painted & starred & stalagmited), Byzantine in the extensive & elaborate mosaics with gold background. Greatest since Sainte [Chapelle] & Sistine Chapel.*

It was intoxicating to think that I might have learned even a bit about how to read architectural and artistic styles (intoxication is as dangerous as *a little learning*). Not having seen a major church carrying the full weight of European artistic traditions in a while, I lingered over the design of the dome, noted various kinds of columns, catalogued the Biblical stories told in mosaic. The mosques of the Near East, impressive as they were, had apparently left me hungry for pictorial narrative. A lone figure knelt in the choir, carefully tracing a mosaic on a large sheet of paper.

And this was just the chapel of the Norman Palace! The cathedral, a classic Italian *duomo*, was vast, silent and grand, with floors of pieced marble. Many of the columns (polished grey marble) had Roman capitals. A half dozen rectangular chapels opened off the nave; most had decorative sarcophagi and small statuary. Large paintings hanging over their altars showed to advantage in the candlelight.

The choir is of old, dark wood, the altar a portico of marble columns framing a marble Christ. Most striking statue is Christ crucified, done in wood, while three marble women, faces aghast, cringe below his gaunt, torn body.

Honoring the illustrious dead was the cathedral's mission: the remains of Frederick II, Holy Roman Emperor, and two Sicilian kings, Roger II and Henry VI, rested in ornate crypts. It was a relief, though, after an hour, to come out into the warm sun and sit on a bench in the precinct under palm trees and the brilliant cerulean sky.

Palermo faces the Mediterranean from a plain east of Monte Pellegrino. A branch of that plain cuts behind the mountain's southern shoulder to emerge at its northwest corner in a half-moon bay. Here is *Sferracavallo*, a fishing village with a youth hostel that we had heard was larger, cleaner, and less crowded than Palermo's, so we spent the night there: our scooters gave us that luxury. The building sat on a ledge fifty feet above the sea, overlooking the village's few houses, a sandy beach edging green water, and the Palermo road.

In the hostel's parking area a young Italian couple stopped necking long enough to ask us a few questions. My Italian came flooding back, and the ability to carry on a conversation in another language again was delicious. Their curiosity satisfied, the couple went back to business. Not to be seen in the Muslim world! Assuredly, we had returned to Europe, where couples, young and unmarried, could display affection in public. "Nice work if you can get it…." Thoughts stirred sluggishly, as after hibernation, of Penny, and, for the first time in months, of Cleo in Naples, a few hundred kilometers north, athwart our way to Verona.

It was a halcyon evening. We wrote letters in the comfortable hostel while a pastel sun sank into the placid grey-blue sea. The quiet village clustered about its idyllic cove - dreamily, I thought, but dreaming of what? In the general store they gawked as if we had been interplanetary visitors. Had the hostel just opened, or did we look stranger than most travelers? I was happy to have to use Italian, yet they spoke a dialect and had trouble with my pronunciation - perhaps a Libyan accent? It was odd to find so provincial a village so close to Palermo, but Sferracavalo was not on a road to anywhere. Glad that it had kept its secret, though not from us, we ate our cold snacks, added the hostel meal on top, and went to bed early.

Feb. 19, Youth Hostel, Palermo, 7:30 PM - Our 2nd & final day in Palermo was full of sightseeing, beauty, sordidness & adventure. We searched for the "Cuba," which we never found, walked to Quattuor Canti, & stopped at Piazza Pretoria, where a ployglot marble fountain writhes before a large old cathedral. Dynamic vs. static. Across the street is the huge, ancient mass of the University, capped by a yellow dome.

According to Baedeker, *La Cuba* is a ruined twelfth-century chateau with an Arabic inscription; he could probably have helped us find it. The scene in the *Piazza Pretoria* seemed familiar, but only later did I realize that the juxtaposition of statues depicting frozen motion with blocky architectural masses was standard in Italian piazzas - the kind of idea that an itinerant student might bring home from his *Wanderjahr*. The university reminded me of what other young people were doing with their time. Back home, second-semester courses had started by now, and my draft board would have received the news that I was a no-show.

A short walk further was Santa Maria dell'Amirralia, 12th century. In spite of this date, & the extremely old appearance of the grey stone outside, the interior is ornate & perfectly preserved.

Later I learned how little I had known then. Much of the mediaeval work had been removed or altered during the Renaissance and restored in the 20th century. The church's name is actually *S. Maria dell'Ammiraglio* (from Arabic *emir*, 'leader,' the root of "admiral"). At one time, Sicily's parliament met there: so, "St. Mary of the Leaders." Now it is usually called *La Martorana*, for the convent that took it over in the 15th century.

Byzantine mosaics with rich golden backgrounds covered the upper half of the chapel; the half-domes and niches without mosaics had painted religious scenes. We both took pictures. Hector shot confidently with high-speed Ektachrome. Using the back of a chair as a tripod and the slowest shutter speed available, I exposed one frame of Kodachrome ASA 25, hoping that its blurred glare of white and gold might be understood as impressionistic.

The representation of four saints surrounding Christ in the dome was done very awkwardly: they were stooping far over, posteriors protruding. One of the favorite Byzantine saint poses, restraining palms facing the viewer & a reproachful expression, looks too much like publicity photos of defensive ends to be taken seriously.

Images such as these suggested that Islam was right to ban representations of the human form in religious art. I still liked the church, and knew that it was impressively old by European standards, but really! By the 12th century CE both Greece and Egypt had declined to Turkish provinces; even the 12th century *BCE* was late in Egyptian history. I was in danger of becoming a chronological snob.

Then out to Monreale, 5 miles from & above Palermo, to see the renowned Cathedral. It was closing as we got there, for a leisurely 2 hours, & we had to be content during that time with the view of the city, the bay, & the hills - which was fine.

We sat on benches in the shady cathedral precinct overlooking Palermo and ate lunch, somewhat pestered by urchins and hawkers. Well, it *was* a tourist site, and the local version of the little ragamuffins who had so bothered us in Naples last fall seemed - after our month in Egypt - relatively healthy and good-natured. Anyway, everyone at the hostel said you *had* to see Monreale.

The Duomo was worth waiting for. Huge, profoundly quiet, covered with Byzantine mosaic, it gave me one of my rare religious experiences. The representation of Christ in the apse was one of the finest examples of Byzantine art I've seen: eyes cast balefully to the left, he looked at once weary & strong, humbled & lordly.

His open arms span the curve of the apse in a welcoming embrace. I read his expression as saying, "Come here to rest, and be worthy of that boon." The momentary sense of contact with the transcendental was worth coming a long way to feel; I had not responded that way to religious art since Paris and Chartres five years earlier. Here, then, Christianity seemed to have been right to allow representation of the divine. It took an effort to pull away from that apse and resume touring.

The sarcophagus of William II ("Here lies William II, called The Good, King of Sicily, who lived 37 years...") was in a side chapel, with that of William I. Ranks of organ pipes gleamed silver; rows of columns were uniformly smooth & Romanesque.

Some of the Greek inscriptions in the mosaics appeared to have been chipped out and replaced with Latin: mute testimony, I supposed, to some remote political, linguistic, or theological struggle. Or perhaps there were just fewer people who could read Greek as time went on.

The Duomo's Cloister, surrounded by double, Islamic-looking columns, was peaceful & verdant. Blue & red flowers & odd green plants set off the bulk of the cathedral well. I'd like a cloister in my back yard.

Well yes, and how about a crew of artisans to set mosaics as rich as *cloisonné* into some columns and carve filigree into others, and a few Sicilian gardeners to plant and tend exotics with spiky leaves and red blossoms bursting like fireworks at the end of long stalks? Oh, and maybe a harem for the intervals between meditations?

That afternoon I revisited *San Giovanni degli Eremiti* (St. John of the Hermits), the old Norman church, with another peaceful cloister. A tall green fir, palms, orange and other fruit trees, ferns, and red flowers set off the pale pink domes that gave it the aspect of an Arab *hammam* (bath). Then back to the Palatine Chapel to see if it was as splendid as I remembered, and to note the details behind the effect.

Hundreds of semi-mosaics line the floors & lower walls (up to the mosaics proper). They are thousands of pieces of cut marble & color[ed] stone, fitted into precise geometric patterns. Here, as in other churches, plaques of polished marble, dark red or green, are exhibited as pictures, framed by decorative mosaic. Very handsome.

On the outer wall, another mosaic - mostly hunting scenes - followed the scalloped surface, neatly accommodating several stained-glass windows. At each end of the room was a bas-relief sculpture of an historical event, with an amazing amount of depth effect among the figures. The main doors, of light wood, had finely carved panels, both relief and inlay. No doubt about it: these guys were good! A prep-school teacher used to exhort us, "Gentlemen, let us be artists, not artisans," but the workers here had been both.

I also returned to Palermo's cathedral for a post-Monreale inspection - as if a new standard had been set there, which must now be applied.

It was a relief to be there again, soothed by its white marble coolness after the glare of Byzantine gold. Although I have no more sympathy with what Catholic art stands for than [with] Byzantine, the style of the art is at bottom more touching to me.

Saying just what each stood for, however, was difficult. I believed that Catholic artists exalted "austere self-denial," but what Byzantine art might refer to, other than "an icon-ridden pantheistic monotheism," was beyond me. It seemed to want to glorify where Catholicism, darker and cooler, consoled and reassured, which suited my mood. And yet, the Byzantine apse at Monreale.... I was out of my depth.

All this cogitation made me hungry, and while eating a cone of excellent *gelato* I decided to drive up Monte Pellegrino, which rears abruptly from the northwest edge of Palermo. Goethe described it (in German, of course) as one of the world's noblest promontories.

It was near dark, the wind, up to gale force, was wicked, & the blurred panoramas [were] increasingly tremendous. I was elated! Stopped at a castle & took a picture: clouds touched with fiery orange, the city dusky, the far hills blue. A few kilometers further up, I was getting pushed around by the wind & darkness was coming on. When I saw a helicopter 200' below me, I knew I was high enough. Reluctantly, I came down toward Palermo's lights.

Whether or not the wind was really "gale force," the top of Monte Pellegrino was thus left to my imagination (which would probably have been disappointed by its array of mast antennae and other communications equipment). That evening it occurred to me that we had now been here for two days and I had been completely engrossed, enjoying myself and feeling no regrets. Astonishing!

We spent the night in the Palermo youth hostel in order to be better positioned to start our first full day of cross-country travel since pulling into the Inn of Pines nine days before. The day provided several reality checks - reminders of why epic heroes tended to stick to the coast.

Feb. 20, Agrigento YH, 10:30 PM - Left Palermo at about 9 this morning & spent an exhilarating day driving thru hills & mountains. A stiff headwind was frustrating at times, & ragged grey clouds made the weather cool, but the scenery expiated all.

Cliffs, precipitous yet green, rose to summits hidden in cloud (think Hawaii); rolling hills held pockets of rich farmland with yellowish soil; small mediaeval towns clung to promontories. This rugged topography would at times open abruptly to sweeping vistas of plain and bay, sea and sky. I beheld this landscape, which gave space for thought and demanded deep breaths, in a kind of three-dimensional delirium. A pair of *carabinieri* passed us on a vintage motorcycle: serious-looking fellows, their carbines prominent. Just before the hill-town of *Castelvetrano* ("old castle"), one of my windshield posts broke and a tire went flat, but a welder and a bowl of *fraggiole* soup set me up again within an hour. I thought how differently that scenario would have played out in Libya.

We had missed the turn to the Graeco-Roman ruins at *Segesta* that morning, and by the time we discovered our mistake were unwilling to backtrack 10 kilometres. What the hell, there were other ruins ahead! Beyond Castelvetrano the road dropped to the southern coastal plain and a side road led to *Selinunte*, whose remains were disappointing: fallen, wasted, fat cylinders that had once been columns, and lots of rubble. Then on along the coast road, east toward *Agrigento*, making good time, sailing before our old enemy the west wind in glorious swoops! We learned that when a truck or bus passed we could pull in behind it and be drafted along, gaining as much as 10 kph. You had to stay close to get this effect, but it had now been awhile since we had had a fall, and young memories are short.

The youth hostel at Agrigento was located in the Greek ruins, which we left until morning. Modern *Girgenti* sat on a hillside a mile or so inland; at dusk we went up there to look for dinner. Young couples and old, packs of bachelors, and whole families were promenading in the mild twilight: the *corso*. We entered a modest-looking *trattoria* and ordered spaghetti. The owner, beside himself with the honor of our patronage, insisted on *giving* us the meal. Very embarrassed, we would rather have left than accepted - he and his diner did not seem prosperous - but situations of this sort are touchy, and difficult to stop once begun. My Italian was serviceable, not fluent, and there were cultural barriers, too. I was reminded of the Papadoupoulos family in Thessaloniki: good will and bad communication.

Back at the hostel, I joined a group gathered around a slightly older-looking fellow, thirtyish, who was telling stories and drawing other people out. "He is writer," a young Frenchman explained. "*Walk the World*?" Sure enough, it was Don Knies, whose book I had finished a week before. Its jacket had said that he was back in the American corporate fold, working for an oil company, but now he was off for Africa and planning another book. When I told him that I had enjoyed his first, he said, "Yes, sometimes I feel like a prophet." I absolved him of responsibility for our *Wanderjahr*, and asked about his job. He shook his head wryly. "Didn't work out. I lasted almost two years, though, and made enough money to travel for a year or so." He seemed a genuinely good person; the inquiring mind and affection for people evident in his book came through in conversation. I should have told him that *Walk the Wide World* had made me re-evaluate my style of travel – although I had not yet acted on that new perception.

In the morning we spent an hour exploring the remains of the ancient Greek colony. Sand-colored Doric temples, better preserved than the Parthenon, stood among almond trees with white blossoms under a sky of pellucid robin's-egg blue. It was almost like being back in Greece, if not better. The sun was warm, there were few visitors, and the temples exceeded expectations, stimulating our photographic juices. I had forgotten how deeply pleasing Greek architecture is, and suddenly realized that I had been missing it.

Feb. 21, YH at Lake Pergusa (near Enna), 9 PM - Too cold to write much. Great day, though: lovely Sicilian hill country, gorgeous mild weather, cherry trees in blossom, craggy hill towns, & snowy Mt. Etna. Scooters cooperated by running like charms. Hostel here is very pleasant, but unheated. Cooked fish soup tonite, & ate cheese & ham sandwich. Good food. Good day.

And with that I tucked into my sleeping bag, again inadequate up there by a mountain lake in the center of Sicily. Still, it had been one of our best days: orchards of fruit trees bearing white clouds of blossom, as if mists were drifting through; fields of parti-colored wildflowers; steep ridges with flanks of soft green fuzz and ancient strongholds on their rocky spines; the road twisting so that all sense of direction was lost and every glimpse of distant Mt. Etna came as a surprise. A country of resonant names that Anglo tongues relished even as they tripped over: *Serradifalco*, *Pietraperzia*, *Caltanisetta*. I drifted off thinking about Enna, a collection of old buildings on top of a hill. There should be a Robert Browning poem about that....

The "warden" overcharged us 65 *lire* for breakfast and I protested. It was only 10 cents, but the *principle*: hostels were supposed to be benign! We took to the road at 8 AM. The driving was pleasant and often spectacular, though cold at first. Trying to stretch my fuel and check the mileage, I ran onto reserve gas 20 kilometers short of *Piazza Armerina*. The last spoonful brought me into town, where the pump delivered the published capacity of the tank. Obviously there were different ways to get into trouble: you could cross the Libyan desert, or just pursue some bright idea. The mileage worked out to 28 kms./liter or 66 mpg: an improvement from North Africa, but still nowhere near my calculations of its performance in the early days.

Feb. 22, YH at Belvedere (near Syracuse), 7 PM - Another long & scenic day of mountain driving ended with a steady descent from the highlands & entrance into Syracuse at 3. I was glad, having [had] my fill of tight curves, hills & bad roads. The land on this eastern slope is neither so picturesque nor so fertile as above Agrigentum. But the omnipresent crown of Etna makes up for other lacks.

The whole island tips southeast, which was our course that day. Mt. Etna stands at the eastern end of the Sicilian massif; south of it the land drops away. At Piazza Armerina, though, we were still very much in the mountains.

It was another old hill town clinging to a rocky escarpment amid green fields. We clattered up steep cobblestone streets to the 17th century cathedral, aloof & austere & beautiful inside; then bounced down & out into the country to see some well-preserved Roman mosaics.

The two stops made a contrasting pair: *Spirit* and *Sense*. In the cathedral, a Mass was proceeding solemnly amidst Baroque splendors that seemed excessive in the context of that cool building. At the villa, most of the extensive mosaics, well-executed even by Roman standards, depicted aristocratic hunting parties. Scholars were at work there; some of the mosaics had been roofed over and roped off.

Then on across ridges and ravines, through *Caltagirone* and *Vizzini* to *Buccheri*, where we stopped to eat. Most of the town assembled for the great event of our lunch. They refused to believe that we were Americans: that must be some unfathomable joke of ours. *They* knew what *Americans* looked like! We decided to take it as a compliment, though they did not intend it as such. Many Sicilians had emigrated to the US, and we did not conform to their notions of *homo americanus*. I think we made them uneasy.

Beginning a gradual descent from mountains to coastal hills, we putted along in cool, hazy-bright weather. Except for an occasional burst of color in a blooming cherry tree, the [fields] were less scenic than yesterday, although not less detailed. The carpets of white, yellow, blue, & orange flowers growing by the road are gone; the land offers more farms, as much greenery as before, & purple flowers that I could no more name than those of the day before (poppies, anemones, and cyclamen, probably). Motoring through these pastoral scenes we came to a railroad crossing. The gates were down, a shapeless old woman in black sat by a little sentry box, and a car waited on the far side, but there was no sign of a train, no sound, no smoke.

"*Signora,*" said Hector, pointing to the gate, "*per favore.*"

She waggled her index finger and pointed to her watch.

"*Ma dove é il treno*?" I asked, with dramatic gestures.

"*Ven' subito. Alle due,*" she answered, pointing to her watch again and holding up two fingers. It *was* 2 PM, plus a few minutes, but the train might still be in Palermo for all I could see. "*Signora,*" we pleaded, but she turned away, wagging her finger. Evidently she lowered the gate on schedule and waited for the train to pass. As did we, and a growing collection of Fiats, whose drivers, after an initial burst of vocables and manual flourishes, were amazingly patient. We got off to stretch and stroll a bit. It was pleasant, once you accepted the situation, walking and talking. Little relationships formed, news and views were exchanged. In 20 minutes or so a small train clacked by, the gates lifted, the Gatekeeper in Black returned to her box without a backward glance, and we all went our ways. A conservative, perhaps with strong views on the perils of thoughtless haste, she probably lost few clients at her crossing.

From 29 kms. away I could see the white gleam of Syracuse, clustered on a jut of land by the sea. Then we were on the plain, the hills behind, thru Floridia, & in the historic old city. Visited the interesting 7th cent. cathedral, built into a 5th cent. [BCE] temple of Minerva. Doric columns are embedded in the cathedral's inner wall -

the first of many reminders that *Siracusa* was once a major Greek colony, the most important city on Sicily. It figures prominently in Thucydides' *History of the Peloponnesian War*. The Athenian expedition against Siracusa in the 17th year of that war ended in defeat by Sparta two years later. Since the 1960s that campaign has been called Athens' Vietnam (or Afghanistan). For Athens and her devotees, this was where history began to come apart. Siracusa was later held by Carthaginians, Romans, Byzantines, Arabs, Normans, Turks - whoever was running the central Mediterranean - but its history is one of decline from the time Athens attacked it. Ironically, the two cities' high points coincided.

Then we came on out 12 kms. to Belvedere, & this excellent Albergho della Gioventu. Splurged 80 cents on a fine dinner.

Belvedere took some finding, though. Asking for "BELL-vuh-deer" produced nothing but frowns and headshakes. Finally it occurred to me that this was Italian for "looks beautiful" or "good views." As soon as I inquired for "Bel-veh-DEH -reh," they said, "*Ah, si*," and pointed the way.

Hector's scootering almost ended abruptly the next morning. He had rotated his front and spare tires, but after about five yards of driving, the Lambretta nosed over onto its front fender with a dull clank. The wheel lay alongside. Oops! It seemed certain that he must have cracked or sheared something, but we could find no damage. He mounted the tire again, tightening the nuts more carefully this time, and it worked fine.

We spent the forenoon seeing the sights of Siracusa: museum, catacombs, theatres, and *latomiae*: ancient quarries, later used as prisons, then turned over to the gardeners. It was there that I lost my patience with the local version of tourism. Our honeymoon was over.

Feb. 23, Latomia [de'] Capuccini - Hector's right: Italy is the worst country for hounding tourists. I had been inside the Latomia for 10 minutes, wandering peacefully, when a "guardian" showed up with a ticket book, demanding L.50. There had been no one at the open gate. Could also point to "parking attendants," juggling of prices on food, ragazzi & the Great Cigarette Quest, etc.

In Monreale a few days before, Italian begging had seemed benign compared to Egypt's. But the Italians were *here* - pursuing me where their ancestors harassed imprisoned Athenian soldiers - and the Arabs far away. This was what I had dreaded returning to when Algeria closed its gates. I wondered where we would have been by now if visas had been granted. Prowling Roman ruins beside *Mare nostrum*? Edging along the Sahara? Or hiding from FLN snipers behind cork oaks up in the Kabylia?

This morning at the Neapolis (part of the ancient city), we visited the Latomiae del Paradiso & [di] S. Venera: grottoes & pleasure gardens. Caves yawn, water trickles down moss, vines wander, huge trees with tentacle-like roots spread shade, ferns & bushes cover grey rocks. Also in this area were a Greek Theatre & a Roman Amphitheatre, both partially hewn out of solid rock.

The theatre, one of the largest in the Hellenic world, had been finely constructed, and was in fairly good repair. The stone-grey orchestra and tiers of seats brought back Epidauros in its Peloponnesian valley, though here you overlooked the town, its harbor, and the Ionian Sea.

Then we drove to *Ortygia*, the "island" (now connected to Sicily by a causeway) that is the site of both the oldest settlement and the modern town. Siracusa can be confusing: *Neapolis*, "new city," is Graeco-Roman. Across the street from the combination cathedral and Temple of Minerva/Diana, the museum housed a large collection of (mainly) pieced-together pottery, broken statuary, and neolithic objects from around Sicily.

A few blocks away, the Fountain of *Arethusa*, mentioned by Ovid and Milton, had unexpected resonance. Arethusa was a beautiful wood nymph and huntress, one of Diana's train. One day, bathing naked in a Greek river, she aroused the lust of its god, Alpheus, who pursued her. Arethusa called on Diana for help, and the moon-goddess (who was once surprised at *her* bath) provided a cloud of mist. The river-god persisted, so Diana changed Arethusa into a stream, and when Alpheus became a river again to join with her, the goddess

> broke the earth, and I plunged downward
> To the dark depths, and so came here; this land
> Received me first in upper air; I love it
> In memory of my goddess. (Ovid. *Meta*. V)

Et in Sicilia dea: Diana had been worshipped here, too! Evidently there was no escaping her. Milton hails the "fountain Arethuse" because Theocritus – traditionally the father of pastoral poetry - was born nearby. The spring itself seemed to have fallen on hard times, though; it was no longer a natural site, having been walled in to form a basin, and the water-level was quite low.

The fountain of Arethusa proved to be a reed-bordered well-pond, inhabited by ducks & pigeons. Lunch across the street at a clean Roticceria, where I ate 2 arancine: warm bread (like potato puffs) stuffed with rice, peas, cheese, & meat with sauce.

At a good time and place for reflection on the difference between mythological interest and physical reality, I discovered that…I was hungry.

YH at CATANIA, 7 PM - This afternoon, after a short visit to the Christian catacombs at Chiesa San Giovanni, we headed for Catania. The headwinds were so stiff that we took off our windshields for the first time since rolling into Tripoli,

lashing them on top of our loads as before. To combat the resultant wind chill I tied my red bandanna so as to cover the lower half of my face. Both procedures were successful. Freed from the drag of windshields, the scooters slipped through the air with glorious freedom, and I looked like a demon on wheels, a motorized *banditto*.

Catania was found across a valley, a range of hills, & another wide valley. Its setting is nonpareil: between the blue sea & the slopes of Mt. Etna. The international campground was closed, but the "Albergho della Gioventú" is handsome & much the same [as Belvedere's hostel]. Took a run into town before dark to see the Duomo & buy dinner.

In the twelfth-century cathedral, Roman columns stood alongside the white pillars of an eighteenth-century renovation. Side chapels had striking, dark-hued paintings framed in marble and gilt; the slanting rays of the low sun produced a transient *chiaroscuro*. Catania dates from the 8th century BCE - the period of "Homer" - but the few material remains of the classical era are unimpressive. Its squares and public gardens were pleasant, though, with their palm trees, Norfolk pines, and views of the famous volcano, standing there like the grandest cathedral dome of all. Another climbable peak that we did not even try to climb! It would be more tempting in summer, when guides are available and there is less snow, for which we were ill-equipped. We drove back to the hostel after dark.

Pulled a hard-headed stunt today. Was determined to eat on 50 cents, after spending $1.50 yesterday - & did it. Cappuccino & a roll for breakfast, 2 arancine for lunch, pizza & a sugar donut for *dinner. "Self-discipline," I told the New Zealand girl here. "I didn't know Americans were like that," she replied pensively.*

I should have told her that most weren't, and that "self-destruction" was a better label for my insistence on eating for a dollar a day, whatever the consequences for my body. Dizzy from malnutrition (and maybe infection), I was in a strange space, seemingly someone else's; the journal entries from that day are hardly recognizable as products of my mind and feelings. I noted how distant I felt from Penny, worried about that unsurprising development, declared a renewed appreciation of the American way of life, and confessed that I was

really tired of travelling. Little enthusiasm for sightseeing, nor for scootering. Best that I finish & get back. At Verona, I hope to rest & read sufficient to get my second wind for Spain.

It is astonishing how independent remembrance can be of its origins. My memories of Sicily are of fair spring days, exhilarating drives, and recurrent exaltation by nature and art, not burn-out. So which is more "real": the tired, saddle-sore week I apparently spent on Sicily, or the golden recollections ever since? I am like a free diver torn between admiring the pearls he has brought up, and recalling the pain of bursting lungs they cost him.

Feb. 24, YH at Giardini, 7 PM - Spent the morning walking around Catania. Aside from some Baroque churches, the best sight was the Bellini Gardens. Had our scooters serviced & left at about 1. Rode slowly up the scenic coast - Riviera de Cyclopi - & watched Mt. Etna's snowy cone in the clear air.

The road followed the undulations of the rocky coast from spine to cove, tiptoeing between Etna and the sea. Never did we lose sight of the great volcano, its white mantle gleaming through the feathery foliage of pine trees; a northeast wind blew snow-plumes off the summit. We stopped by some thistle-bushes to view the *Scogli de' Ciclopi*, a few islets just offshore. Traditionally, this is where Odysseus and his crew were imprisoned by the Cyclops Polyphemus, who killed and ate six of them. Resourceful Odysseus got the giant drunk, put out his eye with a stake, escaped with his men by clinging to the bellies of rams, and made it back to the ships. But classical heroes have to boast: as they pulled away, Odysseus shouted out his name, enabling the giant to curse him properly and invoke the vengeance of his father Poseidon, god of the sea. Polyphemus also threw huge boulders in the direction of the sound: hence the islets. It seemed as likely as subterranean pressures and molten rock. Perhaps the accounts could be reconciled: the Cyclops, "who ply/The black forge under Mongibello's vault" (Dante), assisted the smith-god Hephaestus in the basement of Etna.

Then *avanti*, through more natural beauty in fine weather, to *Giardini*, whence Garibaldi embarked for the mainland in 1860; Baedeker calls it "an insignificant place, often visited by fever." We claimed beds and left our packs at its youth hostel, near the turn-off to *Taormina*.

Arrived here about 3 & took a fast, winding run up the hill to Taormina. It is a civilized tourist village, with some Greek & Roman ruins & a breathtaking viewpoint on Etna & the coast.

Those vistas of mountain and sea have been bringing people to Taormina since at least 400 BCE, though for a long time the fact that it is a natural fortress was part of the attraction. That advantage had been improved with a castle, one of the two principal ruins, the other being the Graeco-Roman theatre. I could easily believe that it has one of the most beautiful views in Italy, as guidebooks say. The horseshoe-shaped tiers face south toward Etna, and from the highest of them the volcano's blinding cone hung as if suspended in the clear air over hazy plains and sparkling seas. Perhaps Coleridge had been there:

> It was a miracle of rare device,
> That sunny dome! Those caves of ice!

What a lovely spot, though tainted by tourism. By framing the view with my hands I could keep Taormina's calculated prettiness out of sight, but when a gay American accosted me shortly after our arrival I took it as a cue to leave. We did, dropping down the hill at a good clip. Even so, a Vespa passed us on a sharp curve, its running board sparking against pavement all the way around, its two local riders cooling it, thinking of something else, careless of their fortune. They say there are only two kinds of scooter riders: those who have fallen, and those who are about to.

The hostel, a ramshackle building near the water, contained an assortment of types. Hector and I and a comely Australian girl mixed a dozen eggs with a liter of milk to make an enormous omelet. It was fun to sit around a common room again with other *studenti*, swapping ideas and stories. The tourist and hostel activity here was the most since Egypt, and seemed to be increasing. We were back in it now, willy-nilly, and needed to find a bright side. Attractive young women would do nicely, we agreed.

Early the next morning we set off for Messina. The northeast coast was so populous that one town almost ran into another. This gathering density, which had begun at Catania, reminded me of the "continuous population belt" that demographers were warning the US Atlantic seaboard to expect. I thought that *Roccalumera*, however, had a better castle than Connecticut could show.

Feb. 25, on the Messina-San Giovanni ferry - Five months ago today we left New York for Italy. Half an hour ago we drove into Messina after an hour's run from Giardini, & in another half hour we should be on the Italian mainland.

"Should be," not "will be," note: I had learned *some*thing along the way. Yet, sipping *espresso* in the ship's café, poised between adventures, admiring the violet mountains of Italy's toe through picture windows as we crossed the strait of Scylla and Charybdis, I found myself reflecting complacently on the trip thus far, and sanguine about the immediate future. All the omens were auspicious: clear skies, the likelihood of a decent road up the coast, a smooth crossing where Odysseus had to dodge dragons and whirlpools - the latter still visible several times daily (on a sub-heroic scale) as tides surged through the gap.

Sicily...Greek, then Roman ruins constitute the chief historical interest. Carthaginians & Greeks warred over the island for much of its early history, both subjugating the natives. Around the 3rd cent. BC, Rome began the conquests which eventually gave her the whole island. Afterwards, Sicily passed to the Byzantine Empire, Arabs, Normans, Swabians, the Holy Roman Empire & the Kingdom of the Two Sicilies before Garibaldi made it part of Italy.

I made notes of the guidebook variety, pointing classics buffs toward Agrigento and Syracuse, Renaissance historians and the artistically inclined to Monreale and Palermo, devotees of church architecture to Enna, Piazza Armerina, Catania, and Syracuse again. (The busy commercial center of Messina, with its churches, forts, and twenty-seven centuries of history, would have to toot its own horn; we had dashed through it with eyes only for the ferry in its excellent harbor.) Lovers of natural beauty might well find the whole island delightful. My readers had to be warned, though, in the spirit of Baedeker, that

In many towns there are no sidewalks. Some do have narrow sidewalks; some a few feet of dirt or stone separating houses from road; & many have old, worn stone houses just sitting at the edge of the paved surface.

Now we were about to set foot on mainland Europe for the first time since crossing the Bosporus nearly three months earlier. Our plan was to head up the coast, visit Paestum, play the tourist in Naples, Rome, and Florence, then crash with Parry in Verona before tackling Spain. That the prospect of a long winding drive north was not exciting proved my weariness: the thought of such a scooter holiday would have electrified me back in the fall. Well, it was good that the end was in sight, then; no one should be allowed to travel tired through such magnificent country. And when would it happen again?

Our ship's whistle interrupted my reverie. The cliffs above San Giovanni were close. I went up to the vehicle deck and donned my helmet and red bandanna as the ferry nosed against soft pilings. When they lowered the barricade we started the scooters and guided them gingerly down the steep ramp to the pier. I looked back questioningly, but Hector waved me on: no need to stop here. I found the coast road north and opened up. At the edge of town a sign said "NAPOLI 527 km." First, though, we'd need to get by a place called *Scilla*, 10 kms. up the road, of which some disturbing old stories were told.

Hotel in Cetraro, Italy, 7 PM - Rushed up the west coast of southern Italy this afternoon with amazing rapidity. In spite of mountainous terrain & winding roads almost the entire way, we covered 215 kms. between leaving the ferry & pulling into Cetraro at 6. The countryside was absorbing enough to prevent a repetition of Libyan boredom.

Near *Palmi*, workers were pruning olive trees in the deep shade of a cavern-like grove. Further on, the road traversed orange orchards where the sweet tang of citrus blossoms hung in the air like an invisible veil. Our first day on the road had delivered the boon of rich, full scents. To scooter now through this landscape was to pass through repeated waves of sensuous experience, from which we distilled, moment by moment, the purest of pleasures. To our left, Stromboli and the other volcanic Lipari islands jutted hazily from the sea, their starkness softened by distance.

We had talked of spending the night in the small port of *Pizzo*, but, arriving in the early afternoon and learning that the hostel (an old castle) would not open for another week, we lunched on pizza, coffee, and rum pastry - as if we weren't already high enough! -

& pushed on. Amantea & Paola went by as we kept setting our sights higher. We discussed camping, but couldn't find uninhabited country. Arrived here at sunset & talked the man down to L.400 (65 cents) apiece for a triple room with basin.

The chill of driving without windshields, the beauty of the landscape, our pushing, and various uncertainties – mainly what might transpire in Napoli - kept me shivering all afternoon. I was cold, tired, and a bit dizzy as we unpacked, but revived during our brisk walk after dark to find food. The evening promenade - the *corso* - was in progress, so the streets were filled. As always, it excited me; I kept looking around for some event or catastrophe, which is what it would take to produce such crowds in my culture, but here people came out every night just to see and be seen, talk, stroll, and enjoy being alive and at leisure after a day of work. The Arabs call it *kayf*.

Salerno, & even Napoli, seem possible goals for tomorrow. Without windshields, we are running much more satisfactorily.

Indeed, the stripped-down Lambretti ran like dreams over the hilly, winding coast road, as if they knew that home was near, and we reveled in the kinetic pleasure of it. But I was vaguely ("dimly" would be more to the point) aware that the pace of which we were so proud - and yearned to increase - was sinful. Nearly every hamlet that we had blasted through was a natural beauty spot, and had enough historical interest to rate a guide-book entry; from many of them, side roads led up to other intriguing places in the mountains. One could spend a happy month loitering through the country we transited that day, mere birds of passage. Slow down and live, man: *piano, piano*!

Forte, forte, we left Cetraro before seven, breakfasted on bread and coffee half an hour up the road, and resumed our sprint, whirring smoothly through curves and over terraced hills in country of extraordinary beauty. The sun cleared the eastern wall late, and with little color of its own, but brought out the orchards' green and the smooth sea's aqua. From the top of the hill beyond *Sapri* - a fishing village on a small bay sheltered by promontories - the vista back down the coast unfurled its great banner: jagged peninsulas like anchored warships, each a slightly fainter bluish-grey than its northern neighbor, in a row that extended clear to the horizon.

Where the road turned inland, through the mountains behind Cape *Palinuro* (Palinurus was Aeneas' helmsman who fell asleep and then overboard on the voyage to found Rome), there was a bad stretch over roads in poor repair, especially on curves and hills. Steep grades and unbanked turns demanded close attention, derrieres grew fatigued, and the fact that we were now openly pressing for Napoli added to the nervous strain. It was as tiring a three hours as I could remember on the scooter.

After a late lunch in a roadside café near the ruins of *Paestum* on the plain south of Salerno, we spent an hour among the Greek temples. Paestum is the Roman name from the 3rd century BCE; three centuries earlier it was *Poseidonia*, after the sea god to whom the principal building is dedicated. The temples sit in a meadow that shelves gently toward the sea a quarter of a mile away like a welcome mat spread for the waves. Simple, classic, the Temple of Poseidon had the most deeply grooved Doric columns I had seen anywhere. A most perfect excellence, it seemed to be waiting silently for its time to roll 'round again in the great circle of the ages. Paestum is said to have the finest Greek temples outside of Athens; they would likely be our last. Green salamanders ran over the brown sandstone, and buttercups were blooming in the grass.

Napoli

Feb. 27, Biblioteca Nationale, NAPLES, 1 PM - It's a strange feeling to meet yourself coming around the mountain, but I experienced it yesterday as I recognized the faded yellow apartment houses of

Salerno. The chill grew stronger as shafts of sun lit the Amalfi hills & Vesuvius. We passed "Scooter" de L. Castino, & the Albergo Astoria, resplendent with a new sign. Unpleasant as some of the memories are, this is where it started, 4½ months ago. The wheel has come full circle. We covered 312 kms. & made Naples at 5.

The run along the coastal plain from Paestum to Salerno was fast, but then the Apennines stuck a finger out into the sea. Having gone around its tip (the Amalfi drive) in October, we chose the straighter, faster route via *Nocera* this time. Up in the mountains, one of the Mersa Matruh saddlebags - rotted through by leaks of oil and gas - gave up the ghost, spilling mechanical paraphernalia along the highway. We found places for the stuff - anywhere! - and pressed on to Napoli. An Italian Line ship was at anchor in the bay, the *Conte* something. Could it be?! No: 'twas the *Conte Grande*. In *Posilipo*, a hilly neighborhood on the city's western edge noted for toney villas in Roman times, we bespoke a couple of beds in the crowded, lively youth hostel.

The ease with which we located this boon, whose very existence we had not suspected in October, showed that something had been learned in those eventful months since we blundered here, anxious and naïve, ignorant of what to see, of how to find places to eat and sleep. Some of the potential of our fledgling days had been realized, some of their hopes dashed. I knew more but felt jaded, was less restless but sadder: somehow both richer and poorer. It was a natural time - and the quiet reading-room of the National Library a good place - for stock-taking. I thought again how much I liked the church-like repose of libraries, without the implied obligation to Believe.

My general condition is not good: some infection around both knees & my hip, saddle sores painful, clothes worn & dirty, & one of my saddlebags torn up. But, with frequent rests, I'll try to work on up through Rome & Florence [to Verona].

To be back in Napoli, yet feel so different, was unsettling. It was a city of ambiguities and bittersweet memories: Giancarlo and Jeff, our first scooter excursions, thrill and trauma, Bruno and Cleopatra. Ever since turning north I had been thinking about her and what to do. She was probably still here studying - might walk into the reading room any minute! A cold feeling invaded my stomach. What was I up to? Up for? *The glands know.*

Could I just call on her as a friend? Yeah, right. And seeing her might make it worse. Or, if she had broken her engagement and become available, what then? I had nothing to offer. The first time she crossed my path I stumbled on her, hurting Penny. This time I was fully conscious of the risks, able to expose myself to temptation or not. To chance upon Cleo or Calypso or Circe or Diana is one thing, to return and pay her a visit quite another. It needed careful thought.

So I thought about it - that day while looking around the city, at dusk while photographing the sunset behind Ischia, and that night - without making a move. In Victorian poems about the Virtues of Action, the protagonist's flaw is to be too passive, but I was not convinced that it would be right to act on *these* feelings; there might be times when passivity was a virtue. Victorian poets didn't know everything! And yet…Penny *had* cut me loose. How about a brief fling? I knew that was not my style, and doubted it was Cleo's: we were both serious, intense types, not dabblers. The next morning I went to the Naples Museum - which we had not visited in October - and carefully lost myself in studious admiration of the collection.

Feb. 28, Nat'l Archeological Museum, Naples - I'm fortunate in having been able to visit some of the world's great museums on this trip: Athens, Istanbul, Cairo, & now Naples. This one is excellent - particularly struck by two river & sea deities reclining; "Prometheo Crea l'Uomo" in relief on a sarcophagus; & a Roman praetor on a horse. Aesculapius is always a good subject. Did Christianity kill off good sculpture for awhile by killing off its best subjects - the gods?

The hall of colored marble was displaying the best collection of mosaics I had ever seen (including some mosaic columns like those at Monreale), black bronzes, many frescoes, and a scale model of the excavations at Pompeii.

A fine museum, but the first floor far exceeds the rest. Two books which would mean something now are Last Days of Pompeii and Decline & Fall of Roman Empire.

By the time I emerged, a decision NOT to *chercher la femme* had been made, somehow; I just knew I wouldn't. That afternoon we went to look for Jeff and Giancarlo. Neither was at home. We left a note for Jeff, who called us later at the hostel and invited us to come by his office on our way out of town the next morning.

As amiable and natty as ever, he surprised us by announcing his engagement. We congratulated him, and in return offered the short version of our winter travels. "Ah, the Lambrettas. You know your friend Giancarlo is a son of a bitch," he said. "He took a commission on your scooters, 15,000 lire each." Hector and I blinked. 30,000 l. was $50: a month in Greece or Egypt! We said hasty farewells to Jeff, who bid us *buon viaggio*, and set out for Giancarlo's with no plan except to speak our minds and let events take their course.

Fortunately he was again out somewhere, his time of return unknown. We considered waiting, but, having seen the local attractions, wanted to head for Rome. Why should Giancarlo be allowed to delay our trip? We settled for a terse, angry note that made no allowance for Mediterranean commerce. I picture him reading it with a smile at American moralism, or perhaps hurt that his friends would address him that way. Had he been home, he would probably have disarmed us with his suave surprise that we could think business would be done in any other fashion. Didn't the middleman always get a cut? Ignorant not only of Mediterranean business, but of business in general, we left Napoli as we had Turkey and Egypt: with the sour taste of venality in our mouths.

That made a poor start to a leap year's extra day, but it was still young. And there was a route to plan! We were so used to there being only one highway that it came as a shock to look at a map and see that we had several choices. It was almost as if all roads *did* lead to Rome.

Roma

Feb. 29, YH in ROME, 8 PM - Back in Rome (I threw a coin in the Fountain) & so the paths cross again. Had a funny feeling as I drove by the airport, first point of contact with the 1955 trip. A comparison of then & now was irresistible: 10,000 hp Constellation vs. 6½ hp Lambretta; the Hassler Villa Medici vs. the hostel; sport coat & tie vs. sweatshirt & sneakers; chateaubriand vs. spaghetti.

I had felt something similar as we cruised back into Naples, but the poles of comparison were farther apart here - a quarter of my life! - and involved such radical differences in "lifestyle" and socio-economic levels that it was more contrast than comparison.

Left Napoli at 9:45 & drove north through the Campagna admired by Alaric & the Goths 1500+ years ago. Crossed a long plain not far out of N[apoli], then skirted some high, bare hills, notable for castle ruins on the slopes. Also one well-preserved castle on a promontory overlooking the sea.

I had by this time acquired a copy of Henri Pirenne's two-volume *History of Europe*, a magnificent work of prison literature (written in a Nazi concentration camp) that provides general historical contexts, though it does not discuss particular castles in the manner of guidebooks.

Crossed another plain - low clouds made it cool & obscured the view - & ascended the hills ringing Rome. Good views of the green fertility of the handsome Campagna. A brief stretch of cobblestone & then into the Eternal City on smooth new roads. Familiar landmarks & little chills: the Coliseum, Forum, St. Peter's dome, the Spanish steps.

Familiar, yet changed by things seen, felt, or learned since 1955. The Coliseum was a bit less impressive after El Djem's; the Spanish steps were darkened by the knowledge that John Keats died nearby at the age of 25. And I wondered how my growing agnosticism would affect the old power that St. Peter's had had over me.

After buying a guidebook we took a walk through the Pincio Park & Villa Borghese gardens. Both were cool, verdant, pleasant - & both I missed when here before. I saw little then; was worthless as a traveller: 90% was wasted on me. I'm not much better now, but being on my own I'm having to make the effort.

For the next five days we were tourists in Rome: what I had been dreading ever since the Algerian axe fell in Tunis. Yet the city pleased and even moved me; there were, it seemed, solid reasons for many roads to lead there. Between revisiting favorites from 1955 and finding new attractions, I covered most of what guidebooks recommended and a few sights they omitted. There were also good times that had nothing to do with tourism.

March 1, Rome YH, 7:30 PM - Festival!! The streets were littered with ribbons of colored paper as I walked home at dusk. Kids in party costumes & make-up wandered around making noise & throwing confetti. It was some fête, & the spirit spread like electricity; streets were thronged with hurrying gay people. I succumbed to the atmosphere & bought a big ice cream cone with whipped cream.

The *fête* was Mardi Gras or *Carnevale* ("farewell to the flesh"), the pre-Lenten bash that was then just a name to me; I knew nothing of its colorful, riotous observances throughout the Latin countries. We observed it in female company. Hector had a letter from Parry, written after hearing that we had turned north, telling him to look up one of his old girlfriends in Rome, a student who would be a good guide to the city. He had also written Inge, and she, it turned out, was willing to accept the assignment.

Wound up spending the [day] with Hector & Inge. She's a Latvian-Australian art history student (sounds more interesting than she is) who was sweet & pleasant. She kept us walking all day, poking into "the real Rome," coming up with little stories about this Romanesque tower or that fountain. I enjoyed it.

Although I made light of Inge at first, she did show us around Rome and brought it to life; not since Leo had we had such a guide. Inge knew lots of interesting stories - from Romulus to Fellini - about the places we went, reminding me why early American writers tried to populate the landscape of North America with myths and legends (such as Irving's Rip van Winkle) as food for the imagination.

That day she took us to *Piazza Navona* with its three fountains (one of which is Bernini's "Four Rivers"), to *San Pietro di Vincoli*, which has Michaelangelo's muscular Moses, to the columns of Antonius and Trajan, to the Coliseum and the Forum. We debated whether the monument to Victor Emmanuel was imposing, gaudy, or monstrous, settling on "neo-Godawful." From there I walked back to the hostel via the *Piazza del Populo* in an hour and a half. Rome was a city of smells, like Istanbul; you could gauge your progress by sniffing. Over half the shops sold food of some sort. There were (attention, Gilbert and Sullivan) *ristoranti, alimentari, trattorias, rosticcerias, pasticcerias, pizzarias, gelati,* "bars," cafés, fruit and vegetable stands. Which of them would I give up for Lent? Did a lapsed Episcopalian have to do that?

I spent Ash Wednesday morning in St. Peter's: making notes, sketching the design of one column's stonework, and climbing to the cupola. After lunch, it was *Castel' San Angelo* and the Papal Apartments, followed by a long ramble over the Janiculum Hill, humming Respighi. A fountain with shade trees made the courtyard of *St. Onofrio* cool and pleasant on a warm afternoon. Inside St. Peter's on the Mountain was a well-executed but poorly preserved painting of Christ flagellated, and a chapel by Bernini. Casa Dante turned out to have had nothing to do with the poet until 1920, but was still a fine mediaeval house-castle, with a tall, windowed tower and crenellated top. On the way back to the hostel, I noticed Romanesque towers everywhere now that I knew what they were: thanks, Inge! This might yet be a useful *Wanderjahr* - if I went into architecture.

On the 3rd Hector and I visited Hadrian's Pantheon, which offered a great volume of enclosed space but not much else. Nor was I moved by the *Farinesa* and *Chancelleria* palaces with their symmetrical Renaissance façades. Aha! So an aesthetic that learned judges pronounced beautiful, harmonious, and graceful might leave me cold, whereas mosques that no one I knew of had praised pleased me deeply. Perhaps the build-up, the expectations, were the problem? After lunch I returned to the Villa Borghese gardens and sat in the sun with the red and white cyclamen, shade trees and pines of the Pincio Park at my back, overlooking the city and writing in my journal. *Touristy* Rome might be, but this wasn't bad.

4 PM, Nat'l Gallery of Modern Art - Vastly enjoyed my visit to this museum, the finest of its kind I've seen: oils done with a high degree of competence, the statuary brilliantly lifelike. Perhaps the thrill was in seeing whole, undamaged works in good frames & on pedestals; maybe the spacious, modern building was influential. At any rate, it was a really absorbing hour, even without getting to the Klee exhibit.

Inge's agenda was culinary and social as well as historical. The first day she led us to a clean, inexpensive place off the Corso, *Vini e Cucini*, where Hector treated us to a lunch of pasta, eggs and fruit. "What a difference it makes to have good food in your stomach," I noted profoundly. A couple of days later her ambitions had grown to a full evening of dining…for four. A *date*? For *me*? I clearly remembered my last one - with a married woman in Beirut. Hector and I each hauled out the One Good Suit from the bottom of the pack and scootered to Inge's apartment in our wrinkled finery. As we parked across from her place, a tall, well-turned out young woman crossed the street. We looked at her appraisingly. Low heels, nice legs, tailored clothes: the whole package. She entered Inge's building. "Your date, probably," said Hector, deadpan.

"Yeah, sure," I laughed, but as we went inside she was entering Inge's apartment, and in a few more seconds we were being introduced. Her name was Evelyn, a philosophy student from New Zealand. She was lovely; I was dazzled; Inge smiled. Forget prostitutes, I thought: here is this handsome, healthy young woman all but dumped in my lap. With any luck she will have been *liberated* by crossing the oceans and studying in Rome.

March 4, Rome YH, 6 PM - The last 24 hours have been full of everything but sleep. Hector & I & my date were taken to dinner by Inge at Il Mio Cavallo, a gourmet Roman-Sicilian restaurant. A uniformed guard directs parking, the waiters wore red, white & black Sicilian peasant costumes & doubled as dancers & musicians. Inge says the place is patronized by high Rome, & the "entertainment" sparked with gaiety. As the guitars thrummed, the wine made everything grow throbby.

Two guitars, tambourine, shepherd's pipe and jug, in fact: presumably a Sicilian combo. We made a stab at a bacchanale, but were out of practice. The true, the blushful Hippocrene, beaded bubbles winking at the brim (knowing themselves full of more than the warm South), had its way with Hector; he grew affectionate with Inge, who seemed not averse. Evelyn became alarmed. "Isn't she supposed to be his brother's girl?" she whispered behind her hand.

"I thought so. Maybe ex-girl?" But this revelation of a moralistic strain was chilling. Though she was excellent company - humane, intelligent, warm, vivacious - I sensed no values that were not thoroughly middle-class, and as the evening progressed we were in danger of becoming friends. But things were going worse for Hector, who excused himself and disappeared. Later I found him out in the parking lot, taking the air and quite unwell.

I downed fettucini (ample & excellent), bread, beefsteak, salad, ice cream & cake. One of the guitarists, a sad-eyed fellow, was good, & I got him playing Spanish music by donating a Spanish (spastic) one of my own. Once primed, he was almost pathetically eager to play, & regaled me for 20 minutes with classical guitar.

It had been months since I had even held a guitar, the wine that loosened my inhibitions was no friend to small-muscle coordination, and the Sicilian guitarist was suspiciously enthusiastic about my "*Malagueñas*," but that night my musical juices began to flow again: west, toward Spain and its wide array of affordable guitars. I got high enough to write a poem in French, and the others were high (or kind, or weary) enough to praise it.

We stayed from nine until almost two; by the time we deposited Evelyn at her place it was three. She was renting what looked like a garden cottage: unlikely digs for Rome, but pleasant. I had offered to make this run on my own, but she and Inge insisted that I would get lost coming home by myself: the kind of thing women cook up to avoid awkwardness. Well, we mustn't be awkward! We talked about meeting again; she would consider riding to Florence with me, but… Don't call us, we'll call you.

By then it seemed pointless to go back to the hostel, so the three of us spent the rest of the night drinking coffee and talking about art in Inge's apartment. What made it fun was that by then we could all draw examples from what we had seen in Italy. After a while Hector fell asleep and I mostly listened to Inge, who did, after all, know a lot. When day broke, Hector and I went back to the hostel to change clothes, and then to the Sistine Chapel,

much superior in effect to '55, when it was spoiled by 300 other tourists, walking around craning necks like birds in mating season. Today we had it to ourselves, & scanned carefully the dark-hued, tapestrylike paintings along the walls; wondered at the power of Michaelangelo's work in the vault (Creation through Flood) and The Last Judgment. There's a lot there you can't explain.

After our all-nighter, I could not have explained the sunrise, let alone artistic genius. We paid a brief visit to the Vatican Museum, but in the afternoon the works at the Gallery of Modern Art began looking so unfocused that I gave up and lazed "home" to the hostel to catch up on sleep.

March 5, Rome YH, 6:30 PM - Our final day in Rome; Hector & I covered a lot of territory. Enjoyed it immensely. By 9 on a raw windy morning we were on Capitoline Hill, overlooking the Forum. It's one of the Seven Hills, a site of ancient buildings &

terminus of triumphs. Now it houses the Senate, & the Capitoline & Conservatori Museums. We visited the former - a few good statues.

Owing Hector a meal, I treated him to brunch at Barrington's Tea Room on the *Piazza di Spagna*. The prices, a notch or two above our usual level, bought us pleasant surroundings, good service and excellent food (an order of French toast, a cinnamon toast, and drinks for $2.25). He then persuaded me to come see one of Inge's favorites, the Villa Borghese Museum. Its collection, dominated by Bernini's statues, was as impressive as he said. Bernini's subjects were almost an anthology of our travels: the brilliant "Apollo and Daphne" evoking Greece, especially Delphi; "David," our brush with Biblical lands; "Aeneas Carrying His Father," Turkey and Carthage. The museum also had a superb "Victorious Venus" by Canova, and powerful paintings by Reubens, Bernini, and others.

Then we picked up Inge & went to the Baths of Caracalla. Their scale is huge, imagining the former luxury a staggering game. Aïda there must be fine. Leaving the others, I visited the Forum & Chiesa St. Ignazio, where a striking Baroque mural by de Pozzo, St. Ignace Ascending to Heaven, covers the ceiling of the nave.

Standing in the Forum, watching all the years go by - stubs of dark-red Roman columns in the foreground, a Baroque church in the middle, a mediaeval Romanesque tower in the background - I wondered how would it feel to grow up amidst all that history: inspiring? Oppressive? Would I want out from under it, or feel that I could live nowhere else? That one had to go in the Unknown basket, with the art of Michaelangelo and a number of other issues.

Read history for awhile on the Spanish Steps, then browsed in a bookstore. Found an illustrated history of music in French that was first rate: began to wonder why I'm spending all this money traveling when I could buy books!

This was a remark such as Hector occasionally alarmed me by making, so I had some comebacks ready: if you stayed home and saved your money, would you *really* spend it on music books? Would you find *this* one? And didn't travel help form your taste for such a purchase?

But the best answer came the next day: an exhilarating and joyous day of travel. We checked out of the hostel early, bought food, and went to Inge's for breakfast. She was coming with us; Evelyn, alas, was not. I made a ham omelet, and while eating that, Corn Flakes, and bread with strawberry jam, read the first chapter of *On the Road* (*The Dharma Bums* had made me a Kerouac fan). Perhaps I was a rolling cliché, following my cultural guru, but it still seemed the perfect send-off. I felt (as on some mornings in Egypt) that what I was doing was right for me at this time and a huge boon, exciting and rare. Almost gloating over my good fortune, I could have hugged the day from sheer desire to keep hold of all it was worth. The months of travel fatigue fell away. I could taste the morning.

March 6, George & Kitty's farmhouse near Asciano, 7 PM - Left Rome in high spirits at 10:30 & drove into the hilly interior with a buffeting wind. At Viterbo got gas at one of those big Agip gas stations/bars & went in for refreshments. It was a scene straight out of <u>Giant</u> or <u>The Wild One</u>: juke box blaring, scooters drawn up outside the window, us in cold-weather-grubby travel outfit, Inge in black slacks & sweater, etc. Drank cappuccino, ate donut; loved it.

An Italian *Giant* or *Wild Ones*, with Lambrettas instead of Harleys. Inge, or rather her close-fitting moll's uniform, was the object of all eyes, especially those of the toughs at the bar. It was the *scene* that I loved: not just the doughnut. Then back outside to our struggle with the wind. As we climbed into the Apennines along a chain of lakes - Bracciano, Vico, Bolsena - toward the hill towns, the softness of the coastal lowlands disappeared; we were caught in the heat exchange between mountains and sea. Even with windshields on it was a buffeting ride, but we were making good time, despite Hector's double load, and enjoying ourselves hugely. During a rest stop, I dropped down on the warm pavement and did 50 push-ups out of sheer exhilaration. I'd never done that many before - but there was less weight to lift now.

Pushed on into green hills, marked by towns (perched on crags as in Sicily; houses of brick & mortar), occasional snowfields way up, rivers, some cultivation & a few handsome old castles (Radicofani). Headed for Asciano, home of a couple of Parry's friends, on a 17 km. tertiary side road. Ran the last 15 on reserve.

Almost as empty as parts of North Africa, *this* was not the Italy I had been dreading. The dirt road offered marginal traction; we barely made it up one hill. There were lovely views through leaves down onto jumbled hills and meadows, but I was glad to see Asciano and its gas pump.

The town's nestled in a valley between hills; a stiff climb brought us to George & Kitty's rented no-heat, no-[running] water farmhouse. George, a painter, isn't home yet, but Kitty has welcomed us sweetly & is preparing to feed us.

I like it here. Darkness crept in as we sat in the warm kitchen. When we went to the well, the cold wind whipped us; obscurity covered the hills, in which lights from other hilltowns twinkled like stars. Outside is cold - inside is light & warm, & I know our good fortune.

George did not return until we had eaten. He was excited by a nearby archeological site where they were uncovering a necropolis, but his own life interested me more. Two years in the Army had earned him enough to bring Kitty over, marry her, and rent the farmhouse for a year: a time of grace, as halcyon as an artist-in-training is likely to find. An admirer of Italy's frescoes, George wanted to learn their secrets; the stucco walls of the farmhouse were his studio. He also needed to understand terra cotta and the minor crafts, so he visited local digs, studied ancient artifacts and modeled from the same clay. It was basically the *Bauhaus* story: the artist learning to know his materials and what can be done with them - a kind of *Sitzenjahr*. Kitty, a salt-of-the-earth Minnesotan, was seven months pregnant. It was late when we finally called a halt to the talk and crawled into sleeping bags spread on the thin rug.

At seven the next morning, sky and hills and houses seemed to have been brushed clean during the night and their hues brightened; details on the far side of the valley stood out as if magnified. We rolled up our sleeping bags, broke our fast and said goodbye to Kitty and George, already old friends, with grateful thanks.

March 7, YH at Florence, 7 PM - We stepped from scrambled eggs & sausage into a cold, windy morning at 9 AM. George & Kitty were friendly to the last; we left them wine & bread. Shivering & swaying with the wind, we wound over dirt & gravel roads, bouncing from hill to hill, farm to farm, village to village: backwoods Tuscany, poor in soil & population, rich in color & history.

My family had been chauffered from Rome to Florence in 1955, but no clear memories of the countryside remained. What made landscape more striking from a scooter on a rough back road than from a car on a highway? Was scenic beauty enhanced when you had to pay for it? I had begun to believe that, and was now more convinced than ever that pain and adrenaline were related to aesthetic experience.

Found the strada nationale & buzzed into Arezzo. Saw its main art attraction, the frescoes of Piero della Francesca, at the Duomo & Chiesa S. Francesco. Though faded & badly lit, their quality comes thru. His use of his mistress' face on the Madonna, & the occasional face in a crowd scene staring out at you, mark him as the maverick artist. The architecture of several churches & buildings gave the back streets a 13th century, Dantean flavor. Ate lunch at a restaurant (decorated like a church) alongside Chiesa S. Francesco.

While we had clearly not "discovered" Piero, he was a good deal more out of the way than, say, Michaelangelo's or Bernini's work in Rome, and it was fun to have tracked this provincial genius to his original haunts and to find him as interesting as Inge had said.

Firenze

In the afternoon we ran a windblown 75 kilometers through densely populated hills to *Firenze*, whose ruddy cathedral dome appeared in the Arno valley about 4:30 - another point of contact with my 1955 trip. I had time to mail a letter and cash a check before driving to the hostel, an old country house in the hills near *Fiesole*, about five kilometers from the city center. The *Villa Camerata* was the most luxurious hostel I had ever seen. Situated on a wooded rise, surrounded by spacious gardens, it had a peri-style colonnade, a verdant courtyard, and inside, a three-story dome with frescoes. The place was clean, well-equipped and well-organized: meals were available at reasonable prices, cooking was allowed, there were hot showers, and good music played on a big radio in the common room. Glad that Firenze had much that really ought to be seen, I settled down there with a sigh, as did a goodly number of other young travelers. No need to rush off anywhere.

In the morning I indulged in the hostel breakfast (with hot chocolate!), meeting a Canadian who knew a college friend of mine, and went to see the sights with Hector and Inge. We began, naturally, at the *Duomo* - which has Michaelangelo's unfinished "Descent from the Cross" - and Baptistry, with Ghiberti's superb bronze doors and a baptismal font mentioned in *The Inferno*. I learned about the Renaissance trick of suspending the inner dome separately from the outer so that each will have the optimal aesthetic effect, an idea that Wren borrowed for St. Paul's. Then a start on the Uffizi Gallery, from the earliest paintings up to the 15th century, notably Botticelli. I envied his main characters' "attitude of strange repose, surprisingly detached from events." To an art historian this was a characteristic of the painter; to me, an enviable way of handling the real world, with cool, Stoic aloofness.

After lunch at the railroad station, I revisited the gloomy Medici Chapel and its Michaelangelo statuary, then walked to *Chiesa S. Marco*, a quaint old monastery full of religious frescoes. Those by Fra Angelico and Fra Bartholomew seemed well executed, but in an unpleasing style, and most of the others struck me as silly, hyper-pious, or sadistic. Perhaps I had reached my limit for religious art? The way back to the hostel led across the *Ponte Vecchio.*

March 8, Florence YH, 8 PM - Hot shower tonight. Felt very good, but gave me another of those rare looks at my body: painfully thin, knees infected, sores on my rear & legs, fingers swollen with a rash, hip raw. Immediately my economic resolve went out the window (I've been eating on L.450/day): I had a full Hostel meal plus milk & a vitamin pill. I'm now scared enough of my false economy to eat what I need, keep my health, & go home sooner if need be.

Thus my first day in Florence ended with a decision to scrap the old dollar-a-day goal for food (though I was down to about 30% of my original funds and still had to buy a ship passage home) and try to regain the sense I was born with – the one about self-preservation.

In the morning I scootered to the Russian Church, resplendent with domes of blue marble, gold mosaics, and jagged Cyrillic script. Next on my list was little *SS. Annunciata*. A mass was being celebrated, but I tiptoed over to an interesting fresco in the left transept. Like S. Ignazio in Rome, it continued the architecture of the church onto the ceiling; the illusion that the church lay open to the sky was nearly perfect, thanks to the Baroque device of "overflowing clouds." Filled with paintings, statuary, marble work and chandeliers, Annunciata managed to seem both over-decorated and attractive.

S. Lorenzo was larger and comparatively bare. It did contain, though, a strange mural, filled with reverent body-builders, dripping muscle. I wondered, not for the first or last time, how those two strains in Renaissance Christianity - the world-hating, all-flesh-is-grass view derived from Paul, and the humanistic, flesh-loving, all-creation-is-good outlook - managed to coexist in the Church. Another enjoyable hour at the Uffizi, working from Flemish painters up to del Sarto, did nothing to solve that puzzle.

After lunch I rendezvoused with Hector and Inge. Grey clouds by then hanging low overhead only made Florence look richer. We went to *Piazza Michaelangelo* and walked to *S. Miniato al Monte* at Inge's behest. She showed us the details of construction and decoration that made it "Romanesque": wooden cross-beams supporting the ceiling, marble inlay, geometric patterns. Remembering how Diana and Lucinda had taught us in Greece, I wondered if she could be another moon goddess. Alabaster windows behind the altar admitted a yellow light; Della Robbia terracottas could be seen here and there. It was an interesting church, we agreed, walking to *Santa Croce*. By then I had had my fill of churches, though, and could not respond to it, but the tombs of Michaelangelo and Machiavelli, and monuments to Dante and Galileo (once a resident of Fiesole and visited there by Milton, said a learned Brit at the hostel), were another matter. Byron called Santa Croce "The Westminster Abbey of Italy."

Rain drove us into the USIS library, where we read until time for a concert at the *Palazzo Vecchio*. The Symphony of Florence made Prokofiev's *Classical Symphony* sound stodgy, but did better on Milhaud's *Concerto for Violin and Orchestra*, with its echoes of jazz and Stravinsky. Wagner's *Siegfried Idyll* was so gorgeous that I found myself tearing up in the friendly darkness. It had been a long time since my last classical concert; evidently I had missed such harmonies, as rich and warm as the cello's burnished gleam. The antique rooms of the old palace, hung with faded tapestries, doubtless helped the effect, and the thought that this was a lot of Italian art for a guy who had just wanted to see Africa may have entered into the emotional mix as well. The concert ended upbeat with de Falla's *Three-Cornered Hat*, which sounded like a summons to Spain. Afterwards we all ate together. I drove back to the hostel in a cold rain after dark, quite miserable with itching fingers, pains in my knees, the wet and the chill.

March 10, USIS Library, Florence, 11 AM - USIS libraries are becoming welcome havens, refuges from sightseeing, the elements, & sometimes foreigners. The one in Tunis was quite good, this one even larger & better equipped. Both, however, are guilty of the charge that the books are predominantly in English, not in the local language.

Of course if there *were* more in the "local language," the libraries might no longer be "refuges" from "foreigners," i.e. natives, eh? Yet the USIS said that its mission was to lead non-native speakers to English. Then they must be taught to read it! But by whom? It was probably during one of these sessions - warm and dry among magazines while the heavens fell outside - that I remembered my fondness for books, renewed my growing resolve to carry my education further, and realized (looking at my swollen, cramped fingers) that playing music ought not to be in the forefront of my thinking any longer. I could go on to make a life out of libraries; could qualify myself to teach English, find a post abroad, and contribute by teaching it to - no, *I* would be the foreigner - to those who came to the foreigner.

This morning, after a hot shower, I came into town & lasted an hour at the Pitti Palace. George & Inge are right: the manner of display - crowded & poorly lighted - is really bad, the general interest of the art is sub-Uffizi, & the place is quite chilly. Takes dedication to stick with art or music in the damp or cold.

Giving it the old college try, though, I filled pages with notes on painters' names, dates, and subjects, on my favorites - Memling, Murillo, Sustermans - and my reactions ("sick of everyone wearing a gold halo" in mediaeval Tuscan religious paintings). "2nd half of 15th century was really full of good artists," I exclaimed, discovering the Renaissance for myself. But I could not forget my physical discomforts.

Am ready to leave Florence & get to a doctor. My infections are worse & worry me; the swelling & itching of my fingers (M. calls it chill-blanes) is distracting.

This was the first I'd heard of chilblains, obviously; I couldn't even spell it. "M," another lovely New Zealander, was a classic sweater girl in the style of 1940s films; males at the hostel called her "La Magnifica." I would have been glad to carry her northwards, or in a direction of her choosing, but there was a long queue, and she maintained a cool, queenly distance from all suitors, never going anywhere without her very plain girlfriend in tow. We had a *tête à têtes* one night on a dark bridge near the hostel, in vain.

Uffizi, 3 PM - Through a mud-spotted pane, I look out over the vaulted red tiles & angular roofs of Florence. They are wet with rain, & smoke from chimneys merges in a few seconds with murky grey clouds. Somehow, watching this, I feel a kinship with it, as if it gives me knowledge how to live. Perhaps, in unhurried, rainy moments such as this, I can create; my melancholy may come from not trying now. On drizzly, indoor days, I miss leisure, music, writing, & friends. But most I miss Penny.

Years later, Wordsworth's poetry helped me understand that my vague sense of "kinship" with domestic smoke rising to the clouds on a dark day was neither unique nor unnatural.

Most evenings I read at the hostel, or talked with an Italian friend there, an art critic and teacher. One day he led me on a private tour of his favorite paintings in The Gallery.

March 11, Florence YH - Yesterday as I was leaving the Uffizi, the history of art teacher from Rome who has been so friendly collared me, & guided me thru paintings of the Siennese & Florentine schools, 13th-15th centuries. They are his specialty, as well as being those I dismissed quickly as stereotyped, distorted, "too much gold." Obviously a real <u>afficianado</u> [sic], he showed me the texture of the wood [the painted surface], the lines marked for the painter to follow (which, like any kid, he often missed) & demarking his area from that of the gold-leafer, explained the function of the gold (depth), & pointed out details of head & hand position, expression, architecture & landscape. In two curiously rigid portraits by della Francesca, he showed me that the "movement" was not human, but "quick, dot-da-da, that of light."

What he had to say was interesting and stimulating, and I believed that *he* believed it was true, but I could seldom see or feel what he claimed to see and feel. My gut reaction to the subject matter remained the same. Still,

I was more responsive to similar paintings in the Academia di Belli Arti today. They depicted the usual subjects of the period: annunciation, madonna with child, massacre of the innocents, etc. There is a great deal to them, if you look closely: they are the painful labor of love. But I still don't like the shifty eyes, pseudo-Oriental faces, & set poses. And I detest the whole Catholic emphasis on death, gore, & martyrdom. That is not part of my religion.

"My religion" immediately sounded false: did I even have one any more? If so, what were its pictorial traditions? Perhaps you needed to have been raised Catholic to respond to these works. Then I was culturally alienated from that *school*, but not, fortunately, from all Italian art.

Also in the Academia was the best Raphael I've seen: Sn. Giovanni in the wilderness. The play of light, & the position & motion of the body, were superb. The gallery's prize, however, is sculpture by Michaelangelo, notably David. He is depicted as a nude, alert youth, slim but muscular. Some of the other statuary, unfinished, has tremendous impact. I could see the figures emerging from the stone, as if from Michaelangelo's imagination.

All this intense gallery-going gave me an appetite. Fortunately the *mensa studentes* at the University of Firenze's student union served a substantial lunch of bread, spaghetti, meat and potatoes for about 40 cents, and I looked like a student. That afternoon Hector, Inge and I visited the National Museum, which was exhibiting bronzes by Donatello and Della Robbia terra cottas. Later we went to the Pozzi Chapel, whose Renaissance façade and Della Robbia decorations pleased me more than they did my friends. I glanced at the bare cloister and small museum before walking back to the hostel. It was our last day in Firenze.

The next morning we rendezvoused at a gas station on the outskirts of the city; Inge came along to say goodbye. After she left to catch a bus I started to show Hector the choice of routes to Bologna and Verona on our map, but he shook his head, saying just lead on and he'd follow. Having heard that a secondary road stayed lower than the main one - which might be important if the past three days of rain in Firenze had been snow in the mountains - I chose that, and we headed northwest on the *autostrada* to pick it up. A few kilometers down the freeway we passed an accident: policemen and a truck driver looking at a smear of metal and glass on the road. You could just tell that it had been a scooter. The truck looked unmarked. At *Prato*, we turned north into the mountains and began to ascend Dante's "vale wherefrom Bisenzo's waters flow."

When Italian maps say "*secondarie*," however, they mean it. Grades ranged from steady to steep; hairpin curves abounded; "pavement" was a bad joke. It began to look like a bad choice on a bad day. Dark clouds impended, threatening precipitation, keeping us cold and hampering vision. The road became a continuous muddy pothole in the dim beam of my headlight. It looked more like northern Greece in November than anything we had seen since. In the bottom of a wooded ravine below a tight curve, a big semi-trailer that had gone over the precipice lay abandoned, jackknifed in agony.

But we had dressed warmly, the Lambretti were climbing better than most other traffic, and the weather began to improve three-quarters of the way up. Clouds broke apart, opening patches of blue that admitted shafts of sun. At the same time the road smoothed out: to our amazement, it had been recently resurfaced. And just as we reached the pass, the remaining overcast yielded to bright sun in an azure sky. All around lay a countryside dressed in fresh snow, the first time since Mount Lebanon that we had driven through such a scene. Vistas opened of broad white plateaux, the valley of the Po, blurred mountain ranges beyond: the sentinels of the Alps! I breathed in pure exhilaration as from an oxygen mask. As gloomy as the world had been an hour before, by so much more was it joyous now. High villages were digging out from under the snowfall; bare trees thrust up pruned branches like stiff brown squid. The road was dark-banded with trickling melt. All was washed clean, vibrant with smiling nature and life resurgent. "He makes each day a resurrection," says *The Koran* of Allah. With joyous whoops we fell down the long grades of the northern slope onto the plain.

At the bottom we turned west for awhile, leaving Bologna for another time. Lunch was pasta, bread and water in an expensive roadside café - welcome to northern Italy! - then north again toward Verona on tree-lined roads. Though my engine began to run roughly, we crossed the flat Po valley, Dante's "sweet plain," quickly, entered the city of Romeo and Juliet at four, and soon located our long-desired haven. Though I did not realize it at the time, Hector and I had had our last day of scootering together. It was a good one, worthy of its predecessors.

> The journey, not the arrival, matters;
> the voyage, not the landing.
>
> Paul Theroux

XI. Solos

There is no world without Verona walls…

says Romeo, exclaiming against banishment as a loss of his world, of his life. Later it occurred to me that Shakespeare's sentence *could* mean that every place has walls to imprison or exclude, but on first arrival I was inclined to feel about Verona much as Romeo had.

March 13, Parry's Verona home, 9 AM - Made it, by God, & what a blessed relief! Parry is hospitable & interesting; his apartment is warm, pleasant, & furnished with cots & a kitchen; there are good books & records! It's all too fine for a tired traveler.

We drove from Florence to Verona between 9:30 & 4 yesterday with a minimum of difficulty. A few bad moments over the mountains, but soon we had both sun & a good road. Bright sun on fresh snow has a unique beauty, & I thoroughly enjoyed that stretch.

Already the previous day's trials had begun to recede into a rose-colored distance where anxiety and discomfort paled in the after-glow of good memories.

Parry lives on the 4th floor of a big house with a courtyard off a tree-lined street. His pad will be a near-perfect haven for rest & study.

Suddenly, the concerns that had vexed us almost daily for months did not exist. Down the hall was a hot-water bath and a clean toilet; down the street was a laundry-woman eager for work. We could eat nearby at one of Parry's favored restaurants, buy food from the local grocery or from the PX at the American Army base outside of town where he had privileges, or forage in his kitchen, where I soon had a stash of eggs, cheese, milk, cereal, and other favorites.

Best of all, Parry says they can meet me in Barcelona, so my path is clear. I'll go in a couple of weeks, buy the guitar, & have 2 weeks before the caravan arrives.

I would scooter to Spain on my own, they would follow in Parry's VW bug when his leave began, and the three of us would tour Spain by car at Easter time. It sounded great! But other folks were making other plans on my behalf.

Got a telegram from Dad this AM: I'm 1-A again. Don't believe, however, that it's cause for either haste or alarm; just due process.

Though I made light of this news, my period of grace was clearly almost over. The draft board had responded predictably (perhaps angrily) to my abandonment of student status and could not be trifled with now: if they continued to call up at their 1959 rate, I might be drafted as soon as September. In a month or so I would have to return and do something to head off that development, or lose my freedom of action. Though we didn't know the term yet, it was a "reality check," and not the only one that greeted us in Verona. We had mail from our ladies.

Penny's letters, waiting for me here, were lovely. They recharged my feelings at a propitious time, when memory was growing hazy & confused. She got the telegram, but still no word about the sweater.

And whatever Andrea had written Hector troubled him. During the winter, she and Penny had talked of going to the west coast, finding jobs, rooming together, but that had not happened; they were both still around New York and sounded restless. There was a hint of foot-tapping challenge in their letters: what'll it be, guys? There was, of course, the issue of other suitors. Knowing that they existed, that they *had* to, and not hearing about them, was unsettling. Mine weren't the only eyes that could rove. So that was anoher reason to go home and make plans.

Will now settle down to 2 therapeutic weeks [of] rest, good food, writing, study of history, Spain & Spanish, reading, & a trip to Venice Wed. to hear a Gregorian chant concert.

Unlike most segments of the trip, the interval in Verona unfolded much as planned: great quantities of rest (i.e. lazing about the apartment with a book), study, and writing (letters, journal, sketches for stories). And there were also other, unexpected pleasures, one of which was exploring the city, with a guide or without. One night Parry

took us to some bar tucked in Verona's side streets. Each Mon. the local musicale gathers, unofficially, for 2 hours of operatic arias. Performers seem to materialize from nowhere, & perform with much energy & heart to piano accompaniment. Besides being great fun, it's insight into this Italian musical tradition & its grass-roots support.

When, a few years later, Nikita Khrushchev dismissed Italy as a land of peasants and opera singers (an odd insult for a Russian communist to fling), I remembered that night, and thought, You might better hail the country in those terms than scorn it. Such unpromising, seedy-looking little people would rise out of the smoky shadows when their turn came, set their music before the pianist - or not, because everybody knows this one - and belt out a fair rendition of some favorite aria *con gusto e amore*. And when it was over, what bravos and gesturing, what tearful hugs and kisses for the singer! It was impossible not to be moved, not to feel that you had been vouchsafed a revelation. We have baseball; they have opera.

The day before I set off for Venice

Hector & I scootered out to the main Army post in the rain for a couple of hours of B[asket]ball. It was great, but gave me a chance to weigh myself: 152. That's almost 20 lbs. lost since the beginning. I <u>am</u> eating more now

and paying less for it at the PX, where we did a big shopping after basketball. My share came to $2.70. This was a company town with a difference: the company was the US Army, and the groceries were subsidized by US taxpayers.

I decided to hitchhike to Venice for the performance of Gregorian chant, and perhaps to Ravenna as well. It would have been easier to take my scooter, but ever since reading Don Knies' book in Tunisia and realizing what we had been missing, I had wanted to get out and meet more people. Here was the perfect opportunity: a circle trip, not too long, involving only myself. The routes were well traveled, and my spoken Italian seemed good enough to make the experiment without undue embarrassment. If not now, when? Parry and Hector were driving to the Vicenza Army base that morning, which would give me a head start. I packed light.

The road followed the northern edge of the fertile, well-irrigated Po valley, skirting the base of green hills that rose toward the Dolomites and Alps, somewhere back in the clouds. Parry pointed out the ruined castle of the Montecchi - Shakespeare's Montagues: Romeo's family - about halfway to Vicenza. Before dropping me off, he reminded me that I was *autostopping*, not hitchhiking. A thumb out might not be understood; the correct gesture was a downward motion of the hand. Also, I was not to sail past *Padova*, but stop and see the sights, especially the *Cappella degli Scrovegni*. As it had already become clear that he knew his stuff, I agreed, and took my position at the right of the road.

March 16, Venice, 3 PM - Got a ride with Parry as far as Vicenza, then hitched to Venice in 2 hours. Stopped in Padua to visit the Capelli de Scrovegni. The small, vaulted church contains several walls full of frescoes by Giotto. Where the colors - deep reds, blues - have held, they are very striking, & facial expressions are well done everywhere. The subject matter is the life of Christ. The Last Judgment is interesting as a precursor to Michaelangelo's.

Next door was the *Eremitani*, with frescoes by Mantegna, and this was just to scratch the surface. A few blocks south was the university, founded in 1222: long the greatest center of Italian learning, and the foundation of Padova's importance in the late Middle Ages. There were also churches, a cathedral, public gardens, old walls, major works by Donatello, and so on. It was an ancient town, once a rival of Rome, later a magnet for artistic and financial ambition; Petruchio in *The Taming of the Shrew* has "come to wive it wealthily in Padua." Beneath his mercenary exterior, though, lies something else with which I could easily identify. Asked what has brought him from Verona, he replies:

> Such wind as scatters young men through the world
> To seek their fortunes farther than at home,
> Where small experience grows.

One might easily give a week to Padova - and I had the means to do so, without asking anyone's consent - but the wind still blew, and Venezia called from down the road.

Autostopping was easy that day: a steady stream of Fiats flowed east, and one always pulled over within minutes. Most of the drivers were alone and glad of company. Initially I was struck more by the stimulation that hitchhiking afforded, its wealth of social contacts, than by its inconvenience, and exulted in knowing enough Italian to send and receive simple messages. One of my benefactors was a tired salesman who seemed bored until he heard where I was going. "*Ah, Venezia é comé un sogno*!" he enthused, gesturing dramatically. It was better than a travel poster.

Venezia and Ravenna

Two rides brought me to the edge of Venezia by 12:30. Hiking randomly, I wandered up several dead ends, in one of which was a Mensa Universitaria. What the hell, says I, & eats a good meal of "risotto al spinachi," roast beef, mashed potatoes, bread, & apple stewed in juice - for L.300. [under 50 cents]

Another hour's walk brought me to Piazza S. Marco. Like the rest of the city, it's a mixture of quaintness, grandeur, & antiquity, but the pigeons are like a squadron of dive bombers.

I was happy wandering around the city, delighted to reach the famous piazza and basilica of San Marco, the Bridge of Sighs and Ducal Palace, all celebrated by poets and familiar from pictures, but neither *Teatro la Feniche* nor *Chiesa San Marco* knew about a performance of Gregorian chant. I took the *motoscafe* out to *Isola Giudecca*, whose large *ostello* was closed until 5. It was siesta: there was nothing to do except wait in a café until the hostel opened or I heard chant wafting over the water from somewhere.

Venice YH, 7 PM - Finally found the concert in Basilica S. Giorgio Maggiore, Isola S. Giorgio (I'd been by it twice on the launch). A well-trained choir of about 30 black-frocked priests sang 17 chants. Their stage presence, pitch, & interpretation were excellent. The music carries you along in effortless motion, with never the tension of Western music. Perhaps this is the failing of cadential music (or at least its effect): you exist from cadence to cadence, drawn by real or implicit tension, seldom able to experience the music purely of the moment, but more in regard to what has preceded or will succeed. Chant has the ambulatory quality of a hike in the woods; cadential music seems like a ride along an autostrada with mileposts.

Sitting in a drafty room with dark heavy tapestries, letting the stream of plainsong wash over me, I was strongly attracted to it, but hard put to translate my feelings into thoughts. I do not entirely understand my own words now, but they made sense to me at the time. I saw that context and interdependence were woven into my musical culture, and found their absence or diminution refreshing in chant, where the spoken and musical phrases seemed to coincide naturally, as if the musical form was not pre-existent but an expression of the verbal idea. The music arose from and wrapped itself around a word or sense in the text; rhythms were irregular, as in speech. Further I could not go. The differences could hardly be that black and white, but the emphases were certainly distinct.

While listening, I had a musical idea: a fantasia on a gregorian chant for guitar. Begin with a chant theme, pick one [phrase] & repeat pensively. Then harmonize it, major & minor, make a fugue of it, orchestrate it; finally repeat it as chant, & end quietly & simply.

I jotted down a theme that looks suspiciously like "Willie, Take Your Tiny Drum." (The trouble with my "original compositions" was frequently their resemblance to earlier work. "An original idea? That can't be so hard," says Stephen Fry. "The library must be full of them.") The *idea* is not worthless; it just needs imagination and industry.

After an hour the choir finished and I came outside. Venice's domes and towers were silhouetted against a blood-red sunset below tiers of variegated rainclouds. In the splashiest ceremony of the glory days here, the Doge of Venice wedded the city to the Adriatic. That would have been something to see, especially on an evening like this. Another motorboat ride brought me back to the hostel, where a large assortment of motley folk had assembled. Two young Mormons returning to the US from two years of missionary work in South Africa caught my interest. Having heard that Mormons took a dim theological view of dark skin as Hamitic, I asked them how that had worked out, but could not make sense of their answer; they had already learned how to be diplomatic and evasive.

Cold rain streamed down all the next day. I plodded around doggedly in my poncho, trying to absorb and enjoy historic sights, quaint corners, and dead-end canals whose water looked sullen and dirty. This city of Tintoretto, Vivaldi, Byron, Thomas Mann and many other Big Names could bloody well work for me, too! So I kept at it all day, caught a slight cold, and went to bed early without even making a journal entry. The next morning's weather looked the same, and revealed the limits of my romanticism. Enough of this *Death in Venice* stuff! I packed up, took a *motoscafe* to the mainland, and began waving at cars. I could write about Venezia just as well in Ravenna.

March 18, courtyard of S. Vitale, RAVENNA, 3:30 PM - Left Venice about 8:30 & passed through Padua & Ferrara, getting here at 2:30. Really enjoy the hitchhiking: fared pretty well, & had fun talking to my benefactors. Besides, it's a nice day

and the countryside on the Padua-Ferrara leg - hilly and rich in feudal castles, some of them in good condition for mediaeval structures - was interesting. One driver pointed out the hilltop palace of the Hapsburg Emperor Franz Joseph, built around 1810 when Austria ruled there.

In the mellow afterglow generated by some pleasant social contacts and a warm dry afternoon, Venice at once began to sit more gently on my mind:

My one full day in Venice, tho' plagued by rain, cold, & bad hostel hours, was memorable. Spent an hour in the chill, drafty rooms of the Palazzo dei Duchi. Begun in the 9th century, [it] figured prominently in Venice's history. Now it is a combination art gallery, military museum, palace, & dungeon. The art is not very good & the weapons are familiar, but the tortuous walk thru the dungeon-passages chilled my spine. What a place to freeze to death!

Know this of me: seeing a prison alone on a cold wet day in March gives a keener sense of what it means to be incarcerated there than a crowd of summer tourists, enjoying its shade, could ever have. A small chapel in the palace offered amazingly realistic "painted-on architecture," shadows and all: an incongruous baroque effect, only a few walls away from the dungeons.

Chiesa San Marco - St. Mark's - disappointed me in a way that St. Peter's, Notre Dame, and St. Paul's had not. The baroque exterior seemed overdone, more seaside pleasure pavilion - Brighton-on-the-Adriatic – than cathedral. Inside, though, some of the gold mosaic was well-preserved, especially in a chapel on the right that also had a bronze of Christ. Afterwards I wandered in the drizzle for an hour, eating at the *Mensa* again before tackling the *Galleria della Academia*.

It has a large & high-quality collection of paintings, mostly Venetian, dominated by Tintoretto. Trying hard, I could see a little more to him. His best was of 4 senators adoring the Babe.

To a modern accustomed to historical costume, the richly-attired Venetian grandees looked bizarre in a Palestinian manger; Tintoretto lived in an age innocent of research into period and regional dress. Or maybe the senators packed one good suit in their luggage for special occasions, as we did! There were also impressive canvases by Piero della Francesca and Giovanni Bellini, who had a special gift for creating memorable faces, full of character.

Ravenna YH, 7 PM - In Ravenna I went right to San Vitale. Built by the Ostrogoth king Theodoric in the 5th cent., it is octagonal & straight Romanic. The famous mosaics are all in one alcove. Some are portraits, & have the familiar gold background. Other groups, notably scenes from the Old Testament, are refreshingly free of gold, the primary colors clear & fresh.

The mosaics that had brought me here - Ravenna's treasure - closed another circle. When our *Wanderjahr* was young, the Byzantine mosaics of the east Roman empire (Greece and Turkey) had dazzled us. Now, in the trip's latter days, came this startling reprise of that tradition in the *western* empire: there were Justinian and Theodora, looking as splendid as ever! It was classic ABA construction, the return of the first theme of a truly grand sonata. You could see from one remaining patch that the worn red brick of the walls had once been covered with white marble; a Baroque fresco in the dome, with its open-to-the-sky effect, looked grotesquely out of place. San Vitale and the piazza in front of it were almost deserted.

Afterwards I went to the small, simple tomb of Dante and to Piazza Byron, where the English poet lived in 1819: both, in different ways, exiles. There was the 13th century *Chiesa S. Francesco*, a basilica with a Romanesque tower whose windows arched over the column between them like Emperor penguins looking down on their chick. The tomb of Theodoric, a circular, two-story monument northeast of the walls and the railroad, looked tired and weather-worn, reminding me of my own fatigue. Yet I had vivid memories of the day's hitchhiking.

You do meet the people this way. [Four] Italians today took me for German, & I had the pleasure of setting them straight. One man told me that Americans didn't hitchhike 'cause they're all loaded. Another couple was dazzled by my Italian; a woman selling fruit told me I had a lot of courage!

Well, *coraggio,* 'heart,' anyway. I didn't try to explain that I was a privileged member of a mobile, affluent society, while she had been born to limited circumstances: my Italian wasn't *that* good. It also failed me when one driver waved his hand at the verdant river plain and conjured up a vision of total industrial development: factories, chemical plants, increased GNP. (Smog?) He wanted to trade in his Fiat for a Cadillac, and found my resistance to these ambitions inexplicable. "It would be just like America!" he exclaimed. I shrank back in the corner and hid behind silence.

The next morning I visited Ravenna's other mosaics. What distinguished them from San Vitale, and recommended them to me, was their being part of a total plan, not isolated figures, or confined to a small part of the church.

March 19, S. Apollinare in Classe - A true basilica: [plan]. Romanesque tower: [drawing]. The most symmetrical & unified [mosaics] yet. Outline of whole is square, in center of which the apse is inset: [drawing]. The principal theme, besides religion, is pastoral, presumably because S. Apollinare was in that field. There is not much gold, & it is generally unobtrusive. Preservation is perfect.

Golden backgrounds, which impressed me at first, had come to seem garish, their absence refreshing. St. Apollinare, a good-shepherd figure, occupied the center of the apse, surrounded by sheep and trees. Around them was a sort of proscenium arch on whose face were mosaics of Christ, angels, saints, evangelists, and sheep. The full name of the church was *Sant' Apollinare in Classe Fuori*: "outside (the gates of) Classis." Ravenna began life as *Portus Classis*, a haven for Rome's Adriatic fleet. Dante mentions pine forests "along Chiassi's shore," presumed to be the same word. But Ravenna was moving inland, i.e. the coast was rising and the sea retiring - fast. When the English geologist

Charles Lyell visited in 1820 it was already 5 miles from the sea. Baedeker (1928) had Ravenna's canal to the Adriatic 6 miles long; our 1959 map showed the road to the marina as 7 miles.

YH in BOLOGNA, 9 PM - S. Apol[linare] in Classe was my favorite mosaic work. S. Apol. Nuovo, another "true basilica," had frescoes down the side walls of the nave, above the pillars. There were saints, angels, & Christ along the right; virgins, magi, angels & Mary with Jesus to the left. Built also by Theodoric (6th century), it shows his palace & the walled Ravenna. Very good work.

There were also finely detailed representations of Classis and Justinian. Theodoric reigned from 493 to 526; they don't know when the different buildings were started. My guidebook said that the figures in the frescoes on the side walls "reflected the Church's division of men and women" - its seating plan, or a broader sexism? And what were the magi doing on the women's side?

Left at 12:30 for Bologna. Made it in 2 rides, via Ferrara, at 3:15. Spent most of the PM wandering with my pack on. Did climb the 90-meter Asinelli tower (1109), one of the "due torre" which are Bologna's landmarks. It & its shorter, leaning sister were built by 2 rival families, the other being Garisendi. By Dante's time, Bologna was a forest of these towers.

The plain brick towers, built "for defensive purposes," gave a vivid image of how insecure and viciously partisan life in mediaeval Bologna must have been. From the top I could have thrown a rock down onto *Torre Garisenda*, which was only half as high. It seemed incomprehensible that the shorter tower was built a year *later*: could that be right? If so, was it not a Height of Foolishness? Garisenda has such a pronounced lean (7 feet in 154) that Dante thought of it when the giant Antaeus bent over him in Hell:

> Such as the Garisenda seems to men
> Beneath its leaning, when clouds pass on high,
> And counter-wise it seemeth then to lean,
> Such seemed Antaeus...

Evidently I was not aware at the time that the Asinelli tower also leans, some 4 feet in 318 - but others' biases are generally easier to see than our own.

Will be happy to see Verona <u>*domani*</u>*. My infections are still going, & am worried that I have it in my whole system: every little scratch infects.*

Sunday morning was devoted to examining Bologna's plenitude of churches, most of which were full of worshippers; a Canadian from the hostel ("one of the simplest people I've ever met") kept me company. After lunch I started *autostopping* to Verona.

March 21, Via Anzani, Verona - Lazing around the house, recuperating from 4½ tiring, exciting days on the hoof. Spent yesterday morning browsing Bologna, skimming the cream off its treasures: massive S. Petronio on the main square, where a mass was progressing in the ornate interior; S. Domenico; S. Francesco, in French Gothic style, with a beautifully carved altar screen; & S. Stefano, another of those superimpositions of several centuries & styles, which was too packed for looking. Brief visits to the Museo Civico & the Galleria Nationale; the latter had much good painting.

San Petronio seemed an allegory – of what, I was not sure. The Bolognese, determined to have the grandest church in Italy, started it in 1390, but eventually gave up and stopped work around 1650. So did it stand, finally, as a monument to overweening pride and ambition, or to two and a half centuries of dogged perseverance?

Left Bologna at 2, & had a tough time hitching. One good ride to Modena with 3 friendly Italian kids, who went out of their way to take me to a 6th century church.

I had plodded two miles from Bologna with my pack when they stopped for me. The boy was out for a drive with his girlfriend and wanted me to occupy her warm-blooded kid sister - sent along, presumably, as a chaperone - in the back seat. Sis was a mature fifteen and very friendly; her dark eyes sparkled with mischief. I could have gone farther with them, but declined to proceed past my planned point of departure near Modena. They left me on a lonely secondary road at 5 PM, and my next ride dumped me unceremoniously when I didn't laugh at his stupid jokes. Apparently there might be *dis*advantages to knowing some Italian. A scooter would have been welcome then.

Then 2 short rides, & finally a long one to Verona (with a man coming from Rome) just as I was about to give up. Arrived back at warm & comfortable #3 about 8 PM, with 95 lire left.

What "giving up" would mean in that context is uncertain. With only 15 cents in my pocket on a Sunday night, my choices were to keep waving at cars or crawl into my sleeping bag under a bush beside the road.

Ancora Verona

I spent four more days in Verona, savoring the luxury of staying in one place long enough to grow familiar with it. The idea of returning to the Old World to live and teach, and my attraction to reading and writing as occupations, grew stronger. Whatever teaching *per se* might prove to be, the preparation was greatly to my liking. I seemed to flourish mentally - but not physically. When my sores actually began bleeding, Parry insisted that I see an Italian doctor on the Army base; he gave me shots and pills for the infection. I promised to wash every day and eat reasonably, and did. The sores closed and began to heal.

Parry's many contributions to our welfare quickly earned him a place alongside Laurent and Leo in our Pantheon of Benefactors. Whatever goods and services he had access to via the Army were ours to command, and he included us in his social life. One evening he took us to dinner with an Italian-American couple and their friends: a cross-section of American-Army-in-Verona society. The Italian wife won my heart instantly by complimenting my pronunciation of her language. On the way home Parry chortled over how many extramarital affairs her husband was having. That can cut both ways, I thought, wondering how the attractive young bilingual wife spent her days.

A lean, sharp-faced intellectual, Parry turned out to be as interesting as my first impression had suggested. He spoke fluent Italian, knew lots of art history, read widely, aspired to be a serious writer, and was a keen Lothario. His thought and manners were uninhibited. Within minutes of our arrival he quizzed Hector about Inge, and quickly divined how things had gone. "Oh that's okay, that's great," he exclaimed. "I don't mind. We're finished."

Inge belonged to the large category of his exes: my moralizing had been misplaced as well as excessive. One afternoon a young Italian woman rang the bell, went straight into Parry's room and closed the door behind her. Hector grew uneasy and left, as I should have. But, being absorbed in my book, I just put *Bolero* on the phonograph and kept reading. In half an hour or so they came out. She said "*Ciaou*" and departed, her purpose achieved.

It was fascinating (for a psych major) to observe how the brothers' relationship worked; they seemed genuinely fond of each other, despite fundamental differences. One day when Hector was doing his usual set of push-ups, Parry stood over him, yelling like a drill instructor at a Mensa camp - "Hector, if you'd train your mind the way you train your body, you'd really be in good shape!" - until Hector collapsed on the floor, laughing. After observing us for a few days, Parry professed amazement that Hector and I were still on such good terms. "If I'd traveled that long with somebody, I'd hate him and he'd hate me," he said.

March 23, Verona - Life here proceeding as per intent: rest, food, reading. Monday I contrived to see Dr. Noto about my ailments. His verdict: not serious, but a good move to come see him. Told me to keep 'em clean & take Ledermicin [anti-biotic].

For much of my time in Verona and northern Italy the weather was somber or wet, but a few sunny, moderately warm days sang a song of spring, of mild southerlies and the reviving earth. We had made it to the equinox!

Today, breaking away from the steady diet of [reading Henri] Pirenne & Kafka, I took a longer walk. Verona affords a lot to see: the musing baroqueness of Piazza Dante, the umbrellas & delicious bread smells of the market, the crenellated walls & "teatro romano" of Piazza Bra, & the unique S. Zeno Maggiore church.

A Romanesque tower overlooked the statue of Dante "musing." He lived in Verona for years, patronized (in the good, old sense) by Can Grande, after his political enemies exiled him from Florence. The fruit and vegetable market, *Piazza Erbe*, Baedeker calls "one of the most picturesque in Italy." Surrounded by venerable *casas*, *palazzi*, and *torre*, it was the ancient Forum, and would be the place where partisans of the Montagues and Capulets met, bit their thumbs at each other, and clashed - all of which played second fiddle to the smell of fresh-baked *panini* when I was hungry. It was good to find that people still used the old name *Piazza Bra* (a corruption of Latin *pratum*, "meadow"), rather than the later *P. Vittorio Emanuele*. Of the churches, I found San Zeno the most interesting.

This gaunt old basilica, finished around 1000 & built over earlier temples or churches, is a curious combination of Romanesque & Baroque, with 3 naves, wooden crossbeam ceilings, elevated choir [and a] multitude of statues, columns, frescoes. The effect, although not harmonious, has a disorderly sort of power when the vaulted emptiness cuts you off from spring sunshine.

Yes, but…outside, *in* the spring sunshine, resided a different, more natural power, perhaps even a different religion, and that was the one I wanted and needed now.

Ah, blessed vernal equinox, I worship thee! Pour down thy rays, & warm a chilled body! O long-awaited time, fulfill me with joy & love, spring & warmth, hope & strength!

The River *Adige* curves through Verona, crossed by half a dozen old bridges. Both the *Ponte di Castel Vecchio* and the "old castle" itself are constructed of red brick and picturesquely crenellated. A dapper angler in a sport coat, homburg, and waders stood in the sunny shallows by the bridge, one hand on his hip, his pole held high. He seemed to have the right idea. "The coming in of spring," says Thoreau, "is like the creation of Cosmos out of Chaos and the realization of the Golden Age."

The walk took me past the plaque with the quotation from *Romeo and Juliet* that begins, "There is no world without Verona walls." At first that had suited my mood, but now I was feeling almost *too* comfortable, and getting restless. When Parry said that a young woman was coming for the weekend and we should find alternative lodging, I heard my cue to set off for Spain. On Friday the 25th, well-rested and eager again, I said *arrivederci* to them and set out on the last leg of my scooter journey.

Hit the Road, Jack: Kerouac Days

Above in beauteous Italy lieth, walled
By the Alps behind it, Germany's confine
 Over Tirol, a lake Benacus [Garda] called.
Through a thousand springs and more between
Pennine
And Garda and Val Camonica is besprent
The land by streams that in that lake resign.

Dante, *Inferno* (trans. Lawrence Binyon)

Heading north to see Lake Garda, a famous beauty spot - Parry's recommendation - before turning south toward the Mediterranean, I followed the Arab practice of making a short first day. It wasn't far to the *Brenzone* hostel, and the weather did not invite lingering out of doors.

March 25, YH at Brenzone, L. Garda, 6 PM - Back on the road & cold again! Drippy skies & chilly weather made my drive up Lake Garda difficult to enjoy, & the hostel has no heat. Traveling & cold seem to go together.

Wound up 2 weeks in Verona today, vacating the apt. about 3. Much has been accomplished: knee infection cured, 8 pounds gained, scooter serviced & insured, Vol. I of [Pirenne's] History [of Europe] read, as well as some Capote, Kafka, & Chekhov. Right now I just want that guitar, warm weather, & a flamenco environment!

Lake Garda is, I'm sure, beautiful in good weather. Today there was little to see. The hostel has a fine situation looking out on the lake, & I can see high snow-decked peaks. Here's hoping for good visibility tomorrow as I go up & around the lake & head south.

Actually I could see mountain*sides*, not peaks, which were in the clouds. Long snow gullies hung down from the overcast, marbling grey cliffs with a white tracery. I cooked a small supper on the hostel's hotplate and read for awhile before bed. The hostel was almost as primitive in its lighting as in its heating, but then it *was* technically still closed for the winter; there were no other guests, reinforcing my (not unpleasant) sense of isolation. In the drafty dormitory I put my sleeping bag inside the bedclothes. Some body heat would be welcome, though - just imagine if Evelyn had decided to come along…or La Magnifica! No, no, better not. The bag was soon warm and comfortable anyway.

I rose at dawn, bought some eggs from a shop down the road, made breakfast, and packed my gear in a silence broken only by the muffled dripping of rain-soaked eaves. Outside, the morning was misty, chill, and dark. Tying on quickly, I paid and said goodbye to the hostel-keeper in (what seemed to me) flawless Italian, started the motor, wheeled out onto the wet black shoreline road and turned north. My sense of self-sufficiency had never been stronger, and the snail's pace at which I putted along was a deliberate exercise of my new freedom. Hector liked speed and was often far ahead, which created pressure to keep up, so now I trolled along at 25 mph beside the grey lake, drawing out the moment and enjoying what views the weather afforded. "Travel is at its best a solitary enterprise," writes Paul Theroux, who would be a difficult travel companion.

Behind *Riva*, at Garda's northern tip, mountains reared up into the clouds, challenging the traveler, yet also inviting exploration. I stopped to check the map. Garda and the other Italian lakes were clearly glacial trenches; if the Adriatic ever drowns the Po valley, they will be fjords again. A road led north to *Bolzano* and over the Brenner Pass to Innsbruck. New ground! Winter conditions were certainly up there, and not far away, by the look of the clouds. How about it? For a few heady minutes I considered turning north - *because* it looked cold and snowy, *because* it was unplanned, *because* I was on my own. Because I could. Of course it would negate my arrangement with Hector and Parry – obligations still existed. In a few minutes, though, confident of my independence, I decided to go on south: what I most wanted was warm weather and a guitar. So, left, not right. Talk about your roads not taken!

Halfway down Garda's western shore I stopped to photograph the lake's dull sheen and the great cliffs whose white network of canyons disappeared into clouds above the snowline. A soft rain blurred all contours. Beyond the ceiling of altostratus, imagination took over, building peaks of fabulous height upon this massive base. I could *feel* those summits, hidden in the overcast. It was a delicious moment: self-reliance was something I could taste, and very tasty it was. The scared neophyte of those first days at Naples was just a faint memory. My whole trip seemed to have been pointing toward the moment when I would come to these mountains as if to a magic mirror, which said, "Look! You stand where you were, your vision limited by clouds of self-doubt, but now your mind's eye sees the mighty world above, and, seeing, you are there!"

I stepped back and shook my head to clear this reverie, or revelation, or whatever it was. Whence came all this?! It was not my first out-of-body experience in the mountains – I already knew that I was emotionally susceptible to them – but the *content* of this epiphany surprised me. Was I working through a crisis of self-doubt of which I had been unaware, or trying to fend off the doubts and criticisms (real or imagined) of others? It seemed odd that I hadn't even known that I *needed* this reassurance.

Time to move on, to close other circles. I completed my circumnavigation of the lake in the rain, noting as much German as Italian on the signs. Trying to climb the hills south of Lake Garda, the motor died suddenly, but as usual coughed back to life with the next kickstart.

March 26, YH, GENOA, 6 PM - Wet day! Drove 340 kms., all but the north end of Garda in the rain. Left at 8; the lake, even under overcast conditions, is spectacular. Sheer crags & grey-white snow up high gave it the aspect of Yosemite Valley flooded. Riva, & Garda yesterday, were pretty towns on bays. The entire lakeshore [has a] resort atmosphere: bars & albergos everywhere, little "lungolago" parks of trees & benches, beribboned piers.

Then, in steady rain, I came down to Brescia & Cremona, where I ate lunch & looked at the old tower, reputedly the highest extant in Italy. It is a campanile attached to an old cathedral.

The *vecchio torre*, with its Romanesque windows and steeple, was picturesque, though I was too drenched and chilled for more than a glance. A hot lunch was Cremona's main contribution to my welfare, after which I faced the miserable weather again in ridiculously high spirits.

Purred on across flat country in a grey, steady rain: Piacenza, Voghera, & an autostrada to Genoa. Pushed it up to 86 kms./hr.

The rain discouraged stops but did not impede progress, and with the scooter running well the *autostrada* was great fun. On a straightaway I drove at full throttle and briefly hit the official top speed: 54 mph. Even the coastal range did not slow me down much, thanks to the freeway; when traffic backed up approaching a tunnel I moved onto the center line, passed a string of slow-moving vehicles and sailed on into Genoa. Only later did the imprudence of this maneuver occur to me. It was my longest run since our Benghazi-to-Brigadoon day in Libya.

The delightfully warm, dry youth hostel in Genoa was crowded with young travelers, among whom were two South Africans looking for a scooter. They promptly offered $150 for mine, which set off a flurry of soul-searching, though we needed to find out if my insurance was refundable and whether customs was a problem. This was Saturday night: the answers would not be available until Monday. I spent Sunday - which was sunny - sightseeing and thinking about the offer. Hector and I had discussed selling our scooters at the end of the trip to avoid the trouble and expense of getting them back to New York, where their value was less certain. But my trip had not ended!

Logistics & emotions say "Don't." Hitching to Barcelona with all this junk will be a pain. And I just haven't had enough scootering. If I do sell it now, I'll <u>always</u> miss it. If I don't, I may have trouble selling it for anything later without much red tape.

Thus, as in October, Genoa was seen through a haze of turbulent thoughts and feelings. The agonizing was needless, however: once the Automobile Club of Italy office opened on Monday, we learned that a vehicle with export (EE) plates *could not be sold in Italy*, which I should have known. Once I had! The feeling of happy relief that flooded through me showed that this was the "right" answer; I rushed back to the hostel to pack and leave before it occurred to Piet that he might follow me to France and buy it there. "I haven't had enough scootering" was the bedrock. Would I *ever* get enough to quit willingly? Face it, man: you love riding the thing, and won't give it up either to meet more people or to make money. The term "scooter bum" whispered its slurs: *dropout, ne'er-do-well.* Even another motor failure on the freeway through the hills west of Genoa was only a momentary scare. It restarted at once and I pressed on in the rain: a new storm had moved in.

March 28, YH in NICE, FRANCE, 5:30 PM - Bonjour, et tous recueillements du beau pays de la France! It was a lousy day: chilly, with low clouds & steady rain. Couldn't keep my spirits as high as the other day & make myself enjoy it. Passed thru Savona, Imperia, San Remo, Ventimiglia....

The weather discouraged halts in these old resort towns, which would otherwise have been quite pleasant. San Remo was once the largest winter resort in Italy, much frequented by boreal Europeans, but I just could not enter its genteel-looking cafés in my boots and dripping poncho, toting my red helmet - and having to leave my pack out in the rain. Instead, near *Ventimiglia* (20 miles or 20,000 paces from somewhere) I found a roadside cave where we could all dry off together. "Perfect!" I thought as it presented itself.

Ate a roll & ½ a pack of Petit Beurre biscuits in a cave. The psychological characteristics which give the Italian & French Rivieras their appeal: isolation & security. Each resort is snuggled in a cove, sheltered from the weather & other towns by the arms of land enclosing it. You easily believe it's the whole world you're seeing -

or so it seemed to someone snug in a cave, sheltered from the weather and the world. Where had I done this before? Delphi! Washing down my bread with swigs of water, I meditated on the irony of my "bold journey to Africa" finally devoting more time to Italy than to any other country. Still, I felt as isolated and secure as a Riviera cove-resort, and quite happy with how things were going, despite (or because of) the steady drizzle out there.

Hit the Italian border at 3. Formalities were swift, & the officials pleasant & impressed with my trip. Harder rain. The French side was as fast, but I can't speak French any more.

The handsome Italian officers, seeing that one of their common domestic scooters had been round to Egypt and back, clucked and pursed their lips appreciatively. They asked if I could speak Arabic. I said no, not really, but taught them a few words anyway. Then, a hundred meters down the road, with *Buon viaggio, amico*! still ringing in my ears, I was trying to make sounds meaningful to a Frenchman and envying Europeans their linguistic facility. After more than a month of thinking in Italian, I suddenly had to close those switches and use a new set. That took time, even with my premier foreign language, and in a few days I would have to speak Spanish! Surely it was only people who had grown up under this linguistic patchwork quilt who could produce one *or* another on demand in adjacent speeches, as if they were interchangeable.

Driving slowly through a continuous resort strip, bedraggled in the downpour, I passed Monte Carlo and the high brown walls of the Principality of Monaco before pulling into Nice at 4:30. Another circle closed, more memories stirring. The hostel, set on a hill above the white town, was well populated, and hot showers were rumored to be available at 6 PM. Great! And yet -

Could easily get lonely - find that I want to be doing something each minute - or go to bed. When I can't take time alone with myself anymore, it's a sign....

So there were limits to the appeal of solitary travel! That high had already dissipated. It was easy to see that reaching the Cleopatra Coast had brought this on: Genoa, Nice, with Cannes and Barcelona to come. Along here I had been under her spell, and now I was soloing. There was a sound of music from the main room, and I went to join the singers and a guitarist. In the course of the evening a fellow-traveler asked if he might ride toward Spain with me, and to my surprise I said Yes. Well, Pat would be company, and he was a prodigious dispenser of good dark chocolate.

The next morning was clear and mild. While tying on the two packs - a fresh problem! - I talked with an American girl who had scootered from Paris. Seeing the route of my trip crayoned on the windshield-flap she began asking questions. Telling her about the wilds of Greece, Turkey and North Africa, I felt like a veteran, a father-figure to neophyte vagabonds - a Don Knies! Then Pat boarded for our trial run. Fortunately the first mile was downhill, after which I had to stop and re-tie the packs.

March 29, YH in Arles, 7 PM - Un beau jour passé en traversant le paysage provençal. It was lovely, & I felt in control of things for once. I know the language, scooter is running well, money & weather look good. It may all fall about my ears tomorrow, but I don't care.

How quickly we forget! In the Arab lands I would not have dared to write thus without some sort of *inshallah* clause. Was it pride, or self-confidence, that went before a fall? And how quickly I had come to "know" French again! Just the day before I "couldn't speak" it.

Carried Pat, the red-headed NH boy, from Nice to Arles. Had seen him in Rome, & he turned up last night. A heavy load - he weighs 180, & his pack is heavier than mine. The mountains gave trouble, but on the whole the bug performed admirably. We breezed through the corniches of Nice & Cannes under blue skies, then cut thru rugged little mts. (but beautifully green) to Fréjus. The flood damage is sobering: mud flats, roots, overturned cars, rotted timbers.

I had read of the flooding at Fréjus a month earlier, but seeing it was a revelation. Tree roots like huge birds' nests, ends of cars, and house beams jutted at odd angles from vast mud flows, not dry yet. The battlefield was almost deserted; the dazed survivors were still somewhere else.

Then 80 miles thru increasingly Provençal countryside toward Aix-en-Provence. In Brignoles I bought bread, & we had a splendid lunch of bread, cheese & margerine alongside the road on a white wall by a Shell station. We reflected on our good fortune in life thus far; & Pat fed me chocolate.

Ordinarily I would not *choose* to eat at a gas station, but this one, where we had refueled and been well received, was different. It was delightful to be able to converse with the proprietor; I had no sense of alienation or struggle, only of competence and international amity. There was a residue of good will for Americans left over from the Liberation, he understood my French, and by the time he invited us to *pique-nique* on the low wall of his rural station it was almost like being asked into his home. Wasn't this what Philip Wylie had called for? That day I, even I, could enjoy the present moment, there and as we drove on through the verdant foothills of the Provençal Alps. The *paysage* was so pleasant that we barely paused at Aix-en-Provence.

We slighted old Aix horrendously & buzzed on to Arles. It is lovely "provincial" country, with red roofs & green firs: the France of Flaubert, Stendhal, Gide & Cézanne. In Arles we took peeks at the baths of Constantine, Roman theatre & Roman arena. The brown swift Rhone, missing so many bridges, was more interesting.

Vincent Van Gogh, a print of whose "Bridge at Arles" hung on a wall at home for many years, can be added to the list of artists.

Arles was the largest Roman settlement in the Rhone delta, but broken bridge-ends and missing spans gave mute testimony to the death throes of another empire just 15 years earlier. Fréjus and Arles, nature and man: Provence had had its share of knocks. The youth hostel was a trailer on blocks and a cottage beside a hard-packed dirt square with trucks and pastel gypsy carts parked on its perimeter; some old men were bowling-on-the-brown.

Among the few other guests at the hostel were a good-looking American divorcée in her thirties, her five-year-old son Juan, and a husky, handsome Norwegian about my age who were cycling from Spain to Italy. Juan had spent the winter as a shepherd's apprentice in Andalucia, and said he loved it. After dinner I tried to speak Spanish with them, but thus far my practice had been silent, and conversational ability requires conversations. I began to prepare for another linguistic battle, reminding myself sternly that the recurrent necessity for such engagements was one of the most appealing aspects of this mode of life.

I also struggled to sort out my feelings about this irregular "family." Bourgeois society would no doubt see a woman living in sin before her son's eyes, and judge her harshly (at least Melody of Mykonos had eventually married her son's father). Of course this *might* be a platonic arrangement - but if not, what was wrong with it in broad humanistic terms, regardless of received codes of conduct? Where was the harm? An intelligent, adventurous couple were finding satisfaction together and educating Juan liberally. The social and ethical freedoms they had taken or found were daily being passed on to a mature, self-sufficient boy. As for the future, she said that she had some money in the U.S. and would go there in a year to put Juan in school and find work for herself. Of course there were other ways of regarding the matter, but for myself I could not make objection. We are advised to judge a work of literature on its own terms: why not people and relationships?

Still, this *ménage* did rankle somehow. It could only be envy, jealousy: I wanted an older woman to take *me* in hand, teach me the ways of the world, and a tanned, curvaceous blonde like this one would do nicely. To my amazement she called herself Lu. Lucinda, is that you? Were there moon goddesses everywhere, then, and was I to be ever at their mercy? Yes, please! The old heroes were not long on fidelity - Odysseus, allegedly pining for his wife, slept with Calypso every night for seven years "on his way home" - but that league had folded and we had moved on. Hadn't we?

The next morning we headed in opposite directions. Pat and I drove west toward *Montpellier* on a flat road skirting the northern edge of the *Camargue*, a huge marsh known for wild horses. By taking that route we missed *Nîmes* and its Roman ruins, including the famous *Pont du Gard* aqueduct. From Montpellier the coast road led to *Sète* and the *Étang de Thau*: a strange, wild region, like the Camargue but more barren, whose few inhabitants spoke a dialect not taught in textbooks of Parisian French. The weather remained good, though it looked darker ahead.

March 30, Perpignan, 6 PM - Back on adversity trail, but still glad I didn't care yesterday. Beginning in the hills between Montpelier & Sète, I had a series of half-engine failures. While there was a load on the engine, or just after, [it] would lose power. I could cure it by downshifting or rest. I think it's a combination of overload, hills & wind, leading to overheating. I may deposit Pat tomorrow

- and could have done so that day. Our agreement was that if his weight seemed too much for the Lambretta he would be on his own. That seemed to be the case; the cutting-out was worse than usual, and when the engine had to be restarted there were two of us to dismount and reboard. Once the rain began, these episodes infuriated us and we swore impotently. Yet I could not make myself leave him on a back road in sparsely populated country, as had been done to me in Italy. He had become a friend, and it was fun having someone to talk to en route; we would jaw about Mussolini, Charlemagne, the scenery or our travels most of the day. I was still working through Pirenne and enjoyed pointing out landmarks of which I had just read. So I coaxed the scooter along, the Apostle of Individual Effort having become the booster of good company.

Shortly after Narbonne, 30 kms. from Perpignan, rain became a downpour. Drenched, we pushed on into town before 4. After ½ hour hunting for the hostel, it was full. We're spending 500 francs ($1) each for a hotel room. It's not a bad idea on a cold, wet day: heat & hot water & privacy. I'll get my money's worth & read.

Another good road lunch today: sardine sandwiches, bananas & chocolate, by a bridge over a stream near Narbonne.

Though we limped into Perpignan in 3rd gear, with a coughing engine and soaked through, good reading lights and the memory of a picnic in a warm meadow did much to compensate for the adversity. Perpignan, once the capital of the Kingdom of Mallorca and culturally the frontier of Spain (French "only" since 1659), deserved more than the night we gave it, but with Barcelona just over the horizon I was even more goal-directed than usual. Parry and Hector were due to arrive in less than two weeks, and that was my interval to live and learn.

March 31, YH in BARCELONA, SPAIN, 9 PM - Olé! The scooter trip is completed; I've reached long-thirsted-for Barcelona. Spain is beautiful & exciting: tomorrow I will probably find a pension & buy a guitar. Many roads seem to close behind, & much opens up ahead. I'm on top of the world & feeling everything!

Up at 6:45, Pat & I made short work of packing & breakfast, & left Perpignan before 8. Almost immediately we had views of majestic white peaks along the border: the Pyrenees. Toiling thru green precipitous foothills, we crossed the border at 9, had passports checked on the Spanish side & drove 4 kms. to the customs village.

At first Spain struck me as colorful and funny. Every few kilometers, policemen in three-cornered hats slouched along in pairs, one on each side of the highway. Gilbert and Sullivan extras in faded green uniforms, carrying bolt-action rifles, played "the Spanish Army," marching single file or riding in wooden wagons drawn by burros. I didn't know much about Gen. Franco and was slow to recognize a *European* police state, even after our time in Egypt. Who could believe that these feckless-looking men in their silly get-ups represented a real evil on this green and rolling farmland dotted with quiet villages, haystacks, old churches, fields of daisies and red poppies; upon quiet paths through pine groves with the Pyrenees for a backdrop? It was all so peaceful. A few miles inside the border, though, someone had painted on a huge roadside boulder the motto, "*No existe libertad sin orden*": 'There is no liberty without order.' You could see how that might be abused.

We passed Gerona, possessor of a beautiful sylvan park (stately sycamores by moss-green fountains), & bought lunch. Ate in a pine grove just off the road. Over bad roads, thru a one-minute rain, up & over abrupt little hills, the bug ran like a mad thing.

As well it might on its last real travel-day, though a snapshot of our picnic, showing the luggage heaped on the rack, makes me wonder how it ran at all. The 230-pound scooter, which usually carried a load of around 200 pounds, now had over twice that. Gerona - like Perpignan an interesting old town that merited more attention than it received - hosted some of Salvador Dali's earliest exhibitions. He was born nearby, in *Figueres*, through which we had passed earlier.

> 'Boy, boy,' interrupted Don Quixote in a loud voice, 'go straight ahead with your story, and do not go curving off at a tangent; for it requires much proof and corroboration to bring a truth to the light.'
>
> - Cervantes, *Don Quixote*

Barthelona

Came to the rugged Costa Brava, then flattened along the sandy beach stretches leading to Barcelona. Had to stop once & run out & feel the warm water. [Into] Barcelona at 3; found the hostel. All Spanish YH's are part of Franco's youth movement. This one is semi-palatial, semi-villa, with a swimming pool. But the beds are terrible, the administration [is] despotic, & it is several kms. from downtown.

We drove there, to American Express, together; then I went off on my own to price guitars and *pensiones* along the lower Ramblas boulevard and vicinity. It did not take long to find clean, reputable lodgings, but after visiting five guitar shops I realized that making a choice would be difficult. The district, with its little *calles,* brought on a version of my nostalgia in Naples, plus: both cities were associated with the journey's commencement, but Barcelona would also be my last chance to realize dreams and make choices that had been woven into the rationale for the trip. The pressures of the future and the pull of a past already coming to seem idyllic made the present vibrate with their competition.

Now I actually had a chance to grasp at what I'd been wanting for six months! It was the eve of April.

April 2, Pension Puerta, Barcelona, 2 AM - Having satisfied myself that no livable accommodations were available for less than 25 p., I came back [here] & took a room. Then (being in high spirits on a translucent day) I rushed back to the hostel, packed up & had a memorable ride down into Barcelona: Paseo del Graiia, Ramblas, Calle de Escudelleros. The room, on the 2nd floor looking onto an interior court, is small, but large enough for push-ups. The walls are partly green, partly off-rose. The lights are fair. I have a clothes-closet, basin & mirror; hot showers are included; the court for my scooter, & friendly people running the place. But I should have known that the elation couldn't last; depression was bound to follow. Last night I got an acute attack of Raskolnikovitis & sacked out at 6 PM.

April Fool! This attack was a direct result of finally *Buying the Guitar*. I visited two more music stores that morning, and returned to the previous day's for second looks. A walk and a piece of apple strudel helped me decide to buy one of the 1300-peseta guitars at 28 San Pablo, but there was something wrong with its head-nuts that would have taken a day to fix, so they let me have a 1500-p. beauty that I had played and admired for 1300. I made the mistake, however, of going back to one of the rival shops to purchase the soft cover. "!*Como es pequeno*!" laughed the proprietress there. I shriveled, but it was what I deserved after spurning *her* guitars for this...dinky child's toy! Then I went back to my room and tried to play it.

When you have looked forward to something as long as I have this, a let-down is almost sure when [it] is finally achieved. Immediately after the purchase, I felt as I do Xmas morning after I've opened all my presents. The distressing thing is how I sound on it...terrible.

And I had thought of a career as a *guitarist*?! The months without practice, cramped fingers with chilblains, and my basic mediocrity, conveniently forgotten, now appeared to present their bills. I could not even play my old repertoire, let alone the demanding sheet music (Bach, Beethoven, Albeniz, etc.) I had bought. All that agonizing over the right instrument! The fault, dear Brutus, lies in ourselves...

Fortunately the city outside my window did *not* let me down. I fell head over heels for it.

Barcelona is, by day, a spacious, well-ordered, attractive city. The stores are good, prices low; parks & promenades are plentiful & pretty. But at night it comes crackling to life. There is excitement hanging in the air at restaurants, at flamenco bars, in the streets.

The Ramblas and its side streets became my turf, to be prowled, savored, harvested, gleaned. There were music stores, cinemas, ticket offices with posters for upcoming events, good-looking women, and a whole plethora of food outlets: groceries, snack bars that specialized in *caracoles* (snails), cafés, and restaurants ranging from within my means to well beyond. Yet all this I defined as diversionary: back in my room, the guitar waited, frowning.

April 3 - What has hurt me these last 2 days is my inability to do anything on the guitar. I was ready to get rid of it yesterday, but it's not the guitar's fault. If I ever thought that I was good, I was sadly deluded. I can't play anything. Scooter riding hasn't been good on my fingers. I'm having to do some re-thinking about a musical career -

As well you might! my parents would say. Of course I had re-thought it often during the trip. Why not go to one of the nearby *escuelas de musica* and find a teacher, though? I assumed he would be too expensive for me, and behind that lay the trauma of early piano lessons, and the fear that a *maestro* would just confirm my lack of ability, or laugh at a no-longer-young *gringo* tackling a Spanish instrument. Self-taught thus far, I would *not* seek help, but would try to master Segovia's diatonic scales and editions of classical pieces on my own. Whatever illusions I had had about my talent, the idea that I could turn from months on the road to playing Bach and Sor on the guitar, and show improvement in a few days, was at least as unreasonable.

Yesterday I spent time in the USIS library, ate at the U. of B'lona student restaurant or hogar, bought a ticket for a futbol game today, & went to see Haydn's Creation at the Palace of Music at 10:30 last night. It was not well performed, either by the 3 soloists or by the B'lona Orch., but is a fine piece of music, ranking somewhere behind Messiah & Fauré's Requiem.

Actually I could speak of only the first half. Dining hours in Barcelona society were late, 8 or even 9 PM, so a 10:30 start made sense, though that put intermission at midnight, with the second part beginning around 12:30 - made sense, that is, with a siesta. Without one, I was unable to follow Haydn into the wee small hours. Still, if that was the price of being out early on clear, mild spring mornings when the low sun flooded the narrow streets, so be it. I would go to a workmen's café where it was acceptable to dip a hunk of fresh bread in your tall *café con leche*; then buy bananas for 1 or 2 cents apiece and a little milk and sugar to take back to my room and the cook kit's dishes. And Barcelona offered a lot to see and do all day long, including the siesta hours. The next afternoon found me in a palm grove in a beautiful park under blue skies, writing my journal.

April 4, Park of Montjuich, 3 PM - Went to 11 AM Mass in the Cathedral yesterday. Wonderful gloomy atmosphere for the pomp & the men's choir, whose music is very close to Gregorian chant. Great dark arches of columnated stone look like heavy-duty bridge cables in a theatre backdrop. The cloister, a hangout for painters, has one good Pieta sculpture by Llimona.

In the Plaza del Rey nearby I walked thru excavations of the ancient Roman city: a 2nd cent. building, a 4th cent. Xian basilica & a 5th cent. Gothic temple. The Mares Museum next door had a huge collection of medieval Xian art, mostly sculptures of the Crucifixion & Madonna con Niño. Too many: Spanish Xianity dwelt on the stern aspects. Other items [included] Arabic carving on door lintels.

This was the first example of Arab influence I could recall since Sicily, though as we went south into the former kingdom of the Moors there would be more. *They* had not taken No for an answer in Algeria, but had completed their North African traverse, and then some.

At 4:30 I joined a huge crowd thronging toward the Estadio de C[lub] F[utbol] Barcelona. Surprisingly, almost everyone wore a coat & tie. I stood up top with the noisy preferente de pie [standing room] crew & enjoyed a hell of a good game: they're amazing soccer players. The Spaniards, really sarcastic, sometimes clapped loudly for bum plays. Barc. 2, Valencia 1.

Since I had previously seen only American amateur soccer, this was a revelation - like going from sandlot baseball to Yankee Stadium - and broadly educational: my introduction to a genuine world sport. Numerous young men in Barcelona strutted around town in sweat clothes and sneakers, looking like jocks on campuses back home. But this was not *Yanqui* cultural imperialism; Franco's youth movement was modeled on the Nazis' 'strength through joy' program.

A drunk American soldier dragged me around for an hour last night. Poor bastard: I felt as if he were sent me as a warning not to go Army.

This bored, unhappy fellow probably had other purposes on the planet than a special embassy to me, but I was facing the military decision (along with others) in the next few months and so took him personally.

Today I spent mostly trying to find a ship home. Being tied to Barcelona with [the] guitar, I can't go to Cadiz for work or a cheap passage. The Italian Line wants $80 for the scooter. May take a freighter.

Fear of attempting a scooter trip with the guitar slung on my back restricted me to the port of Barcelona, which (said the clerks in shipping offices) had less traffic than Cadiz or Le Havre. I still had a faint hope of using my Able-Bodied Seaman's papers to work my way; failing that, I needed to find a low fare. Lévi-Strauss remarks that we travel in space, in time, and in social hierarchy. If I had not been pinching pennies it would have been a much different, much easier trip, but I would have met fewer of the good folk in the maritime business or the *preferente de pie*.

Walked to the Plaza de España & the spacious park & palace of Montjuich this afternoon. It is imposing, with good views of the city from all over the hill. The Fine Arts Museum is in the Palace; in a half hour I saw only enough to find out I need to go again.

The language situation here is interesting. They speak not of "Spanish," but of "castellano" & "catalan." The latter is really another language, as much as Portuguese, & has a lot of French in it. Most people in B'lona speak both. And I heard a few "aywa's!" at the football game yesterday. Language, like art, has logic in its associations with history.

The Archeological Museum proved more interesting than I had expected. Some early cave paintings from Santander (or copies of them?) exhibited close observation of nature and impressionist touches; again I was struck by how the work of talented artists can delight you across the centuries. There were also Neolithic artifacts from near Madrid, red and brown clay-ware from Valencia, burial finds from Almeria and Ibiza, and primitive pottery. Of course the Greeks, Carthaginians and Romans had been here, but that Greeks were making fine pottery with geometrical designs in Spain ca. 1000-800 BCE came as a surprise, as did bronze eagles and snakes from Mallorca. And what was an Etruscan sarcophagus doing here? Again the yawning temporal vistas stunned me.

Still frustrated by the refractory guitar, I grew restive and thought of going somewhere else for a bit. Collecting information about ships to Ibiza, I went to a showing of *Los Hermanos Karamazov* to consider the matter. It was dubbed in *castellano* Spanish with no subtitles, so the action was difficult to follow, but Maria Schell and the dark singing of the Russian Orthodox Office for the Dead were reward enough. By the time it ended I somehow knew that Ibiza would cost more than a *short* visit could justify. Then the Pension Puerta management announced that they no longer had room in their courtyard for my scooter, which was kinder than attacking my guitar-playing directly and helped me decide to give up my room there. I was sorry to leave, though: the baths were lovely, and the Señora had helped me with Spanish, cautioning me not to trill *all* my r's, turning *pero*, "but," into *perro*, "dog."

Just 6 kms. from the city was a campground that an American at the hostel recommended. I improvised a strap out of some cord, slung the guitar across my back like a rifle and drove out there - very slowly. Like our Naples campground in the fall, the *terrano* was not crowded: just two trailers and three orange tents scattered here and there. Nights would be cool and long, but I could play or read in the daytime, and probably no one would steal the guitar.

April 6, campground at San Adrian, 7 PM - The Fine Arts Museum has lots of 13th-14th cent. on-wood painting on Xian subjects. Also sculpture, wood-carvings, altar screens of the Crucifixion, Madonna & child, Salomé, etc. More interesting is my new friend the guide: a language professor who speaks English, French, & Italian. He is intelligent, quite observant...

The guitar is going better. A 2-hr. session yesterday was very profitable, & I progressed on the Bach. Perhaps yet, who knows? Otherwise,

I've spent time reading history, strolling the city streets, & enjoying a pleasant couple of hours in the Parco de la Ciudella zoo.

By the time I returned to visit the park's art museum, I had moved again. The campground charged a peseta more than the youth hostel, and when my friends left there was no reason to stay. The guitar attracted them initially: a French family (mother and daughters), an English girl, and an Italian-German boy who had been robbed of almost everything in Almería and was waiting for money to be wired from Berlin. He told me about Elvis Presley's hold on German teenagers, which appalled me. One of *les françaises* had just bought a guitar, so we had a sing-along. The type of American music that they - like all musical foreigners I met - knew and asked for was Negro spirituals. I taught them some chapters from the gospel according to Josh White, and they were thrilled. The ringing emptiness of the campground after their departure soon sent me packing.

April 8, Barcelona YH - Morning a study in contrasts. From 9 till 11, I was casing the docks, making inquiries about jobs to the States. In my own mind & under the pressure of a sketchy Spanish vocab, I became a poor student with not enough money to get home.

Then to the Modern Art Gallery in Park de la Ciudella. There is an exhibition of Picasso sketches & oils. He exudes imagination. Small marble & bronze statuary by Gargallo & Llimona, of high quality. Best of the rest were landscapes by Joaquin Mir. Some paintings are comments, others are insights, some are revelations.

Almost as enjoyable as the exhibit were my own strong, hair-trigger responses to it: much of the collection moved me. Somehow, mysteriously, I had regained my freshness. Maybe my destiny in the arts was not to be a performer but an enthusiastic member of the audience – with any luck, one of those who could afford to buy a ticket.

Another reaction to my inability to sound like Segovia was the resurfacing of the desire to write. "Strands," a group of stories about the trip, started percolating again. There would be "Deck Passage," "Border Post," and "Tea in the Desert" for sure. In Tunis I had imagined an incident in a *souk* that could be anywhere in the Arab world. The plots and ideas of these sketches remained vague: they were all surface and decoration - which did not keep me from writing them. I visualized myself going home and telling my parents, "I've decided to become a guitarist or a writer - haven't decided which." Yet they - and not only they - would be expecting answers from me in a month or so.

I may be beating myself around too much on future plans. Don't know that you can just sit down & reason it out. Perhaps, when all the necessary data is there, the cards just point - somewhere. Choices keep jabbing my mind: psychology? music? teaching? the Air Force? Windhome? If I only had something I could dig into.

More desperate flailing around! Psychology? My college major had been an academic convenience, not a vocation. Music? But how? Teaching? What? The Air Force would be a way to avoid the draft and learn to fly, not a career. "Windhome" was shorthand for David's offer of future employment - but only in summer. So what *was* I going to do with myself? One thing was certain: Dad detested "drifters."

The hostel, almost full now with the approach of Holy Week, *Semana Santa*, offered lively, diverse scenes. The loudest guests were three guitar-toting Angelinos, Kingston-trio clones full of themselves. They had a gig at a local bar, and crowed that they were being paid in the flesh of B-girls. From what I heard of their stuff, it was a fair valuation. Peter, a thoughtful architecture student, called them *tipos*, "types." He showed me *Casa Felipe*, a workman's restaurant down in the street beyond the soccer field: a crowded, noisy eatery that served the meal of the day and a glass of *gaseoso* - carbonated lemonade - for about 25 cents. Eating there at long tables with tradesmen, I realized how deeply these down-to-earth Spaniards had worked their way into my affections. Their speech was like a rich loam.

April 9 - Barcelona...so much color & variety. The band playing outside the Cathedral after Mass for country dances...the band with flat trumpets practicing near the athletic field...students bullfighting with red capes & mock horns on the field...18th-cent.-German-looking frescoes on a bar off the Ramblas, sprites coyly holding banners saying "America"...the fellow in the bread shop near Pension Puerta in his undershirt...the demented girl with the bad eye selling lottery tickets "iguales para hoy" around Calle Ancha...

A snapshot shows an aspiring young matador practicing his passes, and a contraption that could be steered at him: bulls' horns mounted on a sort of wheelbarrow. Older students watch with appraising eyes; you never know where the next Great One will emerge ("I saw him when…Even then…"). I had no interest in bullfighting, no desire to see a *corrida*, yet clearly this was a cultural characteristic, as Spanish as the guitar, that ought to be examined.

Palm Sunday I spent mostly in the art museums. Picasso was the star attraction of the Modern Art Gallery, but - as on my previous visit - an unfamiliar artist, Nonell, caught my eye with his dark, somber gypsies. At the *Museo de Bellas Artes*, el Greco and Velasquez lived up to their reputations, while Vaccaro's presentation of flesh suggested Italian Renaissance painting. The professor-guide was on duty, and quite friendly - until I asked his views on Franco and Spanish politics. His answer was so prompt that it might have been prepared, or given before: "I don't know you that well, and good jobs are hard to find!" He remained polite, but kept a cooler distance thereafter, as if he thought I might be CIA. When I had recovered a little from having made such a gaffe, I realized what a revealing answer it was: what more could a long discussion have told me?

The next morning I walked down to Antonio Gaudi's *Iglesia de la Sagrada Familia*, Church of the Sacred Family, which looked like an idea for a spaceship. Peter suggested that it might have been built for "some Higher Power other than God." Its four tapering spires, lizard and turtle gargoyles, and bizarrely carved symbols on the façade could have formed part of the landscape of *1984* as I pictured it; "War Is Peace" and "Freedom Is Slavery" inscriptions would have fit right in. Below a ceramic Christmas tree, blobs of stone seemed to drip from the portals like melting flesh. Down in the dim recesses of the subterranean chapel, arches cut parabolic paths of light overhead, and more "bridge cables" supported the roof. I could see it being called a work of genius, but it seemed more movie set than church, and the idea of finding something to worship there was problematical, even frightening.

That evening I was sitting on my bed in the dormitory, plucking at the guitar, when a familiar voice said, "There he is," and two gentlemen from Verona were bearing down on me. I had all but forgotten them. "!*Bienvenidos a Barthelona, amigos mios*!" I said, giving my best imitation of a Spanish roll on the guitar. They stopped and looked at each other.

"Whoa, he's gone native on us," remarked Parry.

"He'll do that," Hector replied calmly.
My solo was over.

Trust thyself - every heart vibrates to that iron string.

- Emerson

44. The compleat angler: Adige River, Verona

45. Lake Garda in rain and snow

46. Farm country and mountains in northeastern Spain

47. Barcelona: the Ramblas

48. Matador in the making: Barcelona youth hostel

49. Detail of Gaudi's Holy Family Cathedral, Barcelona

50. Granada: The Generalife, Alhambra forest, and Sierra Nevada

51. *Caballista,* horse, and bull: Seville

52. Guitar among the olive trees, Andalucia

53. Spanish information highway

XII. Semanas Santas

this strange world
Is such that but to live here is to dream

- Calderón de la Barca, *La Vida es sueño*

Then I am riding along the *Costa Dorada* on a balmy night in the back of a VW beetle, its windows open to the heady perfume of orange and lemon groves, not altogether sure how so novel a situation came about, or what to think of it. Is this the *Ode on Melancholy* again: "Beauty that must die?" The wind on my face is warm/cool, delicious/poignant, like my final days in Barcelona. Our weeks in Spain - holy or not - will be different from their predecessors. The team has grown to three, it is no longer a scooter trip, and spring has come full upon us. Spain is exuding warmth and color beyond my expectations. And the shadow of The End is lengthening: before leaving Barcelona I booked my passage home.

April 13, Casa Campobello - Tues. AM I put in for a place on the Agnete Torm Apr. 30, Parry bought books, we ate at Casa Felipe & pulled out at 2. Trying to make time, we raced south through mountains to Tarragona & onwards. The coastline was sometimes magnificent: sheer rocks, blue sea. Olive trees everywhere. Here & there a castle in ruins on a hill; & the towns, tightly clustered about a cathedral of faded rose or brown, took on a Spanish aspect.

At dark we paused in Castello de la Plana, but it had little, so we pushed on to Sagunto. A full moon rose over the sea, & orchards of smells, sweet, lush, stole in windows. We ate in a workman's restaurant, & finding no beach, took a room for 25 cents each.

Of this room I have no recollection. Things were moving too fast to catch and hold: Hector and I had never, could never have dashed across so much country in half a day, and did not travel at night, going past who knows what at 80 or 90 kph. It was an intoxicating rush, but a rush nonetheless, in order to reach Granada by Thursday night. Alone, I might have investigated "Castle of the Plain," and might have taken a side road to *Onda* to find out why a village several kilometers inland had been named "Wave."

In the morning, though, we had a good long ramble through the mighty fortress of *Saguntum* - a place that the Romans, Moors, and Spaniards had taken turns building up and defending - in the hills behind Sagunto. Everything was fresh to the senses, with a fine washed clarity: a salamander basking on a mottled brown boulder; crenellated ramparts overlooking an expanse of mountain, plain and sea; a stunted olive tree standing alone in a field; a lace of cirrus high over the impassive sea.

Just down the road was "Valencia of the slender towers" (and some stout ones as well). It had also given birth to many of the guitars I had seen for sale in Barcelona, including mine. We examined

a 15th c. tower with Arabic designs & a pot-pourri cathedral: Roman, Arab, Gothic & Renaissance. Bare brick poked thru the white facing of interior pillars; a Bellini-like altar canopy commanded the middle of the transept; Arab designs along the architraves. In the museum, a magnificent Goya of St. Francis contending with Evil for the soul of a dying man. Combining realism & mysticism, it had more power than any other painting I've seen except the <u>*Transfiguration*</u>.

I had been feeling somewhat disoriented by the pace of our sprint, but was set right again by the enormous goodness of the Goya. It had (among other virtues) the impact of a gifted journalist's report on a war zone.

We ate lunch on a fine beach and swam in the sea, but the surf was full of something, marine refuse, and the feel of foreign bodies sliding along my skin was unpleasant. Whence came this stuff, and what was it? Could it be natural, or was someone putting garbage into *Mare Nostrum*? I could not capture any of the evidence. Tourism seemed only embryonic here, and most of that was European. Weren't *they* supposed to be clean, careful folk?

The beetle was soon rolling again. Our road crossed a windswept plateau, wove among hills pitted with caves, and dropped to a coast of fishing hamlets, emerald coves, and serried ranks of watchtower peninsulas. I fell hard for the countryside: orange orchards in perfumed profusion; horse-drawn gypsy carts with direction signals trundling along the sides of the road like lost prairie schooners; yellow-brown houses with red tile roofs; big tawny haystacks in the fields; crinkled, blue-gray or shrub-green mountains that interrupted broad valleys and ran headlong into the sea; color splashed on color.

At dusk we found the "*Costa Blanca*" and *Casa Campobello*, an international hostel full of sottish idlers, marvelously insouciant, whom I both envied and despised -

a refuge of travelers, alcoholics, fat stomachs & inexpensive, dissipated living. A few interesting people - like Bill, the vagrant Australian for whom a beard & the sun were enough. With a bottle of wine & a chunk of bread, however, I was quite happy getting in 3 or 4 hours of starlit guitar. Some blonde pulled me inside to play for the drunks, & we sang for an hour. I did get some free rum & cokes.

Perhaps that made me a professional? The evening seemed a moral fable, though. Outside, under the starry heavens, I sipped wine and played Bach; then came a friendly young woman - like those who target hot prospects at fraternity parties, or befriend epic heroes far from home - to coax me inside where the liquor was harder, the repertoire pop or folk, the company swinish. Thereafter the scene grows hazy: consciousness was dulled, conscience lulled. But I knew that in all our hostel-roaming we had never chanced upon one this hedonistic before. An allegory, for sure.

Early the next morning I was sitting outside on a low wall, playing my guitar in the warm sun, when three Spanish boys, around ten years old, approached me. They were very polite, and after an exchange of pleasantries one of them asked if *he* might play my guitar. I was not enthusiastic, and rather condescending: 'Be careful. Very careful.' Cradling it perfectly, he played through "*un canthion de Albenith*" (he informed me) with a facility that I knew at once I would *never* have. It was more depressing than my solo sessions in Barcelona. If you started early, you might get this sound; if not.... He had a *maestro*, he said, for which his family paid 5 pesetas a week. This was a system that could produce another Segovia. Was it conceivable that I should present myself to a *maestro* as a mature student, his oldest beginner by a decade or so? Perhaps – if he really needed the money. Ashamed and deeply discouraged, hoping they had not heard me faking *Malagueñas*, I reclaimed my unfaithful guitar, which had yielded its treasure to this *boy*.

We drove into Alicante, a brightly flowered resort and port, walked around for two hours while the car was serviced, then headed inland. Almost at once the coast's verdure was just a memory; the rutted road began to twist around arroyos and hills rising to brown, barren mountains. The map was full of "*Al-*" place names here in the country of the Moors: Alcoy, Albacete, Almansa, Almeria. With more Arabic I could have opened up their meanings - the farm, the oil press, et cetera. Above Murcia, a huge marble Virgin blessed us from a hilltop, but the landscape felt Arab to me. Perhaps some place we had missed, Algeria most likely, also had wide, rolling plains, dotted with palms and cacti, red-roofed homes and farms, enclosed by

wrinkled mountains of brown, grey, purple, dark red and faded blue. It was a less Picasso-Van Gogh landscape than the coast, more hostile, more Spanish? We ate a roadside lunch by a ditch in a field.

Soon after, the white Sierra Nevada peaks became visible across wide valleys. We returned to the sea at Almeria, guarded by a ruined castle above. Each peninsula of the jagged, precipitous coastline was crowned with a cylindrical watchtower, remnants of Moorish or Christian vigil.

At Motril we turned north into the mountains. It was a lovely twilight drive, lit by a flaming sunset, culminating in the never-to-be-forgotten spectacle of Granada's lights twinkling softly & with perfect clarity out of the purple foothills.

Ah, but not so fast. Remember the mountains rising clean against the northern sky as dusk falls on the ascent, the little car snaking among canyons; the countryside dimming as the crisp line of the sierras etches itself upon a field of glowing amber, red and violet; the sunken sun sending up orange shafts as on a Japanese flag, illuminating the underside of the mauve cloud-deck. We twist and crawl in the darkness until our rebirth: the interior plain spreads before us, the city winks through air as soft as velvet, and the snow-mantled summits, above and behind us, hang over the capital of the Moors' Spanish kingdom like tokens of Divine Favor.

As we approach Granada the night becomes irresistibly scented, vibrant with freed longings, and, once we join the crowds streaming toward the red castle (*Al Hambra*) on its wooded slope, strangely poignant and confused. Something has set this place and time apart from ordinary life: a *domaine* outside familiar rules. Unseen streams born in Sierra snows splash down runnels among the trees; at intervals lanterns highlight a branch, making the grove seem darker. Separated from my friends, I am not lost or lonely, but caught up with a host of strangers, bound to them almost carnally by mob excitement as the first drum rolls, trumpets blare maddeningly, and a red glow illumines the great keyhole of the Gate of Justice. After a single drummer-boy and a splendid *caballero* issue from this portal into another world, grotesque statues, caparisoned horses and hooded cross-bearers follow for more than an hour, until it is all too much, and we go jostling and scampering down forest walks and back streets to find them again below, winding in three great lines through the milling masses in the plaza.

The processions blend pomp with casual irreverence. A hooded *penitente* leans his cross against a lamppost, removes his dunce cap to wipe his brow, trades jests with an onlooker, then resumes his re-enactment of Christ's passion. Is Spain crazy, or is this the people's Catholicism, or what? Snare drums roll and a gold-tasseled maroon standard looms into view bearing the legend *S.P.Q.R.*: *Senatus Populusque Romanus*, 'the Senate and people of Rome.' Two thousand years ago it was the motto of the Roman republic. I am ecstatic, being unaware that Mussolini resurrected this slogan to inspire modern Fascists, including Franco.

There is singing in many languages that night, laughter, tinkling glasses, a bullfighter from Perpignan, a girl's smile, the smell of musty casks and dark wine. Above the reveling city is the Alhambra, above that the Sierra Nevada, and above them are the stars. At last I make my way back to the campground on the edge of town and find oblivion in our yellow tent. I feel enriched, but my wealth is in a foreign bank account that I cannot touch.

In the morning come warm sunshine, food, languor: a halcyon day, but bereft of magic. Snow-glare from the high Sierra Nevada washes over the fortress and the gardens of the *Generalife*. The light seems to enable, and perhaps even demand, a naturalistic understanding of the previous night; the Alhambra's poetry has become prose. I sit down wearily, hopelessly, to write about the ineffable and vanished night. The first thing that bobs to the surface is, tellingly, a popular Tony Bennett song.

April 15, GRANADA, 9 AM - "Moonlit Granada" lived again last night. It lived in the flickering candles & sputtering pyrotechnics of the Holy Procession issuing from the Alhambra, & in the shrill trumpets & inexorable drums of the military bands. It lived in the bizarre terra-cotta figures of the floats, the milling thousands in the streets, the beautiful & aristocratic faces of the black-laced doñas & the ghostly nighttime Alhambra...it was a spirit & a mood, a motion & a shadow, not to be caught. I was a tabula rasa, soaking up impressions

and buying it all. Normally I would have held back, played the cultural critic, but such was the power of the drama that I could not keep my footing, was caught up and swept along. Even the morning after, when second thoughts are natural, I just wanted to recapture the images and emotions of that wonderful dream. It was a day of names, dates and floor plans as we toured the cathedral and the old city - much as one might take the backstage tour after a marvelous evening of theatrical illusion to see how it was all done, and regret the disenchantment. Among the turrets and arabesqued courts, spring flowers glowed brilliantly in the flawless air of Good Friday, yet I could not shake a feeling of loss.

6 PM - We saw the Alhambra today: the old, fortified portion of the Moorish town, set in a deep forest full of coursing little torrents. It consists of the [Alcazaba], the Palace of Charles I, the Arabic Palace & the Generalife. The latter two are thoroughly Moorish in their doorways, decorations, courtyards & fountains. Very interesting & a lovely spectacle, when combined with numerous gardens.

Yes, "very interesting": a damnation of faint praise, after the transcendant apparition of Maundy Thursday night.

On Saturday we drove to *Sevilla*. In mountainous southern Andalusia, from the coast to Granada, we had been in troglodyte country where inhabited caves were outlined in white or blue paint, like made-up eyes. Now we came down from the hills, across dry rolling fields with white villages, into the broad plain of the *Guadalquivir* (another Arab name: *Oued el K'bir*, Big River), its meadows full of wildflowers and olive trees. Behind us, the snowy heights of the Sierra hung in the air for a long time, a last reminder of Granada's magic. We reached Sevilla in time to secure a room before the evening's festivities, but hit a snag; none of my Spanish words for "bathroom" impressed the owner at all. She firmly denied that there was one, anywhere. Finally Parry resorted to Italian in disgust: "*Cosa per urinare*?" "Ah," she said, and led the way down the hall to the bathroom.

April 17, Easter Sunday, SEVILLE, 10 AM - After a beautiful drive yesterday we arrived in Seville & installed ourselves in a pension near the center of town. The last procession of Semana Santa began at 7, & we watched it till dark. It was not [as] moving as Granada: the novelty was gone, as well as the life-giving darkness, the Alhambra forest, & some spirit in the crowd. We ate at a too-expensive restaurant & got started on a wine-fling for 3 shops, but I got tired, & when the others started girl-hunting about 11 I retired.

Parry seemed puzzled, even disturbed, by my reticence in this area. My aversion was instinctive, and I had to interrogate myself in search of reasons, apart from congenital shyness. We had all admired the beauty of many Spanish women, but they would not be going after the fine *doñas* and *señoritas* who embellished the processions, and I had always found the idea of using prostitutes repellant – instinct again. Finally I told Parry that I did not think they would meet my needs. Anyway the quest was unsuccessful, they said.

The Granada-Seville drive was thru a quality of light, a translucence, I've never seen before. Hills & valleys, white villages & far-rimming mountains, olive groves & onion fields stood out in etched clarity. Near Seville were wide plains, & a fine road ran thru lanes of cedars. We ate lunch on a hill looking over a broad & colorful plain.

Easter is beautifully clear & warm, & I am bound for Mass.

Not, I must confess, out of piety, or even to celebrate the end of Lent - which had begun for us in Rome - but in a spirit of cultural and architectural curiosity. And when I sat down later to write the final entry in the journal begun at the Siwa oasis, my thoughts turned first to the

lovely flowers in the fields yesterday: red, purple, lavender, yellow, white. The flowers are <u>making</u> Spain, whether in fields, parks (as here in Seville), or in a thousand tiny bright gardens behind the *white brick-&-earth houses in small villages. They & their honeyed scent recur as one of the main themes of the symphony of Spain. Another is the incredible beauty of Spanish women of all ages.*

Yes, some of them were beauties, but then of course we were seeing the most fortunate at their best: all made up, dressed to the *nueves* in Easter finery, topped off with *mantilla* lace. Let's see, what was this holiday all about?

Then I remembered that I had also been to church.

Mass in the Cathedral proceeded simultaneously in the main nave & in a small chapel. Like Granada's, the Cathedral is 5-naved, the centre one being given over to (front to back) a chapel; the chief altar, decorated in great quantities of gold & fenced by a golden railing; the choir; & an altar canopy 75 feet high, in 3 colonnaded stories, topped by statues of 2 crucified men, too high to see their identity. The "bridge-cables" were gone; otherwise it was Spanish Gothic.

An architect might reject "five-naved," but four rows of columns divided the nave into five aisles, each large enough to *be* the nave in most churches. "Bridge-cables" was my shorthand for the massive sheaves or bundles (*fasces*), executed in stone or concrete, that I had seen supporting arches in Barcelona and elsewhere. The untrained eye has to understand novelties by analogy to known objects, but enjoys the liberty of being impressionistic.

April 18, Casa Dora, Seville, 1 PM - Never, I think, has my time been so meaningfully used or so quick to fly as in the last few days. Spain, alive with color, rich with spring, is performing the impossible by outdoing my dreams!

Somehow my doubts, cares, and road fatigue were being changed to joy by the harmonious powers of *Semana Santa* in Andalusia - as if dregs were transmuted into a glass of full-bodied wine. Apollo did his part, causing skies to glow luminously and warm airs to comfort. Beauty in many forms - human, botanical, architectural – acted as a tonic. Excitement floated freely among natives and visitors alike; we were glad to be alive, glad to be *there*, in this season of *fiestas*, parades, music, and blossoms.

After Mass yesterday (allowing time for stops in Pension Arenal to play a few notes), had a lunch of meat, potatoes, salad, bread & gaseosa (16 cents) here in Casa Dora. In company with my travel buddies, Brian (South African, very sharp), Buck (an American dwid), & Tom (Dutch), walked to the Alcazar, an old Moorish palace with beautiful, peaceful gardens.

I don't know what Hector and Parry were doing, but the city's hostels, pensions and restaurants were full of young travelers during Holy Week. ("Dwid," a common term of abuse among adolescent males at the time, was "pimp" spelled upside down and backwards. Unlike "dork" and "nerd," it has passed away.)

At the Alcazar

I got us student tickets (3 instead of 15 ps.) - as much fun as getting a "student discount" on our wine in a bodega Sat. night. I thoroughly enjoyed the Islamic architecture of the Alcazar: hidden courtyards with tiled fountains, domed ceilings & alcoves full of shell-like depressions in rich polychrome, & proto-Romanesque arches.

But the gardens were most soothing & lovely, abounding in shade trees, pools [and] flowers. In the palace's decorations, a most unprecedented thing: paintings of animals & people - strictly against Mohammed's interdict. They seem to have been added later.

If asked to point out "Mohammed's interdict" in the *Koran* I could not have done so: it was something I had read or been told about, probably by Leo, and may belong to later Islamic tradition.

In Spain, Easter Sunday is, among other things, a fine day for a bullfight. On my own I might or might not have gone, but in view of Hemingway's *The Sun Also Rises* and "Death in the Afternoon" it was unthinkable that a young American with literary ambitions - meaning Parry - would pass it up. And so we went.

At 5:30 it was time for a Corrida de Toros de Domingo de Fachuada - my first! The arena was whitewashed outside; inside, the tawny sand was enclosed by bleachers low down & a colonnaded mezzanine, all white. In a hot sun & festive atmosphere the glittering preliminaries took place, strutting matadors & horses.

As the ritual trumpets squealed, I felt myself drawn in. Not even in opera had I seen such passionate bravado elevated into dignified, formal rites. Patriotic spectacles came closest, but lacked this gallant, supremely confident style, which drew animal roars from the crowd. Then came the fighting, led off by the *caballista*, an equestrian bullfighter, who, unlike the matadors, meets a fresh bull.

The caballista showed off his horse, who was exceptional. Then, fighting from his horse, he took on the first bull. It was the afternoon's most exciting & skillful fight: each time the bandelleros were shorter, each pass at the bull gave him a broadside charge at the horse. The last Bandollero was a knife in a rose, deftly planted between the shoulder blades. He finished him on foot.

It was hard to believe what we were seeing, to imagine the breeding and training required to produce that level of teamwork between man and horse. Acting as one, they teased, outmaneuvered, wounded, enraged and weakened a glossy black *toro* with rippling muscles, though every pass must have violated the horse's deepest instincts. Whenever they galloped across at an angle of about 45 degrees to the bull, he had a fair shot at the hindquarters of the beautiful palomino, who seemed to swivel on his own as the *caballista* leaned far out from his saddle to drive a *bandollero* down into the bull's shoulders at the instant of closest approach. Each intersection of bull and horse was a breath-catching moment of truth for the crowd. My misgivings about this "sport" were in abeyance for those few minutes. And a rose on the knife, !*Dios!* Women were swooning.

The rest of the afternoon was, I'm sure, second-rate bullfighting. The bulls were not especially good; the bandolleros, picadors & matadors were worse. Our chief complaint: the bull had too little chance. Between 4 or 5 stabs by the picadors (fat slobs), & ½ a dozen lances in his back, the bull was in no shape to face a matador.

We had the usual outsiders' illusions about this being a sport in which the bull *should* have a fair chance - rather than a ritual killing. I started hoping that the bull would gore a "fat slob." Despite my ignorance, I was prepared to play the critic, mainly on the authority of the *gentilhombre* on my left, who kept groaning and putting his face in his hands. Finally I asked him if the bullfighter was bad? "*Toro malo, matador malo, todo malo,*" he moaned.

Didn't like the way they finished him off: running him into the ground, then standing around watching his death throes. It's a pagan spectacle, but could be powerful with the right men & bulls.

Despite this nod to Hemingway, I felt that the *corrida* raised questions about his taste. He had celebrated the matadors, who tormented and killed a wounded bull, but not the *caballistas.* Had he seen none, or no good ones, or referred to them so casually that I missed it? I was glad when the bullfight, which had given us its best first, ended, and left the arena feeling sullied, not cleansed or uplifted.

At 10:30 PM we went (with Brian) to a night club to see some flamenco: touristy, much watered down & dressed up, only fair. But it's interesting, as Brian said, that Spain's two great diversions - bull-fighting & flamenco - use many of the same motions, & reflect the same proud air of nobility, tinged with passion.

As subjective and debatable as cultural criticism generally is, the similarity of carriage - arched back, tilted head, sidelong glance, strutting walk, etc. - between the matador and the (male) flamenco dancer is difficult to deny.

Monday morning I bought some mantilla lace for the *doñas* at home and walked through the Maria Luisa gardens. Every Spanish city we had seen possessed fine large parks with lots of benches and quiet promenades. Though the palms and palmettos made them look subtropical, in Sevilla some parks, as sleek and verdant as those of central Europe, were laid out like formal Italian gardens, with columns, statues and reflecting pools. It was difficult to pull myself away, but the pressure of time began to make itself felt.

After lunch we crammed into the car and headed for Córdoba. As inexorably as a clock's hand passes six, the car trip swung through its nadir and began climbing back toward Barcelona, where the music would stop. We eased off Sevilla's low plateau onto rolling plains and into gentle green hills bright with flowers. At a rest break I sat in long grass under an old olive tree and plucked a few songs. Often and almost anywhere those days I would play: in fields or hotel rooms, on balconies, at lunch, between events. Sometimes, to my surprise, came several good notes in a row. I was letting go of illusions about a six-string career, but the scarifying days in Barcelona had given way to a mellower mood in which the guitar became a pleasurable diversion again, instead of a miserable task.

We found Cordoba sprinkled whitely between two ranges of hills. So far, its only attraction has been the [Great] mosque, which Christians turned into the Cathedral. Cordoba having been the seat of the western Caliphate, this is a very fine mosque, huge & solemn. The Christians did no better than the Muslims with the [buildings] they converted: the dominant spirit is Islamic, the adaptation superficial. Best is the choir, a mass of carefully carved mahogany, which occupied a 17th cent. artist for 62 years. Finest Moorish remnant is an opulent side chapel, encrusted with colored mosaic.

It was depressing - though no longer surprising - to find that the religion in which I had been raised showed as little toleration of or enlightenment about mosques as Islam had about churches. History could not be revised; Ataturk's "museum of the history of civilization" approach seemed to me the most defensible modern attitude.

The rest of Cordoba has not been friendly; only Los Portales, a market square surrounded by a colonnade & frequented by prostitutes, was interesting. We ate a good meal there, & I told a rubbing prosty, "No de todo." She gave a big laugh & punched my arm as she left.

Parry and Hector laughed too as I rubbed my arm. Like the streetwalkers of Barcelona and Naples she could have taught me something, but I couldn't get beyond my revulsion.

Though my journal is hard on Córdoba, it had its graces. Baskets of flowers hanging from wrought-iron brackets brightened narrow whitewashed lanes; the setting sun made the old arched river-bridge, with its thick piers and crenellated rectangular watchtower, glow with a golden light. In this quiet atmosphere, the noise and color of the last few days in Andalusia seemed even more remarkable.

The spirit of Granada's & Seville's "religious" processions [was] quite secular. Both were disorganized, with ranks constantly breaking & being infiltrated. In Granada everyone crossed himself as a float went by; in Seville fewer did. Soldiers saluted as Christ's figure went by. Perhaps Spaniards live more closely & simply than we with religion, & feel no need to attend it with pious reverence.

These phenomena were beyond my comprehension, and this was only one striking instance of a point that could have been made anywhere in Catholic south Europe, where religion was treated with a freedom for which the Protestant solemnities of America had not prepared me.

On the morrow we climbed out of the valley of the Guadalquivir into the *Sierra Morena*, the Dark Range in which the Knight of the Sad Countenance spent some time, and headed north - along empty stretches where peasants with donkey-carts and strolling pairs of *Guardia Civil* were events of note - toward the *Montes de Toledo*.

April 19, Pension Fonda Alcazar, TOLEDO, 8 PM - After a breakfast of hot milk & bread goodies, we left Cordoba about 10. For an hour we were in hills, beautifully poppied & olive treed; then ascending into barren steeper hills, red plowed fields & few flowers. We ate a hilarious lunch by the roadside: good old cheese, bread, & gaseosa. Shortly after, we moved into the more pleasant La Mancha tableland, a land of rolling fields, hills, red earth & green grassfields, & an occasional ruined castle on a hill.

Maps show *La Mancha* a bit farther east, but never mind: the grand sweep of the plateau compelled wonder and humility. Among these sun-blasted slopes and rocky crags I could sense how it might feel to belong to the earth as passionately as to a lover, and thus what the Civil War (1936-39) must mean to Spaniards. In a famous documentary film on the conflict, Hemingway's narration identifies the foot-by-foot reconquest of land that others have taken from you as the central issue. The rich brown earth - as fruitful, succulent, and intoxicating as the Spanish peasants' character and tongue - worked far into you before it was perceived to have entered at all. Gaunt broken castles on distant summits did not leap out as on a poster, exotic and garishly romantic, but were integrated parts of the landscape.

Our trio had by now achieved a warm *camaraderie*. We joked or argued through long hours in the car, were awed, edified, entertained or disgusted more or less in concert, pooled our bits of learning, shared road lunches, and sought the pause that refreshes on a treeless plain between a railroad and the main highway in conditions of desperate urgency. Like wars, comic exigencies create bonds.

Toledo was found clustered on a craggy hill, half surrounded by a bend in the river. Just like El Greco painted it! We went first to the Casa & Museo El Greco to see some of his work. Best are the portraits of Christ & 11 apostles, but his stylistic characteristics are immediately clear everywhere: thin, sensitive faces, dark eyes, semi-luminous clothes, & elongated bodies.

His canvases appeared to be peopled by so many Don Quixotes. And perhaps it is because of El Greco's landscape vista of Toledo that I remember the first imperial city of Spain as chilly winds sweeping through gloomy ancient streets. Narrow cobblestone lanes, steep grades, and surging crowds after dark suggested a colder Sicilian hill town.

But this Toledo was not El Greco's; it had sold out to Mammon. I had to face the question of presents now: what did social obligations and common sense dictate? Nearing the end of the trip and traveling by car, I *could* carry some gifts, but that activity I associated with my parents' generation and style (the tourists in Toledo's souvenir shops looked like friends of theirs). The work in steel and gold thread for which Toledo is famous - knives, bracelets, boxes, etc. - was abundant, and some of it superb; with money, one could buy really fine things. But the trade was geared to the tourist industry, prices were high, and the scene put me off. I had not traveled in order to return and lay a shiny toy at anyone's feet like a retriever. Conceived under the sign of Philip Wylie, my trip had been born anti-touristic; the idea of *becoming one of them* at the last rankled, and brought out my moralistic side, never far below the surface.

April 20, Pension Piso, MADRID - Toledo yielded its art treasures to us this morning, but wound up leaving a bad taste in my mouth. As we covered the town on foot, it became plain that here was a city immersed in tourist mud, from glittering gift shops to its entrance fee for churches & points of interest. Dante put people in the 5th circle for that.

Actually the 5th circle was for the merely wrathful. Those who charge admission to churches would be with the other frauds down in the 8th circle - a level that must be very crowded since the advent of tourism.

We found El Greco originals in St. Vicente Museum & St. Tome. In the latter was "The Burial of Count Orgaz," often called his masterpiece, a huge canvas comprising 25 or 30 figures, including the Count (twice), St. Francis of Assisi, Mary & Christ. Most of Toledo's nobility are there; & 3 clergymen, in the embroidered & encrusted ecclesiastical robes of the time. The painting is excellent for composition, for the expressiveness of faces, for the soft lines & mystic symbolism of the upper part. S. Vicente had 15 more originals, several very striking.

To my surprise, Spain was proving a locus of great painting, even before Madrid and the Prado: Picasso, Miró and others in Barcelona, El Greco here. Toledo also has a huge Spanish Gothic cathedral whose immense wealth of architectural and artistic detail ought to have rated an entire day. The numerous reliefs of the altar screen, unfinished Baroque figures at the rear of the sanctuary, and a giant fresco of a man - perhaps Christ - were just the most interesting parts of a grand whole. And I was intrigued by the bare building called *Santa Maria del Blanco*, which began as a mediaeval synagogue and whose architecture was clearly Moorish. In 1960 we thought of "Jews" and "Arabs" as hostile polarities, yet here was evidence that the cultures had once mingled in ways of which I knew nothing.

Madrid - our last major city, and Spain's largest - sits at the center of the country. If not quite *every* road leads to it, at least every other Spanish city has a road to the capital. Toledo's was not very long.

Left after lunch for Madrid. Coming down from the mountains, we crossed a wide undulating plain. It was cold & cloudy, a sprinkly day. Madrid, white & wide-spread, appeared over a rise at the same time as snow-topped mountains northwest. Following a fruitless mail check, we drove to Plaza Mayor, beginning of Old Madrid. Grim brown 3-story buildings & 4 strange towers completely enclose the square. Half a block away we found a pension, which [had] a room with 2 beds for 40 ps. a night. I'll sleep en el suelo [on the floor].

Even before the car had stopped, delicious food smells were wafting in from the Old Quarter, promising good meals. Stashing our bags and walking west a few blocks, we found the vast granite bulk of the *Palacio Nacional*, with its Renaissance façade and imposing aspect. And some blocks north of that, past a series of fine gardens – the Lepanto, *Cabo Noval*, and Sabatini - rich in pink blossoms and white statuary, we chanced on an

excellent bronze of Don Quixote & Sancho Panza in the Plaza [de] España. Both are mounted on realistic steeds, & could have come straight out of Cervantes' mind. DQ is up out of the saddle, pointing to something with an expression of concern. Sancho looks on with a faintly indulgent smile, worldly, humorous. They express perfectly the faith-reason dichotomy over which Miguel labored so long.

Don Quixote is not just pointing but calling a halt or trying to stop something. Windmills? Sexual assault? And you might quibble with "faith-reason" (altruism-indifference?), but it remains a fine statue. The contrast between the gaunt Don rising in Rocinante's stirrups and the fat squire overflowing Dapple's saddle may be as good a piece of literary appreciation as bronze has ever provided. A stone rendering of Cervantes looks down on them.

That night I jotted down notes for a story about an architect who devotes his career to designing and building a cathedral, only to find at the end that he no longer believes in the god to whom it is consecrated. It must have come from thinking (and dreaming) about Gaudi's *Sagrada Familia*, though I knew nothing about his eventual attitude toward that strange and enigmatic church.

Creators and creativity were the themes of the next two days as we tackled the Prado Museum, set in gardens about ten blocks from our *pension*, past *La Casa de Lope de Vega*. The Prado offered as exciting a collection of paintings as any gallery I had seen in Italy (or France). It was not just a Spanish but a European collection; royal patronage had attracted major artists from many countries. As usual I worked through the rooms in order, making notes, discovering or rediscovering Van Dyck, Reubens, Brueghel, Murillo, March and Ribera, but was most taken with the work of *Francisco Goya y Lucientes*.

April 21, The Prado - Goya: the famous tableaux of the "Episodes" of 2 & 3 May 1808 are alive with horror, darkness, blood. He paints people the way he sees 'em - an ugly Maria Luisa, a cruel Ferdinand VII, a beautiful Mary in a Holy Family, a nobleman who looks like Jack Benny. Then the "Pinturas Negras," to me the essence of Goya's power. The landscapes & their inhabitants are mystical, psychological. The closer you look, the more awful they become. They could be the projected hallucinations of a schizophrenic.

Ah, the artist as madman: the way we try to explain away Swift. "Lay not that flattering unction to your soul," Hamlet warns his mother, "That not your trespass but my madness speaks." Goya's dark psychodramas had plenty of company among Flemish painters of the turbulent 15th and 16th centuries such as Patinir and el Bosco, whose Temptations and Edens were full of death, retribution, and gruesome detail.

Completing the rooms on the ground floor, I discovered that serried ranks of Raphaels, del Sartos, Titians, Rembrandts and Tintorettos awaited me upstairs. When El Greco's tendency to paint virtually the same face on all his subjects began to annoy me, I broke off and went to see some more of the city.

April 22, Pension Piso, Madrid, 9 AM - The Prado is an immense storehouse of fine paintings, & 3 hours there yesterday was not enough. We are all going back this morning.

Afterwards, took a walk through the vast Botanical Gardens. There aren't a great many flowers, yet the peacefulness of shaded paths & inviting benches [is] as welcome as ever. It's a pleasure to see people <u>using</u> their parks, strolling & playing with their children - as in Seville, Valencia, Barcelona, Rome, Cairo, etc.

I exited into *Plaza de la Independencia*, whose triumphal gate is pockmarked by old French cannonballs, and walked down *Calle de Alcala* to *Plaza de Madrid*, ringed by tulips. Traffic orbited the central fountain, an 18th century marble group: the chariot of the fertility goddess Cybele, drawn by a team of lions. Around here, at least, Madrid seemed a gracious cosmopolitan city, rather like Paris.

That night we ate dinner at *Meson de la Segovianna*, a find of Parry's, rich in atmosphere. There was flamenco dancing to the music of three guitarists worth listening to, and (by 10:30) the food tasted great. My share of the bill came to 70 cents, which I considered steep! Spanish prices were for the most part in line with those of Greece and Egypt.

9 PM - Spent 2 more hours in the Prado this morn. Waded thru multitudes of Titians, Reubens, Murillos, more Goyas, & French, Flemish, & Spanish schools. Liked Bruegel's "Triumph of Death" very much. The "flamenco school" is interesting for its reliance on line & tone, & absence of color.

On a washstand in the men's room was a sliver of soap. My own had disappeared from the bathroom in our hotel the night before, so I wrapped this one in a bit of paper towel and pocketed it. Before I left, though, the old custodian noticed its absence and started crying out shrilly. I first pretended not to understand her, then said I hadn't seen it. She called in a guard and complained bitterly. By then I was scared, but it was too late to own up. The woman seemed genuinely distraught, as if the soap were a major loss. Finally I convinced her that I wasn't guilty and hurried from the Prado, shaking. For days afterwards I felt soiled, and stewed in guilt over my offense. What sort of ethical standards allow such a quick fall from Titian and Goya to petty theft? I wondered if I could go back and donate a fresh bar without her noticing. Not bloody likely. Or present it as a gift? That would look suspicious.

This PM we drove out to El Escorial & Valle de los Caídos. The former is a gigantic grey 16th cent. palace, originally built by Philip II "for God." The façade is simple, harmonious, impressive. The palace is a showplace of fine tapestries, painting, & one amazing 100-foot mural depicting battle scenes. The Main Chapel is lofty & solemn. The Pantheons contain the remains of Spanish kings from Charles V to Alfonso II, with separate chapels for Bourbons

but I was just going through the touristic motions; in truth, *El Escorial* seemed dull and grim. Well, at least *El Valle de los Caídos* was not dull! Literally The Valley of the Fallen, i.e. of those who died in the civil war, it was usually Englished as the Valley of the Dead. We called it the V.D., and our similar responses to it constituted another bond.

The Valley of the Dead was constructed by the Franco regime: a piece of landscaping-architecture more monumental than religious, so modern as to give a "brave new world" tinge to its pretensions. A huge grey marble cross has been erected on a small rocky mountain. Around the cross's base are 4 large statues. Behind the mountain is an immense 4-story square "monastery." Along the front of the hill is a marble colonnade, reminiscent of Hatshepsut's Temple at Luxor.

The prevailing spirit seemed Egyptian/eclectic. From the center of the colonnade, a basilica had been driven into the mountain, reaching under the cross; it was about six or seven hundred feet long, and perhaps sixty feet high. Bronze doors had been carved in a neo-Byzantine style, while the horseshoe-vaulted ceiling suggested Moorish arches. A pair of bronze angels guarded an ornate steel gate that began the temple proper. Inside, gilded organ pipes were arranged in trios of quartets, one above the other, at intervals along the walls. From loudspeakers behind them, recorded Gregorian chant resounded down the corridor, unceasingly.

Statues of black-hooded men overlook the pews, a large terra-cotta of Christ crucified spoils the altar, & a dome of glittering gold mosaic completes the chief decor. It is a bit frightening, & joins the [Sagrada] Familia as monuments to a religion apparently quite confused about the modern world -

if it was a religious building, which I had begun by doubting. Comparison with Gaudi's church was futile: Franco's folly combined Christian, militarist, and chthonic or Dionysian elements in a unique way. We agreed that he could have spent the money better. Driving home, I wondered what had made him raise that grotesque monument to "the fallen," many of whom he had had killed. Was it an apology for the Civil War that his party had visited on Spain, an admission of guilt? It was unlucky thought, bringing to mind my own. What had moved me to filch the old woman's soap, anyway? Why hadn't I just bought a new bar? The only possible explanation was laziness, and my (artificial) poverty. I had grown so accustomed to pinching pesetas that it seemed natural to pinch that bit of *jabon*. So that was what it was like to be poor! And why the poor so often wind up in jail.

> 'Now I declare,' exclaimed Don Quixote…, 'that he who reads much and travels much, sees much and learns much.'

Parry's strong literary instincts caused him to carry a large black notebook in which to write at all hours and places. I was permitted to see it once. His models seemed to be Truman Capote and Ezra Pound. As the *literati* of old took a Byron or a Browning tour of Europe, so Parry used Pound's *Cantos* as his guide to Italy, though his prose had the lyrical, impressionistic resonance of modern Southern writers. I opened to a passage on the fogs of Venice that was quite good. He picked up *my* journal one day and curled a civilized lip at its empirical chronicling. It did not occur to me to defend myself by arguing that our travels were of different kinds. Instead, stung by his response, I tried to record more imaginatively, to be more like him.

And in fact a new strain did appear in my journal, a sort of *fin de voyage* melancholy. The last days of the trip would end a phase of my life, so I tended to view them apocalyptically, with anticipatory nostalgia, as Tom Lehrer says. For once, I could feel that my present was gloriously happy, while the future looked, well...foggy. It seemed a feeling worth having, or having had, once.

April 23, Igualada, Spain - The high, arid plains the first 100 miles east of Madrid were dry & warm. The road undulated over rolling tableland or mesas & down into wide, colorful plains. On one of these mesas, which looked down on a lunar landscape of blotched plains & eroded gulleys, we watched the old Spanish A. F. bomber wheeling slowly & dropping weighted parachutes. I shivered, because it brought to mind earlier wars & isolated attacks on lone cars,

and because the parachutes were falling near us, and because the airplane, a 1930s Ford or German tri-motor that might have flown in the Civil War, looked like a time machine in 1960, when western air forces were well into the jet age. Either Spain really was, as I had been taught, a backwater, or we had strayed into a weird piece of science fiction.

But down here, over the mountainous crest on the Atlantic watershed, it is rainy & cold. Mediterranean air, rising to meet us, chills, & formed frightening purple sky ahead. It darkened, poured; & the fiery sun behind gave the sky an orange glow thru the dark screen. We twisted down, between rocks, to the green valley below Monserrat.

Knowing how memorably harsh and magnificent that drive would have been on a scooter, I half regretted the comfort in which we viewed it. We covered most of the distance to Barcelona, but stayed in the last hill-town in order to visit the famous monastery at Monserrat in the morning.

Lunch today was as pleasant as I've ever had in male company. A green carpeted apple grove by the road; a rushing torrent of brown water, feet hanging over; crowds of daisies, buttercups, & one red poppy. Warm sun, blue skies.... I ate bread & cheese & bananas, played the guitar, drank from my bottle.

How to capture so many vistas of grey hills & red-brown plains? Why record reminiscences of Greece & Libya, stolen by new scenes? Only to hope that the image in mind will be true, & fresh, in less lovely times.

Yes, that is the rationale, the theory, and sometimes it works, but the whole process of memorializing is tricky. My pictures from that day show a town amid orchards, and barley fields before a limestone escarpment - of which I have no memory. Yet I do recall a noble vista over grassy plains to distant rangeland - of which there is no photograph. And none of these is mentioned in my journal.

April 24, Barcelona (Pension Puerta) - Monserrat, a vast disappointment, was educational. The monastery, perched on a ledge of a brown rockface, will always represent to me the travesty of organized religion, the greatest blasphemy I've seen. The grounds Sunday morning were covered with tourist buses & cars & scooters. At least a thousand tourists swarmed over the gardens, thru the buildings, into the church. They were dressed for holidays, picnics, cycling; they wore packs & cameras; all [were] talking loudly. A steady stream flowed in & out of mass, heedless, in rolled-up pants & cycle helmets, of the consecration of a bishop.

I was amazed, angry. Catholicism never before has sunk so low as to permit such a degrading of their rites. We soon walked off. Parry: "I wouldn't stay here an hour to see God. Not that he'd come." Monserrat served to confirm two opinions this trip has strengthened: 1. My religion embraces God through nature, not through the Church, & 2. Where tourists go in quantity, I do not belong.

Perhaps, in my New England Puritan/Protestant aversion to Spanish Catholicism, I over-reacted; certainly I have seen worse "blasphemy" since. But the Tennesseans responded similarly, and we bolted without waiting for the art gallery (whose reputation had partly drawn us there) to open.

During the pleasant drive down through verdant mountains to Barcelona, Hector and I discussed Jewish and Arab rights in Palestine. Not surprisingly, given our backgrounds and information sources, we agreed that Jews had the stronger claim. Leo – and many a later friend - would have been disappointed.

In the city, we took a triple room at Pension Puerta (which I wanted to show them) for $1.25 a night, and dropped by the hostel. There I learned that two guys had inquired about my scooter, news which again produced conflicting emotions. I left word that I would talk to them on the morrow, after learning more about ships to the US.

On our final evening together, then, I was preoccupied with questions about the scooter and my trip home. I did notice, though, how little the Spanish landscape figured in my journal, how spotty the narrative became when I traveled by car. It was a story of places, but without connections. Nor was it just a question of technique; I had *felt* less this way. I had come to believe that open-air riding gave access to something rare and valuable, even unique; now I *knew* it. The visual sweep, the thrills and frights, the scents, the physical discomfort and almost carnal knowledge of the land came as a package or not at all.

"But so what?" I muttered. That was history: the scooter trip was over. The issue now was the future of the machine. Would I take it back?

My preoccupation was hardly noticed, however: making the most of our central location, Parry and Hector went out in search of women. I saw little of them, falling asleep before they came in, and the next morning they left for Verona. At parting, Hector and I, both looking for ships to New York now, agreed to rendezvous there and settle any accounts. Parry, who would be finishing his Army stint in a few months, promised to keep in touch through Hector, and I thanked him for the ride around Iberia. Then they departed, leaving me to search for answers to my questions.

At the shipping offices near the port I learned that the *Agnete Torm*'s sailing had been postponed until early May. Its whole situation seemed confused, and the cost was likely to be higher than previously announced, so I canceled my booking. Now what?! Discouraged, I went to the hostel in low spirits, but the buyers had evaporated, so I would be taking the scooter home with me after all. Again I felt glad – though I still needed to hit upon the right ship.

> "In my opinion," said Don Quixote,
> "there is no human history in the world
> which has not got its ups and downs."

Making the rounds of maritime agencies and finding fault with every ship, however, I realized my deep ambivalence about heading home. Throughout the trip, Hector and I had debated the pros and cons of every big decision; now the dialogue had to be interior. A mediaeval writer such as Dante would have presented my dilemma allegorically, using characters such as *Prudentia* and *Audax* to stand for my warring poles.

Audax: Sure, there are things to do and folks I want to see back there, but I still have my scooter, my health, a few dollars, *some* time, and loads of confidence!

Prudentia: Wait: this isn't December in Beirut, you know. With Selective Service on my case, I can't fly off the perimeter of the trip, find work and stay for a year or two.

Audax: Well, no, but how about an expedition to the Pyrenees…Andorra, Pamplona? Or drive up through France to Mont St. Michel?!

Prudentia: Is there really even *that* much time? If I want to go back to school, I need to apply *now* for September, or risk missing a whole year…doing what? Getting drafted!

Audax: (*wailing*) But I haven't had enough! When else in my life will I have a chance to do things like these? And can anything back home replace the happiness, independence and learning of the last seven months?

Prudentia: But do I want to risk becoming one of those long-term travelers (some of them surprisingly dull) for whom travel is a negation or an escape? Do I want to be a scooter bum? Or an Army private?

And so on, and on, point counter point, in a circle that might have been endless had I not received another fine letter from Penny and found a good deal on ships.

April 26, Barcelona YH, 7 PM - All my running around has borne fruit: am reserved to leave tomorrow night on the Augusto for N.Y.; my scooter is to pass thru customs tomorrow & be shipped on the Agnete Torm May 3rd. If both prices hold - $206 for me & $43 for the scooter - I'll have the best of both worlds.

Just three and a half days passed between our return to Barcelona and my departure. I packed into them all the strolls along the Ramblas, good food and music, guitar-playing on my balcony over the narrow street, and baths in the rich Spanish language I could manage. In the warmth of clear days and sunny evenings I took my final walks in the *Parc de la Ciudella*, along Calle Ancha's cobblestones, and through the effervescent flamenco-and-pastry neighborhood of Pension Puerta.

Then I moved back to the Youth Hostel: less colorful than the *pension*, but affording more company and with better provisions for the scooter and for exercise; the sunny soccer field behind it allowed pleasant late-afternoon runs. And, after all, hostels had played a major role in our trip. From there I made final visits to the *Museo de Bellas Artes* to say goodbye to my friend the guard (more guarded now), to Gaudi's unearthly cathedral, and to the hill above Barcelona for its vista of sea and plain and the city I had come to know and love best - though it troubled me to see women collecting garbage, and blind or crippled vendors selling lottery tickets on the street corners.

There was a young maid at the hostel - so a lubricious limerick might start - with mischievous brown eyes, often turned in my direction, and shapely legs. Any dalliance would have to be conducted in Spanish, but I felt up to that, and if the hostel could not accommodate us, I knew places to go downtown. Or perhaps she had resources of her own! One day I was sitting on a parapet behind the hostel with two other young American men when she walked by and gave us - me? - a conspiratorial smile.

"Hmm, nice," I said. "And she knows it."

"Jail bait," said one of my companions.

"You think? Might be worth the risk."

"Oho, line forms on the right," said the other. "Take a number." I looked at him. "She's been around."

A pro? Somehow it took the wind out of my sails (I could almost see Parry rolling his eyes: "With you it's always *something...*"). Was she angling for dollars, then? Or a ticket to the States! How about just a scooter ride? It became another of those things that would not be known.

That evening, my plans made, I sat down to assess what the trip had meant, and where it left me.

The string is running out, Huck. In a short time we'll be in a black cave of unknown promise, the link cut with what lies behind. My feelings are confused. I feel proud that I could do it, happy - I'll draw on the experiences the rest of my life - & grateful. I am lonely: no one can ever entirely share the past 7 months. I feel guilt that I did not go as far as I wanted or see all I could; & nostalgia: so many laughs & frowns [and] sun-lit curves, more than one man's share of soaring spirits & wind on face. This trip means more to me than anything I've ever done. Sad to see it end; yet happy to be going back to Penny, to friends, to chances to do something valuable. At once frightened that I might ultimately derive nothing but memories from the trip; & hopeful that somehow it will make me a deeper person.

The image of Tom Sawyer and Huck Finn in the cave might seem more apt for the start of the trip, as we launched ourselves into the unknown. But just then, marriage, a family, a vocation, or at least a job were the great mysteries for me. In comparison, the months of travel, for all their exciting uncertainties, seemed broad daylight and simple problems. Perhaps they *had* been an escape; the big questions (and their answers) resided at home, as Penny had written. Here then was the deep cave, and no more twine. Voyaging had made me look into myself, but now I had to drop that string and grope forward. With luck there would be a second entrance, and I would come out on the other side. At least that's what I *think* I meant.

On my final afternoon in Spain I went to see a new Brazilian film, *Orpheo Negro* (*Black Orpheus)*, hoping it might flesh out the mythic dimension of Spain, which had seemed slender. Rarely has such a hope been so generously fulfilled. The tale of Orpheus and Eurydice was set in modern Rio during *Carnevale*, of which Rome had given me just a taste. Orpheus, a happy-go-lucky, guitar-playing trolley conductor, likes to serenade his lady ("The Shadow of Your Smile") and the sunrise from a hilltop, but he and Eurydice are stalked by a sinister death-figure in masquerade costume. At the end, with the lovers dead and Hades triumphant, the boy who has inherited Orpheus' guitar sits on the hill facing east and strums the sunrise into existence. (Was it mere accident that the actress who played Eurydice was named Marpessa Dawn?) I came out into the sunny evening stunned with the gift that had been given, and knowing how I would spend my last Spanish dawn.

Do not awake me
If I am dreaming! Do not let me fall
Asleep if it is true!

- Calderón de la Barca, *La Vida es sueño*

XIII. Home from the Sea

Of wandering, and the earth again.

- Thomas Wolfe

The Italian Line's *Augusto* was newer and sleeker than the *Conte Biancamano*, and the title once given to Roman emperors a couple of notches above a Count, but its itinerary was shorter and less exotic: Gibraltar, Lisbon, Halifax, New York. Still, it should give me time to order my thoughts, reckon my accounts, and prepare some answers for the home front without too many distractions. Distractions? I fervently hoped there would not be another Cleopatra, who would be very inconvenient at this juncture. Eyes straight ahead, then! Embarking in late afternoon, I showered, attacked the dining room - determined to consume the cost of my passage - and turned in early without having met anyone dangerously attractive or interesting.

April 28, on board Augusto off Spain - In one of those frenetic bursts of activity which seem necessary to my days of departure, I yesterday bought my ticket ($215), took my scooter thru customs, left it in a shed for shipping ($10), packed up & boarded at 5:45. Some joker sent me a half-mile out of my way down the wrong dock.

One part of the scooter I kept with me. A dockhand pointed out that my windshield, with its unique map-decorated flap, was unlikely to survive loading and unloading. It was easily removed, only a bit awkward to tuck under my arm, and might be a good conversation piece at sea.

Took some nostalgic walks thru my favorite off-Ramblas section. For lunch, showed the latest batch of Californians to Casa Felipe, & said goodbye to my waiter-friend. They're really nice people there. My Spanish has improved, too.

This AM, as we coast south along Spain, is a perfect day for staying inside. The weather is grey & drizzly, the decks gleam wetly in diffuse light, & nothing is visible more than a few hundred yards away.

My mind was disposed to roam over the whole trip. Sense-memories bubbled up spontaneously, as if the subconscious were conducting its own poll on what to keep. Buying a juicy red apple from a roadside vendor in Arles and sitting down on a warm curb to eat during an idyllic day of scootering in the *Midi*, when it was bliss just to accept the spring sun after the chilling North African winter. Other road lunches: by a stream in a Spanish meadow, on a grassy ridge outside Tunis, in a pine forest in Cyrenaica, on a rocky promontory in Lebanon. Tougher kinds came back too: a damp cave near Ventimiglia, a sand-whipped bridge in Libya. Early-morning excursions (Hector's specialty) featured prominently in these reveries: a cloudy dawn at Delphi, a foggy one in Istanbul, the Sphinx watching the sun rise. A cool November morning on Mykonos, eating hot bread and honey with friends on the green porch. And so on: I was past-tripping, and getting sentimental.

My first night aboard, excited and wakeful for hours after midnight, I tried again to resolve my various dilemmas. With the morning came a vague recollection of having decided that it was a very complicated situation that could not be untangled all at once, but I had either reached no conclusions, or had subsequently forgotten them. Aiee! It was like being back in Aswan, months earlier. What *was* I going to do with myself? Or tell *them*?

Inspired, perhaps, by the purser's daily schedule for the ship, I set about planning my own life on board. Nine hours of sleep, two of eating and one of exercise should restore my body's trim. Two hours of guitar, two more for reading, and one of language study: so much for mind and spirit. That left seven hours for laundry, thinking about life's quandaries, watching the ocean, and sundry other tasks. It sounded as feasible as most sets of New Year's resolutions.

After eating my first breakfast - fried eggs, steak, rolls, butter, jam, orange juice, *café latte* - and realizing that it would have cost about 30 pesetas at a modest restaurant in Barcelona, I tried to calculate what the ship's meals were worth to me. Lunch (three courses plus dessert and wine) would come to another 30 ps. Three more courses, with fruit, ice cream and more wine, for dinner: perhaps 35 pesetas. This more than doubled the 45 pesetas a *day* I had averaged in Spain, where my month of travel - like those in Greece and Egypt - had cost $50. (The absolute centrality of favorable exchange rates to this bargain-basement existence had still not occurred to me.) Still, ten days at 95 ps. ($2.40) a day left the Italian Line a comfortable profit margin on my fare, which I hoped they would put into salaries and maintenance, as well as food and fuel.

That afternoon we skirted the *Costa del Sol* from Almería to Malaga under threatening skies that produced occasional squalls. As each approached, my stomach tightened and I tasted adrenaline, but the *Augusto* handled the storms better than a scooter, or a canoe on an Ontario lake. Glimpsing the coast between clouds, I remembered driving past those old watchtowers, down into coves and obscure fishing villages, and up through the cave-pocked hills behind Motril. As a surveyor places a point by triangulation, so we learn to know a place by seeing it from different angles over time.

Gibraltar harbor, 11 PM - Gibraltar, an apparition by night. Lights float in a semi-circle around the ship, red & yellow, winking green & white. The town, on the water at the Rock's side, piles up in tiers, each row of houses lit by unseen lights in the street or the row in front - like the white villages on Greek islands. Towns in Spain gleam faintly at intervals along an arc; planes roar off from the airport to blink towards Morocco. High above, floating detached, shine the Rocktop beacons: a white, & a pair of reds, like 2 eyeholes in the mask of hell.

Gibraltar has been strategic for control of the Mediterranean at least since the Phoenicians (not content with Carthage and Sicily) placed a settlement there and pushed on to Britain. In 711 AD the Arab warrior *Tarik ibn Zijad* fortified the Rock, thereafter known as *Jebel al-Tarik* ('hill of Tarik'), hence Gibraltar. The British took over in 1704, and the Rock became so crucial to the Royal Navy's Mediterranean mission that Thackeray saw it as a British lion, guarding the strait for Queen Victoria. For the nineteenth-century French writer Théophile Gautier, it was a sphinx, watching Africa '*avec une attention rêveuse et profonde.*'

Meanwhile the world is much with us, in the form of 3 or 4 motor skiffs alongside, from which vendors hawk bright scarves & cameras in magnificent multilinguality. Sing out once & you'll have the price in your language & currency at the going *cambio. The boats roll in the slow-heaving waters, their underwater parts clearly visible in the glare of spotlights on clear green seas - soon to be mixed with blue Atlantic.*

We sailed at midnight, passed between the Pillars of Hercules and headed into the Gulf of Cadiz. I did not stay up to watch this passage; the idea of leaving the Mediterranean - our hub for all these months - was too depressing. The emotional impact of The End, which had been running smoothly, like a *tsunami* in mid-ocean, finally hit my coast that night. I was still unhappy the next day, slept for half the afternoon, and took this dark mood ashore in Lisbon, where I bumped into an old nemesis: myself.

April 29, at sea, 11 PM - We docked in Lisbon at 4:30, & I set off in a direction opposite to that I took last October. Interesting what I missed then! I saw a tourist's map of the city, planned a route, started picking out cheap eating spots, pricing pastries, [noting] mixed-gas pumps. All these went by me before.

'Twas strange to sit in the little park near the port & look at the exact spot where I stood 7 months ago. I was a different person then: happier, more hopeful, perhaps better balanced. In contrast, saw myself now richer in experience & memories, sadder & disillusioned with myself, older but little wiser.

But what was all this?! My *Wanderjahr* was supposed to settle me down, clarify priorities, straighten me out, point the way, teach and form me. If all I had to show at the end were sadness and disenchantment, then wouldn't the whole project have to be considered a failure?

As I later walked, despondent, thru steep cobblestone streets, all the feelings I've been battling the last few days seem[ed] to come to a head. I've been fighting to realize my own nature, which still escapes me. I know those things - music, reading, writing, flying - with which I want to surround my life, but not what to put at the center. I am becoming a dilettante, rooted in nothing, good at little. And I require that hub around which to turn. I must have a central idea soon, to which I can direct my energy, my - me.

At least this candid self-criticism identified real problems. The trouble was that my predicament demanded some kind of solution *right then.* In a few days I would be meeting people who loved me, and they would want to know what I had decided. Well, I had decided nothing, and had discovered no firm basis for deciding. More failure.

It is a difficult choice, with a multitude of possible answers. None of them is clearly better than the others. But as I walked thru a hilltop park, a few ideas fell into place. I decided to make a start... of studying music, with the intent of teaching. It will thus combine two of my desires, without ruling out writing (for which I believe I am unfit as a vocation). It will be very hard, perhaps frowned upon, perhaps interrupted by [military] service; but I need something now & believe this is where I will find myself, if anywhere.

Under pressure, my abhorrence of a vacuum was paramount: "I require" a hub; "I must have a central idea soon"; "I need something now." And, as C. S. Lewis wrote, when the demand is very strong, a poor thing in the way of supply will be greedily embraced. I half understood that a decision reached in this way was likely to be shaken by fresh inputs of reason, information, or perspective, but wanted to put my worries aside and enjoy the crossing.

Obviously all this had little to do with the city of Lisbon, which, despite my preoccupation, I quite enjoyed.

Lisbon, built precipitously on several hills, looks large for 850,000 inhabitants. Steep, irregular cobblestone streets & no symmetry of plan. City of angles. Saw the St. George Castle on [its] hill, Moorish architecture, & some new parks. Otherwise covered the same ground, but liked it better this time.

I felt no need to *visit* another castle at this point, though St. George looked impressive across a valley from the deep shade of a park with wrought-iron railings. Elaborate iron grillwork appeared to be a specialty of the city: fencing property, arching over narrow lanes, holding signs, decorating turrets. The "Moorish architecture" was modern, and quite tasteful. But my favorite graces were the parks, studies in *chiaroscuro* where shafts of sun angled down between shade trees, illuminating red flowers and children at play as I sat trying to figure out my life.

At dusk I reboarded the *Augusto*. As the huge cruciform statue of Jesus, which had seemed to welcome us in October, gazed again across the broad Tagus, it was just possible to imagine that it was blessing our departure.

Took my guitar to the cabin of Frank and his brother tonight - <u>hermano</u> sang some <u>canciones espanoles</u> & I played: we touched flamenco, alegrias, pasadoble, & bolerias. Some fun.

The listing of flamenco in general with a few of its subtypes is odd; perhaps I misunderstood what they said in Spanish. This report does not mean that I had mastered the complex rhythms of these songs and dances, even in my imagination. I was just faking it, imitating like a monkey. That, of course, is how they are learned - starting when you're about four, and watching your uncles and their friends! "Frank" (aka Francesco de Valencia) and his brother were the first friends I made on board; the guitar and a modicum of Spanish were central to the relationship.

Perhaps it was the Valencians who set me to reflecting on the human types I had met during the trip. The next afternoon, as the empty Atlantic stretched east and west, I started trying to classify the attitudes toward people and values we had encountered.

One school holds that every person is in some way fun or interesting or valuable if you look long & deep enough. They excuse apparent stupidity or lack of taste as idiosyncrasies which represent only a portion of a person or misrepresent him. They are "omni-accepting."

Peter, the Chicago architect's son I had driven around and learned from in Barcelona, went to that school, and Diana was probably its top girl, but I had met other adherents all around the Mediterranean, including "Ernie Kovacs," our benefactor in Istanbul. Diametrically opposite them was a group

critical of anyone who doesn't accord with their standards. Feeling a need to judge everybody, they are quick in forming opinions, sometimes superficial. This group, narrower in outlook & sterner in criteria, probably comes closer to a just assessment of human conduct because they are ready to admit the bad. Yet they tend to be intolerant.

These "stern-judgers" included Parry, and, less certainly, Leo, who had gentler moments. But they were preferable to the relatively small group of "nationalists," who knew what to think of someone as soon as they knew what country he came from. Several Germans had been that way, and so, to my surprise, were some Californians. That left the rest of us, whom I called "happy mediums" or

moderate liberals. We try to be tabula rasas, to accept everyone we can for what he is, & to castigate only the obviously foolish, tasteless, or uninternational. We are slow to judge or accept.

"Uninternational" was my label for nationalists or cultural absolutists. This attempt to construct an ideal group (and stick myself in it) smacks of a background in social psychology. Perhaps I was just establishing my credentials to write the next judgmental paragraph.

In Istanbul I wrote a long eulogy on the traveling student set. Most of what I said I still believe: it's a fine movement, & I'm glad to be in it. But in certain cases I do renege. I have been surprised by the number of dull-witted, uninteresting or objectionable kids - esp. Americans. My expectation that anyone who had the initiative to travel this way was of necessity interesting has proved ill-founded.

The *Augusto* passed just north of the Azores, within a few miles of *Terceira*. It looked a good deal like Flores: another mountain rising from the floor of the sea, confronting it with high cliffs against which waves crashed in great thumping explosions that resounded across miles of ocean and sent sheets of spray high in the air and far downwind. I imagined that Pitcairn Island, the final refuge of the *Bounty* mutineers, would have looked much like this. Atop the cliffs, white houses were scattered across broad, sloping green fields, some of them terraced, but the mountains outclimbed all verdure and touched low clouds. Later we sailed between two more of the islands, and white sea gulls escorted us for a few miles before turning back to shore: the first and last European land of my trip.

Poor weather settled in - rain and cold on the last of April, several line squalls on May Day - but I didn't mind; the sea- and skyscapes were spectacular, and the *Augusto*'s regular pitching pleased me. It also kept most passengers in their cabins, which translated to extra food in the dining room and more seats in the lounge. Finding places to read, write, and play the guitar had been problematical: after Lisbon I had five roommates, one or two of whom were usually dozing in their bunks, lights out, when I wanted to play or exercise. And this ship had no quiet reading lounge like the *Conte Biancamano* - only a big room set up with tables for card-playing.

But I got in my 2 hrs.+ on the guitar today, mainly by getting up at 6:15 & playing an hour before breakfast. Went thru the Minuet del Sol, the Bach Prelude, the 1st Bach Minuet, & played thru the Allemande the 1st time. Difficult, but cool.

My decision in Lisbon, however unrealistic and benighted it might prove, did cause me to practice the guitar as if that were a skill I would have to possess. Reading back over my journals, I saw how strongly I had been inclined early in the trip to a career in music. After Egypt, though, that feeling had ebbed, and in Spain came the reality check of buying the guitar and trying to play it. I still had to work through the implications of *that* setback. A musician needs an instrument, and I played no other.

May 2, at sea, 2 PM - Roughest day yet, with line squalls, wind, & at times fairly heavy sea, has done a fine job of clearing out the dining room & lounge facilities. As long as my stomach remains unshaken & we [arrive] on schedule, I'm all for it.

Storm-petrels of some kind - dark birds with one white patch - appeared that morning and kept us company for hours through wind and rain, hundreds of miles from land, as if the ship flushed out their prey. These sea-nomads made their search for food look like daring play, a sustained aerial exercise full of casual skill and grace. One would drag a wing coolly over the rough, slate-grey surface, disappear into a deep trough, and then, when I thought it had miscalculated and gone in, dart up in a graceful swoop. Or it might fly right under the tumbling white crest of a comber and shoot out from beneath the spray at the last second. What glorious sport! It looked like first-class surfing. Maybe these were shearwaters? That was a good description of their behavior, but no one that I asked could tell me.

I went to bed early that night and rose at 5 to photograph the sunrise. By the time I came topside it was already light; if clouds on the horizon had not partly obscured the sun, in effect delaying the dawn, I would have missed it entirely. The clouds dominated, robbing the sun of color and limiting its glory to bright spots of gold and yellow shafts, but spray from ship-crushed waves, turbulent, hissing white and green boils of foam, heaving swells, and the sky's variations on the theme of grey rewarded my effort.

May 3, at sea - Really rough today, wind from dead ahead & we pitch accordingly. I now know what "restless Atlantic" & "deep troughs" mean. The wind is strong enough to whip the tops off white-caps & turn the propeller spray into a long diaphanous veil. You keep falling out of chairs, walking is exciting & writing difficult.

Hey, this trip wasn't over! The crew tied heavy ropes across the lounge and other open areas to assist walking, but passengers were scarce, especially at meals. The cooks and waiters seemed glad to see us - The Few - and to serve as many portions as we wanted. Like the petrels, I led a charmed life, immune to the turbulence of a world full of menacing personifications and images of strife. Warrior-waves marched against us in endless ranks. We smashed them but staggered, and more followed, while clouds stormed around and the wind ripped us all. What a corking voyage! I hung onto a forward railing and rode my rearing sea horse *Augusto*. Maybe days like this begot stories about the wars of gods and heroes. I vaguely remembered an episode in the *Inferno* where Dante meets Odysseus in Hades. The hero tells him that Ithaca grew dull soon after his return, so he set off on one last voyage, through the Strait of Gibraltar and west across the Atlantic, where a great storm did them all in. Hold on, though: that was after he got home! I've made no heroic choice.

May 4, at sea, 11 AM - Grey clouds cover the sun; a cold wind whips the deck; the weather continues bad. But no matter: Halifax tomorrow morning & New York the next day.

Inshallah! Showers hit us glancing blows and moved on; the ship and the elements were still at odds. If this was May in peacetime, what was winter like for the convoys of 1942-44, freighters and corvettes rolling about here, coated in rime ice, waiting for the wolfpack? I continued to enjoy reading, playing, and eating, though. Daydreams - of Penny, of the first few hours, days, years back, of tentative steps toward a career – were part of my daily regime. But after greeting Penny and my family, telling them… whatever I was going to tell them, what next? Short term, middle term - a summer job would be good, a few dollars. Read my mail: a terse note from the draft board, perhaps. Yes, but whence would come the guidance that I still desperately needed? Aha! A light broke. I must go back to Debrew, seek out my favorite, most trusted former teachers, and lay my dilemma at their feet. *They* would tell me what to do.

The 5th dawned cool and clear, with a light smoke haze on the horizon. Peace at last! But the day's program read "Halifax at noon": four hours behind schedule. If we did not make up most of that time, said the purser, we would reach New York too late on Friday to clear customs. At 0930 the coast of Nova Scotia emerged from the haze: dark rocky cliffs with stands of pine and fir overhanging the surf. In the lee of the land, the ocean had the silky tranquility of sheltered New England bays on calm summer mornings. Earth-smells wafted across the glassy surface, on which kelp and seaweed rocked in obedience to currents, tides, the moon, and far-off winds. We steamed into the large bay that narrows after a few miles into Halifax harbour. On the barren shores were a lighthouse and Coast Guard station, beached small craft, a few frame houses, some roads. The stillness of the air after the Atlantic wind tunnel was almost shocking. We eased against a pier at 11.

Halifax must be chiefly a manufacturing & commercial burg, judging from warehouses, factories, etc., & not a big one at that. The houses rambling up the slopes are almost all frame dwellings, blue or green or rose. A large bridge is visible further [on], also several churches & an urban center. I'd guess that its woodsy & isolated situation has made it a rather left-field city....

A New Yorker's view! Of course I should go ashore: after all, it *was* a foreign country and doubtless had its own traditions, of which I knew nothing. But Canadian was not exotic enough to tempt me at that point, and we would stop there only three hours. Callous enough to pretend that little could be seen in that time, tired of being a diligent traveler, I was willing to imagine Halifax from the appearance of its harbour. Mentally, then, my trip was over. I lounged on the passenger bridge in the wan sunshine, enjoying the fresh river-breeze and scenery, but carefully not making the acquaintance of a shapely brunette standing nearby. At 2:30 the ship began to tremble slightly and our ropes were cast off. Next stop: New York. *Inshallah.*

At dusk the next day, May 6th, the *Augusto* passed through The Narrows between Brooklyn and Staten Island into Upper

New York Bay, making for the Hudson River piers where we had embarked in September. Lights began to glow in Manhattan. My native city looked strange to eyes eight months abroad; looked, in fact, like Franz Kafka's "Amerika." He had somehow intuited the place, had grasped its essence without ever crossing the Atlantic. Descriptions in *Amerika* that had seemed surrealistic when read in Verona recurred to me as we passed uniform ranks of apartment buildings reflecting the sunset from windows like dead staring eyes; cars racing frantically along their concrete treadmills; the wharves and brick-boxes of New Jersey, already in deep shadow.

And here came another surprise: the goddess of Liberty - last of many representations of mythical deities on the trip - still had power, even for me. Her torch glowed and she was silhouetted against the final ruddy daylight above dark clouds in the west. Italians, Spaniards and Portuguese, seeing her for the first time, began to dance for joy on the afterdeck, forcing me to look with fresh eyes. She was no backyard cliché or historical exhibit to them. Their tears and songs and kisses, although (or because) they excluded me, were unexpectedly moving; it was as if they, not I, were coming home. But I was, and could see in my mind's eye the myriad desecrations they could not: slums, dirty streams, paved meadows, the lost people in the South, injustice, violated promises, the derelicts for whom the American dream that my shipmates still dreamt had faded.

They seemed much like that callow me of eight months ago who walked off a ship in Naples, and what I might say to them now of America would correspond roughly to what they could have told me then of their lands. And I would not have been satisfied, would have gone to find my own version of the country, as they would do here. Each of them - student, shoemaker, entrepreneur, singer - had hopes, might find what he sought, or something else, and was in no way to be discouraged. Was my Greece any less real than Jeff's? Would Francesco's America be less true than mine? I did not think so. It was good to have mingled, to be mingling, in this way, laughing over our various tongues, hoping and dreaming in each other's lands. Whether we came to believe that different nations had more uniting or more dividing them would be a matter of personality as well as of fact. Either way, we had met, and might meet again, as brothers - mostly (I made mental exceptions for Dmitri, the warden of the Athens hostel, and Zeki Ozkurt on the Turkish-Syrian border).

It was right to have gone, and right to have come back in this third-class company (fourth not being available). When the gangplank went down I was the first ashore. Faithful Penelope was on the pier, hand at her mouth to see this gaunt fellow with his backpack and scooter windshield waving at her, and our arms closed the last, best circle.

> And so the seasons went rolling on into summer, as one rambles into higher and higher grass.
>
> Thoreau

54. City park in Lisbon, Portugal

55. Welcome: The Statue of Liberty